8th Version

The

BEST

Deals & Steals In San Diego

by Sally R. Gary

Pacifica Books, Etc.   San Diego

8th Version
Best Deals & Steals In San Diego

by Sally Gary

The content herein is based on the best available
information at the time of research. The publisher
assumes no liability whatsoever arising from the
publishing of material contained herein.

If a phone number has been disconnected,
please call the Information Operator at 411
for possible new listing. (However, some companies
 may no longer exist. *Sorry.*)

TABLE OF CONTENTS
Best Deals & Steals in San Diego (8th Version)
by Sally Gary

Continued next page . . . . . .

"We bought this book in Horton Plaza. I can't tell you how fabulous it is! We save on everything, and I always look in her book before buying.

Also, the chapter on free and bargain things to do is so wonderful. I can't believe she did all this research for us! I highly recommend it for families.

It also has so much information in it that we can benefit from for saving on vacations, and the chapter on classes and free money for college really opened a lot of doors for me.

My husband loved the section on autos and auto insurance, and I love the resale shops. Great book. You will use it often."

Anita G.
San Diego

PROGRAM SPEAKER
Sally Gary, author

8th Version
The Best Deals & Steals In San Diego

PRESENTATIONS FOR

Staff Appreciation Day   Charities
Professional Growth Day   Social Organizations
Brown Bag Lunches   Professional Groups
Secretary's Week   Church Group
Staff Development   Seniors
                                                              PTAs

FUN AND INFORMATIVE TOPIC
"It's like a pay raise . . ."
Sally Gary
2726 Shelter Island Drive, Suite 94
San Diego, CA 92106
Tel. (619) 222-8489/ Fax (619)-222-3800
Email: SallyGary@aol.com

Chapter 1
GOODS & SERVICES *FOR LESS*

Everyone loves a bargain, regardless of station in life. Even multi-gazillionaires want to have the very best *and pay the very least*. Research shows, and you're gonna love this, that people who run around tracking down bargains are actually HAPPIER people. They report less depression and more general satisfaction in life! My philosophy is: You can truly live better *for less* if you know where the fabulous deals and steals are. So, whether you want to create a down payment on a house, pay off your mortgage and retire early, or just have a few extra thousand bucks in the bank at year's end, this book is for you. Read on. Make all your dreams really come true.

In this chapter, you will find endless options for shopping below retail. Discover the multitude of alternatives to the traditional malls, which many are complaining are so repetitive (not to mention, expensive!). San Diego is home to many factory outlets and within driving distance to multitudes of others. We have national chain discount and off-price stores, two membership warehouses (Costco & Sam's Club) that sell at wholesale plus 4-10% markup, clearance centers that deal with liquidation and surplus merchandise (cheap-cheap-cheap), local manufacturers that hold huge parking lot sales to clear out inventory to make room for the next season, and several swap meets that sell new (and used) merchandise. Then we a large "resale" market including consignment stores and other used outlets that sell "previously owned" or "pre-owned" merchandise. The used market is experiencing a huge boom. Clothing from some of the best closets in San Diego and furniture and household items from all over the world are being recycled through consignment shops, resale stores, antique stores, thrift shops, auctions, estate sales, swapmeets and yard sales. You'll find resale shops that specialize in clothing for men or designer apparel for women, or vintage clothing, formal and bridal wear. Then there are resale shops for babies and children with clothing, furniture, toys, books and maternity wear. Others specialize in sporting gear, furniture, used CD's and videos, office furniture, equipment, etc. In this chapter, you'll also find catalogs, TV shopping and web sites for those who prefer the convenience of shopping from home. Check out all your options. The bottom line is: if you shop around (let you fingers do the walking and always get six to ten price quotes), you can almost always find whatever you are looking for, *for less*. With the competition out there, someone is always ready to offer you a better deal, just for the asking. So, what have you got to lose? *Surely*, your Mama told you: *"You better shop around."* ♫

You're gonna love what's ahead for you in this chapter. . . it will enable you to save a ton of money on everything you need or want, so enjoy! Ask me if I had fun putting all *this* together!

Antiques & Collectibles

Ya' like antiques? Practically everyone has at least one if not a whole house full. When you buy new furniture, about 50% of its value is gone the moment you take it out the door of the store. With most antiques, though, the value remains; and, in most cases, will go up! So, whether you're an addict or a novice, if you want to spend a day browsing for that treasure (or cash in that old heirloom), Ocean Beach, Mission Hills, Adams Avenue, Downtown San Diego, South Cedros, Highway 101 from Del Mar to Oceanside, Carlsbad, Escondido, Lemon Grove, La Mesa, and La Jolla offer some of the best places to spend an afternoon:

OCEAN BEACH ANTIQUES
Newport Avenue in Ocean Beach has become an antique haven! After browsing, take a walk out on the O.B. Pier to the café for lunch or coffee and enjoy that great fresh ocean air. Also, on Wednesdays from 3 p.m. to dark, you can shop for fresh produce at the O.B. Farmer's Market. **Ocean Beach Antique Mall**, 4847 Newport, (619) 223-6170; **O. B. Attic Clearance Center**, 4921 Newport, (619) 223-5048. **Mallory & Sons Antiques**, 4926 Newport, (619) 226-8658. **Newport Avenue Antique Center**, 100+ booths, 4864 Newport, (619) 222-8686. **Newport Avenue Antiques**, Over 25 booths, 4836 Newport, (619) 224-1994. **Vignettes**, 4828 Newport, (619) 222-9244. **Mallory Consignment**, 4916 Newport, (619) 226-2068. **T's Antiques**, 4878 Newport, (619) 226-6789 **Homer's**, 4871 Newport, (619) 222-5834
ADAMS AVENUE ANTIQUE DEALER
Kensington Antique Parlor, 4222 Adams, (619) 563-6440. **Antique Seller**, 2938 Adams Avenue, (619) 283-8467.**Adams Avenue Cottage**, 2873 Adams Ave, (619) 281-9663. **Revival**,3220 Adams Ave, (619) 284-3999; 5000 sq. ft; antiques & used.
Country Cousins, 2889 Adams Ave, 284-

3039
MISSION HILLS/HILLCREST ANTIQUES
House of Heirlooms, 801 University, (619) 298-0502; Comprehensive selection of antiques, including 18th C. English. **Mission Gallery**, 320 W. Washington, (619) 692-3566; **Papyrus Antiques**, 116 W. Washington, (619)298-9291;**Private Collector Enterprises** 800 W. Washington, (619) 296-5553;
CARLSBAD ANTIQUE DISTRICT
Carlsbad Village offers charm and a couple dozen antique stores. Stroll down State Street from Beech Ave. to Oak, plus Carlsbad Village Drive, and Roosevelt St. There are a couple dozen to check out!
MISCELLANEOUS ANTIQUES SHOPS
Unicorn Antique Mall, 704 J Street, downtown, (619) 232-1696. Three floors of antiques and collectibles, American and European furniture, jewelry, clocks, deli. Over 100 dealers, 30,000 square feet; restaurant & deli. **Olde Cracker Factory Antiques** 448 W. Market St. near Seaport Village downtown, (619) 233-1669. Large, three floor complex of antique shops including Oriental Treasure Box, (619) 233-3831, and Bert's Antiques, (619) 239-5531. Bert and Olga are great people who also run estate sales. Ask to be

on their mailing list. Tell them Sally sent you. **Glorious Antiques**, (benefits the San Diego Humane Society & SPCA), 7616 Girard Avenue, La Jolla, (858) 459-2222. Consignment shop with furniture, lamps, Tiffany, Lallique, Baccarat. Items from $25-$15,000 with proceeds benefitting the animals. **The Ark** 7643 Girard, La Jolla, (858) 459-7755. A consignment shop with antiques that benefits several pro-animal groups. Run by the same gals who started Glorious Antiques and ran it for 30 years, giving over $250K to the Humane Society. Buy or sell your antiques here! **Country Friends** This is a non-profit consignment shop (over 46 years) which donates over 1/4 million dollars profits in grants to 35+ human service agencies each year. The two large shops, staffed by volunteers, with fine quality items including sterling, crystal, antiques, rugs, lamps, more. Located at 6030 El Tordo, Rancho Santa Fe, (858) 756-1192, fax

(858) 756-0111. To consign an item, call for appointment. **West Sea Co.**,2495 Congress, Old Town, (619) 296-5356; large selection of fine quality marine antiques and art. **India Street Antiques**, 2361 India, (619) 231-3004; ever-changing array of European armoires, buffets, tables, chairs, etc. **Antique Warehouse**, 212 S. Cedros, Solana Beach, (858) 755-5156; 101 dealers; antiques, collectibles, memorabilia. Closed Tues. **Escondido Antique Mall**, 135 W. Grand, Escondido, (760) 743-3210; 60 dealers; antiques and collectibles. Open daily. **Hidden Valley Antique Emporium**, 333 E. Grand, Escondido, (760) 737-0333; 52 dealers; complimentary coffee, tea and popcorn. Open daily. **European Antiques**, 2135 Industrial Ct, San Marcos, (760) 598-0581. European and American antiques. **La Mesa Boulevard** Three blocks of antique shops in the heart of the charming village.

Temecula has become another mecca for antique browsing. Many shops and malls worth the drive up for a fun day. Many wineries, too.

Whether you want to buy or sell an antique, you'll find bargains galore in the *Union-Trib* classified ads for Garage Sale/Moving Sales #2070, Antiques & Art #3060, Thrifties #3190, Auctions #2000, Collectibles #3050, Estate Sales #2010, Furniture/Accessories #3280, Jewelry #3105 and Miscellaneous For Sale #2050. Very interesting, unique stuff for sale!

To locate an antique appraiser to appraise the value of that vase Aunt Bessie left you, look in the *Yellow Pages* under Appraisers. Some appraisals are free; others are $10-$15 and up, depending on the article and its value. Butterfield & Butterfield of Los Angeles will do free appraisals by mail. Send a photo of your item with description to: 7602 Sunset Boulevard, Los Angeles, CA 90046 or call (858) 755-2743 and get their email address and send it to them. They come to San Diego from time to time and offer free clinics and appraisals. Call (949) 673-2199 for date ($30 for five items or less). Another free, informal appraisal by mail is offered to those who send photographs and brief description to: Sotheby, Parke, Bernet, 9655 Wilshire Blvd., Beverly Hills, CA 90212; (310) 274-0340, or visit their web site at sothebys.com. The Antique Road Show, the extremely popular TV show of appraisals, came to San Diego in June 2001; many San Diegans got free appraisals.

To locate buyers who are willing to pay cash for all kinds of collectibles, check out the Wanted to Buy #3300 column in the *Union-Trib* classifieds.

Also, check one of the *free* antique newspapers at any antique dealer which usually have buyers advertising for things they want, and a calendar of events listing antique shows in San Diego, and much more.

For a free catalog of hundreds of books on antiques with pricing guides for furniture, pottery, porcelain, china, stoneware, ornaments, items from occupied Japan, dolls, Barbie, Disney, jewelry, Indian, Depression glass, and much more, call: Collector's Books, (800) 626-5420 or L-W Books, (800) 777-6450. *Kovels Antiques & Collectibles Price List* is a very popular source book, as well as *Lyle: There's a Fortune in Your Attic.*

The Collectors Information Bureau tracks prices on 30,000 collectibles from 300 companies. The bureau operates a hotline to answer questions about plates, figurines, bells, prints, ornaments, dolls, etc, (616) 942-9CIB.

Some of the community colleges offer one day seminars on antiques and collectibles. The nearest certificate course in antique appraisal is offered at the College for Appraisers in Placentia (N. Orange County), (714) 579-1124. Home study program for certificate is available, too. Modules include Orientals, Primitives, Glass, more. Web: collegeforappriasers.com

The Antique Repair Shoppe, 10639 Roselle Street, (619) 677-0094 offers restoration and refinishing, stripping, sanding and woodcarving plus cane, wicker and rush repair. Don's Antique Refinishing & Repair, Hillcrest, (619) 298-5429.

The internet has become an incredible place to buy and sell antiques, and you can tour a dozen auction houses in less than half an hour. Here are some sites to browse: Dixon & Dixon (dixon-antiques.com) and click on the "Best Offer" icon. Butterfield & Butterfield (butterfields.com); Christie's East (christies.com); Harris (harrisauction.com) and you will find dozens more web sites for auction houses with telephone numbers and links to individual web sites at: auctions-on-line.com. Another site is Onsale Auction Supersite (onsale.com). Probably the most popular site for the mid-price buyer/seller is EBAY (ebay.com).

Apparel for Women

San Diego offers a wide assortment of places to shop for great clothing with affordable prices, whether you want designer clothing or designer knock-offs, new or used, dressy or casual. San Diego has great mega-malls with fine department stores that have sales-sales-sales (and always a clearance rack with markdowns up to 90% off), factory outlets (with savings 20-70% off suggested manufacturer's price), discount and off-price chain stores that sell overstock (some of the same merchandise you find in malls at the same time but at much cheaper prices), CLEARANCE stores (some REAL buys, here), and the really hot trend: the resale market. The truth is: you can dress like a million for as little as a few bucks if you know where the bargains are, so check out all your options. Incidentally, a true bargain is something you love that you can wear many places and flatters you non-stop (NOT just a price tag!)

Tip: Most department stores offer a discount on your first day's purchases when you open an account. For example, Macy's offers a 10% discount on all purchases the day you open an account. With a little planning you can buy a whole new wardrobe for the season *on sale,* with an additional 10% off for opening a new account!! Mervyn's offers 15% off your first day's purchases with a new account. Some stores allow 90 days deferred billing with no interest. Most stores offer "instant credit" with a Master Card or Visa. Another tip: if you buy an item that goes on sale within 2 weeks (time varies with stores), most stores will refund the difference (with receipt), so keep all those receipts (even if it's in a bowl.)

Here are some great options for shopping for quality women's apparel at less than retail prices. You have a lot of choices from top of the line designer clothing at the Versace Factory Outlet to mid-range bargains to resale to unique finds. They are in alphabetical order. Check them out!

A Nite On The Town, 8650 Genesee Ave, #222, Costa Verde Center, (858) 457-1233. Great selection of the latest party and formal dresses, cocktail wear, eveningwear, purchase or rent. Women of all ages can find unique, beautiful and affordable special occasion clothing.

Anne Klein Factory Outlet Desert Hills Outlets, near Palm Springs, (909) 849-1114. If you like the upscale designer Anne Klein, you're gonna love this place. Blazers, $149 (were $300), leather jackets, $299; were $499). Suits, skirts, sweaters, turtlenecks, denim pants, regular sizes plus petites and missy sizes. Accessories including handbags, wallets, scarves, fashion jewelry, sunglasses and perfume at least 40% discount for openers, some with an additional 10% or 25% off; $75 sweaters for $22. Lots of items for petites. Clearance racks, 40% off *discounted* price. To see the Anne Klein's collection, go to anneklein.com. This is their only factory outlet in Southern California.

Ann Taylor Factory Store, Citadel Outlets, (323) 725- 7033. This store carries the famous quality Ann Taylor outfits that are exclusively in their own retail stores in malls. All items are markdowns from the retail stores, and are a season behind. Suits, dresses, evening dresses, jeans. Turnover is about three days in the store and it's gone. Cashmere, wool or silk sweaters ($9.99), suit jackets ($29), matching pants, $19-$39), dresses $19 up. The Ann Taylor Loft stores carry a completely different line from the lines in their retail stores. Other outlets at Ontario and Cabazon. Check the Ann Taylor line at anntaylor.com.

Ariana's, located upstairs in the Bazaar del Mundo in Old Town, near the Juan Street entrance, (619) 296-4989. They no longer have the clearance store, but, there is a well stocked clearance section in the store with prices 30-70% off (ask where it is). Ariana's is the exclusive fashion store in the Bazaar that sells upper lines of ethnic fashions, bright sportswear, separates, novelty t-shirts; western clothing, Indonesian batik prints; hand painted art to wear, jewelry, from hundreds of different sources.

Armani Outlets Desert Hills Outlet Stores, (909) 922-3400. This is one of are only four Armani in the U.S. outlets. Exclusive designer Giorgio Armani has two outlets in Desert Hills, one for casual wear including separates and one for more elegant fashions called the Black Label line. These items are from the famous Armani boutiques, one of which is in Beverly Hills. What you will find is excess inventory of what was in the boutiques LAST year, at 40-60% off the tag price. Some dresses, suits, bags, jeans that were $100, shirts, handbags, sandals that were $300, for 25-60% off. This line is found at fine department stores. See the collection at giorgioarmani.com. As we go to press, there were 2,019 Armani items for sale online at Ebay.

BCBG Max Azria, Carlsbad Company Stores, (760) 929-2735 and Citadel Outlets, (323) 727-7284. Very hot fashions from prom dresses to suits; tote bags, clutch bags. Carried at Nordstrom, Macy. BCBG Retail boutiques are in Fashion Valley, Horton Plaza, Beverly Hills, and are carried at Nordstrom & Macy. Everything is last season's overstocks, deep discounts, off the racks from their boutiques. Web: BCBG.com.

Banana Republic Las Americas (San Ysidro), (619) 934-7244; Carlsbad Co. Stores, (760) 804-0802; Last season overstocks. About 10% of merchandise is Banana Republic merchandise from their retail stores in malls, discounted 30-50%. The rest is a line made for outlet stores. Pants, dresses, shorts, jackets, blazers, suits, shoes, accessories and a clearance table. An outfit that was $118 is $60 in the outlet. Size 0-16/XS-L.. About 2/3 of the store is for women; men's and home items, too. Very few irregulars. Check their site at bananarepublic.com. Shop online, too. Sales!

Big Lots (formerly Pic N Save) is the largest broadline closeout retailer in the U.S. with over 1300 stores with shipments from many familiar names like Valentino and Marilyn Monroe lingerie (50% off), top of the line bras like Playtex (save 53%), workout wear, Capezio handbags,($9.^{99}) and much more. Things go fast, so jump when you get their ads in the mail or in the *Union-Tribune*. Sign up at biglots.com for an enewsletter containing a link to their site where you can view the print mailer the day it is mailed.

Brighter Side, 439 S. Cedros Ave., Solana Beach, (858) 481-7565. Boutique devoted to helping women cancer patients look good and feel good about themselves. Specialty clothing and lingerie, prostheses, swimsuits, hair alternatives, turbans, hats, slumber caps, wigs, wig liners, wraps, scarves; inspirational tapes, videos, more.

Brooks Brothers Outlet Las Americas Outlets (619) 934-4580 and Carlsbad Company Stores (760) 930-8066. About 10% of the merchandise is overstock from the regular stores, and the rest is manufactured by Brooks Bros. for their outlet stores. Mainly casual wear. The "real" Brooks Bros. Store is in Fashion Valley with suits and career wear and more.

Burlington Coat Factory Clairemont Town Square, Clairemont Mesa Blvd & Clairemont Dr., (858) 272-1893. La Mesa, 7938 El Cajon Blvd., behind El Torito, 619) 460-7624; Vista, 650 Sycamore, Vista, (760) 727-6422. More than just coats, Burlington is relatively new to San Diego and is part of a national chain started in 1932 that has grown to over 240 stores. The San Diego store is a superstore *(big)* and they offer name brand clothing for women. Women's, men's and children's fashions, too. Excellent source for famous label suits, career wear, dresses and sportswear, handbags, blazers, sweaters, coats, jackets, accessories, sleepwear, etc. Linen pant sets, $29.98; spring dresses, $29-49; coats, $99 (value $200). All sizes, petite to plus. Same designers as in leading department stores.

California Mart 110 E. 9th Street, downtown L.A. This is where major clothing manufacturers's have their showrooms and display their lines and where wholesale buyers come to do their shopping and ordering for their department stores around the country. There is a monthly sale open to the public where samples, discontinued and overstocks are sold at below wholesale prices. Some of the premier designers include Bisou-Bisou and Rampage. Sportswear, dresses, denim, activewear, childrens and mens apparel, accessories and gifts. Mickey & Co. (Disney) and Pooh for kids. Fubu for men. Shop where the professionals shop. Call (310) 837-6788 for Saturday sale date. Occasionally, the Mart is open to the public on a *Friday*. Call (213) 630-3600 for Friday dates or check online at fashiondistrict.org/shoppinginformation.html.

Casual Corner, Viejas Outlets, (619) 445-9178; Las Americas Outlets, (619) 662-1352; Good selection of petite to Plus sizes. Stock is last year's Casual Corner merchandise at 25% off or more. Sales about four times a year. Some fashions were not in their stores. Up to size 20. Four sales a year with 25% off. Casualcorner.com.

Catalogs You can buy everything from lingerie to outerwear in a wide range of colors and sizes by mail order from catalogs. Especially good for women who don't have time to shop, and it's an easy way to see what's being shown this season. See Catalogs this chapter for 800-toll free numbers for Nordstrom, Bloomingdales, Victoria's Secret and more.

Clearance Centers Check the listing Clearance Centers later this chapter for stores like the Factory 2-U and Big Lots that carry women's apparel at huge savings including name brand lingerie like Oscar de la Renta, Evan Picone, Danskin, and plus T-shirts and separates. Also, the Bargain Center in North Park has a lot of military surplus clothing, funky pants, jeans, shorts, etc. For more, see Clearance Centers, this chapter.

Clothestime, with 13 locations in San Diego County including 3651 Midway Drive, (619) 223-3958; see *White Pages* for a store near you. A leading junior (age 16-35) fashion retailer, Clothestime is a large chain store with over 230 stores nationally carrying discounted junior fashions ranging from 30-70% off with an emphasis on trendy, casual, special occasion and active wear. Lots of inventory with numerous well-known name brands, LEI, Paris Blues, Day by Day, Spoiled Girl. Lots of army and British cowboy look, which can switch to whatever it the hottest next. Jewelry, pantyhose accessories.

Coach Factory Store is at the Carlsbad Company Stores (760) 476-0565. It carries real Coach merchandise which was seen last season in regular Coach stores, at about a 30% discount. They have purses, wallets, watches, jewelry, belts. Some sale items are marked down an additional 20-40%. This is a test store and has some samples and prototypes that may not have been put into production. There and two regular Coach stores in San Diego, at UTC and Fashion Valley Shopping malls.

Costco carries designer labels with good prices. You never know what they will have as their buyers negotiate with different designers including Christian Dior, Bill Blass, Tommy Hilfiger, Ralph Lauren, Act II, Playtex,

Brittania, Jordache, Gloria Vanderbilt, Jones Wear, Liz Claiborne and many more. Of course, they don't have a full line but their buyers buy what is available at the best price negotiable, so what they do get in is at really terrific prices. Calvin Klein jeans, $17.99; Gloria Vanderbilt jeans, $17.99; Gucci and Gargoyle sun glasses; Coach and Prada handbags, $164. Order from their web site: costco.com. I found a Kate Spade purse for $114 online, and Prada purse for $469.; diamonds up to $4700. See Costco & Sam's Warehouses in this chapter.

Costumes   You'll need a costume for that dress-up party. Try Buffalo Breath Costume Co., 2050 Hancock St., (619) 297-1175, with over 25,000 costumes on premise. Some used costumes are on a sale rack in October. The Costume Shop, 2010 El Cajon Blvd, (619) 574-6201. Gypsy Treasure, 8127 La Mesa Blvd, La Mesa, (619) 466-2251, is a complete costume shop. Sale rack around Halloween. The Globe Theatre sells costumes in October, (619) 231-1941. Call for date. Also, people put together great costumes from vintage shops, Salvation Army, Goodwill, etc.

Couture New York Carlsbad Company Stores, (760) 804-5888; Designer handbags inspired by Tiffany, Cartier, Gucci, Prada, Versace, Fendi and more, and fabulous faux jewels.

Discount Stores like Kmart, Marshall's, Target and Walmart have a large selection of mid-range quality sportswear, exercise wear and lingerie, and a much lesser amount of career wear. They carry popular national brands like Gitano, Brittania, Jordache, Bonjour, and many more. Walmart carries Bobbie Brooks, White Stag, Catalina, Jordache plus their own brand. Kmart carries the **celebrity lines** of coordinated outfits by **Jacklyn Smith** (sportswear) and **Kathy Ireland** (leisure, workout) plus other designers and their own brands.

Donna Karan Factory Outlet, Carlsbad Company Stores (760) 804-8190; Barstow, (760) 253-2330. Lots of sportswear with the DKNY logo: T-shirts, sweatshirts, hats, sunglasses. Donna Karan's lines are carried at Nordstrom, Neiman Marcus, Macy's and Saks, and her nearest store is at Southcoast Plaza (714) 557-4408. The outlet has stock that is one season behind the stores. Shirts, blouses, some suits, pants, hosiery, everything 40-60% off the store prices; sale rack with 50% off the discounted price. Blazers, $235 up (originally $400 up.) The Cabazon Donna Karan Outlet, (909) 922-9862 (near Palm Springs) has a better selection and they carry her couture line, "Collection."

Dress Barn, Viejas, (619) 445-7615, also at Las Americas Outlets. Dresses, some suits, mainly casual clothing, denim, coordinates, some pants, sox sleepwear, petites to size 20+. Some name brands, mostly Dress Barn styles. Sales with 30% off + sale rack.

Ebay online fashions. If you're new to Ebay, just click on "how to buy" and in a couple minutes, you'll be able to shop like you've never shopped before. Then, from the home page, click on "Clothing and Accessories" in the left hand column. Just click on one of the categories below and shop-shop-shop. There are brand new items at ebay "stores" that sell over-stocks, and gently used items from closets around the world, catalog returns; department store returns; QVC returns, etc. There is WAY too much here to even try to explain, but everything you have ever dreamed of and then some can be found on Ebay. Must be seen to be appreciated. Click away......

Women
  Accessories
  Intimates
  Maternity
  Misses
  Petites
  Plus Sizes
   Footwear

Vintage Clothing & Accessories
  Accessories (Pre-1980)
  Clothing   (Pre-1980)

Wedding Apparel & Accessories
  Bridal Gowns
  Bridesmaids Dresses
  Flower Girls Dresses
  Grooms Attire
  Ring Boys Outfits

At Ebay, search for "designer boutique," and here are some of the designers that are offered on Ebay, with new and used fashions. Be sure to ask the vendor if they are authentic or copies. As we go to press, the top ten designer boutique sites listed and the number of items they have online for sale (known as "auctions") at this moment were .... *and this blows my mind . . thousands of items, see??*

Gucci - *3258 items*
Kate Spade - *708 items*
Prada - *4323 items*
Chanel - *1674 items*
Downey & Bowker *-items 1366*

Versace - *2526 items*
Fendi - *2142 items*
Hermes - *646 items*
Armani - *2019 items*
Coach - *6619 items*

Not only that, but you can click on the list of designers in alphabetical order and up will come about 200 or more!!! You can buy just about any designer fashions or brand names on ebay!! And, jewelry, watches and more.

Eddie Bauer Factory Outlet, Viejas, (619) 659-0955. Women's pants, wool sweaters, skirts and shirts. Most stock made for Eddie Bauer Outlets and are not carried in the regular store. Some returned items from their catalog, discontinued items and overruns from their retail stores. There are frequent sales in addition to the discounts. Their stock is more limited in selection than their stores, but the savings are good. Classic styles. Duffle bags ($45 for $29). Belts and accessories, socks, a little bit of everything, clearance prices. For a retail catalog, call (800) 426-8020.

Escada Desert Hills Factory Outlets, Cabazon. Exclusive fashions from the Escada boutiques in Palm Desert and Beverly Hills, a season behind. Sportswear, couture gowns, sportswear, sandals, accessories. Fashions come in at 47% off the tagged price, and the store has frequent sales with more off. For more info, call (909) 922-1882. Visit escada.com

Factory Outlets Here are *some* of the fabulous top designer names you will find in the section, Factory Outlets, later this chapter. Designer clothing for *less!* Suggestion: Call before going. Sometimes they are loaded, or just had a big sale!

Ann Taylor	Giorgiou	Nautica
Anne Klein	Gucci	Nike
Barbizon	Guess?	Nine West
Barney's New York	JCrew	Off Rodeo Drive
Big Dog	JH Collectibles	Beverly Hills
Brooks Brothers	Jockey	Off-5th Sak's Fifth
Casual Corner	Jones New York	Ave Outlet
Charlotte Russe	Jordache	Olga
Cole Haan	Koret	Perry Ellis
Donna Karan Co.	L'eggs/Hanes/Bali/	Playtex
Eddie Bauer	Playtex	Spa Gear
Escada	Polo Ralph Lauren	St. John Knits
Ellen Tracey	Leslie Fay	Swank
Esprit	Levi's	Tommy Hilfiger
Etienne Aigner	Liz Claiborne	Van Heusen
Florsheim	London Fog	Versace
Gap	Maidenform	and many more.
Giorgio Armani	Naturalizer	

Factory 2 U is a San Diego based company (since 1980) with 251 outlets including 16 locations in San Diego (Lemon Grove, Kearny Mesa, Santee, National City, Mira Mesa, Oceanside and Vista). Their stores carry overstock, closeouts and cancellations from Kmart, Walmart, Mervyns without tags including some name some brands like Gitano, Bugle Boy, Jordache, Fruit of the Loom. I complimented a woman on a dress she was wearing that was the height of fashion, and she said she got it for $10 at the

Factory 2 U. I rushed there, but, alas, they were all gone. See *White Pages* or call (877) 44-FACTORY for store near you.

Gap Outlet, Carlsbad Company Stores, Carlsbad, (760) 431-2544. Viejas, (619) 445-2974; Las Americas Outlets, (619) 934-7229. Some Gap clothing (tags marked with line thru it). Some things made just for the factory store. Jeans, khakis, denim, boot cut, cardigans and camisoles, jackets, sportswear. Clearance section.

Geoffrey Beene Las Americas (San Ysidro) (619) 934-7358; Carlsbad Company Stores, (7690) 438-2776; Citadel Outlets, (323) 728-2070; Sorry, no designer cocktail wear here for you to wear to next year's Academy Awards. Only office apparel and casual sportswear, skirts, khaki pants, slacks, cardigan sets in silk/cotton blend 29-39; jeans, from $19. Tanks, T-s, capri pants. Very affordable. This line is carried ONLY at Beene outlets and sells for 25-50% less than his other casual lines that are carried at Macy's and Robinson-May.

Georgiou Factory Outlet, Las Americas Outlets, 4201 Camino del la Plaza, San Ysidro (619) 690-2600; Georgiou is a Greek mid-upscale designer with a nationwide chain of boutiques (one is in La Jolla at 1001 Prospect, (858) 456-0402 and one in UTC mall, (858) 452 2218.) This factory outlet specializes in raw silks; there are a few other very fine fabrics (some wool gaberdines, linens, cottons, denim, some polished silk.) They carry a line of coordinates, jackets, skirts, long skirts, blouses, with considerable inventory. Mainly past season, with some seasonal. In the spring, they have a lot of holiday dresses (velvet dress, $59, was $21); A jumpsuit that sells in their local stores for $140, sells here for $72. Minimum 20% off; up to half off original prices. Clearance rack, too with a jacket, originally $159 for $19. Size 0-14. All merchandise is from their boutiques.

Gucci, Desert Hills Factory Outlets, (909) 849-7430; directly from Gucci store. Cocktail dresses, evening dresses, suits, casual wear, trousers, shirts, turtlenecks, shoes, handbags $199-400, which is half retail and they fly out the door. Wallets, sun glasses. Tshirts, $169-$500 (reg. $300-$1200). All 40-60% off. Two or more seasons behind. Size 4-12. As we go to press, there are 3258 Gucci items for sale on Ebay.

Guess, Las Americas Outlet, 4265 Camino de la Reina, (619) 662-3570; Carlsbad Company Stores (760) 934-7216. Jeans, shorts, dresses, tops, sweatshirts, shoes, watches, bags, glasses, long sleeved shirts. Juniors sizes, 3-12. Some regular Guess items, but most clothing here is a special line that is manufactured only for Guess Outlets. They are similar to the fashions that are sold at Macy's, Nordstrom and Guess retail stores, but they are a different line and sell for less. Jeans that sell in the outlets for $39, are about $59 in regular stores. Guess retail stores are in Fashion Valley, Horton Plaza, UTC and other malls. The Guess store in Tijuana on Revolucion is a licensed Guess store, but it carries a different line from those manufactured and sold in the U.S.

Hanes/L'eggs/Bali/Playtex Catalog: Tshirts, sweats, sleepwear, leisure wear, sox, bras, some dresses as well as L'eggs at up to 55% off. Buy 12 pairs and SAVE. Sheer Elegance control top, Alive, Hanes Smooth Illusions, Silk Reflections. First quality, irregulars. All discounted. For a catalog, call (800)300-2600, or visit hanes.com.

Janika Designs International Fashion Bazaar, 2969 State St., Carlsbad, off Carlsbad Village Dr., (760) 729-1840. Selection of Moroccan clothing; hand painted silks, batiks from India and Indonesia, imports from Brazil & Mexico, reasonable. Always a sale rack. Casual clothing, too. Trendy gift items, mirrors, water fountains, etc.

JCPenney, nationwide chain store, carries Jones Wear, a mid-range fashion line by the designer, Jones of New York; Crazy Horse, a mid-line which is designed by Liz Claiborne, plus national designers like Norton McNaughton, Evan Picone, Koret, Sag Harbor and more. Worthington is Penney's own label with good, stylish mid-line copies of high-end designers. Frequent 50% off sales on various merchandise storewide. JCPenney offers a sale: "25% off anything in the store" (regular priced or sale priced) in the fall. I know women who buy all their name brand hosiery, workout wear and sleepwear year after year during this sale. Pick up a Penney's catalog in the store, or shop on line at: jcpenney.com Click online "outlet."

Jockey, Carlsbad Company Stores, (760) 268-0180. Undergarments, sox, activewear, tights, sportswear, sleepwear, found at Mervyn's, Robinson's-May and department stores around the country. Savings up to 30% on undergarments, more on sportswear.

Jones New York, Viejas Outlets, (619) 445-7317; Carlsbad Company Stores, (760) 918-9413 / (760) 268-0632. This factory outlet carries more Jones lines and stock than the department stores. Top of the line Jones New York, Jones & Co., Jones Wear, Country (more casual than career, brighter colors). Some evening wear, career, sportswear. Everything priced at 25-30% less than Nordstrom, Robinson-May, Macy's. Long skirts, short skirts, blazers, dresses, sweaters, pants, vests, costume jewelry, sunglasses. Three or four styles of jackets here for $139-149 that sell in department stores for $199. They receive stock only a few weeks behind the stores. No men's. Size 2 petite to 24. Sale racks: 30% off 50% off every thing on the racks.

Liz Claiborne Viejas Outlets, (619) 659-3887; Las Americas (619) 690-2336. This store carries Liz & Co., Liz Sport, Lizwear (casual, denim twills) Elizabeth (larger size), Villager (Liz's lower line), and Claiborne for men. Watches, sunglasses, blazers. Sale racks. Dressier clothing, trendy sportswear, shorts, purses, wallet, sun glasses, usually Liz's most-in-demand styles of jeans, carefree cotton, twills, linen-cotton, slacks, T-shirts, sweaters, skorts, etc. plus career outfits and coordinated ensembles where 5-7 pieces can be mixed and matched. Sizes 4-16 + petites, larger sizes. Current season fashions, 25% off. Last season fashions are marked down more. New arrivals Monday thru Friday. Web site: lizclaiborne.com

Leather Loft, Viejas Outlets, (619) 659-8929. Belts, jackets, bombers, utility jackets. Clearance table. Most items are 10-40% off retail price; Several of their labels are carried in Nordstrom. Private labels plus Bill Blass and other designers.

L'eggs-Hanes-Bali-Playtex Factory Outlet, Viejas Outlets, Carlsbad Company Stores, Citadel. Hosiery, including Hanes Alive and L'EGGS in 6 colors, lingerie including Bali slips and camisoles, socks, Jog Bras, Isotoner slippers and tights. Shoe polish, shoe strings and related shoe items. Most items are about 30-40% off. Additional outlets in Ontario Mills, Cabazon, Lake Elsinore and Barstow. You can order lingerie and workout wear by phone at big savings; some outlets don't charge postage for mail orders over $50.

Levi's By Most Factory Outlet, 4410 Camino de la Plaza, (619)690-3020, Viejas Outlets, (619) 659-5886. Here you'll find Levi's 501's, $34.99 ($50 at Levi store in Horton Plaza), 550's, 512's 517, 560, $29.99; shirts, shorts, belts, saddles, for men, women and children at a discount. Brans names include Levi's, Dockers, and their own label, Tops By Most. Levi's new brand for men is Slates, $29, which sell in department stores for $50-$80. Frequent sales; a clearance rack. First quality and some irregulars.

Levi's (Original) Horton Plaza, first level next to Macy's, (619) 702-6254. You can have a pair of jeans *made to fit.* In a private dressing room, you will get measured loosely over your clothing: waists, legs, hips, rise and inseam. Large sizes up to 49. This info is put into the computer which determines which jeans will fit you best. Then, they provide you with about 12 prototypes to try on so you can decide which rise, waist, leg width, etc. is most complimentary to you. Several colors and khaki. Within three weeks, you will receive your personal pair of jeans. Cost: $70 plus $10 shipping, or pick up at the store. This is an EXTREMELY popular service and 100% guaranteed. You can re-order by phone. Regular Levi's are available here also.

Loehmann's, Mission Valley Plaza, 1640 Camino del Rio North, (619) 296-7776. Also in Beverly Hills. Loehmann's is an upscale off-price specialty retailer of women's apparel which began in Brooklyn in 1921 and offers current, in-season, brand name designer merchandise at 30-65% off retail prices. There are over 70 stores in 23 states in their chain that buy closeouts from top designers, and several times during the year, they have special sale events when the stores are filled. The assortment is extensive, with lines including DKNY, Alfred Sung, Jones New York, Ralph Lauren, Anne Klein, and famous Italian designers suits, career dresses, evening wear and cocktail dresses. At least two or more arrive in each size, and each price tag has two prices: the suggested retail price plus Loehmann's discounted price. Dress, $59 (orig. $265); shoes $49 (orig. $75); Italian designer sunglasses, $59 (orig. $150); handbag, $49 (orig. $195). Communal and 8 private dressing rooms. Clearance racks with even greater markdowns. All types of clothing from sportswear to cocktail and furs with labels from Geoffrey Beene, Adele Simpson and Bill Blass to Anne Klein, Nippon and others of equal renown. Get on emailing list and click This Week for printable discounts coupons. Join their discount club for all year long discounts Sand birthday discount.

Macy's Fashion Valley (the complete store is apparel and accessories; other locations: Horton Plaza, La Jolla, Grossmont, the Mission Valley store is only home furnishings Chula Vista, North County Fair, Plaza Camino Real. One of the few remaining chain department stores, Macy's has frequent sales with discount coupons in their *Union Tribune* ads. Top designer fashions including Ann Klein II, Liz Claiborne, Jones New York, St. John's Knits, Kenneth Cole, Slate, Ellen Tracy, Dana Buchman, Nautica, Polo Ralph Lauren, Guess? and Calvin Klein. Personal shopper available to hlp you put together a wardrobe, or add to your current one. Open an account and get 10% off your first day's shopping. Frequent sales and discount coupons in their *Union Tribune* ads. Online shopping at macys.com (250,000 products). Sign up for enewsletter of sales, specials..

Maidenform Factory Outlet, Las Americas Outlets, (619) 934-8269 carries all products that Maidenform manufactures: bras, camisoles, shapewear, slips, control garments (girdles, briefs, body shapers), sleepwear, robes and panties, reg. $5 each, three for $9. Bras, 2/$24. There is a variety of prints and colors, and basic colors. The usual savings is about 30% off department store prices: a bra which sells for $30 in a department store sells for $18-19 here Clearance items are in the back of store with additional markdowns.

Marshalls Department Stores, Mission Valley, (619) 497-0773. See directory for store nearest you (575 stores nationally). Marshalls is one of the top ten "off-price" nationwide chain stores for apparel offering mostly first-quality closeouts and leftovers plus special purchase merchandise. You will find some goods marked irregular too. Silk-blend sweaters, fleece wear, dresses, and separates with overall savings throughout the store are 20% to 60%. Marshall's motto is: "Name brands for less," and they carry Evan-Picone, J.H. Collectibles, Carole Little, Chaps, and more. Lingerie, perfumes, leather bags, shoes and boots (9 West and Bandolino reduced 50%!) Occasional buy one, get second product for half off. Great shoe sales (Cole Haan, value $150, $38.) Visit their web site and sign up for email at marshallsonline.com.

Mervyn's has a dozen stores throughout the county. Call (800) MERVYNS for the store nearest you. Over 300 stores nationally, which means they buy in huge lots at discount prices and pass the savings on to you. This is a great place to shop for advertised specials of name brand sports wear, 20-70% off. Gloria Vanderbilt, Bugle Boys, Levi's, Dockers, SideOut, Lee, Speedo swimwear, Nike, Adidas, Bali, Playtex, a Liz Claiborne's sportswear line called Villager, and their own private labels, Partners and Ellemeno. Open an account and get 15% off on your purchases that day.

My Virtual Model (TM) Sign up online and create your own "virtual model" by entering your measurements, and you will be able to "try on" outfits at online sites like Levi's (and many more). See how you would look in their jeans styles to get the right fit and look. Sign up at Levis.com and "try on" jeans, t-shirts and more. You can access your personal model anywhere that features the My Virtual Model(TM) Dressing Room simply by using your username and confidential password.

Neiman Marcus, (619) 692-9100, doesn't have a clearance store per se except in Texas, but their store in Fashion Valley always has sale racks that are loaded with merchandise. Additionally, they have Last Call, their final sale for the season with serious markdowns, and other sales throughout the year with 25-50% off original prices throughout the store on selected merchandise. Even if you don't have an account, you can ask to be placed on the mailing list to be notified of upcoming sales. Shop online at their site: neimanmarcus.com and request a catalog.

Nordstrom, Horton Plaza, (619) 239-1700; (619) Fashion Valley, (619) 295-4441; University Towne Center, (619) 457-4575; North County Fair,

(760) 740-0170. Nordstrom is considered *the* best place to buy women's fashions, period. Not because they are a bargain but because they have a great selection of fashions and are committed to "quality, value, selection and service." Their sales are the *bargain* with markdowns 20-90%, their famous half yearly sale in June and November, their anniversary sale in July, a pre-fall sale with special prices for two weeks (then the prices go up!). Those with Nordstrom accounts are notified of sales by mail prior to notification of the public. Their personal shopper service is free and they will work with any budget. Their Orange County stores are much larger and worth the trip up: South Coast Plaza, (714) 549-8300; Santa Anna (714) 972-2020. The Nordstrom catalog does not have fashions that are in the stores. They carry separate lines. Web: nordstrom.com. Sign up on the web for their newsletter. For a catalog, call (800) 285-5800.

Nordstrom Rack, Mission Valley Shopping Center next to Macy's (twice the size of their old location), (619) 296-0143. This is the clearance center for Nordstrom's stores, and is the place to find unbelievable bargains in better clothing for women (men and children, too), accessories and shoes galore, with 30-70% savings and more on everything. You'll need to spend some time here digging through the racks and racks of clothing, but you'll be happy with the price you pay for goodies from Nordstrom. Even if the ambiance is a bit frantic, it worth it when you find the $29 price tag on a $129 item. There are those who say that some items are not from the store, but ordered in specially for the Rack, and this is true, sometimes up to 50% of stock isn't originally in Nordstrom stores, so ask if you're unsure about what you are buying. Suits, dresses, separates, sportswear, evening wear, petites, lingerie and more for women. Also household items and men's wear. Sales every few months with further markdowns to please the avid bargain hunter. Periodic "See the Dots" tag sales: red, dots mean an additional 35-60% off the last price marked. Take 50% off shoes with brown bars. I know people who take annual leave to hit these sales. Ask to be placed on the mailing list. Go during the week if you can because this place gets busy. Another Nordstrom Rack is located in Costa Mesa, 901 D South Coast Drive, Ste 100, Metro Pointe Center, (714) 751-5901.

Off-5th Avenue Sak's Fifth Avenue Outlet 1750 Camino De La Reina, Mission Valley, (619) 296-4896; People come from all over the world to this one. Merchandise is from the exclusive Saks Fifth Avenue New York stores, but, a lot other merchandise is ordered in and sold here, too. Designer jackets sold at Saks for $475 are marked $129 at the clearance store (75% savings). There is some of everything: sports wear, career, large sizes, accessories, shoes, 40-70%, plus sale racks of various color tags (green is 50% off, mustard is 70%, etc.). Sometimes the store is loaded, and sometimes you might hit it after a sale and everything looks pretty picked over. Try again! (Ask about their mailing list for sales.)

Saks regular stores always have clearance racks, and they offer periodic "Act Two" sales with an additional 25% off already reduced prices on selections throughout the store. Get on the mailing list for advance notice. Shop at saks.com. Sign up for their enewsletter and be advised of sales, and receive coupons for $50 off a $250 purchase, and more.

Off-Price Stores The off-price chains in San Diego are: Loehmann's, Marshall's, Mervyn's, Ross, Burlington Coat Factory and T. J. Maxx. These stores buy name brand factory overruns and department store overstock and sell them at 20-60% below department store prices. On the racks, you will see current in-season fashions that are sometimes simultaneously in department stores, plus last season's fashions. The difference is: the department stores carry a very wide selection of sizes and coordinates, and the off-price stores have less items and sizes to make your selection from. We consumers benefit from the intense competition that exists between these off-price stores, which are particularly good resources for fashions including separates, dressy clothes, outerwear shoes and accessories. Women who love the hunt go often. (They also carry housewares, small electronics, appliances and 14 karat gold jewelry.) For more information, see Discount Gen. Merchandise and Off-Price Stores.

Old Navy Las Americas Outlets (619) 934-7282; Casual wear, tees, sandals, shorts, some career. All merchandise is last's years overstocks from the regular Old Navy lines. Very popular in Southern California. Shop online at oldnavy.com.

Online Shopping Online sales are zooming. Most manufacturers are selling online. Go to froogle.com, which is the merchandise search engine of google.com, a popular and highly rated search engine. Just search for what you're looking for and up will come hundreds if not thousands of sources where you can buy it. Be sure to check with the Better Business Bureau on line (bbb.com) to check for complaints against a company. Most people don't have problems with online shopping, but, of course, there can be problems, so buyer beware. Bluefly.com, one of the most popular online shopping sites, offers over 475 designers at up to 75% off. You can sign up for their newsletter to be notified of their sales. Hot apparel, accessories, etc. **Fashion Net** Fashion and style, and links to designer sites, fashion.net **Looking Great** provides information, resources and advice on eye color and makeup, hair, more, lookinggreat.com. **Fashions**: fashionmall.com. **Discount Designer Handbags Depot,** (Gucci, Prada, Fendi, Kate Spade and more) and designer luggage. Check their site at designerhandbagdepot.com. At **Ebay**, you bid for merchandise, new and used. See above listing.

Personal Shopper The better department stores offer a free personal shopping service. A personal shopper is very familiar with the store. They can update your wardrobe with what's current and what's classic. They can help you pull together a wardrobe that looks great on you, within your taste and budget. You fill out information on your color and style likes, and what you have and what you need. If you need a special occasion dress, or vacation apparel or have a new career and need a new wardrobe for it, a personal shopper can gather up some things for you and have them ready for you to try on at your convenience. Some people use a personal shopper for a special occasion; others use them regularly to maintain their wardrobes with color coordinated ensembles which the personal shoppers keep in mind and they call the customer when an item comes in that might interest them. Nordstrom, Saks, Neiman's and Macy's offer this service. Other department stores like Robinson-May say that their sales associates are happy to pull together some things for you. Call the stores and tell them what you're interested in, they will locate it, and you can drop by for a try-on.

Polo Ralph Lauren Outlet, Carlsbad Company Stores, (760) 929-2898. Viejas, (619) 445-9888. Well stocked with tons of casual wear for women (mainly men's, tho) Large selection of polo shirts, turtlenecks, Oxford shirts, sweaters, some skirts. You'll find blazers at 25-50% off, and other classic clothing for women (but the store is mainly stocked with men's clothing.) Robinson-May, Macy's, Nordstrom, major department stores carry Polo Ralph Lauren, and there is a full retail store in La Jolla. Some things in the outlets are made just for the outlet. The Tijuana store is located behind the Jai Lai Palace, 7th Street and Madero, (Tijuana), within walking distance from the border. However, they do not sell the same things that are sold in the U.S. stores, and the logo is slightly different. Everything is made in Mexico City as they have the Ralph Lauren license from New York.

QVC, the TV shopping network, (800) 345-1515, offers celebrity designer clothing and products including Delta Burke (Plus sizes), Joan Rivers (jewelry), plus fashion designers Bob Mackie, Princess Mirah, Susan Graver, Jessica Holbrooke, and many more. Web site: qvc.com. Many fashions that were bought and returned to QVC because they didn't fit or other reason, are sold on Ebay. Also, if you see something you like on QVC, you can go to Ebay and search for it by designer. (If you just type in QVC, twelve tons of stuff comes up.)

Resale & Consignment Stores You truly can look like a million without spending one if you shop the resale and consignment stores, later this chapter.

Robinsons-May department stores have more sales and more coupons than any store in San Diego! Take in all the "extra 10%, 15% and 20% off" coupons from the *Union-Trib* on Fridays and Saturdays and save on any sale or clearance purchase in departments all over the store. This can really work for you!! Also, sign up at their site to get advance notice of all sales, view their weekend sales ads in mid-week to get ready for the sale, and print out current discount coupons. Go to robinsonsmay.com.

Ross Stores, off-price stores with several locations all over San Diego County including 4760 Clairemont Mesa Blvd, Clairemont, (858) 292-7515, Sports Arena, (619) 223-2453. Ross has name brand clothing and designer fashions at a discount for work, play and an active lifestyle. Labels include Polo, Jantzen, Oleg Cassini, Candies, Cherokee, Diane Von Furstenberg, Vanity Fair and many more at 20-60% discount. Good shoe sales; purses. Frequent and very popular career dress sales, only $15!!

Sew It Or have it made. You (or a seamstress) can make your own designer clothing using designer patterns. Ralph Lauren makes patterns for Butterick for his dresses that cost hundreds in stores. Other designer patterns available in fabric stores are Ungaro, Donna Karan, Calvin Klein, Ann Klein, Perry Ellis, Tamatsu and more. If you don't sew or have a seamstress, ask the manager of a fabric store if she can recommend someone who sews in your area. Mesa College offers classes in Fashion and Design. Most adult schools offer sewing classes, free (or low cost).

St. John Knits Warehouse Sale This is a big annual four-day clearance sale held at their factory in Irvine near John Wayne Airport (Orange County), every year after Thanksgiving. This one is very popular and people park in the lot over night to get a ticket to enter. Call (949) 863-1171 and ask to be placed on the mailing list. They issue 1200 tickets on *Friday* (yup, the day before the sale) at 7:00 am, on a first come, first served basis according to position in line. You want to line up well in advance. Ticket numbers will determine your shopping time and day as the sale is held on Saturday, Sunday, and Monday. They only let in 100 people every 2 hours to shop for 1 3/4 hours. The sale continues the following Tuesday and Wednesday, but you don't need a ticket to shop those days, and of course, not much is left. Your goal is to get in on the first day in the first few hours while they have the most inventory. This is the factory warehouse sale, not an outlet. The sale includes knit and woven apparel from St. John Knit, Dressy and Sport Collections, accessories from the jewelry, shoe, handbag and fragrance collections, as well as items form St. John Home. A St. John factory outlet is in Desert Hills outlets, (909) 849-0130, about 20 minutes before you get to Palm Springs.

Stein Mart Three San Diego locations including Poway, 13644 Poway Road, (858) 513-9309 and Oceanside, 2505B Vista Way; Temecula ((909) 303-8282. Stein Mart is a fairly new name to San Diego, but they have over 200 locations in the U.S. with designer and well-known apparel brands at a discount. Quality casual, career and evening wear. Petites and Women's sizes. Many designer labels including Evan Picone, Jones New York. Imported shoes, handbags, great fashion jewelry. Current season fashions offered at prices 25-60% below those being shown in department and specialty stores. Clearance sales with 30% off the discount price. Large selection of designer sets and separates, $10-$35; selling everywhere for $24-$90. I discovered Stein Mart in Sarasota, Fla., and I am so happy they have arrived here in San Diego! Seniors: first and third Tuesdays, 15% off.

Styles For Less Five locations including Carlsbad, (760) 720-1590, Parkway Plaza, North County Fair, Escondido, Carmel/RB; Lots of fashion for the prices. School clothes, junior, trendy sportswear to career at 50-75% off department store prices. Sizes to 13. Hooded sweaters, $16.99; suede jackets, $19.99; velour pants, $15.99; accessories. Hip music. Always a sales rack, plus frequent sales.

Swap Meets have a number of vendors that sell a variety of clothing for women, including active wear, new clothing from Bali, designer fashions, jeans, shorts, shirts, used clothing, used jeans, imprinted T-shirts, tanks, sweat shirts, casual wear, sportswear, biking shorts, jerseys, jackets, dresses, hats and more. Shoes and accessories, too.

T. J. Maxx, Midway & Rosecrans; Mira Mesa Shopping Center; Mira Mesa Blvd at Camino Ruiz; and Escondido Promenade, I-15 and West Valley Parkway; Carlsbad at El Camino Real. Save 20-60% every day on over 120,000 brand name and designer fashions for the entire family. Misses' dresses, skirts, blouses, shirts, sweaters, slacks, jewelry, accessories, activewear to clothes for going anywhere. Plus, underwear, socks, belts, more. Over 10,000 new items arrive every week. Frequent sales, 50% off store prices. Liberal returns. Individual dressing rooms.

Tommy Hilfiger Outlet, Carlsbad Company Stores, (760) 431-8806 and Viejas Outlets (Alpine), 659-8887; Las Americas (619) 934-9122; Carlsbad has women's line; mainly junior sportswear at Viejas. Prices are about 30%

off department store prices, plus mark downs. Fragrances and accessories.

Versace Outlet, Desert Hills Factory Outlets, (909) 922-9111. Another outlet is coming to Las Americas at the border. This is the outlet for the world famous Versace designer clothing that is carried in Neiman Marcus and Saks (Four lines: Versace, Versus, Instante, and Versace jeans.) When items come in, they are marked down 50% off the department store price, and receive additional markdowns. Most merchandise is past season and overstocks. All first quality (no irregulars). Suits and dresses that retail for $600-$8K are $150 to $3K. Jeans that retail for $160-$325 are 50% off. Tshirts that are in boutiques for $100 are $48 here. All fragrances are 20% off. Shoes and home accessories, sheets, pillows plus men's apparel. Call and inquire about the next major delivery. Versace has signed a lease to be in the Las Americas outlets at the border. And, as we go to press, I checked Ebay and there are 2,526 items listed for sale!

Vogue Italia Las Americas Outlets (619) 428-8332 Many designer fashions here from Versace (pants, $69/orig. $99), Gucci t-shirts, $99; Dolce Gabana, Burberry, Armani, Prada, Coach. Size small up to XL and XXX.

Wearable Art La Jolla Fiber Arts Gallery, 4644 Girard Ave, La Jolla, (858) 454-6732. Art-to-wear, one-of-a-kind fabulously embellished creations, hand painted silks, shibori, handwovens and jewelry by 60 well known local and national artists. This is the only store of it's kind in Southern California. View a few creations at lajollafibertarts.com. Also, visit Carizma, 107 S. Cedros, lots of unique artsy apparel, nice things, (858) 792-2727.

FOR ADDITIONAL FASHION INFO, SEE:

Resale Shops	Clearance	Costco/Sam's	Formal Wear
Catalogs	Centers	Club	Weddings
Leather	Discount	Warehouses	
Shoes	Stores	Factory Outlets	
Jewelry			

Appliances & Electronics

If you're in the market for a major appliance (washer, dryer, refrigerator, freezer, stove, dishwasher, water heater, etc.) or small appliance (toaster, mixer, food processor, microwave), here are a few tips: Check the *Consumer Reports Annual Buying Guide* (available at news stands, drug stores, libraries and online) for reviews, safety, pricing and evaluations of name brands according to performance and defects. Check their website at consumersdigest.com. Also check out: Compare Net at compare.net and Product Review Net at productreviewnet.com. You can also compare prices on the web at comsumerworld.com, bestdeal.com, ecompare.com. Check the online Better Business Bureau at bbb.com. Make your selection based on the above information. Then, check prices at six to ten sources for prices, including Ebay. Inquire about warranties, shipping (sometimes offset by no sales tax when shipped to California) and return policies. Most major appliances offer extended warranties up to 5 years; Maytag offers up to 7 years. (Extended warranties usually cost about $20 per year for 7 years.) Most stores charge for delivery and installation. Whenever there is a Zero Interest sale, usually the price is higher or less negotiable.

Try to negotiate the price. There is so much competition out there, they are usually willing to work with you to get the sale. Many stores have signs that say: "We won't be undersold," which means that if you find the product advertised for less within 30 days, bring in the ad and they will refund the difference; some add 10%. (Computers usually only 14 days.) Don't hesitate to ask if a sale is coming up, and, if you can have the sale price *now*. Ask if they have any slightly damaged stock with scratches and minor dents (always marked down). Maybe the scratched or dented area is on a side that will be up against your wall and won't be seen. Ask about demos and floor models which can also be a good deal, and if you find any minor damage, you should be able to get a better price. Inquire about refurbished appliances and electronics that have been returned and factory rebuilt. Most have full warranties and you can save a bundle here! Discontinued appliances are usually drastically reduced and are being phased out by newer models coming online. Ask for a Raincheck if an advertised item is not in stock. When they get it in, you still pay only the sale price even after the sale is over. (See Ch. 2 for more info on Rainchecks.).

SDG&E offers rebates on energy efficient Energy Star appliances, $50 to $125, when you turn in your old one. For information on Energy Star products, call SDG&E or check their web site at energystar.gov/products. This site will tell you which brands qualify for the rebate, kilowatt consumption, and WHERE energy saving models are available locally.

Because discount stores buy in huge quantities, you'll generally get a good price. Inquire about delivery, hookup and removal of the old appliance which may cost extra and may affect the overall savings. The following stores sell discounted appliance and electronics.

Appliances Direct, San Diego (858) 560-893; Encinitas (760) 634-3527; Vista/Oceanside (760) 631-4500; "Guaranteed low prices" on appliances including refrigerators, washers, dishwashers, stoves, more. Maytag, Frigidaire, Jenn-Air, Magic Chef, free delivery. Repair service, too.

Aztec Appliance, 665 15th St, downtown, (619) 236-0616, has new major appliances and some scratch-n-dent sales inventory with sales up to 40% off and a good selection of appliances.

Best Buy, Mission Valley, Chula Vista, El Cajon, Oceanside. The top consumer electronics chain in the U.S. specializes in large selection of name-brand appliances (refrigerators, washers, etc), TVs, stereos, car audio, electronics, personal computers, phones, cameras, software, videos, CDs. Small appliances (toasters, coffeemakers, microwaves, vacuums, etc). Home office furniture. Frequent sales; lots of clearance items. Low price guarantee. Web site: bestbuy.com

Circuit City, 1608 Sweetwater Road (National City), (619) 477-0093; 3331 Rosecrans (Pt. Loma), (619) 223-2610; 8820 Grossmont Blvd, (Grossmont), (619) 463-0214; 1138 W. Valley Pkwy (Escondido, (760) 738-7400; 3998 Clairemont Mesa Blvd, (858) 272-8444; 1715 Hacienda Drive (Vista), (760) 631-8440; 11710 Carmel Mountain Rd., (858) 675-9111; Encinitas, (760) 632-0050. Large selection of electronics (no longer carries washers, refrigs, etc.). Computers, memory, software, cellular phones, cameras, camcorders, TV's, dishes, phone answering machines, CDs, DVDs and stereos. Office machines. Large stores with frequent big sales. They also have a stock of marked-down opened boxes, scratched, dented, and one-of-a-kind items with full factory warranties. You can return items within 30 days if you are dissatisfied. Circuit City guarantees the lowest price within 30 days or you get the difference. Seven day delivery. Web site: circuitcity.com

Costco & Sam's Club carry a good selection of TV's and stereos, and a few models of refrigerators, washers, dryers, dishwashers, and freezers; major brands or made by major brand manufacturers, at a discount.

Appliance Direct, Clairemont (858) 560-8931; Encinitas, (760) 942-5000; and Oceanside/Vista, (760) 631-4500; La Mesa, (619) 828-1850. Major appliances, GE, Whirlpool, Magic Chef, Maytag, Frigidaire, Jenn-Air, etc. Ten year warranty on some motors; 15 day price protection. Installation and service.

Tweeter Stereo/Video, (formerly Dow) Nine stores including 3445 Sports Arena, (619) 226-3500, San Diego; Clairemont, (858) 277-8003; Rancho del Rey/Bonita, (619) 656-9700; Chula Vista, (619) 426-0300; El Cajon Blvd., (619) 283-2325; Escondido, (760) 747-8700; Encinitas, (760) 634-

1112; Vista/Oceanside, (760) 945-5900; El Cajon/Santee, (619) 444-6177. Price guarantee for 60 days, will match the price. Lots of entertainment gadgetry and audio/visual equipment, many advertised specials, open box clearances. Definitely a place to cruise if you're looking for new sound system or TV setup. Web TV, digital video discs, more. Return policy: within 30 days with box and packaging, manual, invoice, except camcorders (no return) and no return if you install car audio. Sixty day return if defective.

Fry's Electronics, 9825 Stonecrest Blvd., near Interstate 15 & Aero Dr., (858) 514-6400. Relatively new to San Diego, with 21 stores in three states plus California; 5 stores in L.A.. A new store is planned for San Marcos. Their huge stores stock 85,000 items including major appliances with a wide selection of well-known and some not-so-well known brands and models of refrigerators, TVs, VCRs, washers, dryers, stoves, plus bathroom scales, vacuums, cameras, phone answering machines and electronics. Breadmakers, microwave ovens, CDs, videos, software, video games. EVERYTHING. Computers and computer parts including motherboards, fans, relays, cases, etc. Computer books. Guarantee lowest price for 30 days. Huge store; competitive prices. Huge ads almost daily in the *Union-Tribune*. Great sales prices. Ask for items with dents and scratches (and full warranties). Lots of discontinued models. Check manufacture date. I bought something that was dark-ages technology which I didn't use for 45 days, then discovered it wasn't what I wanted but . . oh, well, live and learn.

Good Guys, with 7 locations in San Diego including Sports Arena, (619) 523-2600; Carmel Mountain Road, La Jolla, La Mesa, Chula Vista. Escondido, Carlsbad. Operates 76+ stores along the Pacific Coast and considers San Diego it's best market. Specializes in audio-visual, TV's, stereos, car audio, satellites, loads of cameras, boom boxes, computers, games, telephones. Big selection; good prices; lots of advertised specials. Thirty day satisfaction except cameras. No opened accessories. Can purchase extended warranty. Sixty-day low-price guarantee. Floor samples, clearance items in each department when available.

Kobey's Swap Meet, Sports Arena, (and all swap meets) have a number of vendors that sell audio/video equipment, electronics, components and accessories. Lots of car stereos, amplifiers, woofers, cellular phones, telephones and answering machines, cords, business phones, etc.

Big Lots gets in interesting closeouts of famous brand small stereos, radios, phones and household appliances including vacuums, etc.

Radio Shack, several locations in San Diego; wireless phones, computers, satellite TV, many small electronics; shop online at: radioshack.com.

Sears Outlet, 960 Sherman St. off Morena Blvd., (619) 497-1123. Major name brand TV's and appliances including Amana, GE, Whirlpool, Kitchenaid but mainly their own brand, Kenmore. Some new, but most everything has been sold once and is considered "used;" however, all have a one-year warranty and a thirty-day return policy. Large inventory with savings of 20-50% off One-of-a-kind, discontinued, used, scratched and dented merchandise. Frequent coupons in the *Union-Tribune* for $20 off.

Sony Factory Outlet, Lake Elsinore Outlets, (909) 245-1155. This is an outlet that sells refurbished items that were returned. Telephones, TV's, VCRs, home and car stereos, receivers, CD players, computers. (See Computers for more factory outlets that sell refurbished computers)

Target, Kmart, Walmart, Mervyn's, SavOn, RiteAid, Walgreens and Long's are good places to pick up small appliances like toaster ovens, coffee makers, blenders, mixers, radios, telephones, answering machines, cameras, vacuums, etc., when they are on sale at a deep discount. **Kmart** has increased the number of major brands offered.

Appliance Price Quotes by Phone

Wholesale-by-mail stores will give quotes by phone on their toll-free lines. Shop at local stores, find what you want, write down the make, model, color and call for a price quote. Ask about shipping and warranties. You may save sales tax which can be a substantial savings on items that are shipped from out of state (depending upon the state). Call Percy's of Worcester, Massachusetts, (800) 922-8194, over 50 years in business selling large appliances and more, all major name brands, 30-50% discount; Crutchfield of Harrisonburg, VA, discount up to 60% on name brand stereos, no sales tax outside Virginia, 100-page color catalog of electronics including telephones, home audio and video, and car audio systems, parts and accessories, (800) 336-5566; Web site: crutchfield.com; Damark (liquidation), variety of appliances, large or small. Check their site at damark.com.

Video Review and *Video Magazine* contain ads for many discount mail order companies.

Used Appliances

Check the *Union-Trib* classified ads: Thrifties #3190, Garage Sales/Moving Sales #2070, and Household Appliances #3260 too. Listed are VCR's, refrigerators, TV's, stoves, cameras, and every appliance, large or small, you can think of. I have picked up a lot of small appliances (in perfect condition) at yard sales including a Mini-Cuisinart ($1); a Cuisinart drink mixer in box with warranty ($5); new toaster oven ($5); Rival Steamer/Rice Cooker ($3); new Fry Baby ($1) with no cord (one from another appliance fit!). From the Thrifties, I got a NEW Kitchenaid mixer in the box for $75 (value, $200+). The woman who sold it to me had two and was selling the one she received as a gift from the company that remodeled her kitchen.

Certified Appliances (& Repair), 4456 Vandevere, Suite 9 (619) 280-0601. Late model used and reconditioned appliances, some look brand new. All work is guaranteed. Refrigerators, range, washers and dryers only. Warranty and deliver. Also, in-home repair service. Serving San Diego since 1982, this is a woman-owned and operated company.

Appliance Repair

California Electric repairs small appliances, has cords, parts, manuals (or can order them) and used/rebuilt appliances, some with warranties. Located at 3430 El Cajon Blvd; (619) 283-6488.

Call the 800-toll free number for the manufacturer (usually in the manual or on a sticker near the motor) and order parts, cords, etc. directly from them. Many major companies like GE have a toll free number you can call to trouble-shoot your problem. Sometimes they can tell you if you need a whozit or whatzit. You can order the part with a major credit card and either do the repair yourself or call a handyman or a repair service. If under warranty, they may tell you to return the item and they will replace it, FREE. Go for it.

ABZ Appliance Repair will repair major appliances in your home including kitchen and laundry, refrigeration, air-conditioning, heating and microwave ovens. Warranty for one-year on parts and labor. References from happy customers. No service call charge with repair. In business since 1985. Senior discounts. Visa and MC welcome. For information or appointment, call (619) 280-0044.

Appliance Repair Web Site: repairclinic.com provides solutions for your appliance needs, including helpful hints, tips, troubleshooting and more. .Also, check the Home & Garden Channel's site hgtv.com and search for "repairs." I would also go to google.com and type in "repair a whozit" and see what comes up. Keep trying til you find 10,000 sites that help you repair your own stuff, and the info is all free-free-free. I've gotten a lot of help and how-to's from ole google.com.

PROGRAM SPEAKER
Sally Gary, author of
The Best Deals & Steals in San Diego
(7ᵗʰ Version)

PRESENTATIONS FOR
Staff Appreciation Day   Charities
Professional Growth Day   Social Organizations
Brown Bag Lunches   Professional Groups
Secretary's Week   Church Group
Staff Development   Seniors
                      PTAs

Fun and Informative Topic
Sally Gary
2726 Shelter Island Drive, Suite 94
San Diego, CA 92106
Tel. (619) 222-8489/ Fax (619)-222-3800 Email:
SallyGary@aol.com

Arts & Crafts

Michael's Arts & Craft, 1652 Camino del Rio N. (next to Bed, Bath & Beyond and Nordstrom Rack), (619) 294-5891; 816 Jackson, El Cajon, (619) 442-6666; Other stores are located in Escondido, Oceanside-Carlsbad, Vista, La Mesa, Chula Vista, Clairemont Mesa, Santee, El Cajon, Poway, Carmel Mountain. Large array of floral design, crafts, candles, bird houses, artist supplies, holiday items plus tons of wearables and party goods at savings of 20% to 50% off retail prices. Some wicker and outdoor furniture, pottery and home decor, too. Classes including fabric decorating, floral design, T-shirt painting, stamping, fine arts, holiday decorations, book making, bow-making, stitchery, etc. Specials are featured weekly, and there is usually a 40-50% off coupon in their special supplement in the Sunday *Union-Trib*. Excellent custom framing department. Wait for a 50% discount coupon to appear in their Union ads for framing. One magically appears every few weeks (trust me). Web site: michaels.com

Value Craft, 3825 Plaza, Oceanside, (760) 758-9233; 342 W. El Norte, Escondido, (760) 747-9222. Lots of stock: craft supplies, florals, ribbons, glues, stamps, etc. Lots of specials; good prices.

Dave's Display World, 1306 Kettner Blvd., downtown, (619) 232-3097. carries a large assortment of craft supplies and decorations for parties. Interesting place. Props, silk plants, makeup, costumes, columns. It's been there over 25 years and say their store is "weird as ever."

Shepherdess, 2802 Juan Street, Old Town, (619) 297-4110. Fabulous collection of unusual beads, imports, contemporary glass beads, vintage, basketry and buttons. Beginning classes and advanced workshops.

Check "Art Supplies," "Craft Supplies" and "Florists' Supplies" in the *Yellow Pages* for discounted ribbons, vases, pots, artificial trees and assorted craft supplies. Beads, leather, everything. Ask if there is a mailing list for sales, classes, etc.

Paint and decorate your T-shirt with paints, jewels, etc. Or, If you don't like the colors on screened T-shirts, paint over the colors. Use their designs for starters and go from there. And, you can paint over spots on T-shirts rather than throwing them in the recycle bin (a great idea for children's wear). Tons of design pattern books are available in craft stores.

Most swap meets have a few vendors that sell arts and crafts supplies, rubber stamps, glitters, etc. Check *Kobey's Magazine & Directory* available free of charge at their swap meet, or by paid subscription, for booth locations. For more information, see "Swap Meets."

KPBS TV, Lifetime, and the Discovery Channel and the Home & Garden Channel (my favorite) have a number of craft programs, sewing, painting, watercolors, quilting, and decorating shows. Fabulous ideas. Lots of "how-to's." I'm surprised at how much I'm learning (& gaining confidence!)

Take a free or low cost sewing, jewelry, ceramics, printmaking, drawing, painting, floral design, pottery or craft class at any one of 10 centers of San Diego Community College Continuing Education program. Learn how to applique, quilt and decorate clothing. Enroll any time, (619) 230-2300.

The Learning Annex, and the community colleges including Mira Costa, Grossmont and Palomar offer one-day classes in various crafts including candle making, wreaths, floral design, upholstering, basketry, stenciling and more. UCSD Extension offers interior design, floral design and culinary arts. Some offer classes on how to market your arts and crafts. Get on the mailing list. See "Continuing Education" for college telephone numbers.

Arts College International, 840 G Street, downtown, (619) 231-3900. Wonderful array (dozens) of home decorating and art classes, faux finish, mural art, jewelry making, ceramic tiles, mosaic, bookbinding, clay sculpture, watercolor, drawing, oil painting, fish printing, feng shui, more.

Auctions (Don't Miss Out!)

Auctions are not for everyone because you need a little "know how" before you walk out the door, but you can buy abandoned and unclaimed items galore plus seized merchandise from criminals and money launderers. Articles for auction include everything: fine paintings, TVs, automobiles, vans, motorcycles and other vehicles, bicycles, diamonds, jewels, watches, furniture, appliances, crystal, oriental rugs, antiques, office supplies, tools, fixtures, equipment, furniture, building supplies, store equipment and lots more. Also, when hotels, restaurants and office buildings remodel, the old fixtures, furniture, and equipment are frequently liquidated at auction. U.S. Customs auctions have merchandise that people attempted to bring into the country at the border but didn't have proper documentation for, or the money to pay import duties. Also items that people failed to claim within the one-year limitation.

Auctions are attended by the general public, dabblers, novices, semi-professionals and professionals who buy goods for themselves or to resell (a very good way to raise extra money in your spare time). There is always a list of what is to be auctioned, plus a period for viewing prior to sale. Items are sold to the highest bidder.

There are three methods of bidding. At traditional-type auctions, oral bids are taken from the audience item by item. Then there are "spot-bid" sales, where written bids are accepted item by item, and at a "sealed-bid" sale, bids are offered by mail, and then opened in public. Winning bidders cannot remove property without first paying in full by cash, money order, traveler's check, cashier's check, credit union check or U.S. Treasury check. Novices should plan to attend several times before attempting to buy in order to get acquainted with the auction procedure. A word of warning: you can get caught up in the frenzy and pay too much for an item and end up with buyer's remorse. Get smart quick: pick up a book on auctions at a library or book store, and watch the auction shows on the Home & Garden TV channel and KPBS. Increase your knowledge to lower your risk and to be able to bid with confidence.

Here's an example of a real surprise at an auction: a couple bid $100 on a box that they thought contained tools, only to find it contained several pieces of valuable turn-of-the-century sculpture by a San Francisco artist which the San Francisco art museum wanted, and they were worth boo-coodles of money.

Most people don't know where or how to find out about auctions. Here's how: auctions are publicized in display ads and in the classified ads (Section #2000) in the *Union-Trib*. You can also call and get on the mailing list (free or for a subscription fee) of auction houses listed in the *Yellow Pages*. And, there are tons of auction Web sites. Just type in "Auctions" using a search engine like Ask.com (See auction sites later this section.) Be aware that auctions prompt many online consumer fraud complaints.

Here are some hard-to-find auctions that are not listed in the *Yellow Pages* that sell confiscated goods including everything under the sun, bicycles and vehicles, unclaimed articles and court evidence, surplus items, patrol cars, articles from drug busts, from storage, and much more:

San Diego Police Department Auction General property (stolen and unclaimed merchandise and bicycles), (619) 531-2767 (recording of next date of sale)
General Services Administration (GSA), Federal and local government vehicles are sold by a private company in Oceanside. Call (760) 754-3664.

City & County Coop Auction at 5555 Overland Dr, (858) 694-2920; 1-877-554-0551.Large auction of general merchandise, furniture, equipment, bicycles, computers, late model vehicles, electronics, school & office equipment, tools, refrigerators, musical instruments. Three times a year. Brochure available w/photos. Call for dates and location.

Government Liquidation: hundreds of items each sale including televisions, computers, uniforms, equipment, navy motor boats, more. Call (619) 575-8914 or go to their Web at govliquidation.com for dates.

Government Seized Property Auctions Real estate, boats, vehicles, jewelry, apparel, electronics. This site includes the dates and locations of sale: treas.gov/auctions/customs

County Public Administrator, personal property and real estate, (858) 694-3500. Auction every other month on the third Saturday at 5201-A Ruffin Road. General estate and conservator property including furniture, autos, toys, etc. Call for brochure of real estate. Web: papg.org

McCormack Auctions (handles government auto auctions once a month in Chula Vista + So. Cal. (619) 447-1196.

UCSD Surplus Sales store, 7835 Trade Street, Miramar area, (858) 695-2660, serves as a means to liquidate excess university property including computers (and office equipment, office furniture and more) at auction every Wednesday from 8-2pm.

Goodwill Industries Auctions, (619) 428-7776. Daily auctions, 7 days, 10:00 a.m., 12:00 noon. (Unsold stuff from their stores)

Salvation Army Auctions, 1335 Broadway. Call (619) 239-4037x0; M-F, 9am to 11am; furniture and lots of " as is" stuff.

St. Vincent De Paul Auctions, 6 days, 8:30-11a.m. + M & Th 6pm, (619) 687-1090.

Great American Auction For a current list of auctions, call (800)-85-GREAT.

Museum of Man, Balboa Park, annual Collectors Club Auction of donated artifacts. Benefits the museum; unusual art, clothing, textiles from all over the world, for cheap! Held in October, call for date: (619) 239-2001. Ask about the preview catalog.

Public Storage, monthly sales of items left in storage units at their facilities around the county. Check the classified ads in the *Union-Trib* under Auctions #2000 and more auctions are in the *Daily Transcript*.

H&N Goodies Family Auction, 10 E. 8th St, National City, Wednesdays at 5pm; Preview same day from 9am. (619) 474-8296.

Mr. Auction, 9464 Gimmicky Blvd., Spring Valley, Thursdays at 5:30pm, preview from noon. Web: auctionpreview.net

Online Auctions, all new stuff, Web site at: onsale.com; Go to google.com and search for "online auctions."

Ebay, the largest online auction site, has everything, so if you can't find it on ebay, it probably doesn't exist. Web: ebay.com Click on Safe Harbor and view their policies and protection. You can buy wholesale.lots

Not the most exciting event I've ever been to, but an auction at the Otay Mesa border facility began at 10 a.m. with an hour before hand for inspecting the merchandise. The sale included a computer which sold for $125, several industrial machines, an ocean meter for $260, four boxes of used stereo receivers and tape decks for $140, 96 hot water heaters for a $2,300, a ceiling fan for $25, two cartons of cups and mugs for $30. The real buy of the day was a $5000 bamboo bedroom set that sold for $275!

Sales of Government Real Estate, (800) 421-7848.

The Postal Service holds auctions of unclaimed/undeliverable mail and packages. Call the Mail Recovery Center at postal headquarters in Atlanta, Philadelphia, San Francisco and St. Paul.

Here are some Web Sites for auction hunters:
Take a look at the auctionwatch.com, a metasearch engine which will make a search of ALL the auction sites for you. Type in what you are looking for (diamonds or Levis) and it will search and list all the sites that are auctioning those items..

Union-Trib Marketplace/Auctions . . . http://Auctions.signonsandiego.com
    200,000 local and national auction items.

San Diego County Auctions	co.san-diego.ca.us/cnty
Andy's Garage Sale (new stuff, dirt cheap)	andysgarage.com/misc
Auction Web (since 1995; 4 million new auctions a day)	ebay.com/aw/
Auction Hunters	auctionhunter.com
Antique Trails	netnow.micron.net/`trails/index.html
Internet Auction List	usaweb.com/auction.html
Dixon & Dixon	dixon-antiques.com
Butterfield & Butterfield	butterfields.com
Christie's East	christies.com
Harris	harrisauction.com
Dozens of sites	auctions-on-line.com
Onsale Auction Supersite	onsale.com

Automobiles

This is the one area where you can really save a lot of money if you do your homework. Here are some tips to help you save money on your next car purchase. Keep your car longer than five years, choose a small car, don't trade in your old car (sell it privately), opt for manual shift, limit number of options, reject extra services, pay cash or check into best finance charges in advance and have a sizeable down payment. Shop, shop, shop, and then shop some more. Don't buy impulsively and end up with "buyer's remorse." Wait til the end of the month to make your offer, as salesmen have quotas to meet to get a bonus, and you can negotiate a better deal if they want the sale. More tips follow.

New Cars: Before you make this major purchase, pick up a copy of one of the annual new-car buying guides: *Car Book, Car Driver, Edmund's New Car Prices,* (or check online at edmunds.com, autobytel.com and carfax.com which have links to tons of info and chat areas; carsmart.com;

and Autopedia offer car pricing, insurance, more. Digital Cars offers new and used car pricing and an online calculator to see what those monthly payments will be; Priceline.com offers a "name your own price" deal. All offer info on how a car ranks in performance and what defects appear. They give the dealer's invoice price, and tell you how much you should/should not pay over the invoice price. These manuals are available at libraries, supermarkets, drugstores, newsstands, bookstores, credit unions and banks and online, and will save you boo-coo bucks.

For a printout guide to the dealer's cost for a new car, call Consumer Reports New or Used Car Price Reports, (800) 933-5555, or check their Web site at consumerreports.com. The report will include comparisons of sticker vs. dealer invoice prices, factory rebate information, and other information and tips on how to deal with the dealer. Cost: about $15 for one New Car Price Report, less for additional reports ordered on the same call. Pay with credit card. (This information can save you about $1,000 or more!) If you have a trade in, you can hear the market trade-in and private-sale value of your used vehicle for $10 per vehicle, or you can go to Kelly Blue Book online at kbb.com and get it for *free*. (AAA offers a similar Auto Purchasing Service: one vehicle report, about $15; two cars $22.00; three cars $29.50 plus tax.

Consumer Reports magazine publishes a new-car buying guide each April, listing ratings of features, prices for various models, mechanical problems, etc. Valuable information. Web: consumereports.com

Consumers Digest offers a Web site for automobiles, pricing, ratings, etc: consumersdigest.com.

If you go to autos.msn.com, you'll find everything from the manufacture showcase to invoice to financing to insurance quotes, with calculators for car payment estimates and more. Or log on to CarsDirect.com and find a car, pick a color, choose options and more.

Check the Web sites for the various automakers including Ford, Lincoln, Chrysler, Eagle, Nissan, etc. Just type the make into the "hole" and up will come all models for the year, with links to dealers in San Diego. For comparison prices for autos, insurance, etc., try carprices.com.

Costco's Auto Program is designed for members. Steps to buying a new car at a great deal are: 1) pick up a catalog at the warehouse; 2) make an appointment with the dealer (deal only with contacts listed); 3) show your Costco card upon arrival at the dealership and ask to see the Costco dealer participation certificate; 4) select the vehicle of your choice (several dealers participate), then ask to see the pre-established Costco Auto Program No-Hassle Price Sheet. Trade-in's, too. For more information, call (800) 800-5778. Web site: costcoauto.com. Sam's Club has an autobuying program, too. Check their Web site at: samsclub.com.

New Cars Inc., 7304 El Cajon Blvd., San Diego, (619) 697-2886, plus several locations in San Diego. New Cars Inc is San Diego's largest non-franchised **auto buying service** specializing in acquiring your car for as little as possible. They take the hassle out of negotiating with the dealer. New Cars Inc. customers say they save an average of $1,100 on new cars, not to mention countless hours of comparison-shopping hassle. They enable you to buy a new car, truck, van or recreational vehicle, domestic or foreign, at a price below what you can get the same vehicle for at a dealer. Price quotes include all dealer and broker fees. Contact them after you have shopped and decided on the exact vehicle you want including make, model, colors, finishes and optional equipment. New Cars Inc. will then locate the vehicle to your specifications, frequently in another city, and bring it to San Diego for you. They also have a large inventory of used cars. Free service.

Autoland, an auto broker, over 50 locations in California, new and used, (619) 474-8292 Similar to New Cars Inc., this is another source for new or used autos at a discount. Save the hassle of negotiating.

Luxury cars with a manufacturer's rebate are sometimes cheaper than economy models!

When the new models of cars come out, the unsold last year's models can be negotiated at very good prices. These are brand new cars with brand new warranties that are considered to be "a year old" because a newer model is out. You can really get a deal here, so take your time and do your best negotiating.

Car manufacturers lure customers in by offering interest rates as low as 0.9%, depending on the car and model. This may save you more than a cash rebate, but check the overall price.

Make your new car last practically forever by reading the owners manual and doing what it says, changing oil as prescribed, changing transmission fluid every 12,000 miles, flush and change the engine coolant every year, replace belts & hoses every two years; and replace timing belt at 50,000 miles.

If you lose your keys, no need to call a locksmith. Look in the glove compartment on the back of the lock and there is a NUMBER imprinted. Or, if necessary, you can call the dealer and ask them to look up the key number (by VIN number;) then take the key number to a key maker.

Auto Loans: Every Sunday, the *Union-Trib* publishes the auto loan rates at local banks in the Business Section. Credit unions have excellent auto loan rates, and some offer pre-approved auto loans and have special sales with various dealers. (Some credit unions have restricted membership, but anyone who lives in San Diego can join Kearny Mesa Financial credit union, (858) 292-4851. Anyone with children in a San Diego school can join Mission Federal Credit Union.) The *Pennysaver* is a good source for locating auto loans for those with credit problems. Every week, they have display ads for auto dealers who specialize in financing problem loans. You will, however, pay more interest, so shop around. Check for best loan rates at bankrate.com and click on Autos.

Buying Volvos, Mercedes, Saabs and BMWs factory-direct in Europe: Volvo advertises that you can get your car direct from the factory including a ticket to Sweden and still save money. And, you can fly to Europe to pick up a Mercedes or BMW, complete with California smog specifications. Drive your new car all over Europe, saving on car rental fees which can be up to $400 a week, and then have your new car shipped home! For more information on European delivery, call Volvo, (800) 631-1667; BMW, (800) 932-0831; Mercedes-Benz, (800) 222-0100x4; Saab, (800) SAAB USA; Allow 3-4 months lead time. For other autos, contact the dealer or manufacturer and inquire if they have a plan for buying factory-direct. Not all manufacturers will sell direct; I was unable to find a Detroit manufacturer that sells factory direct.

If you feel you have bought a **"lemon,"** take your complaint to CALPIRG, (California Public Interest Group), (916) 448-4516 or check their Web site: calpirg.org; Also, contact the Department of Consumer Affairs in Sacramento for referrals, (800) 344-9940.

Used Vehicles: Picking a reliable used car can be tricky. Here are some suggestions: Before purchasing a used vehicle, ask if it has been in an accident. Get the Vehicle Identification Number, and call a dealer who can check the computer to see if it has been in a prior collision and salvaged. To find out if a used car has been "recalled" due to manufacturer defects, call (800) 424-9393, or any dealership. *Consumer Reports Used Car Buying Guide* is available in libraries and rates used cars according to frequency of repair information. Cars that have had better than average ratings for the past five years have been the Honda Accord, Toyota Camray,

Volvo, Nissan Maxima, Chevrolet Lumina. Some years they are rated higher than others, so be sure to check this out. Next, have a mechanic check it out before buying (see below).

The National Automobile Dealers Association's *Official Used Car Guide*, which is often called the "blue book," lists the average trade-in and retail prices for most makes and models. Available at book stores, libraries, banks, credit unions, etc. The Auto Club of Southern California (AAA) offers a Used Car Pricing service by phone. One car, $5. Vehicle pricing is also available on the Web at aaa.calif.com/auto-buy. Kelly Blue Book is available at libraries, banks, credit union and free online at kbb.com.

The *Union Tribune* has an interactive section on their Web site to help you buy an auto: signonsandiego.com

Before committing to a used car, take it to a garage that will do a diagnostic evaluation of the condition of the motor, transmission and other parts. AAA offers a **diagnostic service** for members *and* non-members. For around $75, you can have a car tested for various ailments which could save you a bundle of money and headaches. AAA also publishes a free directory of AAA-approved mechanics for members and non-members. Call (800) 713-0003 for more information. Also, AAA sponsors a used-car sale in conjunction with a used-car provider. All cars are warranted for 12 months or 12,000 miles. For members only, call (800) 807-8222. Web site: aaa.calif.com.

KSDO AM1130 sponsors a radio show on Sundays called All About Cars from 10-11am. Call in for advice.

Paul Katson offers an on-site used vehicle pre-purchase mechanical inspection including compression, electrical, accident damage. For more information, call Inspect-A-Car, (619) 259-7555; ASE certified.

Many used car dealers offer extended warranties on used cars. Carefully check what is covered and the time frame. Many things are not covered. You can purchase extended warranties online at: auto-warranties.net.

Consumer Reports devotes an issue every year to auto **repair records** for 288 late model used cars up to five years old, indicating which cars cost the least to maintain. Check here to avoid buying a known loser. Available at newsstands, bookstores and libraries or the Web: consumerreports.com.

Budget Rent-a-Car's rental fleet and leased cars and trucks are sold at; Miramar (858) 623-2300; Escondido (760) 735-2673; and El Cajon, (619)

593-3611. Buicks, Oldsmobiles, Pontiacs, Hondas, Cadillacs, Chevrolets, Fords, Lincoln's, etc, vans, trucks, minivans. Most cars are under factory warranty and you can purchase extended warranties. Mainly vehicles with 20-25,000 miles. Lots of cars. Other locations in Escondido and Mira Mar Road.

Enterprise rental car sales office, 7993 Balboa near Hwy. 163, (858) 277-6600; 850 El Cajon Blvd., El Cajon (619) 579-5566; all vehicles are mechanically certified and backed by 12 month/12,000 mile service policy on engine, transmission and drive train. Large selection; over 80 makes and models of cars, compacts to Cadillacs, trucks and mini-vans; mainly one to two years old, with 10-40,000 miles. Seven day repurchase agreement; no hassle pricing system.

The Federal Government sells over 40,000 **government used vehicles** each year including sedans, station wagons, trucks, vans, motorcycles and buses to the public for nearly $70 million through the General Services Administration (GSA). Information on how to buy **seized vehicles** is sold for $10 and up through the classified ads of local and national newspapers. Do not succumb to advertisements offering to sell you information on "how to purchase government property at insider auctions for ridiculously low bids." What you get for your 10 bucks is a list of addresses and phone numbers of GSA offices around the country, which you can get yourself, free. If you are interested in buying a well-maintained used government car at a fair price, the information on government sales is listed under "Auctions," earlier this chapter. Do not expect to purchase a luxury vehicle for $250 or a jeep for $50, as you may have been led to believe.

Automobile Insurance: Auto insurance is mandatory in the State of California as of January 1, 1997. The new law requires motorists to produce proof of coverage to renew vehicle registration and whenever they are pulled over by a police officer. Violators face steep fines from $1,350-$2,700. If you cannot get insurance, the insurer of last resort is the California Auto Assigned Risk Plan (CAARP) in Sacramento, who will insure anyone.

If you want to save money on insurance, according to one of the "Big Time Financial Gurus," you need to call at least six insurance agencies and compare rates. So, dial on, my friends, and you will be able to save some substantial bucks, usually several hundred dollars. Four companies who have consistently offered lower rates are Wawanesea (619) 285-6000; 21st Century, (800) 443-3100 (21st Century includes coverage in No. Baja); GEICO, (800) 932-8874; Mercury Insurance Co, (800) 579-3467. Do comparison of rates at insurance.ca.gov. Insurance Express has a large computerized base and can locate the best rates for you, (858) 576-3200.

If you carry more than one type of insurance policy with a company or broker (such as automobile *and* homeowners), you usually get a 10% discount.

For advice and information on various insurance coverages, call the National Insurance Consumer Help Line at (800) 942-4242.

Auto Repairs/Paint/Upholstery: If you need repairs, paint or upholstery, get at least three estimates to compare before making your decision. The dealer will usually have the highest bid. You can save money on paint jobs and upholstery in Tijuana. Buy the paint from the dealer and take it down. Get three estimates in San Diego before you go, and use a shop that bakes the paint dry to cure it (or it will flake off!). Your car may have to be left overnight for painting. Some people get the dents knocked out down there and have the painting done up here, if returning to Tijuana to pick up the car is inconvenient. There are dozens of auto body and upholstery shops between the border and Revolucion. I had a car painted down there and I have a friend who restores cars and has had many, many painted and upholstered there. Keep your paint job waxed and it will last many years longer. Many people get radiator and muffler work done in TJ, too.

Thao's Auto Repair, 3400 El Cajon Blvd., (619) 640-4606, and 3752 Park Boulevard and Robinson, Hillcrest, (619) 692-1065. It's owned and run by an oriental woman! This came highly recommended to me, and went there for my car repairs for several years, until I bought a new one.

For used auto parts, call Ecology Auto Wrecking, (619) 409-920, open 7 days; or check "Auto Parts Supplies & Accessories-Used" and "Junkyards-Automotive" in the *Yellow Pages.* (Tip: check the GREEN/BLUE section of topical listings in the front of the *Yellow Pages* first). A great place to get mirrors, doors, seats, axles, fenders, windows, hubcaps, etc. You can locate 1.5 million car parts for cars, trucks, suvs at carparts.com., or search for used auto parts at google.com.

Here are come sites for Auto troubleshooting: troubleshooter.com, autofixes.com; marksalem.com; (host of car radio show); 1carumba.com Automotive Q&A and links, eauto.com; Click & Clack, PBS Car Talk guys, cartalk.msn.com.

Get an estimate from the companies that advertise themselves as offering "Discount" services: Discount Auto Parts, Discount Auto Supply, Discount

Battery Co., Discount Auto Electric, Discount Radiator & Muffler, Discount Tire Co., or Discount Transmission listed in the telephone directory. However, some discount companies aren't always "discount," so do your comparison shopping.

Charge your auto repairs on a major credit card and if there is any problem that you are not happy with and cannot resolve, your credit card will back the charges off your account if you present copies of all bills, correspondence, calls, etc. (Wow, this is a good tip!)

Auto Complaints: If you feel you got stung on an auto repair, call the consumer's complaint and protection agency at (800) 952-5210. They love to help in these matters, and will send you a complaint form and get busy for you, or download one from their site at dca.ca.gov

If you *really* need to save the money, and you have the time to go this route, check into auto mechanic classes offered through community colleges, adult schools, vocational schools, ROP programs and high schools to see if they can take your car as a class project (the teacher oversees everything). It isn't always possible to get your car fixed when you want it, but if you have the time and can coordinate it with a school, you can have the work done for just the cost of parts, fabric, paint, etc.

Discount coupons for a **smog check** are in the *Pennysaver* every week and usually in your neighborhood newspaper, too. Get your car tuned before inspection with new spark plugs, etc. If your vehicle is tested and fails as a Gross Polluter, you must have it repaired and then have another inspection to certify those repairs. Repairs can be very costly. Financial assistance is available for those in need. If a car was made before a certain year, it may be exempt. Call the Department of Consumer Affairs at 800-952-5210, or go to dca.ca.gov and search for Gross Polluter. Unfortunately, you can really get "taken" on a smog check and repairs if you aren't informed.

Discount coupons are always in the *Pennysaver* for an oil change, about $10 off. (It's wise to have your oil changed every 3000 miles in order to "save" your engine. I understand some new cars don't need this, but older ones do.)

Costco has great prices on tires & installation, batteries and auto accessories, automotive tools, (and GAS at Morena Blvd., Carlsbad, Vista, Ranch del Rey). For Costco locations, see "Costco Warehouse."

Swapmeets have vendors that sell car polish, dash covers, seat covers, floor mats, bras, sheepskin and other auto accessories.

Other auto info and tips:

Emergency road service policies are available from the Automobile Club of Southern California (AAA), (619) 233-1000, Signature, (800) 323-2002, Exxon Travel Club & Emergency Road Service, (800) 833-9966. Sears offers a policy, too. I've had an AAA card for almost 20 years and consider it one of the most important "life-savers" around. It pays for itself if you have car trouble only once, and I wouldn't want to be without the peace of mind it affords me. It's the best friend you could have if you have a car problem. For a fee of $64 the first year which includes the $20 enrollment fee, and $44 per year thereafter. Additional adults are $21 adult, and $24 for under 21. If your car needs to be towed, they tow it for you; if you have a flat tire, they fix it for you; if you lock yourself out of the car, they come to the rescue; if your car won't start, they try to start it. If you are riding in someone else's car and it has problems, your membership covers any car you are riding in! Membership includes a packet of local maps and their Travel Club will provide you with maps and a personalized trip plan for any car trip in the U.S., free! You'll also receive their quarterly magazine, and you may make travel reservations and purchase airline tickets and tour packages. I won an American-Hawaii Cruise for two at their Travel Show! AAA membership is a great gift, too. I received my membership as a gift the first year. I love it! AAA also offers auto insurance. Check their site for discounts on a number of services and restaurants (Soup Plantation), shopping, AAA travel guides and more: aaa-calif.com/members/discounts

Discount coupons for a nearby car wash are usually on the back of your supermarket receipts. (Car washes have gotten expensive, but they save you lots of time!!) Be sure to wax it frequently to protect the paint.

Pay parking tickets promptly. Failure to do so may result in an automatic warrant for your arrest. Then, if you are stopped for any reason, when the officer calls in your license number, the computer will show you have a warrant! And, you'll go to jail!

If you are stopped by a police officer for any reason, pull over and wait for him or her to approach your car. Do not reach for your purse, for the glove compartment, or anything until the officer directs you to. The officer may think you are reaching for a weapon. They have to deal with a lot of weirdos (which they are tough on). If you don't want them to be tough with you, be extra respectful, very courteous and polite; address them by their name on their badge (Officer "X"). Tips: never argue with the officer, never touch the officer; never resist an officer, never leave the scene.

If you get a ticket for a moving violation, you usually have three choices: pay the fine before the due date, pay the fine and go to traffic school or fight the ticket. Ask the officer about going to traffic school, or call San Diego Police Department and inquire. If you are eligible to go to traffic school, your ticket won't show on your DMV record and your insurance company won't be informed (for certain violations only, and only once in 18 months). Or, you might want to fight *minor* infractions. I have heard that half the time, the ticketing officer doesn't show up in court due to a conflicting schedule or he/she has the day off, and if he/she doesn't show, your case may be dismissed. I don't know if that is absolutely true, but I have heard from a reliable source that it is possible (as in VERY possible!) If you ignore the ticket, however, you could be charged with failure to appear, and a warrant for your arrest could be issued.

You can go to traffic school approved by San Diego courts on the Internet for $19.95, at trafficschoolonline.com. The course takes between 4-6 hours, and sure beats sitting in a classroom all day. I went to the Comedy Traffic School, taught by some of the comedians in town and avoided having points put on my DMV record for something I did that was STUPID.

You can make appointments at DMV online. Go to www.ca.gov and click on DMV and schedule an appointment (rather than stand in line at the DMV to be served.) If you are an Auto Club member, you can do many DMV transactions at a AAA center, like registering your car. Much easier (and more pleasant) than going to DMV.

Auto lovers will enjoy the Automobile Museum in Balboa Park and at Deer Park Winery in Escondido. Also, the Auto Museum at the Imperial Palace in Las Vegas has more than 800 vehicles and the largest car-related trinket and gift shop in the world, (702) 794-3294.

Bartering

If you own your own business or have something to trade, you will want to consider this one. Join a barter club. A barter club functions as a clearinghouse or bank of goods and services for its members to trade. For a membership fee, you get a list of members with whom and you can trade your "whatever" for something else. The barter club takes a broker's fee for the match-up, frequently in the form of your goods or services, so there may be no money exchanged at all! Businesses from Mom 'n Pop operations to major corporations trade goods and services including optometry, podiatry, ski equipment, broadcast commercials, accounting, massage, trips, hotel rooms, office supplies, restaurants, auto repairs, display advertising, and anything else you can think of. See the *Yellow Pages* for listings of "Barter & Trade Exchanges." Compare membership contracts, costs and services. Ask what products and services are exchanged, and ask for a list of clients. Check to see if they are satisfied. Maybe you have specific needs and can't use tons of restaurant "money/script." You can make your own private deals, too. It's worth asking! A publishing consultation client of mine who lives in Santee said she would drop by my house after going to the chiropractor in Pacific Beach. I inquired why she uses a PB chiropractor if she lives in Santee. She said her husband is a carpenter, so they exchange services with her chiropractor who needed some cabinets installed! If anyone wants to trade something with me for copies of my book, or to speak to your organization, or a consultation on how to publish, let's talk! Call me at (619) 222-8489 and leave a message.

Beauty Supplies & Services

Here are a few suggestions that can put more beauty products and services into your life, and you'll save money, too!

Look under "Beauty Colleges" in the *Yellow Pages* for a school in your area. Great savings on all beauty services including shampoo and set, perms, coloring, facials, manicures, pedicures, etc. You will be worked on by a student, one who is well along in his/her course work, and all the work is overseen by an instructor. It takes a little more time, so go on a weekday...early in the week is best.

The City College Department of Cosmetology offers beauty services performed by students. Huge savings: facial with mask & pack, $10; high frequency (electrical) facial, $10; chemical peel, $20 up; shampoo and set, $5 up; hair cut with shampoo/blow dry, $7+. Senior discounts on hair services. Located in the "S" Building at 16th and C (City College campus). No appointments, walk-in basis. Call (619) 230-2104 for hours of operation and further information.

Many beauty salons need "models" for their stylists to try new products and methods. For a free haircut, maybe even a perm or other service, check "Notices" in the *Reader* classifieds.

Haircuts for men for $4; women, $5.50, at the Associated Barber College, 1045 11th Ave, downtown, (619) 234-7703. All work done by students under expert supervision. No appointment necessary.

For discounted cosmetics and bulk hair care products, look under "Beauty Supplies" in the *Yellow Pages*. You can pick up gallon jugs of salon-brand hair care products, name brand cosmetics and designer fragrances at big savings. Sally's Beauty Supply has several stores. San Diego Salon Supply (SDSS), has top quality products at discount prices, and refills on some products. Several locations including Ocean Beach, (619) 226-6900.

Costco and Sam's Club sell bulk hair products, toothpaste, body wash deodorant, moisturizers and other products in bulk at great savings, too.

Swap meets have a vendors with discounted cosmetics and hair care products with some well known brands including Paul Mitchell. Kobey's Swap Meet has several vendors that sell name brand cosmetics and perfumes, 20-60% off, beauty salon supplies, shampoos, barrettes and hair accessories, toothpaste, hair cutting scissors, hair sprays, deodorants, plus hair and nail service. For vender stall numbers, see *Kobey's Magazine & Directory* available free of charge at the swap meet, or by paid subscription. See "Swap Meets" for more information.

The coupon supplement section of the Sunday *Union-Tribune* has discount coupons for national brand beauty products, hair coloring, cleansers, shampoos, hand creams, toothpaste, etc. I used a $1 off coupon at Von's for a $1.79 bottle of Vaseline Intensive Care hand lotion, which I got *free*, since Von's doubles the coupon value! Visit the Web site of your favorite products and download discount coupons! If none are available, click on "contact us" and request coupons by email or mail.

Target Stores, Kmart, Long's, SavOn, Walmart and RiteAid frequently offer 25-50% off name brand cosmetics. A good time to pick up a few things. See their advertising supplements every Sunday in the *Union-Tribune*.

Cosmetics Co. Store Carlsbad Company Stores, (760) 804-9194; The whole store carries only overstocks and discontinued packaging items for Estee Lauder products, Clinique, Origins and Bobbi Brown cosmetics, and more, normally sold at major department stores. Prices are 20-50% lower.

Perfume "fakes" are copies of designer scents. The fragrance doesn't last as long on the skin because it is made from a lower percentage of perfume oils, but they are extremely affordable, and are in some cases, very much like the finer perfumes. "Fakes" are available at Long's, SavOn and RiteAid Drugs, Mervyn's, Target, Kmart, Walmart and swap meets.

Tijuana is a freeport, meaning you can save 10% on import taxes. Imported designer perfumes from France are available at a number of places including **Sara's** on Revolucion at 5th, **Le Drug Store** at Revolucion and 4th, telephone 011-52-664-685-0374. Both are nice places to shop. In the Plaza Rio Shopping Center, the department stores carry Charles of the Ritz cosmetics, Estee Lauder, Lancome and other top lines at a discount in addition to the 10% import tax. English is spoken at these fine boutiques .

Better name brand cosmetics and fragrances offer special "gifts" with minimum purchase as a promotion at department stores, and boy, that's the time to buy! Ask to be placed on the mailing list and you'll be notified of the next promotion. There's always something coming up. These are very popular, and for a limited time only while supply lasts. Shop early.

Don't forget to ask for your free samples of fragrances when you are in better department stores! Such a deal!

Major department stores have free fashion shows, some with complimentary wine, hors d'oeuvres and a 10-15% discount coupon for anything in the store purchased that day! *San Diego Magazine* has a fashion column with show dates, and there's a fashion column in the *Union-Trib* every Saturday morning with show dates. A great way to see the latest fashions and attendees usually get those great discount coupons for that day's shopping!

Here's a goodie: Get on the mailing list to receive the Beauty Boutique quarterly catalog. Since 1969, they have offered tons of cosmetics and fragrances at huge savings. Name brands like Paloma Picasso, Halston, Fendi, Christian Dior (Poison, $14.99), Jean Patou (Joy, $12.99), Gucci, Versace, Oscar de la Renta. Skin care, cosmetics, some jewelry, savings to 90%. Tons of items. Also, items sold in TV infomercials at a discount. Call 800-497-7463 or visit their Web site at amerimark.com

Cosmopolitan Virtual Makeover is available on CD-ROM. Load your picture into the computer and select from hundreds of options. Try 150 hairstyles, 20 hair colors, makeup. Free demo at virtualmakeover.com. They also have a Virtual Fashion Makeover on CD-Rom.

Fragrances, cosmetics, skincare products online at ibeauty.com

Discover your best colors. Carol Revelli, color expert *extra*-ordinaire, offers a free catalog of books and kits on color and style analysis for your wardrobe. She even has a book and kit on color coordinating and decorating your home! Carol has sold hundreds of thousands of her books. Call (800) 738-3554 for a catalog.

Check out the health spa deals in the chapter on "Health." Even if a day at a bargain luxury spa isn't in the budget this month, you can still treat yourself to spa amenities. Get out a pretty tea cup, an assortment of tea and a scented candle. Buy a good facial mask, some new nail polish, hair conditioner and fragrant bubble bath or oil, and spend a Saturday taking care of you.

Bicycles

Police auctions are held several times a year during which hundreds of unclaimed bicycles are sold. As you can imagine, all kinds of bicycles are there, from beat-up to brand new. My electrician said he took me up on this and went to see what the police auction had. He scored a $2000 custom super-deluxe bike for a few hundred bucks. Was he thrilled or what! Cash or personal check with identification; no credit cards. Call (619) 531-2767 for a recording of sale dates at the Scottish Rites Center in Mission Valley. All sales begin at 10 a.m., with one hour of viewing before. No warranties. No return or refunds. There is always a bike auction a few weeks before Xmas. If you can't wait for the next auction, try the "Thrifties #3150" classifieds in the *Union-Trib*, or the classifieds in the *Reader*. You and your kids can have every size bike on the planet, cheap.

Books

If a book store doesn't have a book you're looking for, fret not, for behold! They can get it for you usually within a week if the title appears in their computer, and they'll call you when it's in, or mail it to you. Book stores usually order books daily to replenish what's been sold, so it's not like it's as "special" as it sounds. There is no charge for ordering it in, and you'll save a lot of time running around town looking for a title you can't live without.

For wonderful books on San Diego, see the chapter on "101+ Free & Bargain Things to Do in San Diego." Titles include *San Diego Trivia, Cycling San Diego, San Diego Architecture, Afoot and Afield in San Diego, the Missions of San Diego; Jackpot Trail: Indian Gaming in So. California* (22 casinos). There are dozens of books with a San Diego orientation; something for every interest. Ask your bookstore manager to see a list of San Diego titles which are distributed by Sunbelt Publications in El Cajon. Unfortunately, no store carries all titles. Sunbelt has occasional sales of returned or damaged books at 1250 Fayette St., El Cajon, (619) 258-4911.

You have probably seen some of the "clearance" book stores that have been springing up here and there. They carry publishers overstocks and unsold inventory. Major book stores usually have a section devoted to this type of book, too, at unbelievable prices. Perhaps a publisher printed 750,000 copies of a book and only sold 500,000 of them. The remainder is sold as "bargain" books at major chain book stores, clearance stores, swap meets, Dollar stores, Ebay, etc. I have a great time browsing around in the clearance books section of bookstores. Large coffee table books, cook books, health, psychology, history, financial, children's books and more. For a catalog of overstock books, write to Edward R. Hamilton, Bookseller, Falls Village, CT 06031-5000, or check his Web site: edwardrhamilton.com.

Libraries: If there is any information you are seeking, and you don't know where to ask, call your local librarian! They *love* to help you locate information, and they have vast knowledge of resources available. I call them all the time. The downtown library is the largest in the County and has more books and services than the branch libraries, but I always call the nearest branch first. Books can be transferred from one branch to another in a few days. Libraries also have audio tapes, typewriter rentals, video rentals, and computer time. The main library downtown offers a short, free Internet class every Tuesday at 2 p.m. in the Science section. Learn how to access the library on the Internet from your home, too. Over 64% of San Diego adults go online, and here is a good place to start if you're not one of them. The San Diego Public Library Web site is: sdplweb.sannet.gov

NetLibrary is a site that offers only electronic books for sale. You download these e-books onto your computer for reading. They are very inexpensive as the publishers don't have to use paper or distributors or book stores to sell their books. Many books are searchable, which is great for reference books. Check it out at Netlibrary.com. There are numerous other ebook sites. Go to google.com and search for ebooks.

Used Books

Friends of the San Diego Public Library, a California tax exempt corporation, is an organization dedicated to the support and future of the public libraries. FSDPL sells the libraries' surplus books plus donations from the public and donations from local book stores at prices you won't believe: hardbacks, mostly $1; paperbacks 25¢ to $1. Great reference books, oversized books, children's books, fiction, etc. The San Diego downtown library has a sale every Friday, Saturday and Sunday. Your branch library probably has an ongoing "off-the-cart" sale, with an occasional big sale. For library sales, call your local library or the Friends' office at (619) 542-1724. City and County libraries are listed in the Government section of the *White Pages*. The libraries raise over $250,000 a year at their sales. They welcome your book donations for their sales at any branch, any time.

A number of **used book stores** are listed in the *Yellow Pages*. These stores are thriving. You can sell your surplus books to them, but not for much. Call first and see if they are interested in what you have. Try making them an offer: so much for a bag full of paperbacks, etc. You can try to locate an out-of-print-book through one of several used book dealers who advertise that they specialize in out of print books. Also, I pick up a lot of great used books, not only for myself, but for others, at yard sales (usually 25¢ to $1, rarely more.). I've gotten some of my "best" books at yard sales! You betcha. I even found a copy of my very own first published book! And I bought it . . . for a quarter . . . because I had sold every last one of them.... . . and I wanted one for my library!

Used book search on internet Abebooks.com has a database of more than 40 million titles from more than 10,000 independent booksellers located around the world. If you're seeking used, out of print or rare books, try here. Also, you can sell your old books here.

Book Appraisals: The Friends of the San Diego Public Libraries has a book appraisal clinic at the central library every April. Bring in your rare books for an official written appraisal by an authentic appraiser. One book, $5, three books, $10. (The price is right!) Call (619) 542-1724 for exact date. Wahrenbrocks, 726 Broadway, downtown, (619) 232-0132, offers free book appraisals by appointment. Email: wbh@ixpres.com.

The San Diego Booksellers Association has an annual **used book fair** every June (since 1998) with about 50 booths in Hillcrest, on 5th Avenue above Robinson. At that time, they offer free book appraisals, up to four books. This is a big event; lots of bargains. Call Bluestocking Books at (619) 296-1424 for more information and this year's date.

Carpets

You're crazy if you pay full price for carpets. There are carpet sales advertised *every* weekend in the *Union-Tribune*. I kept a diligent watch over this for several months and the same companies have sales every month or so, especially around holiday weekends when people have extra time to fix up their homes. Rule of thumb: the deeper, the denser, the better quality and better it will wear. Bend the back of the carpet to see how close together the tufts are. Some wool carpets are so well made they can be handed down from generation to generation; some orientals are hundreds of years old and in nearly perfect condition. Wool is the most expensive (and durable). Nylon (and some acrylics) are the most popular and most affordable. Beware the carpet sharks and deal with reputable firms that have been in business a long time to avoid paying $2000 for $800 worth of carpeting. Many carpets have a 5 year stain warranty and 10 years for wear. Inquire about the store's guarantee regarding customer satisfaction. Call and ask any carpet store how to measure so you will have an idea of how many yards you actually need. Carpet has a grain and needs to be laid all in one direction, or it will look like a completely different color where the direction is different. If you can use carpet remnants, you'll really be able to save. Carpet remnants are roll ends, and are sold at a good discount. They are usually small room size, but I've seen them up to 25-30 feet long. If you put tile, either ceramic or vinyl, in your hallways or just across your door jams, you might be able to use a remnant for each room! It works best if you use only one color carpet, like all beige, with beige tile. Some stores offer deferred billing on purchases over a few hundred dollars with no payment and no interest for 90 days. Here are some carpeting stores to check out:

Cole's Carpets, 1170 W. Morena, (619) 276-5140 and 850 Los Vallecitos in San Marcos, (760) 741-1001; El Cajon, 742 Fletcher, (619) 442-3277. For over 50 years, Cole's has sold quality carpets. They have great sales all the time, plus a remnant section with dozens of very nice quality remnants, many top of the line that are half price. Frequent "free padding" offers or get an extra 5% off, cash and carry, so don't forget to ask about specials. Area rugs, vinyl, laminates, hardwood and ceramic flooring, too. Big Tent sales with markdowns galore. Ask about bonus coupon discounts. Coles offers first year replacement free; some carpets have warranties to 5-10 years for stains, soil resistance and wear. Customer satisfaction guaranteed. Web: colescarpets.com

The Carpet Factory, 1222 Knoxville, (619) 275-1250, mostly apartment grade products. A lot of remnants (room size pieces.) Also, special order.

Sid's Carpet Barn, 132 W 8th Street, National City, (619) 264-3000, has a lot of lower-priced, thrift quality carpets plus lots of mid-priced carpets. Ask about warranties against holes. This is a popular store with many room-sized remnants..

Stone Mountain Mill Outlet, Lemon Grove, 7696 Broadway, (619) 668-9210. Fifty stores nationwide. Lots of carpet remnants (room size) from the mill, some were $38 a yard, marked down 50% and more

Home Depot Expo Design Center, 7811 Othello near Balboa & Convoy, has a good carpeting department with fine carpets, and the local Home Depots & Lowe's have basic carpeting and rugs, too. Good prices.

Costco offers complimentary "In-Home" appointments for Stainmaster carpets. See the Kiosk in the store and call (888) 992-2773 for quote.

Carpeteria Center, 948 Broadway & L St, Chula Vista, (619) 691-0500. Several stores in San Diego (Escondido, Morena Blvd., La Mesa, Miramar, Oceanside.) First quality carpets; lots of remnants (room size). Sales!

You can even buy your carpeting wholesale, factory-direct from the mills in Georgia, have it shipped out, and still save money. Here's how: shop around, find what you want in a carpet store, write down the exact brand name, number, color, and all other identifying information. Then call the following 800 toll-free numbers to see if they can beat local price. You can save on sales tax, too, depending on where it is shipped from. Shipping costs are about $1.20+ per yard, so 100 yards would ship for about $120+, and you'll probably save more than that in sales tax! They send a list of local installers when they send samples, or you can look under "Services Offered" in the *Union-Tribune* or *Reader* classified ads, or call a local carpet company and ask if they have any installers who moonlight. Here are carpet wholesalers to call. Some carry over 50 brands. Most will send you samples upon request, and they can tell you how to measure. Quality Discount Carpet, (800) 233-0993; Warehouse Carpets of Georgia, (888) 419-1710; Owen Carpet, (800) 235-1079; S&S Mills, (800) 363-4036, Web: ssmills.com.

Consider buying a steam carpet cleaner ($100-$300) when they are on sale (Penney's has 25% off sales a few times a year). Your own shampooer can save you lots in carpet cleaning bills and you'll probably do it more often. Some carpets stretch with steaming; consider dry chemical cleaners. Be sure to vacuum thoroughly AFTER the carpet dries to get out any loosened dirt . . or your carpet will look soiled again, P.D.Q. (OK, so I bought a great carpet shampooer at a yard sale, better than my old one!)

Pass on carpeting all together if you have any kind of allergies to dust. I can't wait to get hard wood floors!

Catalog Shopping (Mail Order)

Over 80 million shoppers buy from catalogs and mail order firms each year, and catalog sales are on an upward trend. Busy people are finding it convenient to browse through catalogs at home and phone in an order. We'll all be doing more of this in the future, as shopping by catalog and buying directly from Web sites are so convenient. Tips for catalog shopping: consider shipping fees; pay with a credit card to minimize return problems; understand the company's return policy and save your paperwork. Here are some great TOP RATED major mail order companies. Call and get on the mailing list. Check with ebay to see if someone is selling the returns. Most catalogs do not reshelve and resell returns. I have gotten Coldwater Creek, Nordstrom, QVC returns on Ebay.

Bloomingdale's by Mail . . (800) 777-0000	Patagonia . . . . (800) 638-6464
Brooks Brothers . . . . . . (800) 274-1815	Pottery Barn . . . . (800) 922-5507
Chadwick's of Boston . . . (800) 525-6650	REI . . . . (800) 426-4840
Crate & Barrel . . . . (800) 323-5461	Road Runner Sports . . . (800) 551-5558
Coldwater Creek . . . . (800) 968-0980	Sears . . . . (800) 366-3000
Eddie Bauer . . . . (800) 426-8020	Talbots . . . . (800) 882-5268
Hold Everything . . . . (800) 421-2264	Williams-Sonoma . . . . . . (800) 541-2233
J. C. Penney . . . . (800) 222-6161	
J. Crew . . . . (800) 562-0258	Catalog Link . . . . cataloglink.com
L. L. Bean . . . . (800) 221-4221	*Links to dozens and dozens of catalogs*
Land's End . . . . (800) 356-4444	*Including Fredericks of Hollywood, Barbie*
Lerner Direct . . . . (800) 288-4009	*Collectibles, Porsche, Ford, etc. Browse*
Neiman Marcus . . . . (800) 825-8000	*the catalogs online.*

Nordstrom Catalog, (800) 285-5800. Fine quality fashions with unconditional guarantee. Great selections, and their catalog personal shoppers have the exact measurements and specifications of every item at their fingertips. Free returns if you are doing an exchange; otherwise, it's $4.95. They send a prepaid mailing label to you already made out will pick it up your returns and deduct the postage from your refund. You can order in more than one size and return the one that doesn't fit, or both. The merchandise is not in Nordstrom Stores, but it's great stuff. Nordstrom.com

Wholesale by Mail & Online A thick catalog with more than 600 entries featuring clothing, crafts, sports and recreation, accordions, clothing, artwork, computers, furniture, foodstuffs, vacuums, vitamins, tools, silverware, sheets, all at extraordinary discounts. Selected by *Book of the Month Club, Playboy* and *Better Homes and Gardens* book clubs. Contains information on how to purchase brand names from suppliers. In publication for more than 20 years. Available in book stores for $20.95.

Children's Clothing, Furniture & Toys, Etc.

With children's clothing almost as expensive as adult apparel these days, *my*, how it hurts to pay top dollar, knowing it will be outgrown within a few months (and thrown in the hand-me-down pile!) Here are some great places to check out if you want to save money on children's clothing, accessories, furniture and other expenditures:

One of the best sources for kids' clothes, for both quality and price, is **Mervyn's**. Their buyers purchase national brand overruns and sell them at prices way below department stores that are carrying the identical merchandise. National brands include Bongo, Bugle Boy, Carter's, Gecko, Health-Tex, Levi', Ocean Pacific, OshKoshB'Gosh, Peanuts and Union Bay. Some items are ordered in especially for a sale; other merchandise may be in the store a few weeks and then goes on sale. All sale periods are from Sunday through Saturday. If you buy an item that isn't on sale, keep your receipts and if it goes on sale the following Sunday, Mervyn's will give you the cash difference if you bring in your sales slips before the next Saturday. Their private labels replicate the styles of many designer label fashions found at upscale boutiques domestically and abroad, for a fraction of the price. Their private labels include Color Circuit, LA Baby, Sprockets and Girls Next Door.

Carters Factory Outlet, San Diego Factory Outlet Mall, 4498 Camino de la Plaza, San Ysidro, (619) 690-1106, Carlsbad Company Stores, (760) 804-0254; Viejas Outlets, 5003 Willows Road, (619) 659-0635 offers 30-70% off retail on clothing and accessories for newborns, and playwear, swimwear, sleepwear up to children's size 6x, wooden toys and puzzles. Crib sheets, some lamps. Usually everything 30% off store prices; occasional sales with 40% off. Racks of clearance items, 50-70% off.

OshKosh Factory Outlet, 4460 Camino de la Plaza, San Ysidro, (619) 690-2255; Carlsbad store, (760) 804-1637. Name brand clothing sold at Robinson-May and Macy's for children 0-3 months and to age 14-16. New items are 30% off; periodic sales of 50% off. Buy three items, get additional discount. Infant and toddlers clothing, children's jeans, T-shirts, shorts, some dresses, some sleepwear.

Big Dog Factory Outlet, Viejas Outlets, (619) 659-1655 and Carlsbad Company Stores, (760) 931-7835. Infants and children's up to size 18. Shorts, t-shirts, button shirts, polo shirts, pj's, more.

Strausburg Children, Carlsbad Company Stores, (760) 804-9660. Fast growing chain with 40 stores nationwide with upscale children's wear; fine pima cottons, hand smocked, french seamed sundresses, $32.99; hats, shoes, 100% silk dresses, organza with hand embroidery. All merchandise is 30% off the mall store's prices. Current season clothing. Newborn to size 14 for girls and newborn to size 6 for boys. Visit their Web site at strausburgchildren.com.

Other great places to shop for good prices on kids' brand name clothing for less are: Target, Kids Mart, Kmart, BigLots, Costco, Sam's Club, Walmart, Marshal's, Ross, T.J. Maxx, Burlington Coat Factory's Baby Depot in Clairemont Square, Factory 2-U, Kids Outlet, Kids R Us, Babies R Us, Tijuana department stores, swap meets (get four T-shirts with designs for $11 + plus new furniture, strollers, toys, etc, not to mention the used stuff). Also, check out Nordstrom Rack. Don't miss red tag sales at department stores.

Children's resale shops are such a brilliant idea. Kid's clothes are so expensive; it's no wonder children's resale shops have become so popular. Not only can you shop there, but you can take your kid's outgrown clothes in to sell and retrieve some money from them. Call first to find out what their days and hours are for buying. Here are some of San Diego's best, and if these aren't enough, try some of the baby & kids swaps that follow.

Act II for Kids
8321 La Mesa Blvd.
La Mesa, (619) 460-2606
Baby Trader
5282 Baltimore Drive
La Mesa (619) 461-3321
Baby Exchange
907 E. Washington
El Cajon, (619) 441-1210
Baby-Go-Round
10330 Friars Rd. (near Longs/Black Angus)
E. Mission Valley, (619) 281-BABY
Baby, Too
973 Grand Ave.
Pacific Beach (858) 274-2229
Bizzy Beez Childrens Resale
7885 University
La Mesa, (619)303-6340
Children's Orchard
9430 #5B Mira Mesa Blvd
Mira Mesa, (858) 586-7313
Children's Orchard
998 W. El Norte Pkwy,
Escondido, (760) 738-7296
Children's Orchard
3841 Plaza Drive, Ste 901,
Oceanside, (760) 941-1083
Conceptions
10438 Mission Gorge Road
Santee, (619) 596-2229

Cory's Closet
3745 Avocado Blvd (& Hwy 94)
(next to Long's) La Mesa, (619) 660-1235
Hand Me Ups
12750 Ste 104 Carmel Country Road
Del Mar, (858) 794-7311
Katie's Korner
9662 Wintergardens Blvd.
Lakeside, (619) 390-3152
Kiddie Kottage
681 Jamacha Rd,
El Cajon, (619) 440-1049
Kid's Closet
1601 Kelly Street
Oceanside (
Lil' Britches
5154 Waring Rd
Allied Gardens, (619) 501-5078
Magical Child
967 S. Coast #101
Encinitas (760) 633-1326
Mother's Helper
4810 Santa Monica
Ocean Beach, (619) 224-9960
Outgrown Shop
1163 S. Coast Hwy 101
Encinitas (760) 436-4753
Picket Fences
7431 Broadway
Lemon Grove, (619) 462-7238
Posie's Baby & Children's Resale

365 Birdrock Ave
La Jolla (858) 459-8968
SophistaKids
1815 S. Center Parkway
Escondido (760) 233-7707
Sunkissed
5005 Cass St.

Pacific Beach, (858) 272-5622
Sunkisses
10175 Rancho Carmel Drive, #106
Carmel Valley (858) 385-1805

You can pick up great gently used children's clothing in excellent condition for a fraction of the original cost at **yard sales** (better neighborhoods have better clothes, like La Jolla, Mission Hills, etc.). I've scooped up hand-knit sweaters for 50¢ apiece to give to friends who have infants. One day I saw a couple buy a gorgeous complete layette for a baby girl for $35 at a yard sale at an exclusive home. This couple also bought the crib, stroller, furniture and other items this little Yuppy-ette had outgrown, the finest quality available. What a score! And, I see Grandmas buying second strollers and cribs at yard sales to have on hand when the little ones come to visit. You can afford to have *everything* for your kids/grandkids if you shop at yard sales: fabulous clothing, bunk beds, toys, skate boards, every sporting gear you can think, every game on the market, every book the kids are reading, every size bike known to man, educational toys, microscopes, every musical instruments ever made . . . you can pick up *everything!!* And, if you don't find it this week, well, guess what. . . . .there's always next week! My only regret is: I didn't know about the yard sale/rummage sale/thrift store market when *my* kids were young!! However, I took my grandson yard sale-ing one weekend and he got THREE skate boards. Wow. You should have heard him "heh heh"-ing all the way home. (And, I was QUEEN for a DAY, lemme tell you!)

Rummage sales are great places for grabbing bargains for kids. See a list of some of the best annual rummage sales later in this chapter.

Baby Clothes Swap Meets The Scripps Parent Connection holds a Family Swap Meet a few times a year with baby clothes, strollers, children's clothing, toys, maternity wear. Find something special for families with infants, young children and babies-on-the-way.

Swap Meets have a number of vendors that sell children's clothing, new and used. Great t-shirts, Disney stuff, socks, underwear, jeans, shoes, furniture and toys This is a great place to shop on a budget.

Kids Outlet, 6 stores, 5971 University, (619) 582-1676; (619) 528-8524, Chula Vista, (619) 425-8259, Natl City (619) 474-8073; Very inexpensive prices on children's clothing from newborn through size 14. Many young children's short sets, $1.99. This company buys closeouts and overruns from various suppliers who supply stores like Kmart or Nordstrom, and you will find incredible buys on everything from generic brands to Disney to Starter. You never know what you might find. The most expensive item was a $19.99 jacket for a size 18. Everything else was really inexpensive.

Kid's Foot Locker Fashion Valley, (619) 295 4294; Horton Plaza, (619) 238-0430; El Cajon, (619) 442-7772; National City, (619) 479-5987 **Striderite** Factory Outlet, Carlsbad Company Stores, (760) 476-9061.

Get your baby's first pair of shoes *free* at **Payless Shoes**, and they give you a discount coupon for the next pair. This is great idea for a shower gift. Must give the baby's date of birth.

OH Baby, 1356 W. Valley Pkwy, Escondido (760) 739-0226; guaranteed lowest prices on major brands of children's furniture and clothing for infants.

Baby Depot at the Burlington Coat Factory, Clairemont Town Square, Clairemont Mesa Blvd. & Clairemont Drive, (858) 272-1893. Baby furniture and clothing, name brands, good prices (cheaper than elsewhere).

Goodwill and other thrift stores and resale shops are a great place to shop for **Halloween costumes**. The Oriental Trading Co. is a really good source for holiday and birthday goodies. Call (800) 228-2269 or visit their site at oriental.com

FYI: If you're missing a part to a toy and would like to replace it, call the 800-toll free number for the toy company (frequently printed on the toy itself). You can pick up a lot of toys *cheap* at yard sales that are missing parts and then call the company direct and order the part! Sometimes the parts are free!! This is a such great tip. Don't mention you just bought it and it was missing a part. Just say you have this toy that is missing a part. Get it?! Sometimes NOT saying things will get you farther!

Hasbro, (800) 255-5516   Mattel (800) 367-8926
Little Tikes, (800) 321-0183

Free Stuff For Kids is the title of a great book for children containing hundreds of free and up to $1 things kids can send for by mail including posters, stickers, magic tricks, booklets, etc. About $6, and is published by Meadowbrook Press about every two years. This will keep them busy, and give them valuable "grown-up" skills.

Collect child support at no cost to you through the District Attorney Bureau of Child Support Enforcement office, toll free (866) 230-2273, (619) 236-7600. They can establish a child support order, enforce an order, etc.

Kids 12 and under are free at the Starlight Theater on Thursdays & Sundays all summer when accompanied by an adult. Love it!!

Don't miss these two great kid/family oriented free magazines: **San Diego Family Magazine**, (619) 685-6970, is loaded with great informative articles and a calendar of events for children and families, Web: sandiegofamily.com, and **San Diego Parent**, (619) 624-2770. Both publications are distributed at supermarkets throughout San Diego. Call the magazines for distribution point near you. These are "must haves."

A great Web site for children: refdesk/com/kids. Click on the "Best Sites for Children" (Dinosaurs, Disney, Dr. Seuss, Young Biz (young entrepreneurs), and tons more.

See "Party Supplies" and "Clearance Stores" for good sources for kid's birthday party supplies and gifts. Also see "Things To Do" for hundreds of free and bargain things to do with your kids. See "Health & Medical" for pediatric asthma studies, free shots, health care, etc. See "Factory Outlets" for more children's outlets.

Child Care/Babysitting

This is a tough one, but I was asked to come up with something for people who have sitter needs. So here goes:

Here are some other suggestions for child care: Call the San Diego YMCA Childcare Resource Service and Referral Agency for Child Care Services Parent Referral Line, (800) 481-2151 Call a high school (career counselor or employment office)and ask for a student interested in sitting after school/evenings. The YMCA (see above) offers babysitting classes for teens. Offer to pay for the class. Call the nearest college (employment center) and get a student to live in or out. Call churches to see if you can post a notice for someone to live in or out.

Many seniors would love to help with your children. Call any Senior Center, or call Elderhelp, (619) 284-9281 and ask if there is a senior center near you. They may be lonely, have a need to feel useful or could use the extra money. Strong friendships can evolve from these mutual needs.

I found another mother who was also a SDSU student the day we registered our sons for kindergarten. We arranged our class schedules the next semester so that she picked up my kids on Mondays and Wednesdays, and I picked up her kids on Tuesdays and Thursdays. This way we were both able to continue our college courses and our kids were well cared for. Incidentally, this is how I managed to complete my degree and teaching credential, and how the other mother went on to get her degree and law degree. We are the best of friends to this date (and so are our kids), and this is many years later! To think we all met on the steps of kindergarten! (Today, many colleges have pre-schools on campus.)

Form a Neighborhood Babysitting Coop, where mothers babysit for one another and earn hours of credit toward having someone babysit for their children. The more participants, the merrier. Make allowances for one child versus three children, etc.

Most community colleges have a Child Development Center with a job board. Call your local community college to post a "Help Wanted" position and hire a child development student. They are receiving training and want to work with kids as a profession.

If you enroll at the college, you can take your kid(s) to the Child Development Center while you attend classes. The requirement at some colleges is that you take one two-unit child development course per semester with your child, which is great, because you'll spend quality time interacting with your child during enrichment and developmental activities.

Classified Advertising

The *Reader* still gives one free classified ad per week to private parties and nonprofit organizations that do not charge for their services. Each ad must be printed clearly on a 3x5 cards or on a postcards, and are limited to 25 words. Additional words are 60 cents each. Send to: Reader Free Classifieds, POB 85803, San Diego, CA 92186. Must be received by 7 a.m. Monday, three days in advance of issue. Free ads can be placed online at SanDiegoReader.com until 6pm Monday, and appear only on the Reader's web site. For $8, you can phone, fax or submit your ad online if you miss the deadline for mailing. Also, some neighborhood newspapers like The Beacon and specialized newspapers like Good Life Times and Light Connection still offer some free classified ads. There are many places to put free classified ads online. Go to google.com and search for "free classified ads." The Union-Trib's Thrifties ads are $9 for 3 lines, 3 days, for items under $500. Many serious shoppers are "working" the ads.

Clearance/Closeouts/Liquidation Centers

Clearance stores that carry liquidation merchandise are filled with wall-to-wall bargains. Clearance/closeout/liquidation merchandise comes from manufacturers who want or need to reduce inventory as a result of changes, cancelled orders, product discontinuation or test market products. It is ever-changing and creates an interesting variation in merchandise on any given day or at any given store. Factories and retail stores need to dispose of unsold merchandise in their warehouses to make room for new products. Their excess inventories are sold to liquidators who specialize in buying up these huge overstocks at a fraction of the original cost, and resell them by the truck load to clearance stores who specialize in carrying only liquidation and closeout merchandise. Here are some interesting clearance stores. Notice some are stores that deal only with liquidation merchandise (99¢/and Dollar Stores,) or Closeouts (BigLots and Tuesday Morning); others are clearance centers for their own stores (Pier 1 Clearance Center, Nordstrom Rack, etc.)

"99¢/Dollar Stores" are a 90's concept, and most merchandise in the store is priced at 99¢ or one dollar! Some things are 2 or 3/99¢! But, most of these stores are now including merchandise up to $9.99, so you need to watch the price tags these days. They buy up large inventories of overstocks, unclaimed merchandise, returned merchandise, bankruptcy inventories and close-outs from wholesalers *by the pallet or truckload.* They may not know what is in the truck! Merchandise includes health and beauty aids, tools, toys, children's party favors, housewares, food, hair accessories, picture frames, light bulbs, phone cords, cleaning supplies, candles, lots of small hardware, garden tools & pots, organizers, trash cans, lots of cooking utensils, cosmetics, shampoos, light bulbs, visors, sox, earrings, candy bars and more. I am no longer willing to pay 99¢ or $1 under any circumstances for light bulbs, batteries, Crazy Glue or felt pens because they are outdated and are dried up. I don't buy any food products there for fear they were manufactured in the 60', but I see people buying them all the time. I check anything that has a spray to see if it works. You might ask me why I would buy something again knowing only 7 or 8 out of 10 items will be good, and I would have no good response, other than to say: *Well, I have to do research for this book, right?* But, that is only partially true. I have gotten better at it, and usually 9 or 10 out of 10 things work for me. I can fill up a bag for $10 and most of the stuff is actually pretty good! Particularly good buys are calendars, gift wrap, party supplies, office supplies, candles, paint rollers and brushes (when you can find them - they go FAST). I say drop by often because they get in some really good stuff but it sells out immediately. The 99-Cents Only chain has several stores in San Diego, and they also have a location in Beverly Hills at the intersection of Wilshire and Fairfax. How do you like THAT? I think it humorous that even millionaires shop at dollar stores. There are MANY, MANY neighborhood **99¢ stores**. Drop in for some fun. They are everywhere! I love to shop in any new one I see. There is a wonderful BIG dollar store at Clairemont Mesa Drive and Clairemont Drive. Here are a few, but there are dozens more everywhere: **Max's 99¢ Store**, Ocean Beach, (619) 223-6634; 5079 El Cajon Blvd., (619) 582-1999. Pacific Beach, (858) 272-7751; Chula Vista, (619) 476-1999; Hillcrest, (619) 220-6912; La Mesa, (619) 460-3949; The 99¢ Superstore, Mira Mesa, (858) 695-0243. **99¢ Only Stores** are the "oldest" one price store in the nation with 8 locations in San Diego. Call (888) 582-5999 for a store near you in El Cajon, Lemon Grove, Oceanside, National City, Imperial Beach, San Ysidro, Escondido.

Bargain Center Inc., 3015 North Park Way, (619) 295-1181. This large store has been around since 1961with lots of surplus military items and hundreds of surplus items from all over the world. Shorts, jeans, funky pants, hats, camping bags, flannel shirt, T-shirts, boots, shoes, jeans, pants, wearables and outdoor and camping equipment. Some great buys; unique stuff. Definitely an interesting place.

GTM Discount General Store, 716 16th Street, (619) 234-7122; 8967 Carlton Hills Boulevard, Santee, (619) 449-4953; 7663 Broadway, Lemon Grove, (619) 460-2990; GTM ("Get The Money") is your basic "no frills" clearance store with thousands of items; in business since 1982. GTM buys overstocks, closeouts, discounted and national brand merchandise from over 130 vendors. Much of the merchandise, about 80%, is from Costco (some perfectly good items in damaged cartons, etc.) Also some from

Sam's and Macy's, and from out of state. New bargains arrive daily. Everything is 20-50% off chain-store prices. Health and beauty, toys, food items, paper plates, odds and ends, clothes, TV's, stereos, cameras, drinks, household items, hardware items, stationary, pet food, you name it. Good prices. You might find sweaters & sweatshirts: Members Only, Fila, Smith & Watkins, 30% off; Rice: bulk or bag, 15¢ pound; 16 oz. cans of Snapple, 47¢; PineSol, reg. $2.79, $1.99; Olympus SuperZoom 3000, $207.99 (over $300 value); smoker-grill, $39 (value $38). Limited to stock on hand; open 7 days. The ambiance of the Lemon Grove and Santee stores is nicer than the downtown store.

Big Lots (formerly PicNSave),with 15 locations including 3705 Rosecrans, (619) 260-0109; 1085 East Main Street, El Cajon, (619) 442-2870; 1625 E. Valley Parkway, Escondido, (760) 747-7467; Vista (760) 598-3674; Chula Vista (619) 420-4716; 1655 Euclid, San Diego, (619) 264-6644; 6145 Lake Murray Boulevard, La Mesa; 2017 Mission Avenue, Oceanside; 1410 Plaza Boulevard, National City; 9340 Mira Mesa Boulevard, Mira Mesa, Clairemont and North Park. Call 800-269-9571 for store nearest you. BigLots, is the largest broadline closeout retailer in the U.S., with over 1300 stores. A broadline retailer is one that sells hard goods (appliances, electronics, tools, etc), soft goods (domestics and apparel) and consumable products such as food, household chemicals, health and beauty care, etc. Closeouts are first quality, brand name merchandise found at other retailers, but at substantially lower prices, usually 20-40% below most discount retailers and up to 70% below traditional retailers. BigLots is a paradise for bargain hunters with tons of designer ends and closeouts. People go there for "therapy" whenever they have the urge to spend but don't want to blow a lot of dinero. It's open nights til 9:00 p.m. (except Sundays). The shelves are stocked with household items, sheets, towels and comforters, seasonal decor, cosmetics and sunglasses, candles, wine, books and cookbooks, clothing for men, women and children, food products, wine, tools, artificial flowers, lots of wicker accent furniture, garden things, pet supplies, etc. Recent finds: Remington Paraffin Wax Spa, $9.99 (compare $49.99); Gloria Vanderbilt ladies watches, $7.99 (compare $19.99); 30% off all Gibson greeting cards everyday; tent, $29 (compare $49); gourmet vinegars in beautiful bottles, $4.99 (compare $14.99); Vitabath shower gel or body lotion, $1.99 (compare $5.99); Maidenform 2 pack slippers $3.99 (compare $7.99); phones (always a selection of various priced telephones, new and reconditioned), inflatable family pool, $16 (compare $30); Canon twin sheet sets, $9.99 (compare $19.99); Dirt Devil Vac, $49 (compare $89); park bench $39 (compare $69); boys' corduroy shorts, $3.98, (compare $9), Lily of France bikini panties, $1.69,(compare $6), Danskin and Bali bras, $2.98 (compare $9), Limited Express slacks, $10.95 (compare $38), men's Gitano pants $10.95 (compare $24), silk neckties, $2.98, Cannon potholders, children's activity books and more! This is one of my favorite bargain hunting places, and one of my earliest bargain discoveries, too. I bought some GREAT wrought iron garden ornaments there recently (unbelievably cheap) and a lot of candles. Big Lots has been getting in some higher quality decorator items the past few months and more furniture, too. Their Vista store is large and has more furniture. Some of the stores are nicer than others to shop in -- *mine*, the one on Rosecrans, is *great!* Ask the manager when new truckloads arrive (it's Mondays, and the stuff in on the floor by Wednesday, in Pt. Loma.) And, it's right there with See's Candy quantity store, across the street from a really good Goodwill, around the corner from the new Salvation Army boutique, and a dollar store is in the adjacent strip mall. All are hard to resist if I am in the area. Here is a GREAT tip: sign up on their web site, biglots.com, to receive email notification and view their sales flyers on the same day they get mailed. Recently, I have been getting their ad supplement delivered with the *Union -Trib* on Saturdays. They were mailing them, so it might change again. I hate it when I go in for something a couple days after I get their ads, and they're sold out. Now I can win at the game with e-notification of what's on sale in advance. The Pt. Loma store told me that some items will scan in at the sale price a day ahead of the sale. Sales start on Sundays, and the sale price is in effect until the items are gone. Sales are limited to stock on hand. No rainchecks and they do not accept coupons. However, to ensure that you are fully satisfied with the closeout shopping experience, Big Lots offers this guarantee: if an advertised item is not available on the first day of the ad, they will attempt to locate the item for you at another one of their stores, OR they will give you 20% off your total purchases for that day. No can beat.

Factory 2 U is a fast growing San Diego based company (since 1980) with 251 outlets including 13 locations in the county (Kearny Mesa, Mira Mesa, Oceanside, Vista, Lemon Grove, Point Loma, Murphy Canyon, El Cajon, Santee, Imperial Beach, San Ysidro, Chula Vista, National City. Their stores carry liquidations, overstock, closeouts and cancellations from Kmart, Walmart, Mervyns without tags including some name some brands like Gitano, Bugle Boy, Jordache, Fruit of the Loom. You never know what you might find, occasionally Nike, Oshkosh, Levi's Lee and Adidas are in with the mix. I complimented a woman on a dress she was wearing that was the height of fashion, and she said she got it for $10 at the Factory 2 U. I rushed there, but, alas, they were all gone. See *White Pages* or call (877) 44-FACTORY for store near you. For more info, see factory2-U.com.

Pier 1 Imports Clearance Store 1735 Hancock Street, (619) 291-9920. This store has out of season inventory from the regular stores. Save up to 25-75% off items like candles, vases, bath oils, silver ware, furniture, lots of wicker, wine racks, dinnerware, pillows and accessories; lots of things for entertaining were on sale for an additional 35% off on a recent visit. Clearance items have further markdowns. Christmas items were75% off up to 90% off. I got a fantastic buy on a wicker chair for $80 that was $160 in the Pier One catalog. They receive new shipments twice a week. They also carry some things that are especially made just for the Pier 1 Clearance stores. I know people who love this store. If I hit it at the right time, I do, too. I've had some misses here, so call first to see if their stock level is low or up to the ceiling. I like to here anytime I go to Saffron restaurant on India (which has great saffron chicken cooked over coals, and Cambodian salad to die for.) A big Amvets (619) 297-4213 is in the area, too, on Southerland off Frontage Rd., which is off Washington.

Nordstrom Rack, by Macy's in the Mission Valley Shopping Center, (619) 296-0143, is THE place to find unbelievable bargains in better clothing for men, women and children, accessories and shoes (an excellent source for narrow widths, large sizes), with 30-70% savings and more on everything. You'll need to spend some time here digging through the racks and racks of clothing in their new larger store, but you'll be happy with the price you pay for goodies from Nordstrom, even if the ambiance is a bit frantic. Suits, dresses, separates, sportswear, evening wear, petites, lingerie and more for women. Sport coats, suits and sportswear for men. Children's clothing, too. Some of the items were never in the store; they were ordered in for the sale, but 75% of the merchandise is from the store. Periodic 25-50% off the lowest ticketed price, and Red Tag Sales every couple months with further markdowns to please the avid bargain hunter. I know people who take annual leave to hit these sales! Ask to be placed on the mailing list. Go during the week if you can because this place gets busy. Great buys on sheets, towels, vases, decorator and household stuff. Another Nordstrom Rack is located at Metro Pointe, Costa Mesa near South Coast Plaza, (714) 751-5901.

Tuesday Morning is closeout chain that specializes in items normally found in specialty and department stores or upscale catalogs, but at 50-80% off . They have over 500 stores nationally, and four in San Diego: La Costa Towne Center (760) 634-1790; Pacific Beach (858) 274-3880; Mission Valley (619) 283-7230; Rancho San Diego (619) 660-5126. All first quality. Selections range from room and area rugs to luxury bed linens, some European. You want down comforters ? This is the place! I now have them in three weights. No heating bills for this kid. Imported bath accessories and designer towels; fine crystal, china, decorative accessories, luggage, toys and seasonal decorations or gifts substantially discounted. Birdbaths, gazing balls and other garden items from upscale sources. Gourmet cookware, gadgets, bakeware, serveware and electrics, gourmet foods, olive oils, chocolates. Name brans include Revere, Farberware, Cuisinart, Sabatier, Limoges, Wedgewood, Samsonite, American Tourister, and many more. You never know what you are going to find, but my advice is to get up and GO when you see their sale ad in the *Union-Trib*. If you wait, you might find the place in shambles after the sale and unbelievably picked over. This can be a fabulous place if you hit it right. Is everything great? Certainly not. Some things are kinda strange stuff. Get on the email list at tuesdaymorning.com for advance notice of sales. For snail mail, call the stores.

Sears Outlet, 960 Sherman St. off Morena Blvd., (619) 497-1123. Major name brand TV's and appliances including Amana, GE, Whirlpool, Kitchenaid, but mainly their own brand, Kenmore. Some new, but most everything has been sold once and is considered "used;" however, all have a one-year warranty and a thirty-day return policy. Savings of 20-50% off (or more). One-of-a-kind, discontinued, used, scratched and dented merchandise. Frequent coupons in their *Union-Tribune* ads for $20 off.

As On TV, 7520 Eads Ave, La Jolla, (858) 454-0701. Products you have seen in TV infomercials are available locally at Enternet's "As (Seen) On TV" retail outlet. They also maintain a web site: asontv.com. Quick N Brite cleaner, BioSlim weight loss product, Flowbee hair cutters, Space bags, George Foreman Grills, exercise equipment, 200+ different products at a discount. (I have also seen a lot of infomercial products at swapmeets.)

Out of the area (but let's face it, you do get around):
If you get to New York, you won't want to miss this one. A friend INSISTED that I put this in! Gabay's, 225 lst Avenue between 13th & 14ᵗʰ, (212) 254-3180. Gabays receives clearance items from exclusive department stores in NY, mainly Bergdorf Goodman, but also from Bloomingdales, Saks and Neiman Marcus and sells them at a steal, 50-75% off. The place is a disarray, but sometimes you can find gorgeous quality designer men's and women's fashions, leather jackets, towels, housewares, cookware, some furniture, etc. The best time to shop is after the holidays, when Gabay's receives all the unsold and returned deluxe gift items. Call before going as they may be picked over, but expecting a shipment tomorrow.

The Postal Service holds auctions of **unclaimed/undeliverable mail** and packages. Call the Mail Recovery Center at postal headquarters in Atlanta, Philadelphia, San Francisco and St. Paul. Sounds like fun!

Unclaimed Baggage Center Over one million items a year are lost on airplanes, and these items end up at the 30,000 square foot Unclaimed Baggage Center in Scottsboro, Alabama, where they are sold for about 40-60% of retail. Oprah has been to this one! Changes daily, mostly clothing, but lots of jewelry, expensive racing bikes, tons of sunglasses, tons of books, luggage, tennis rackets, surf boards, skis, and more. Vacation bound travelers buy top quality items: Versace, Gucci, Christian Dior suits. Sunglasses that retail for $50-$100 sell here for $10-$25; $300 cameras go for $75; $200 roller blades, $25; $200 Hermes scarves, $45. The Jackson County Chamber of Commerce receives more calls about the Unclaimed Baggage Center than any other attraction in the area. Located in the North East corner of Alabama, 45 minutes north of Boaz, Alabama, the outlet capital of the southeast. You can shop online or sign up for an event at their web site at unclaimedbaggage.com.

Computers, Software, Classes, etc

The latest models of computers fall quickly from state-of-the-art status. What sold for $2000+ two years can now sell as little as $200. Most families don't need state-of-the art equipment to accomplish what they want on a computer. Newer computers have more capabilities, most of which the average person will never utilize. If you want to keep up with technology, though, Bill Gates says you'll probably want to upgrade your computer every two to three years. Many manufacturers now offer a guaranteed trade program if you buy a new one within 36-48 months. Here are a few places to check out if you are in the market for a computer, new or used, plus helpful tips and other information, too.

If you don't know how to do computers or don't own one, first of all, let me say that you don't *need* to own a computer to *learn* about computers. Most of the people who take introductory computer classes don't own a computer; some, of course, buy one, then don't know how to use it so they end up in a class. Don't waste another minute. Catch up now. I did it. I figured if three-year-olds could do it, there was hope for me. Many people have the computer-phobia thing, as I did, but, I must say: you will learn enough to have fun fooling around on the Internet, using email, etc., not to mention how wonderful it is to have all your letters and stuff on the computer! Some introductory classes are listed later on in this chapter, and you can take them over and over and over again. Most are free anyway. And people of all levels *of fear* are in there. You will be in good company. Like the Nike ad says, "Just do it!" You'll be so glad you did. You can "one-up" your cronies. About 64% of adults in San Diego go online (about 55% nationally). You'll love it, at any age. (Especially seniors who have more time and more friends all over the world to communicate with, free!) You really don't want to fall behind into what is being called the "digital divide." Corporations like Ford Motors are giving all their employees (including carpet layers, cafeteria workers, spark-plug put-er in-ers, etc) a computer and the internet so their families won't FALL BEHIND. There is a new push to get EVERYONE computer literate. AND, if I can do it, let me tell you, ANYONE can do it. I was born before the computer gene was invented, and I have been taking and *retaking* classes for the past 15 years to build that portion of my brain that doesn't exist otherwise. So, you can do it, too. Furthermore, Bill Gates gave two computers to EVERY library in America and you can use them, so you don't have to own one. In fact, you can go to the library and get yourself a free email address/account at hotmail.com or yahoo.com and get your email *at the library!* The librarian will help you do it. I know someone who is currently doing this in Virginia until she gets a new computer. International visitors from around the world check their email in San Diego libraries, free!

Here are some places to comparison shop for computers: The prices on new computers are way down as computer sales have plateaued and plummeted with the uncertain economy. Many computers are offered for under $500 with six months free internet on CompuServe, AOL or Microsoft. If you want to be online, you will pay it anyway., but I got 6 months free AOL with my new Dell recently (my third Dell). Here are some places to check for new computers: Fry's, Costco, Sam's Club, Office Depot, Best Buys, Circuit City, Gateway, Staples, CompUSA, Computer City, Dell. The reason I bought a new Dell is that I like their technical support, 24 hours a day. I had problems with the first Dell, but, after reformatting the hard drive MANY times during a two-month period with their phone-tech, I went to their web site and wrote a LETTER OF COMPLAINT telling them the RECORD would show that I had been thru hell with their computer, and suggested that I would send it to Sixty Minutes and ask them to figure out why I was told to reformat it so many times. I got a call the NEXT day saying they were sending me a brand NEW Dell computer by Airborne Express. I was totally frazzed from the experience, but I guess all's well that ends well. They gave me newer technology, too . . as an even exchange. I am really stoked on their tech support and have learned a LOT. I think my problems are over, so maybe I had a lemon! It sure paid to COMPLAIN. I just bought a new one because it came with all the software I wanted and all would be compatible since they were factory installed. The third time is the charm . .so far, so good. Amazing . . I buy the extended warranty for about $139 that will give me three years of guaranteed parts and labor, and at the end of three years or before, knowing me, I'll find a reason to get another one.

Fry's Electronics has their own web site where you can shop for select products and promotions that are available only online. Thousands of electronic items at Outpost.com.

Sites for buying refurbished computers, laptops, monitors, printers, etc: Compaq sells rebuilt computers on the web: compaqworks.com. Dell Factory Outlet, (888) 783-6965; Dell's web site for rebuilt computers is Dell.com/outlet, IBM sells refurbished computers at ibm.com/products/us. Click on Refurbished.; Hewlett-Packard's site is hpshopping.com. Click on Outlet Store. Be sure to check the warranties. Some of these computers have been returned from lease and may be in excellent working order; some have been refurbished; some have defects.

Gateway is a highly rated, huge mail order computer company that has a showroom in Mission Valley, 826 Camino del Rio N. (619) 574-1107, and in Carmel Mountain 858 879 1144. Select a computer in the showroom to order, and some are in stock. Extended warranties for about $129-159. Ask about their guaranteed trade up. They also sell refurbished computers on the net at gateway.com.

CNET.com is a helpful site for shopping for a computer, building a Web site, free downloads, plus helpful tech information. Also, techbargains.com is a good place to check.

Ebay has some incredible deals on computers and electronics, parts and software, new and used. Some Ebay sellers have complete electronics stores online. I use Ebay if I'm in the market for anything. I do my research and read about products online first. I am so grateful for how the internet has made the search for products and services so easy.

Swap meets have vendors that sell new and used software; new and used computers, and electronics.

Mac, IBM and compatibles offer the best discounts available anywhere to college students and educators at college book stores. Software, too. Lots of stuff is about *half* the retail price, some less than half! Brand new releases. Awesome prices. YOU can buy software (not hardware) at SDSU with an academic ID (it can be your 8 year old's student ID card). That's what I was told! BIG savings; (619) 594-7522. Check it out.

Buy academically priced software at Gradware, 9353 Clairemont Mesa Blvd., Ste J, Kearny Mesa, (858) 569 5995, with a $2 adult school I.D card which you can get at the San Diego Metro Career Center by enrolling in a (free) class. Buy MS Office for $200 that sells for $599 in stores. Shop online at gradware.com.

For a used computer, check the classified ads of the *Union-Trib* (Computers #3020, Thrifties #3190; pick up a used government or corporate or college computer at the county auction (see Auctions, this chapter). Also, look in the *Reader* and *Computer Edge*. Goodwill on Rosecrans has a computer room with a couple dozen used computers; check your nearest thrift stores, too.

UCSD Surplus Sales store, 7835 Trade Street, Miramar area, (858) 695-2660, serves as a means to liquidate excess university property including computers (and more) at auction every Wednesday from 8-2pm.

Computer Edge is a free weekly publication that contains software reviews, how-to articles, trouble-shooting, tips and tricks, and lists computer consultants and software user's groups, classes, etc. for beginner to intermediate. Display ads with computer store sales, used computers and classified ads. Available at computer stores or call (619) 573-031.

The *Union-Tribune's* Personal Technology portion of the Business Section on Mondays contains articles, weekly columns, calendars of computer-oriented classes and meetings, and a section on great web sites. Lots of good tips, and definitely one of my favorite sections of the *UT*. (I can't believe I said that!!)

Anyone can use the computers at adults schools, free, including Mid-City West Center, (619) 221-6973. Enroll in a class or work on your own project, any time during the school year, free. I wrote my first book here before buying my first computer!

San Diego Central Library, 820 E Street, downtown, offers a free internet demonstration/class in the computer lab on one Thursday a month, from 7:15pm - 8:30;m. Call 238-6621 for this month's date. Visit their web site at http://ci.san-diego.ca.us/public-library/

Computer Museum of San Diego, 640 C Street, downtown, (619) 235-8222. Exhibits and artifacts, plus internet classes for children and seniors.

The Centers For Education & Technology (CET) offer FREE short-term, three-hour, join any time, computer classes, located throughout the city. The one at the San Diego Metro Career Center, 8401 Aero Drive, Kearny Mesa, offers morning, afternoon and evening classes on topics ranging from how to buy a computer and introduction to computers to how to design a web page, beginning to advanced Internet, computer care, desktop publishing, MS Office, multimedia, Access, Quark, photo shop, graphics, plus many more. Classes for absolute beginners, intermediate and advanced levels. You might ask: Why are these classes free? The answer to that is: they are sponsored by the San Diego Community College District Continuing Education program which is funded by state and local tax dollars and probably some federal bucks thrown in, too. Any class that is considered "vocational" (meaning you could earn money doing it if you learn the skill) is free. (Note: Gini Pedersen teaches great classes on using the internet. See her class schedule and sign up for her free enewsletter at: iteachyou.com.) For a complete listing of computer classes, check their web site at sandiegocet.net. To request a computer class schedule by fax, call (858) 627-2996. If you go, you want to suit up and show up early and stand in line as these classes are very popular and most fill up. I've been turned away, so I know to go an hour early if I want a class. There are also Career

Centers in El Cajon, Encinitas, Escondido and South Bay offering similar classes. They are all part of a big umbrella organization.

Datel Computer Center, 5636 Ruffin Rd, Kearny Mesa, has a classroom that is used by C.E.T. (above). They also offer free computer and Internet classes. However, preregistration is required. Call (858) 627-2545 to preregister. They fill up quickly and usually have a waiting list for the next class. They will fax you the monthly schedule, or check it out at sandiegocet.net.

Hire a "whiz kid" to hook up your computer, load the hard disc and set up your files from the SDSU Student Employment Office (or other college, community college or high school). You might want to negotiate a flat fee for specific services, or offer an hourly rate. Ask what the going pay is for students, and if you pay $1 more, your phone will ring off the hook.

Adaptive Computer Empowerment Services (858) 244-1226; This is a non-profit, all volunteer organization that repairs and upgrades donated computer equipment, and distributes it to low-income persons with physical and mental disabilities.

For more on computers, see "Auctions" this chapter. For more on computer classes, see chapter on "Continuing Education."

Costco & Sam's Wholesale Warehouses

Sales at membership warehouses (Costco, B.J.'s, Sam's) in the U.S. are booming because warehouses offer cheaper prices on top quality merchandise. They are able to meet all expenses of employees, rent, etc. through membership fees (see below), therefore, markup on merchandise is only 4-14% above wholesale prices (fantastic savings!) Personal or Business memberships are about $45 for you and a second person, and you will probably save more than that on your first shopping trip. There is also a special $100 membership that offers discount services including long distance, mortgages, insurance and more. For more detailed information on membership (recorded), call a warehouse or drop by and see if it's for you, or visit their web page at costco.com and samsclub.com. Even though my family has shrunk, it is very much to my advantage to belong to a warehouse club. Each warehouse is huge. Nearly half the store is devoted to food; many items are in bulk packages or with several taped together, so you have to know how to deal with quantities. Savings can be substantial on their bulk products. Some people arrange to share with a neighbor on a regular basis, or repackage things. There's a fresh bakery with a dozen huge muffins for around $5 and personalized sheet cakes can be ordered. There are fresh and frozen gourmet meats, giant gourmet fruits and vegetables. Beer, wine, liquor and sodas. It's the ONLY place to buy laundry soap, cleaning supplies, trash bags and paper products. Major appliances, small kitchen and household appliances, T.V.s, stereos and electronics, automotive department, tires, optical, pharmacy, 1-hour photo, fresh flowers, plants, outdoor furniture, barbecues, gardening, housewares, hardware, power tools, office supplies, furniture, lamps, down bedding, computers, software, crystal, fine jewelry (great value!), designer watches, seasonal items. Name brand apparel including shoes and lingerie. Many top name brands, plus their own private labels: Costco's own brand is "Kirkland" and Sam's is "Member's Mart." House brand products include nuts, candies, cheese, cookies, hair products, tires, detergent, batteries, shampoo, film, pet food and more. Some locations now have gas stations. You can even buy cars through their discount car-buying program, plus discount cruises and travel! Wow! REAL savings!

Costco Warehouse began right here in San Diego as a Price Club at the Morena Blvd. store in the late 70's, and has grown to over 300 stores in the U.S. and abroad. Costco orders in exciting new products (many VERY deluxe, luxury items at a discount including diamonds, Prada purses!) that are available for a limited time only including pianos, musical instruments, designer handbags, resort wear, silk plants, Southwest jewelry, framed art, garden waterfalls. You can order many items through their special order program (carpets, furniture, blinds, mattresses, diamonds and more). Get on the emailing list and/or shop online at their Web site at costco.com. The Costco web site has purses by Kate Spade, $114; Prada, $469; Coach, $124. You can also search for prescription drugs for prices. The San Diego stores are located at:

San Diego .... (858) 270-6920
   4605 Morena Boulevard
Southeast San Diego ... (619) 266-0915
   650 Gateway Dr.,
Vista .... (760) 631-7255
   1755 Hacienda
San Marcos .... (760) 480-6615
   725 Center Dr
Santee .... (619) 562-2812
   101 Town Center Pkwy
Carlsbad .... (760) 929-0963

951 Palomar Airport Road
Chula Vista .... (619) 427-5468
   1144 Broadway
Rancho Del Rey .... (619) 656-0826
   895 East H St.
Carmel Mountain ...... (858)) 675-0379
   12350 Carmel Mountain Road
La Mesa .... (935) 697-9933
   8125 Fletcher Pkwy
Mission Valley .... (619) 358-4000
   Near Ikea / Stadium off Friars Road

Sam's Club started in 1983 (a division of Wal-mart) and has over 400 clubs nationally. Sam's carries over 4,000 different items. They have two stores in the county and two planned: Encinitas & Chula Vista. Also, shop at Sam's online at SamsClub.com. Bid on their online auctions!

Dinnerware, Pottery, China & Crystal

Department stores have sales on name brand china and crystal, with 20-35% off or more, every month or so. It would be crazy to pay full price if you can wait until a sale, always just around the corner. Their sale prices are very competitive with factory outlets, and frequently, they will have more inventory in a particular line that is ordered in for the sale. Ask a sales associate to notify you of the next sale. They're happy to do it. Some call, some send out cards! Also, you can buy a whole set of china, crystal or silver on their Club Plan and make payments (and some stores don't charge interest!), and some offer a 10% discount if you open an account.

Tuesday Morning, a big national housewares discounter specializing in upscale closeouts, all 50-80% off retail prices. Located in Pacific Beach, (858) 274-3880; Carlsbad, (760) 634-1790; Mission Valley, (619) 283-7203; La Mesa, (935) 660-5126. I love this place if I hit it right, and not just after a major sale when it is in shambles and all the deals are gone. Fabulous housewares, cookware, bakeware, gadgets, cutlery, crystal, books, decorator items, gifts, bed and bath linens, stationary, frames, etc. Closeouts, 50-80% off. Eureka Vacuum, $109 (value $199); towels, $4.99, value $16. Down comforters, $59 (value $300, and I snagged one). Luggage, $39 (value $150). Closeout prices; great sales. Get on their mailing list or email list for advance notice of sales at tuesdaymorning.com.

Mikasa Factory Outlet Store,1660D Camino de la Reina, Mission Valley, (619) 295-0110; Las Americas Outlets, (619) 428-2022. Mikasa outlets carry a large collection of the Mikasa line, from closeouts to current popular patterns at discounts of 30%-60%. There is also a big spring and fall sale with further reductions. Stoneware (Garden Harvest, $29.99; retail $60 a place setting), fine china, bone china (Remembrance, $150 place setting for $79.99), flatware, crystal frames, placemats, tea kettles, crystal stemware ($16.99, value $32-37), silk flowers, bakeware, linens, kitchen, bathroom goods, Xmas items. Clearance room. Most goods are first quality, closeouts or discontinued; some seconds. Occasional storewide sales with crystal stemware starting at $2.49; serveware starting at $4.00; 20 pc. fine china sets starting at $29. Special order, too, from their over 300 patterns.

Crate & Barrel, Fashion Valley, (619) 295-6600 and University Towne Center, (858) 558-4545. Tons of gourmet cookware and unique kitchen gifts. This is a popular place for bridal registry. Fabulous stuff. Check their Web site: crateandbarrel.com. Now there is a Crate & Barrel OUTLET store at the Carlsbad Company Stores, (760) 692-2100. The Outlet store is stocked with about 50% merchandise that came from the regular stores that are discontinued items and seasonal merchandise, at about 30-40% off the regular price. The other half of the merchandise is "outlet merchandise" which is lower priced, but similar items that are carried only in their outlet stores. To view this merchandise, you can go online to their site and click on Outlet Store.

Pottery Barn, Fashion Valley (619) 296-8014; and UTC.(858) 622-9467 Contemporary dinnerware and stemware, vases, huge bowls, table runners, candles, dried flowers and more for California casual life style. Web: potterybarn.com. See "Catalogs" this chapter to order a catalog.

Ikea has incredibly reasonable prices on tableware, utensils and everything you need for the kitchen. I am amazed at their stylish wares at really low prices.

If I were starting over, I would probably have all Pottery Barn, Crate & Barrel and Ikea young, contemporary, uplifting fun stuff! I'd sure be happy with it! I find a lot of things from these favorite stores at yard sales. It has made me realize how people often don't like things they received as gifts, and didn't pick out themselves. One man's trash, as they say . . . . .

Canyon Pottery, 1544 Frazee, Fashion Valley, (619) 298-5400. Previously selling only to dealers, Canyon Pottery is now open to the public offering 40% off retail prices. They still sell to landscapers and interior decorators, but you can take advantage of their discounted prices, too. Over 23,000 sq. ft. of pots, exotic planters, urns, glazed pots from all over the world including China, Greece, Italian, some made in the same fashion they were 2,000 years ago; fountains, statuary, and everything down to plastic pots.

Mex-Art, 1155 Morena Blvd, (619) 276-5810. Trendy and classic pottery, furniture and hand crafted home accents from the interior of Mexico, at good prices (much cheaper than Old Town). Lots of items including colorful ceramics serving pieces, pitchers and decor plus garden pottery (large and small), hanging planters, statuary, fountains, wood furniture, mirrors. Many things are copies of museum pieces. This place is so popular that people are waiting for the truck to arrive from Guadajalara every two months. Things fly out the door.

Costco is a place to check out if you are seeking sets of fine china, pottery, dinnerware and Waterford crystal. See "Costco Wholesale Warehouses" this chapter.

If you're really into cookware, check out restaurant supply houses listed in the *Yellow Pages* under "Restaurant Equipment & Supplies." There are several on both sides of Market Street between 8th Avenue and 13th Street that have large soup pots, tons of dishes, cups, bowls, utensils, pots, pans and tons more, + clearance tables!

Tableware International, corner of 12th & F St., downtown, (619) 236-0210. They may be the largest dealer. Rosenthal china, lots of hotel overstocks, glassware and silver-plated European-size stainless steel flatware. Silverware, linens, kitchen equipment and supplies. On a past visit, they had Bistro china with hotel and yacht club logos; French over-proof dinnerware. Great stuff. Fun place. Order on the web at tablewareintl.com.

Catalogs of Kitchen Accessories Here are some fabulous catalogs for cooks who enjoy unique kitchen accessories: Williams-Sonoma, (800) 541-2233; Crate & Barrel, (800) 323-5461; Pier One (800) 447-4371; Pottery Barn, (800) 922-5507, Ikea (800) (619) 563-IKEA. These catalogs are always a delight and inspiration to receive, and make me want to throw away everything I own.

Dansk Factory Outlet, 1044 Wall Street, (858) 459-2655. Fabulous bargains on dinnerware, flatware, stoneware, vases, pots and pans, food products, cooking utensils, flower pots, all at a discount. You'll love it.

Great News Discount Cookware & Cooking School, 1788 Garnet Avenue, Pacific Beach, (858) 270-1582. Fabulous discount cookware store, this store is absolutely loaded with things for entertaining, kitchen gifts; gourmet food items; newsletter with class offerings, too. If you love to cook, you'll LOVE this place.

Macy's Cooking School, The Cellar, Mission Valley store, offers classes for 110 in a dream kitchen with six overhead monitors. Culinary pros and chefs perform demonstrations, (619) 299-9811x4231. Web: macys.com

Linens'nThings, 8657 Villa La Jolla Dr., (858) 452-4347 and Encinitas Town Center, 1014 N. El Camino Real, (800) LNT-8765; Grossmont (619) 644-0811; Carmel Mt. Ranch (858) 674-1101; Tons of kitchen things; entertaining things; storage things. You'll love this place, too. Tell me you don't. Giggles. Visit and shop at their web site at linenenthings.com.

Bed, Bath & Beyond is also loaded with kitchen, entertaining and storage things. Large superstore at 1750 Camino Del Rio North, Mission Valley Shopping Center (619) 295-9888.; Oceanside (760) 722-8856; Santee (619) 448-3207; Mira Mesa (858) 578-8008; Chula Vista (619) 420-7655. Super good advertised specials in the Sunday *Union-Trib* with discount coupon. I love those 15% off coupons, especially on major items. Shop online at bedbath.com.

LeCreuset, Carlsbad Company Stores, (760) 931-6868; enameled cast-iron cookware from France, professional-quality kitchen tools at great values. I had some of these years ago and miss them!

Waterford/Wedgewood Outlet, Carlsbad Company Stores, (760) 476-1612; crystal bowls, decanters, bookends, ice buckets, candlesticks. No seconds; discontinued American products. Some European products. Wedgewood china in most popular current patterns; some nearly perfects. A large selection of Waterford, Marquis, Wedgwood, Johnson Bros., more.

Kitchen Collection Carlsbad Company Stores, (760) 438-2369; Las Americas (619) 690-2297; Viejas (619) 445-6130; cookware, top of the line to mid line; Farberware, T-Fal, KitchenAid, and other brand names, discounted. Tabletop appliances, table ware, bakeware, cookware, decoratives, gadgets.

Good ole **Big Lots**, mentioned under "Clearance Centers," this chapter, get in shipments of closeouts, overstock, bankruptcy and discontinued inventories with occasional very nice quality dinnerware, utensils, cookware, crystal glasses, serving pieces and more from time to time.

Professional Cutlery Direct, really top of the line knives, cookware and kitchen accessories, discounted, 25-50%. Catalog, (800) 859-6994.

China Finders, all brands and patterns, current and discontinued, (800) 255-6868; Replacements, Ltd., discontinued and active china, crystal, flatware and collectibles, call (800) REPLACE; or at replacements.com. If you want to sell your china, this is a good place to find out what your china is selling for. However, they will only give you 40-50%. If you have some valuable china or crystal to sell, you might do better selling it on Ebay where you get all the profits yourself. You can include a minimum selling price, exposed or hidden. If you sell it at a consignment store, you will get 40-60%. At Glorious Antiques, they give you a larger percentage.

Pottery Shack in Laguna Beach, 1212 S. Coast Highway, Laguna Beach, (949) 494-1141. Take I-5 to Beach Cities turnoff to Pacific Coast Highway to Laguna Beach sign, about 75 miles up the road. Savings are enormous at this delightful seaside location, a landmark since 1936, a "must" if you're into dinnerware. Set the perfect table from the large selection of placemats, china, dinnerware, serving bowls, vases, silk flowers, sets of dishes and china, both fine and pottery. A four-quart giant clam-shaped ceramic serving bowl was $6.98 ($35 at gourmet shops), Oscar de la Renta lead crystal stemware was $9 for large water glass ($12.50 at department stores), and fantastic savings on most name brand items, with a table or two of items marked down even more. A wonderful place to browse, then have lunch along the coast. Really loaded with inventory. Ask about their clearance section. One room has imports from Italy, Portugal, Mexico. Separate garden shop with wonderful things. I fell in love with this place years ago, and have returned many, many times (but, they don't have all the 'seconds" like they used to. Boo hoo. People still ask for them; they were such fun.) Then, you MUST have lunch at the little outdoor restaurant behind Laguna Village, about 10 blocks north of Pottery Barn across the street on the ocean side. You will LOVE the view from above the ocean, and you can see the famous Laguna beach down below and to the north.

Kmart carries **"Martha Stewart Everyday"** cast-iron skillets, set of 3, for $15 and frequently on sale for $10! You can't BEAT a good ole cast iron skillet. The older they are, the better. Be sure to temper new ones in the oven with oil on low heat for 24 hours, or things will stick to it FOREVER. Martha has an 8 piece nonstick aluminum cookware set, $89, on sale for $54. Kmart, Walmart, Target and Mervyn's have great buys and frequent sales on everything for the kitchen, sets of dinnerware, etc.

San Diego Potter's Guild has a large annual pottery sale (over 40 years). One of a kind sculpture, bowls, mugs, platters, each June, (619) 239-0507 in Spanish Village. They sell there all yea, but the big sale is quite an event. You can find someone here to make your custom vase in the colors and style you want for that special spot.

I find some of my greatest treasures for the kitchen at yard sales including copper molds, unique serving dishes, cookbooks and decorator items. My kitchen looks like I'm a gourmet cook (which I am ... in my *fantasy* life!) I bought a fabulous Wedgewood plate for $1 (seriously!) which is great for serving cookies or entertaining, punch bowls, a crystal champagne bucket I had lusted after for years ($3), a white wrought iron stand to put it in (25¢!), a Cuisinart mini-grinder for $1 (value $30!), all sorts of things like rice cookers, deep fat fryers, hot trays, wine glasses, fancy napkin rings, bread maker ($5), cook books galore. . . all at one tenth or less the original cost. My latest score, tho, was at Goodwill where I got 11 pieces of Chantal Cookware for around $25. I checked on ebay to see what they are selling for, and someone had 11 pieces for $400 and included this remark: "Sells for $700 at Williams-Sonama." Ask me if I'm stoked about this.

Discount General Merchandise Stores

Some of the nation's largest discount and off-price chain stores are here in San Diego, offering merchandise at lower prices than full-service retail stores. The discount chains are: Walmart, Kmart and Target and are priced competitively. A discount store is a no-frills, no service version of the old department store, with more merchandise. They buy in huge quantities from manufacturers, offering both name brands and their own brands of merchandise. Usually a little short on trendy clothing, but long on underwear, sportswear and casual apparel. Great for plant sales, inexpensive but fashionable towels and throw rugs, kitchenwares, kids toys and clothes. Their loss leader ads in the Sunday *Union-Trib* are worth jumping out of bed for on Sunday mornings. Then, suit up and show up when the store opens because the advertised specials go fast. If what you raced in for isn't on the shelf, ask the department manager for a "rain check," so you can pick it up later when it is restocked, at the *sale* price. (See "rain checks" in Chapter 2.)

WAL-MART, the largest retailer in the world, with more than 2,200 stores, guarantees they won't be undersold and is known for good customer service. Stores are in Poway, (858) 486-1882; Santee, (619) 449-7900; 3382 Murphy Canyon, (858) 571-6094; El Cajon, (619) 561-0828; College Grove Center, (619) 858-0071; Oceanside, (760) 631-0434; Vista, (760) 966-0026; Chula Vista (760) 691-7945, Palm Ave (619) 428-4000; and more to come. There is an optical department, pharmacy, appliances, hardware (drawer pulls, too), footwear, bicycles, jewelry, and men's (McGregor, Manhattan, Wrestler, Wrangler), women's (Brittania, Jordache, Bonjour, Beverly Hills, Vassarette) and children's clothing, and their own private store brands. Name brand electronics, computer software and electronics. Their loafers look like they are a much more expensive brand. There is only one price marked on tags, so you don't know how much things sell for at other stores, but they guarantee they won't be undersold. Leather purses, $15 (a great buy); T-shirts, $6.94; cotton slacks, $15; Bill Blass beautiful bras, $5.94; Playtex bras, $12. If an advertised item is not available, Wal-Mart will sell you a similar item at a comparable price, or reduction in price if the item is on sale, or you can receive a "raincheck." Some exceptions. Call (800) WALMART to receive monthly mailer of sales items, or receive e-notification and shop on line: walmart.com. (Over 500,000 items)

Kmart, 8730 Rio San Diego Drive, Mission Valley, (619) 298-9916; 7655 Clairemont Mesa Boulevard, (858) 279-6823; 5405 University Avenue, (619) 286-9733; Spring Valley, (619) 420-9315; Carmel Mountain (858) 485-1954; Chula Vista, (619) 482-2765; El Cajon, (619) 442-6651; San Ysidro, (619) 428-0303; Oceanside, (760) 630-7601; Call (800) 866-0086 for location nearest you. Kmart is a general merchandise discount superstore, selling quality goods at bargain prices, 20%-50% below regular retail. The stores are filled with name-brand goods in all departments. Name brand apparel for men, women and children includes Jacklyn Smith, Kathy Ireland, Maidenform, Sasson, Gitano, Candies, Hanes, Botany 500, Wrangler, Nike, Gloria Vanderbilt. Shoes and accessories. Small appliances and electronics: Sunbeam, Black & Decker, GE, RCA, Sony, first quality merchandise at below retail prices. Garden centers with great plant sales, pharmacies, portrait studios, jewelry, watches, housewares, food items. If you haven't been there in a while, you might be surprised. Kmart revived their "bluelight" special sales (reduced prices), some for limited time, some always.. Kmart will issue a "rain check" for any advertised item that is not in stock. See the Sunday advertisements online and sign up for email at their Web site: kmart.com or bluelight.com (30,000 items)

Target Stores, a leading discounter, with over 1000 stores nationally, and several locations in San Diego including 3245 Sports Arena, (619) 223-2491, Mission Valley (619) 542-0292; Escondido, Oceanside, Encinitas, Kearny Mesa, Clairemont, a 2-story building in Grossmont, plus El Cajon and Poway, National City and Chula Vista. Call (800) 800-8800 for location nearest you. Open seven days a week from 8 a.m. to 10 p.m. Target offers national brands, from upscale to moderate-priced, at discounted prices. Target has great advertised specials every Sunday in their multi-page supplement in the *Union-Trib* that are worth giving up your afternoon for. Housewares, vacuums, irons, great organizers, domestics, bedding and curtain rods that don't cost a fortune. Their garden department has good sales on house plants and flowers, garden tools, bird houses, BBQ grills, beach chairs. Good prices on sporting goods, skates, camping gear, food items, cosmetics, shampoos, auto accessories. A great place to buy inexpensive but stylish watches on sale (Timex, Casio, Gittano, Brittania, Gloria Vanderbilt). Sale-priced name brand telephones. Many quality labels (Sanyo, Zenith, Sony, Panasonic, Hanes, Fruit of the Loom) and many made expressly for Target stores including Honors, Stanza. Clothing for the whole family. Lots of work out wear. Every Wednesday, items are placed on end caps for clearance. Target offers credit, with 10% off an entire Target Guest Card purchase. Target Corp. donates millions to the community, schools, scholarships, etc. Shop online at target.com (15,000 items)

Off-Price Stores

The **off-price chains** in San Diego are: Loemann's, Marshall's, Mervyn's, Ross, Burlington Coat Factory and T. J. Maxx. These stores buy factory overruns and department store overstock. On the racks, you will see current season fashions that are simultaneously in department stores, plus last season's fashions. The difference is: the department stores carry a very wide selection of sizes and coordinates, and the off-price stores have less items to make your selection from. We consumers benefit from the intense competition that exists between these off-price stores, which are particularly good resources for fashions, housewares, small electronics, appliances and 14 karat gold jewelry.

T. J. Maxx, the largest off-price retailer with over 700 stores in 48 states and 5 stores in San Diego including Clairemont, (858) 483-1286; Escondido,

(760) 746-9528; Pt. Loma, (619) 224-2754; Encinitas, (760) 942-1275;
Santee (619) 956-0851 and Temecula. Save 20-60% off retail; name
brands and designer fashions for the entire family and home. Fashions
include separates of Jones New York, Guess, Calvin Klein, Ralph Lauren,
Liz Claiborne, DKNY, Ralph Lauren Polo. Men's, women's and children's
clothing, home accessories, luggage, shoes, fragrance, jewelry, lingerie,
hosiery, hair accessories, gifts. Three truckloads of merchandise arrive a
week. Casual wear year round; cocktail wear arrives in the fall.

Burlington Coat Factory, with 315 stores nationally, is the second largest
off-price apparel retailer in the U.S., and by no means is their inventory
limited to coats. Although they have tons of coats for women, men and
children, including wool, leather, and down ski jackets, they also carry high
quality fashions for the whole family including suits, sportswear and shoes
plus linens and baby furniture and accessories, up to 60% off. They boast
that over 5 million people bought coats at Burlington last year, moderately
priced to designer coats The San Diego store is located at 3962 Clairemont
Mesa Blvd. At Clairemont Drive, (858) 272-1893.

Loehmann's, 1640 Camino del Rio North, Mission Valley Center, 296-7776;
La Mesa, (619) 460-7624. Loehmann's is an upscale off-price specialty
retailer of women's apparel. There are over 70 stores in 23 states in their
chain that buy closeouts from top designers, and several times during the
year, they have special sale events when the stores are filled. The
assortment is extensive, with lines including DKNY, Jones New York, Ralph
Loren, Anne Klein, and famous Italian designers suits, career dresses,
evening wear and cocktail dresses. At least two or more in each size arrive,
and each price tag has two prices: the suggested retail price plus
Loehmann's discounted price. Communal and 12 private dressing rooms.

Marshall's Department Stores, Mission Valley, Mission Valley West, (619)
260-0981; Solana Beach; Fletcher Pkwy, in El Cajon, (619) 462-1530;
Carmel Mountain Plaza, (858) 451-2883; 8657 Villa La Jolla Drive, 587-3984;
Chula Vista, (619) 425-6006; Balboa & Genesee, (858) 467-9330;
Escondido, (760) 480-1534; Carlsbad, (760) 434-8900; Mira Mesa, 549-9060,
Marshall's is one of the largest off-price nationwide chain store (over 575
locations in 37 states) offering mostly first-quality closeouts and leftovers plus
special purchase merchandise. About 90% of their stock is "overbuys"
(goods that are returned to the vendors by the stores because they over
ordered). Marshall's motto is: "Name brands for less." They carry Evan-
Picone, J.H. Collectibles, Carole Little, Chaps and more. Suits and
sportswear for men, women and children. Silk-blend sweaters, fleece
separates, career and casual dresses, men's dress slacks. Cookware,
leather portfolios, leather bags, shoes and boots (9 West and Bandolino
reduced 50%!). Overall savings throughout the store are 20% to 60%. Men's,

women's and children's clothing, shoes, housewares, linens, gifts, lingerie and perfumes. They had a sale on down comforters for $49, a real steal.

Mervyn's, with several stores throughout the county including 3345 Sports Arena Boulevard, (619) 223-8111; Horton Plaza, Escondido, Balboa Ave., Carmel Mountain Road, College Avenue, Fletcher Parkway, Chula Vista, Mira Mesa, Plaza Bonita, Saturn Blvd., Oceanside. Call (800) MERVYNS for a store nearest you. Since 1949, with over 264 stores in 14 states, and 124 stores in California. Mervyn's slogan is: "Big brands at small prices." Mervyn's buys in huge lots at discount prices and pass the savings on to you. This is a great place to shop for advertised specials on name brands including the same items that are sold in Express, Victoria Secret and the Limited. L. A. Gear, Reebok, Nike, Jockey, Hanes, Playtex, Danskin, Jantzen, Gloria Vanderbilt, Ocean Pacific, Van Heusen, Bill Blass, Arrow, Levi's, Lee's. Excellent for children's clothing, name brand sports wear, lingerie, sox, linens, bedding, towels, fine jewelry, and housewares. Mervyn's own store brands are Partners, clothing and shoes; Celebration, domestics and linens. Layaway available. When you open an account at Mervyn's, you get a 15% discount on all your purchases that day. "Rain checks" available for advertised items that are not in stock. Keep the receipt; if the item you bought goes on sale with in 12 days, they will refund the difference. All sales are from Sunday through Saturday, and are advertised in a special supplement in the *Union-Tribune* on Sundays. Mervyn's has teamed up with the Women's Sports Foundation to offer $1,000 scholarships to 100 female high school seniors to further their education and help them excel in their athletic pursuits. Applications are available at all Mervyn's stores. Web Site: mervyns.com. Mervyns is a subsidiary of Target Corporation.

Ross (Dress For Less) is one of the top three off-price store with 507 stores nationally and 14 in San Diego: Sports Arena, (619) 223-2453; Chula Vista, (619) 420-1245; La Jolla Village Square, (858) 450-1233; Oceanside, (760) 439-4040; Clairemont, (858) 292-7515; Escondido, (760) 480-0307; La Mesa, (619) 698-9222; Santee, (619) 258-0301; Solana Beach,(858) 259-2208; Carmel Mountain (858) 451-9716; Rancho San Diego; Vista, (760) 758-6992; and Mission Valley. As an offprice retailer, Ross offers first-quality, in-season, name brand and designer apparel, accessories and footwear for the entire family at everyday savings of 20% to 60% from department and specialty store regular prices. In addition, the same savings can be found on a wide variety of merchandise for the home. Fashions for the men, women and children, businesswear to active wear to clothes for going anywhere. Ross buy overruns and sells them at 30-50% off. Many buyers, previously employed by Lord & Taylor and other major east coast stores, have great contacts, and they are able to get many current season things. Many high end fashions including Adrienne Vittidini coordinates, Jones of New York, Bali, Lizbeth, Liz Claiborne, plus their own labels. Five truckloads arrive each week. Markdowns every week. Bed and bath, home accents, luggage, shoes, fragrances. They only advertise on TV. Seniors day every Tuesday, 10%, age 55.

Stein Mart Two San Diego locations including Poway, 13644 Poway Road, (619) 513-9309 and Oceanside, 2505B Vista Way (760) 433-7440. Stein Mart is a new name to San Diego, but they have over 265 locations in the U.S. Designer and well-known apparel brands for women, men and children. Casual, career and evening wear. Beautiful fabrics. Petites and Women's sizes. Italian imported shoes, handbags, delightful fashion jewelry. Current season fashions offered at prices 25-60% below those charged by department and specialty stores. Housewares, gift items, luxury linens, goose down, all discounted. Baby boutique. I discovered Stein Mart in Sarasota, Fla., and I am so happy they have arrived here!

Dry Cleaners

A friend called snorting mad because she put a few things in the cleaners and found out it would cost her $62. She insisted I find something for this book on dry cleaners. OK, so here it is. Check your *PennySaver* (see chapter on *Resources)* for discount coupons as there is *usually* a coupon every other week for your area.). Wait a week if there isn't. Also, there are usually discount coupons for dry cleaning *on the back of your supermarket receipts!!* Another suggestion is to take your clothes to Tijuana. Limpiaduras (cleaners) are everywhere. I took a suede jacket to TJ that they wanted an arm and a leg for to clean up here. I was pleased with the great job they did. Also had it redyed for about half what I could have had it done for in San Diego.

The *Entertainment* book has several coupons discount coupons for 50% off the regular price of your dry cleaning order, one for every month.

There are no more "do-it-yourself" dry cleaners in California because there were problems with the cleaning chemicals catching fire, but there are some new products on the market called "Dryel," "FreshCare" by Clorox, "Custom Cleaner" and "Dry Cleaner's Secret." They run around $10-12, and you will find $2 discount coupons in the *Union-Trib* Sunday coupon supplement every few weeks. For wools, silks, knits & rayons, sweaters, skirts, blazers, pants, dresses, blouses and other "dry clean only" garments. Not meant to be a *full* substitute for dry cleaning, but works on some fresh stains, and refreshes. Available in supermarkets, Kmart, etc.

Tip: dry cleaning can be hard of clothes. To save $$ *and* your clothes, hand wash your better things and invest in a good steam iron.

Be sure you *know* the fabric is dry cleanable because if it isn't, cleaning fluids can ruin it. Check your *label* first.

Small Claims Court is flooded with dry cleaner cases. There are more dry cleaner cases, and hair salon cases, than any other type of small claim.

Try some of the commercial spot removers available in supermarkets. Heloise, the helpful household lady, has several products on the market that do the job. Home Depot has a whole rack of killer grease and glue desolvers and removers that *work.* They dissolve dried masking tape glue and even take chewing gum out of delicate fabrics like silk; carpeting, too.

A student in one of my bargain hunting workshops told me the fabulous outfit I had just complimented her on was an unclaimed garment from her dry cleaners and that her entire wardrobe when she was a teenager came from dry cleaners because her parents owned one! Ask your dry cleaners when they sell unclaimed clothing, usually once or twice a year, sometimes for just the cost of cleaning. If your little cleaners says they don't sell them, call one that is part of a chain.

Energy

GASOLINE For the cheapest gas pumps in town, check out this web site at fueltracker.com. Americans burn an average of around 600 gallons per car per year. Multiply that by the cost per gallon to see what you spend per year. To save on gas costs, keep your vehicle in top running condition. Use the proper octane according to the manufacturer (only 18% of cars need the highest octane). Consider a smaller, more energy efficient model (the Toyoto Echo gets about 38 miles per gallon, and I've seen new ones on sale for around $10K+).

ELECTRICITY: Get your Home Energy Savings and Comfort Kit from SDGE which contains "100 Ways to Save Energy" plus info on approximately how much each appliance in your house is costing you and information on the energy-saving programs. Call (800) 711-SDGE or visit their web site at sdge.com to get your free kit. It also contains info on rebates for replacing old refrigerators, washers, air conditioners, pool pumps, etc. with new energy efficient ones. Any appliance with the Energy Star is eligible for a rebate, including washers, dishwashers, air conditioners, furnaces, insulation, hot water heaters, pool pumps, programable thermostats and more. The SDGE site at sdge.com has a list of Energy Star appliances eligible for rebates, or go to energystar.gov. Also, SDGE will come to your house and do an "energy audit" and show you where and how you can save on utilities. They check leaks in doors, windows, even refrigerator gaskets and tell you to turn off lights in rooms when you leave them. I had this done YEARS ago. It's a free service. (There is an online, do it yourself version you can fill out.) It may take some time to get an appointment these days due to the energy crunch, so call soon. SDG&E also provides a list of approved contractors to do energy saving home improvements which qualify for a rebate. And, they will arrange for qualifying low income seniors to have their houses weatherized and retro-fitted for energy savings thru a federally funded program.

Since 2000, I have been saving 5% on my electric bill by switching to electricAmerica, which provides green energy. However, the Public Utilities

Commission in California has suspended signing up people for this service. When that is settled, you will be able to switch to electricAmerica and get either regular service at a 5% savings, or purchase green energy which will cost about twice as much. Do call and get the latest skinny on this at (800) 353-2874, or go to the Utilities Consumer Action Network at ucan.com and see their latest on it.

UCAN (Utility Consumers' Action Network) offers consumer information on electric bills, phone bills, water bills, cable bills, internet. They want to know of any complaints you may have against a utility, and they will go to bat for you, taking your issue to state and federal legislation agencies. This is a nonprofit organization founded more than 20 years ago. Call (619) 696-6966 or visit their web site at ucan.org

Compare current rates for gas and electric utilities and more at www.lowermybills.com.

Your major energy pullers are your heater (especially electric heaters), your refrigerator (especially non-enery efficient ones) and your freezer. People don't realize the amount of electricity a refrigerator uses, even a small one. Fill empty plastic jugs or plastic ziplock freezer bags with water and fill up in the freezer. A full freezer and refrigerator are more energy efficient. Take some of the frozen jugs of water and rotate them into the refrigerator for more efficiency. Replace them in the freezer after they thaw. Check into a Power Saver which you plug into an outlet, then plug your refrigerator or washer into it, and save up to 20%. Available at home improvement centers for about $40 or check powersavers.com. Also, vacuum the coils on the refrigerator and vents on all appliances, heating systems, computers, even hair dryers. Keep them dust free and efficient.

Compact flourescent lights (CFL) use 75% less energy, provide the same amount of light and last longer. They cost about $8-$20, 60, 75 & 100's. (Available at Home Depot, Costco, Walmart, etc.)

Since you know this energy problem isn't going to go away, the name of the game is to FREE yourself from the clutches of the utility company. I went "au naturale" years ago and had the heat ripped out of my house, and am thrilled to say I have met many people the past year who have told me they haven't used heaters/furnaces in YEARS either. I felt rather eccentric, but it's actually healthier and I haven't had a cold in 30 years. It will be hard for some people to make small changes, but I have loved every one I have implemented. Here are some ways to stay warm in the cold months without turning on the heat. Invest in three weights of down comforters (light, medium and heavy...on sale). Tuesday Morning has sales all the time. Add a feather bed (sale price, $49.) That should do it for sleeping, as down keeps ducks warm on *ice ponds!* Wear thermal underwear around the house under sweatshirts, sheep lined Ugh boots, wool sox. I LOVE my wool sox. They are my new best friends on "winter" days. I like light weight zip front hooded SLEEVELESS sweatshirts so I can move around without being confined, or a sleeveless down vest is great. Apply lots of heavy hand and body creams to keep warmth in. Use candles in groups in metal containers (you'd be surprised how much they heat a room). I have several groups of candles, being sure they are never unattended and are in a container or bowl that can catch hot wax (which can start a fire.) You can buy them by the dozens at the 99 cent stores, BigLots, Kmart, drug stores, etc. Drink lots of hot drinks like herbal teas. I just drink brewed bottled water with lemon, all day. Cook a lot of hot soups and bake bread to warm up the place. Wrap up in a "granny shawl" while watching TV or reading. I have a small down baby comforter for my legs while I'm at the computer. Put "storm windows" over your windows on the North side of the house. Home Depot sells 4x8 ft. sheets of clear acrylic you can cut, frame and put over large picture windows. Consider double pane windows if you're going to be there a while. Plug up all leaks around windows and doors. Get drapery liners, I put double pairs of drapery liners on sliding patio doors and large windows (from JCPenney). They really help insulate a cold glass window. Consider wood shutters which don't conduct cold. Keep your windows uncovered during the day on the South and West side and let the sunshine in. Cut back trees that block the sun. *Turn a light on all day in a really cold North room.* You'd be surprised how much chill that bulb can take off the air. Get SDG&E to come out and show you where your doors are leaking and allowing in cold drafts. Stick a small rug or towel up against the bottom of an outside door to stop a draft. Consider additional insulation in the attic. Where there is crawl space under the house, get under there and staple thick insulation to the subflooring. Lay a room size rug or throw rugs over carpeting to cover floors, especially concrete slab floors which are ice cold. Hang a sheet over a doorway and keep the warmth confined in the family room if you are not using the living room.

In summer, cover the windows on the South and West to protect from direct sun. Invest in large trees in large pots with wheels that can be rolled in front of a window to protect it from the sun in the summer and removed in the winter. Put in awnings, hang plastic exterior blinds, or place a patio umbrella in front of a window to protect it (makes a tremendous difference). Create cross ventilation by opening windows in several rooms. Open double-hung windows, top and bottom. Put an air vent on the roof to take hot air out of the attic (Sears installs them and they're cheap.) Install Casablanca ceiling fans in every room from Home Depot, etc. My mother used to put a bowl of ice in front of the fan on the kitchen counter to blow cold air on her while cooking! No wonder I am the way I am.

Here are some other energy savers may be adaptable: Wash in cold water, and only full loads. Use a clothesline instead of the dryer. You can fluff line-dried towels in the dryer without heat. Install solar outdoor lighting outdoors. Put a hot water blanket around your hot water heater or make one out of thick insulation and attach it with bungee cords. See if you can lower the setting. Install double pane energy efficient windows on select windows. Call *Yellow Pages* under Windows. They give free estimates.

If you're interested in renewable energy (wind, solar, bionmas, geothermal, check this web site: http://environment.about.com and click on renewable energy. Personally, I would get a windmill in a heartbeat, and look forward to being a part of any research project on this. Such independence! If I were building a new home, I guarantee you it would be designed by an architect who would know how to capitalize on the sun for heat, and have transom windows for ventilation, atriums, adobe walls, moveable trees in roll-around planters, solar heated pool, hot water, etc. Many things are eligible for 50% off the purchase price with the California Energy Commission rebates, 15% California State income tax credit, and an extra 10% federal tax credit for using solar on qualifying homes and businesses. Learn everything you need to know about solar/electric grids for do-it-yourselfers at Fallbrook Community Center (they hold classes).

Fabric Stores

Designer Fabrics, 530 Broadway, Chula Vista, (619) 422-2340; fine importers of fabrics and lace, buttons and trims from around the world, for bridal and evening wear. Wholesale and retail.

Calico Corners, 4240 Kearny Mesa Rd., Kearny Mesa, (858) 292-1500. Top decorative fabrics for the home at a discount. With 115 stores nationwide, their buying power can offer you good prices. Call and get on mailing list to be notified of sales which occur about 7 times a year. Call (800) 213-6366 to receive great catalog with fabrics, pillows, accessories and furniture frames to upholster Web site: calicocorners.com.

Jane's Fabrique 7547 Girard Ave., La Jolla, (858) 459-5828. Fine designer fabrics. Silks, cottons, shirting, suiting, linens, woolens, cottons, lace. Jane's Fabriques has been around for 35 years, and has now combined with Sew & Sew. Lots of unusual trims, ribbons, buttons, costume fabrics, tons of white fabric for brides, custom bridal headpieces.

B & B Laces, 117 E. Park Avenue, El Cajon, (619) 440-4569, is a factory outlet with laces, ribbons, elastic, fabrics, rhinestones, satin roses, fringe, sequins, velvets, velcro, baskets. Fabrics, upholstery. Sales, good prices.

UFO, 1919 Hoover Avenue, National City,(619) 477-9341, and 1120 N. Melrose Drive, Vista, (760) 941-2345. Open Mon-Sat, 9-5:30 p.m. UFO stands for Upholstery Fabric Outlet and they carry everything you need in the line of decorator and upholstery fabrics for home and auto; foam rubber, too. No seconds, no closeouts, all first quality. High end ($79-$100+ a yard) plus mid line, inexpensive, everything! Very few sales but there is always a clearance table with markdowns. This is a huge place! Drapery hardware, tassels. Special order books to look through. They will supply you with a list of upholsterers.

Discount Fabrics, 3325 Adams Avenue, Normal Heights, (619) 280-1791; 6,000 square feet of decorator, upholstery, curtain fabrics. When manufacturers make clothes and furniture, there is always about 10-12% of the fabric left over. This store (old theater) sells the leftovers at good prices, in season, because the furniture was manufactured 6 months ahead of season. They have a second store down the street at 3580 Adams, with apparel fabric and trims. Remnants, mill ends, sample cuts, lycra, good deals, (619) 282-6920.

Cutting Corners, 5150 Convoy near the 52 freeway; (858) 560-5831. A fabric discount supermarket and mill outlet (big store) with decorator fabrics for upholstery, draperies and specialties. Current fabrics, colors, styles. They also do custom draperies and bedspreads. Ask to be put on the mailing list to receive advance notification of sales.

Fabric Villa, 6364 El Cajon Boulevard, College Area, (619) 286-4364. Imported, hand woven fabrics, Guatemalan cottons, cottons from India, Dashiki panels, fabrics from Bali, tie dyes, batiks, African prints, silks, Cuna Indian molas. For clothing, pillows and curtains. They haven't had a sale in 20 years because they say their "prices are right."

 Get on the mailing list for sales at **Jo-Ann's Fabrics and Crafts**. Stores in Pt. Loma, (619) 224-2331, El Cajon, La Mesa, Lemon Grove, Escondido, Oceanside, Chula Vista, National City, Poway. For a store near you, call (877) 465-6266. The company owns over 1200 stores nationwide with frequent sales, 30-40% off and more; always a sale for three weeks and sales within the sale! Tons of fabrics, notions, crafts, candles, decorator items, seasonal decor with big discounts. Discount coupons, 40-50% off the regular price of any one item in store, are in mailers or online at joann.com.

Beverly's Craft & Fabric store, 6185 Balboa Ave, in the Ihop shopping center, Clairemont, (858) 278-8072; fabrics, wearable art, seasonal, quilting, notions and trims plus crafts. Always a holiday weekend sale, and frequent coupon offers. Check their Web: beverlys.com.

We-R-Fabrics, 963 Lomas Santa Fe Drive, Solana Beach, (858) 755-1175. Really fine decorator fabrics and trim for the home. Some furniture and accessories. Ask about clearance/remnant items (there is usually an interesting pile.) Classes on how to make pillows, slip covers, valances.

Yardage Town (5517 Clairemont Mesa, (858) 278-5662 and 11 other locations in San Diego. Large stores with tons of fabrics, patterns, notions, home decor, crafts, great prices, frequent sales. At the National City Giant Store & Warehouse ((619) 477-3749), you can get a Discount Card for the asking which will give you 20% off regular prices, daily. The last Saturday of the month, everything is 30% off; holidays sales, 50% off certain items including bolt ends. Wholesale and quantity warehouse in National City. Discounts for quantities, schools.

There are several **wholesale fabric**, notions and millinery supply stores in the Los Angeles Garment District, including B. Black & Sons, 548 S. Los Angeles Street, with imported fabrics for men's and women's clothing, trimmings, shoulder pads, dress forms and more at below retail prices for the general public. Discounts given to teachers and classes. Many San Diegans go to L.A. for the huge variety.

Walmart has fabric roll ends, $1 a yard, and a friend got beautiful decorator fabric at Kobey's Swap Meet from a weekly vendor, for $3 a yard.

Discount fabric by mail: Locate the decorating fabric you want in stores. Write down specific information including mill, color, design, fabric number; then call the Fabric Outlet, (800) 635-9715 to see if you can buy it for less by mail. No California sales tax. They carry Waverly & Robert Allen fabric up to 60% below retail, plus 35 major brands.

Silk Surplus (Scalamandre), luxurious upholstery and drapery fabrics with up to 75% savings. Also, cottons, velvets, woolens, brocades and weaves. Call with ordering information or send a swatch. Since 1962, (718) 361-8500.

Factory Outlet Malls

If you're not familiar with the terminology, a factory outlet is a store that is usually owned and operated by the manufacturer; therefore, there is no middle-man markup. Some call themselves "company stores" or "factory stores." By any name, they are directly connected to the manufacturer. Factory outlets are usually located in malls that are removed from the center of town so they don't compete with department stores that are carrying their merchandise for full price.

If you're into fashions created by famous high end designers, or nationally known name brand merchandise, you'll be thrilled to know that right here in Southern California, we have these famous name outlets (& more):

Versace	London Fog	Leslie Fay
Gucci	Ralph Lauren	Liz Claiborne
Anne Klein	Fieldcrest/Cannon	Olga
Off-5thSaksFifth Ave.	Swank	Oneida
Off- Rodeo Dr./BevHills	Etienne Aigner	Royal Doulton
Sony	Brooks Brothers	Donna Karan Co.
Georgiou	Izod	Ellen Tracey
Guess	Maidenform	Jones New York
Jockey	Sergio Tacchini	Playtex
Levi's	Florsheim	St. John Knits
Maidenform	Naturalizer	Spa Gear
Mikasa	Nine West	Lenox
Nike	Barbizon	Noritake
Van Heusen	Carter's Baby Clothes	Pfalzgraff
Black & Decker	Chicago Cutlery	Royal Doulton
Corning/Revere	Cole Haan	Bose
Big Dog	Geoffrey Beene	Ritz Cameras
Esprit	Jones NY	Ann Taylor Loft
Eddie Bauer	Jordache	Charlotte Russe
Gap	Koret	and many more.

Here are a few things to know before you go outlet shopping: There are different types of outlets. Some only sell the overstocks and discontinued merchandise they manufacture and sell to department stores, chains and boutiques. Others sell merchandise that they manufacture for department stores, plus a few other lines that you will never see in retail stores, some of which is manufactured FOR the outlet stores. Then there are stores that rent space in outlet malls that sell apparel exclusively and only in outlet malls! These lines are never seen in any department store or elsewhere and are found only in their own "outlet mall" stores.

Most manufacturers make several lines: high end, middle and low end, all or some are sold under different names. Some of the low end may be copies of their own high end, created in different fabrics and sold under different labels. Some merchandise may come from a designer's exclusive boutique. Some things are overstocks of the designer which may be a line made especially for a high end department store. Some items from a designer are made expressly for the outlets and won't be seen in designer boutiques or department stores. Ask a sales associate if you aren't sure what you are looking at. Outlets carry mostly first quality merchandise. Irregulars should be well marked. IRREGULARS have only minor imperfections, like some stitching missing; SECONDS, on the other hand, have more prominent irregularities.

Factory outlet prices usually range from 20-30% off the suggested retail price that is printed on the price tag. Items are marked down further the longer they are in the store, with clearance racks up to 90% off the regular retail price. Although a relatively new concept in San Diego, on the East Coast, there are tons of factory outlet shopping malls. People spend their vacations going from one factory outlet center to another all over the East Coast! Some say you can do just as well at department store sales and this is often true....if you want to wait for the sale to come around! Some factory outlets won't have all the styles that a department store has. But many outlets have *more* styles because they carry the whole line which department stores usually don't. Some outlets sell things that are currently seen in department stores. Some outlets get the same things that are in the department stores, only three to six weeks later. Others only have things that are from the previous season's line (or even last year's line). You never know what you might find, so call first and find out. I always ask if they have a lot of inventory, or just had a sale and are empty. You might find out they just got in a huge shipment of designer purses tomorrow or next week. They can usually tell you what they are expecting and when. Ask how often they get in new truck loads. Ask if there is a sale coming up. Before going, make a list of the stores you want to visit and what you're looking for because it gets very confusing when you just plop yourself in among all the stores without a plan. Many outlet malls offer a discount coupon booklet at the mall office, so be sure to drop by and pick one up.

San Diego has three factory outlet shopping malls. Most of the ones that were in the old San Diego Factory Outlets in San Ysidro have moved across the street to the new Las Americas Outlets that opened in the fall of 2001. The Carlsbad Company Stores opened in 1997, and the Viejas Outlets that opened in the late 90's. There are also several other factory outlet malls in Southern California within a few hours driving time from San Diego that are definitely worth going to because of the designer fashions and name brand outlets. Telephone numbers are provided so you can call the outlet and find out if that St. John's knit or Armani outfit you saw in

Nordstrom, Neiman Marcus or Saks is available for less at their outlet, or if the Liz Claiborne sweater you saw in Vogue is available at the outlet yet.

Carlsbad Company Stores

Carlsbad Company Stores. . . . . (888) 790-SHOP 5620 Paseo Del Norte behind Anderson's Windmill off Interstate 5 and Palomar Road. Opened in late 1997, the Carlsbad Company Stores mall offers many upscale designer and manufacturers outlets, plus restaurants. Here's what you will find:

All area codes: **760**

Designer Fashions & Sportswear
Banana Republic 804-0667
Barney's New York Outlet 929-9600
BCBG Max Azria 929-2735
Bebe Outlet 929-8625
Big Dog Sportswear 929-7835
Brooks Bros. 930-8066
Cashmere Elite 918-6711
DKNY/Donna Karan 804-8190
Ellen Tracey 602-8224
GAP Outlet 431-2544
Geoffrey Beene . . . .
Guess? 602-0803
Jessica McClintock 476-3611
Jones New York 268-0632
Jones New York Country 918-9413
Kasper ASL 930-9839
L'eggs Hanes Bali Playtex 804-0723
Maternity Works 804-0387
No Fear 603-8643
Oh, La La 804-1896
Polo Ralph Lauren 929-2898
Puma 438-4711
Reebok 804-0200
Robt. Scott & David Brooks 804-0296
The Territory Ahead 918-0575
Thousand Mile Outdoor 804-1764
Tight Assets 268-1000
Timberland Outlet 602-8495
Tommy Hilfiger 431-8806

Home Furnishings
Crate & Barrel Outlet 692-2100
Kitchen Collection 438-2369
LeCreuset 931-6868
Polo Ralph Lauren 929-2898
Lenox 929-1260
WestPoint Stevens 804-0160
Waterford Wedgwood 476-1612

Footwear
Adidas 804-0667
Barney New York 929-9600
Cole-Haan 804-0290
Factory Brand Shoes 804-9170
GH Bass
Hush Puppies 804-0701
Johnston & Murphy 602-5065
Kenneth Cole New York 804-3793
Nine West 930-8955
Reebok 804-0200
Rockport 804-0154
Skechers 918-0040
Vans 804-0190

Children's Fashions, Toys, etc.
Big Dog 931-7835
Carter's 804-0254
Gap Outlet 431-2544
OshKosh B'Gosh 804-1637
Polo Ralph Lauren 929-2898
The Right Start 804-3840
Strasburg Children 804-9660
Striderite 476-9061

Leather, Luggage & Accessories
Coach 476-0565
Dooney & Bourke Handbags 476-1049
Franklin Covey 476-3401
Kenneth Cole 804-3793
Samsonite 804-0053
Wilson's Leather r431-5297
Specialty
Bose 438-4820
Carlsbad Book Company 804-0467
Cosmetics Store 804-7979
Carlsbad Book Co. 804-0467
Designer Fragrance 903-9653
Four Seasons Sunglasses 804-9122
Sunglass Outlet 476-9019

Viejas Outlet Center

Viejas Outlet Center .... (619) 659-2070
Located at 5005 Willows Rd., Alpine. The Viejas Outlets were built by the
Viejas band of Kumeyaay Indians. The mall is designed in a Native
American village motif with lush landscaping with natural water features and
massive rock formations. Each evening in the Show Court (weather
permitting), visitors are treated to a spectacular seasonal water show with
music, laser, lights and pyrotechnics. Web site: shopviejas.com

All area codes **619**

Aerololes 659-0620
Bass 445-9616
BonWorth 659-1564
Book Warehouse 659-3282
Big Dogs Sportswear 659-1655
    Casual Clothing
Black & Decker 659-3413
    Tools & appliances
Carter Children's Wear 659-0635
    children's
Casual Corner 445-9178
Claire's Accessories 445-6454
Country Clutter(decor) 445-2656
Dress Barn 445-7615
    missy & women's to size 20+
Eddie Bauer 659-0955
Factory Brand Shoes 659-3897
Fragrance Outlet 445-4195
Gap Outlet 445-2974
Geoffrey Beene 659-9540
Tommy Hilfiger 659-8887
Jones New York 445-7317
    This factory outlet carries more lines and
    stock than the department stores. Top of
    the line Jones New York, Jones & Co., ...
Jones New York Country 445-6814
    New line, more casual than career store,
    separate jackets, jeans, carried at
    Nordstrom, 25%, 2-16.
Kitchen Collection 445-6130
Koret 659-3476
    high end women's clothing
L'eggs/Hanes/Bali/Playtex 659-3428
    lingerie
Levi/Dockers 659-5886
Liz Claiborne 659-3887
    Outlet store that carries Liz & Co., Liz
    Sport, Lizwear (casual, denim twills)
    Elizabeth (larger size) Villager (Liz's
    lower line), Clairborne for men, last
    season and in- season, watches,
    sunglasses, blazers.
Naturalizer ....
Nautica 659-3266
    men's and boys, from East; wovens, solids,
    all casual, khaki pants, jackets, pullovers.
Nike Outlet 659-3460
    athletic shoes, wear
Nine West 659-1391
    women's shoes
Osh Kosh B'Gosh
Reebok 659-8160
Samsonite 445-5709
    luggage
Socks Galore 445-2560
    sox
Sunglass Hut.............. 659-3602
Tommy Hilfiger 659-8887
    mainly sportswear, knits, chino shorts &
    pants, men's only, 30% off stores, then
    marked down from there.
Van Heusen
Vans Shoes .... family shoes

Las Americas Factory Outlets

Las Americas in the new factory outlet mall at the border. Phase I opened in November 2001 and includes a 630,000 sq. ft. open-air factory outlet mall and retail complex, entertainment facilities, duty-free shopping and restaurants. Phase II will open in 2004-5, and many tenants have already signed leases including a Versace outlet. Proposed plans include a 300-room hotel and conference center, an office building, transportation terminal and a 2,000 car parking deck. Also planned is an International pedestrian bridge which will begin at Louisiana St. in the factory outlet mall, cross over the Tijuana River and end at Avenida Revolucion in Tijuana where there will be new Mexican shopping mall. Plans include having U.S.Customs officials stationed here. Driving Directions: Take Interstate 5 South, exit at Camino de la Plaza, make a right turn (head west). The outlets are on the left.

STORE NAME	AREA CODE		
619 A&W/Long John Silvers	428-6619	Kitchen Collection	690-2297
Adidas Outlet Store	662-0955	Leather Outlet	662-3506
As Seen on TV, Radio	662-9110	Levi's Outlet by Most	690-3218
Babylandia	) 690-1122	Liz Claiborne Outlet	690-2336
Baja Duty Free	662-3010	Magic Step	662-2887
Banana Republic Factory Store	934-7242	Maidenform	934-8269
Bass	934-7367	McDonald's	690-2989
Bath and Body Works	690-4702	Mikasa	428-2022
Benzene	428-6174	Motherhood Maternity	428-0229
Big Toy Box	662-3890	Nautica Jean Co. Outlet	690-4881
Bridal X-Press	428-5998	Nike Factory Store	428-8849
Brooks Brothers	934-4580	Old Navy Outlet	934-7282
Buster Brown Kidwear	r 690-6400	Pac Sun	428-7669
Candles ' N Things	690-9366	Pac-Net	011-52-634-3480
Casual Corner Annex	662-1352	Papaya	662-3800
Charlotte Russe	934-7221	Rayless Shoe Source	662-1294
Claire's Accessories	934-7154	Perfume and Cosmetics Co.	662-1900
Consumer Electronic Outlet	662-2900	Perfume Outlet	662-1500
Crescent Jewelers	428-0516	Polo Jeans Co. Factory Store	662-6111
D.C.C. Sunglasses	934-0673	Reference Clothing	934-7175
Designer Studio	662-9571	Rice Garden	662-1818
Dress Barn	690-5368	Sally Beauty Supply	934-7541
Factory Brand Shoes	662-2485	Sam's Auto Care	428-8328
Gap Outlet	934-7229	Sam's Handbags	428-8328
Geoffrey Beene	934-7358	Sam's Mobile Plus	428-8328
Georgiou	662-2600	Samsonite	934-7261
Glamour Shots	662-1090	Sunray	934-7576
GNC	690-1418	Skechers	934-7340
Guess	934-7216	Springtail	934-7543
Haggard	428-0805	Starbucks	690-5144
Harry and David	690-4593	Stride Rite	934-7258
Hush Puppies	662-1492	Subway Deli	428-8500
IHOP	690-9411	Sunglass Outlets	690-2211
IZOD	934-7362	Tilly's	690-5200
		T-Moblie	271-2122

Tommy Hilfiger	934-7182	Wanna Taco	690-6270
Van Heusen	934-7363	Wet Seal	934-7196
Vanity Plus	662-3799	Wilsons Leather	428-7766
Vitamin World	934-7607	Zales the Diamond Store Outlet	662-2500
Vogue Italia	428-8332		

San Ysidro Village *(Formerly San Diego Factory Outlets)*

San Ysidro Village 858-592-6287/619-572-2485
Formerly the San Diego Factory Outlet Mall. Most stores moved across the street to the new Las Americas Outlets when they opened. This mall is bringing in a Marshall's and Ross in addition to the Kmart store already there and they will be getting in more factory outlet tenants, too. Located near the Mexican border at 4498 Camino de la Plaza, San Ysidro. Take Interstate 5 South or Interstate 805 South to the last exit before the Mexican border which is Camino de la Plaza. Go right on Camino de la Plaza one block to the mall. Here's a list of their stores:

All area codes: .... **(619)**

Just For Feet	690-3338	KB Toy Liquidators	428-4826
Reebok	690-9006	Nine West Factory Outlet	428-8838
Anna's Linens		Van's Shoes	690-2725
Carter's Baby Clothes	690-1106	Walking, skating, tennis shoes,	
Infants to girls 14, boys 7		canvas	
OshKosh B'Gosh	690-2255	shoes, found at department stores	
Infants to age 7, some adult		Kmart, and coming: Marshalls & Ross.	

Citadel Factory Stores

The Citadel (Los Angeles) .... (323) 888-1220
The Citadel factory stores are located behind the historic Assyrian castle wall, a familiar landmark just off Interstate 5, at 5675 E. Telegraph Road, Commerce, CA 90040. Take Interstate 5 North about 20 minutes North of Disneyland. Just after you cross the L.A. line, you will see the Citadel on your right. Take Atlantic Blvd. North off-ramp; take a right on Telegraph Road and you will see Citadel to your left. Hours, Mon-Sat, 10 a.m.-8p.m.; Sun 10 a.m.-6 p.m. Drop by the office for a GOOD discount coupon book

Women's Apparel		Benetton, United Colors of	(323) 721-3676
A&Y Leather	(323) 728-2690	Benetton Clearance Outlet	(323) 721-3641
American Brands	(323) 724-4654	Big Dog Sportswear	(323) 722-1589
Ann Taylor Factory	(323) 725-7033	Eddie Bauer	(323) 725-1858
Attitudes	(323) 887-8405	Geoffrey Beene	(323) 728-2070
Balboa Beach Company	(323) 837-9999	IZOD	(323) 832-5394
BASS (323) 887-9436		L'eggs, Hanes, Bali Express	(323) 724-8391
BCBG Max Azria	(323) 727-7284	London Fog	(323) 887-9322

Maidenform . . . . (323) 887-8906
Max Studio . . . . (323) 721-2200
Old Navy Outlet   . . . . (323) 726-0621
Quiksilver . . . . (323) 887-1574
Reebok Outlet Store . . . . (323) 724-2248
SU . . . . (323) 887-3817
Van Heusen . . . . (323) 722-9642

Men's Apparel
American Brands . . . . . . (323) 724-4654
Balboa Beach Company . (323) 837-9999
BASS . . . . (323) 887-9436
Big Dog Sportswear . . . . (323) 722-1589
Eddie Bauer . . . . (323) 725-1858
E-Street . . . . (323) 728-2543
GH. Q. Men . . . . (323) 887-0993
Geoffrey Beene   . . . . (323) 728-2070
IZOD . . . . (323) 832-5394
London Fog . . . . (323) 887-9322
Old Navy Outlet . . . . (323) 726-0621
Paolo Giardini   . . . . (323) 721-6400
Reebok Outlet Stores . . . (323) 724-2248
Quiksilver . . . . (323) 887-1574
Van Heusen . . . . (323) 722-9642

Children's Apparel & Toys
Big Dog . . . . (323) 722-1589
Carter's . . . . (323) 887-8640
Old Navy Outle . . . . t(323) 726-0621
Reebok . . . . (323) 724-2248
Toy Liquidators   . . . . (323) 722-1998

Footwear
Ann Taylor . . . . (323) 725-7033
BASS . . . . (323) 887-9436
BCBG Footwear . . . . (323) 887-8677
Street . . . . (323) 728-2543
Nine West . . . . (323) 724-7723
Old Navy Outlet . . . . (323) 726-0621
Paolo Giardini . . . . (323) 721-6400
Reebok Outlet Store . . . . (323) 724-2248
Two Lips . . . . (323) 722-1228
Vans Shoes . . . . (323) 887-7435

Leather, Luggage & Accessories
A & Y Leather . . . . (323) 728-2690
Geoffrey Beene   . . . . (323) 728-2070
Leather Revolution . . . . . (323) 726-4060
London Fog . . . . (323) 887-9322
Prime Time . . . . (323) 724-1550
Samsonite Company Store(323) 722-4255
Van Heusen . . . . (323) 722-9642

Home Furnishings & Specialty
Bijoux Bijoux Jewelry . . . . (323) 726-9888
Book Warehouse . . . . . . (323) 722-7210
Corning Revere   . . . . (323) 725-3155
Fragrance Outlet . . . . (323) 725-3942
Kitchen Collection . . . . . . (323) 722-3272
Linen Club . . . . (323) 721-2444
Prime Time . . . . (323) 724-1550
Vitamin World . . . . (323) 721-1197

Factory Merchant Outlet Plaza - Barstow

Factory Merchant Outlet Plaza (Barstow) . . . . (619) 253-7342
Manufacturer's outlets plus restaurants are located at 2837 Lenwood Road, Barstow, on the way to Las Vegas. Take Interstate 15 North to Lenwood Road Exit, Barstow, CA. Hours: 9 a.m.-8 p.m. every day. Closed Thanksgiving and Christmas. Outlets include Etienne Aigner,

Lake Elsinore Factory Outlets

Factory outlets, plus restaurants, are located at 17600 Collier Avenue, Lake Elsinore, CA 92330, (909) 245-4989. Less than two hours from downtown San Diego! Take Interstate 15 North to Nichols Road. Left on Collier. Open 7 days, Sat, 10-9 p.m.; Sun 11-6 p.m. Outlets include Sony, Florsheim, Elisabeth (Plus sizes by Liz Claiborne), Casual Big & Tall Men, Esprit.

Open 7 days, Sat, 10-9 p.m.; Sun 11-6 p.m. Outlets include Sony, Florsheim, Elisabeth (Plus sizes by Liz Claiborne), Casual Big & Tall Men, Esprit.

Desert Hills Factory Stores at Cabazon (near Palm Springs)

Desert Hills Factory Stores (Cabazon) . . . . (909) 849-6641
Factory stores, plus restaurants, located at 48650 Seminole Road, Cabazon, CA 92230, about two hours from San Diego. Take Interstate 15 North to 215 North to 60 East to 10 East. Exit Field Road to the factory stores, 20 minutes West of Palm Springs. Hours: Sun-Fri, 10 a.m.-8 p.m.; Sat 9 a.m.-8 p.m. Exclusive designers include: (all area codes are (909): Anne Klein, 849-1114; Giorgio Armani, 922-3400; Gucci, 849-7430; Versace, 922-9111; Coach, 849-0277; Versace, 922-9111; St. John Company Store, 849-0130.

Ontario Mills Factory Stores

Ontario Mills . . . . (909) 484-8300
Southern California's largest mall with anchor stores, factory outlets, restaurants and entertainment located at One Mills Circle, Ontario, Ca. Located at the intersection of Interstate 15 to the Interstate 10 in Ontario, Ca., about 2+ hours from downtown San Diego. Hours: M-S 10 am - 9:30 pm / Sun 11 am - 7 pm. Featured stores not elsewhere in Southern California are the Charlotte Russe Outlet, 481-3411; bebe, 980-7660; Ritz Cameras, 481-8020.

Additional autographed copies of
"The Best Deals & Steals In San Diego"
+ *So. California*
are available by sending $21.50 (includes tax) to:

Sally R. Gary
2726 Shelter Island Drive, Suite 94
San Diego, CA 92106
Postage will be paid by publisher

Food & Beverage

OK, so let's get down to the *really* important things in life .. like FOOD! Yes, food *is* a major item in many household budgets but there are *TONS* of ways to save money on food if you want to. And, it's all so *fun!* One of the secrets is to shop at a variety of *types* of stores and the bottom line is, you''ll save-save-save. No longer are people going only to the nearest supermarket. In fact, Americans now only spend 53¢ of every food dollar at the supermarket, down from 62¢! The competition for your $$$ is fierce. In addition to chain supermarkets, your options include warehouse *clubs* (Costco & Sam's Club) and food warehouses (Food For Less); food specialty stores like Henry's, Trader Joe's, Barron's and oriental markets like the big 99 Ranch Market at 7330 Clairemont Mesa Blvd. (great fresh fish!); natural and whole food stores that feature organically grown foods and whole grains like Whole Foods (they carry more than 600 kinds of cheese, 300 beers, 600 wines and 200 self-serve bulk bins) at 711 University in Hillcrest, (619) 294-2800 and 8825 Villa La Jolla Drive, (858) 642-6700; Ocean Beach People's Food Store, GreenTree, Jimbo's, Annies, Harvest Ranch Markets, House of Natural Foods, Johnathan's of La Jolla and farmers markets. Take advantage of these unique shopping opportunities and add variety while spending less.

If you want to save money on shopping, never shop when hungry. Use coupons. Buy rice, beans, potatoes, pasta in bulk, and simple fresh vegetables. Learn how to make lots of money-saving stir fries, soups and stews with only small amounts of meat. Avoid expensive cuts of meat and prepared foods. Learn to make your own pizzas. You'll save money and have a healthier diet. Here are tons more tips below.

Shop at two or more stores for better savings. Plan meals around the ads. Make your list so you don't get seduced by everything on display. If an advertised item is not on the shelf, ask for a "rain check," which will allow you to buy the item at a later date when they are restocked, at the lower advertised price. Note that weekly ads often contain coupons for discounts on photo-developing, tickets to events, etc.

Errors in pricing occur less than 2% of the time, although it sometimes seems like more, doesn't it? It is your responsibility to check your receipts, preferably before you leave the store. Notify the manager of errors. Some managers won't charge you at all for an item if it was priced wrong in the computer.

Get your frequent shopper membership, free of charge, for in-store discounts on tons of items at Von's and Ralph's. It's only a matter of filling out info on where you bank. And Voila! You will get automatic discounts on special items throughout the store. Some really excellent savings here, especially on meats. When you use your "membership," you are also automatically signed up to win money, cruises, plane trips, and receive cash rebates, etc. Note that supermarkets offer discounts on tickets to Six Flags, Universal Studios, the Fair, Seaworld & ski slopes from time to time.

Natural food stores carry natural **foods without preservatives** plus organic foods (grown without pesticides), and meats raised without hormones. Here are some natural food stores in San Diego: Henry's, many locations in San Diego; Whole Foods; Daniel's Market (Del Mar, Alpine, Ramona); House of Natural Foods of La Jolla ;Harvest Ranch Markets (El Cajon, La Jolla, Encinitas); Jimbo's Naturally (North Park, Del Mar); Ocean Beach People's Natural Foods Market (Ocean Beach); Barron's, (Encinitas, Pt. Loma, Del Mar).

Henry's Marketplace is a natural/health food store with 17 stores including Pt. Loma, (619) 523-3640, Their locations include 1260 Garnet, Pacific Beach, (858) 270-8200; 6091 University, College area, (619) 582-4343; 734 University, Hillcrest, (619) 295-4569; 6091 University, College, (619) 582-4343; 3332 Sandrock, Serra Mesa, (619) 565-1714; 152 N. Second, El Cajon, (619) 579-8251; Chula Vista, (619) 476-1032; and Vista, (760) 758-7175; 4630 Palm Avenue, La Mesa, (619) 460-7722; UTC, 3358 Governor, (858) 457-5006; Poway, 13536 Poway Rd., (858) 486-7851; Escondido, 510 W. 13th Avenue, (760) 745-2141; 1327 Encinitas Blvd., Encinitas, (760) 633-4747; North Park, 4175 Park Blvd., (619) 291-8287. Their meats have no hormones; their organic vegetables have no pesticides (the other veggies were grown with pesticides), and their prices on produce are some of the best in town. Even in winter, you will find weeks when lettuce is 3/$1; broccoli crowns, 2 lbs/$1; tomatoes, 4lb/$1; Portabella mushrooms, $2.99 lb; cucumbers, 4/$1 navel oranges, 3 lb/$1; fresh baked French bread, 99¢; meat specials, large eggs, $1.19 a dozen about every other week; good Costa Rican, Columbian and Kenya coffees, $4.99 a lb., (reg. $6.99); Henry's own croutons are the BEST. Great ready-to-heat-and-eat gourmet specialties and a nutritionist on hand to help you make your selection of prescription alternatives, vitamins, minerals, herbs, aroma-therapy plus skin care, etc. In-store cholesterol, blood pressure and bone density tests, and more. Ask about their calendar of events and lectures On Wednesdays, they honor both last week's specials and this week's (a VERY popular shopping day.) See "Health & Medical" regarding their Wellness Fair with health screenings, expert lectures and exhibits.

Trader Joe's, La Jolla Square Shopping Center, (858) 546-8629; 1211 Garnet Avenue, Pacific Beach, (858) 272-7235; Oceanside, (760) 433-9994; Carmel Mountain, (858) 673-0526; La Mesa (619) 466-5998; Encinitas, (760) 634-2114; Hillcrest, (619) 296-3122. Trader Joe's is a food and spirits store for the gourmet bargain hunter, with an emphasis on cheese, nuts, chocolates, imported items and gourmet foods at amazingly low prices. If you're not on the mailing list, give them a call, and you will be. The wine and beer list is superb, with their own brand as well as others. Virgin olive Oil from Italy, $3.^{99}/liter; Extra sharp cheddar, $3.^{99} lb., fresh pecan pie, $3.^{99} shrimp & lobster ravioli, $3.^{19}; Sherry from Spain, $3.^{99}; Toblerone Swiss chocolate; Gouda $3.^{29} (value $4.^{99}), individual quiches, $1.^{59}; seafood, dips, spaghetti sauce, oils, gifts, more.

Barron's Marketplace, a specialty food store with good prices on eggs, fresh deli, wines, cheeses, nuts, coffees, wines, liquors. Pt. Loma, (619) 223-4397; La Mesa, (619) 697-7063; Del Mar (858) 481-2323; Encinitas, (760) 942-9881.

Buy bulk at membership warehouses like Costco, Sam's Club ($35-$45 membership); and Food For Less and Smart & Final for big savings. Also, most supermarkets now carry a number of bulk items so ask where they are. Repackage them in smaller quantities if necessary or trade with friends. Usually, the larger number of items in the package, the more you save per unit. Some products you can get bigger savings on in bulk are: milk, eggs, flour, bouillon cubes, olive or canola oil, coffee, sugar, instant potatoes, mayonnaise, peanut butter, rice, soy sauce, spaghetti, rice, tuna, vanilla extract, bread, cleaning supplies, paper goods, light bulbs, detergents, etc. Shop smart: don't stock up on items that supermarkets often put on sale for less. And skip items that you can get cheaper in supermarkets using manufacturer's coupons. Here are some items that most supermarkets carry in bulk are: Pepperidge Farm Cheddar Cheese Goldfish, about $4 for a 38-oz. package, or 10.5 cents per ounce, or half as much per ounce as the 6-ounce package. Cereals, cleaners, large jars of mayonnaise and pickles, multi-packs of paper towels and more. Some products are a good savings, but compare the per ounce price. Some are just larger sizes at *no* savings.

Smart & Final at Midway and Rosecrans, (619) 223-5381; 720 15th Street, downtown, (619) 239-3377; 5195 Clairemont Mesa, (858) 541-2090; 5245 El Cajon Boulevard, (619) 286-0688; Escondido, (760) 746-5490; National City, (619) 477-4126; Lemon Grove, (619) 668-0220; Mira Mesa, (858) 689-6242; and El Cajon, (619) 562-4151; Carlsbad, (760) 434-5036; Chula Visa, (619) 427-0202; Smart & Final is a warehouse-type operation that deals in bulk for businesses, clubs, organizations, plus you and me. There is no membership fee. Over 10,000 items to choose from. A five pound bag of shredded cheddar, mozzarella or jack cheese, $10.49; 4 lb chicken party wings, $4.99; 5 qts. ice cream, $4.49, and these items go on sale for less. Three pounds of grade AA butter is around $2 a pound and butter freezes *great*. Good place for paper plates and party supplies, giant cans of nacho cheese, chili, canned fruit; cleaning supplies, brooms, frozen meats, restaurant quality cheesecakes, baking goodies, gourmet foods in holiday wrappings, much more. Get on the mailing list and receive occasional discount coupons ($5 off $25 purchase works for me!). Cash-and-carry since 1871; in California and Las Vegas. Web: smartnfinal.com

Costco warehouses devote about one-third of the floor space to food and beverage, mainly in bulk. There is a fresh bakery with muffins to die for. You know the fabulous muffins that sell for $1.50 in muffin shops? At Costco, they're only about $5.50 or so for a *dozen!!* I thought I was misreading the price. And, a huge bag of fresh rolls, $3.79 for 50 oz.; a doz. croissants, $4.99; 9 huge danish, 3 lbs, $5.49 and a variety of fresh baked cookies. Personalized sheet cakes ($14-$16..99) that serve 30-48 people, fresh and frozen restaurant quality beautiful gourmet meats, stuffed salmon, bulk cheeses, gourmet Chocolate Raspberry Decadent Torte ($20) is a hit to take to parties, for sure; large fruit tarte that is beautiful, $15; and cheesecakes ($13) (whadda deal!), gourmet restaurant quality fresh produce (huge strawberries, apples, huge avocados that are *not* prepackaged), sodas, booze, canned and packaged goods in large sizes, paper goods (their large paper napkins, paper towels and T-paper are the best and cheapest). Party trays from the deli are an outstanding value and can be ordered ahead (veggie trays, $17), shrimp ($39) or selected meat and/or cheese trays ($23), and their selection of frozen gourmet hor d'oeuvres in bulk quantities are outstanding for entertaining: 60 mini-quiches, $9.99, 6 lb. meatballs, $9.59, chicken wings, more. Extra large eggs, 18 count, $1.31. Their ready-to-heat-and-eat selections for dinner range from pastas to rotisserie chicken, twice-baked cheese potatoes, chicken cordon bleu, Caesar Parmesan pasta salad, grilled marinated vegetables, steak stuffed with shiitake mushrooms and sun-dried tomatoes, ready-to-bake pizzas (an 18" fresh pizza, loaded, and ready to cook, $7.99), a magnum of festive Cook's champagne (5.99). I wouldn't dream of leaving without a one-pound jar of fresh grated Parmesan for about $5.35 (put parmesan on *anything*, and they will think you are a true gourmet cook!) Costco only carries a limited number of brand names for a single item like jelly, there isn't every kind of soda known to man, and there isn't a variety of sizes, but Costco only buys top quality items that they can get the best buy on. This translates into a low price for you, with an overall markup of about 4-14% over wholesale. It pays to know thy prices and plan what to buy at Costco. Stick to your list or it might take you all day to unload the car. The only complaint I ever hear about Costco is that people spend too much. (Come on, kids, use some self-discipline!) I think everyone should shop at Costco once every six weeks to two months, minimum. For locations, see Costco Warehouses, this chapter.

Vons.com and **Albertsons.com** offer over 20,000 products and groceries online. Produce (very fresh, large, beautiful quality), dairy, meat, fish, deli, brand name products. Order 24 hours a day, as late as 10pm for next day delivery. Select a delivery time window. You automatically get a discount on your first order (with a minimum purchase). Order by 9:30am for same day deliver. There is a fee of around $10 for delivery. They will deliver to your kitchen counter if desired. Great for busy people, those who live with stairs, etc, or if you're laid up with a leg in a cast. **Priceline.com** offers grocery shopping from the Ralph's site at Ralphs.com. Click on priceline.com for terms and conditions. From an online list, make an offer of what you are willing to pay for each item and within 30 seconds, you'll know if your offer is accepted. Print out the list and take it to Ralphs. You can also use your coupons for additional discounts! **Recipe finder** site: recipefinder.com. Wow, everything is here.

Use your grocery coupons at a double coupon store. The first coupon was issued in 1895 for 5 cents off on a Coke, and today, coupon manufacturers produce and distribute over 278 billion "cents-off coupons." The most used coupons are cereal, soap and deodorant, and about 7 out of 10 households cash in on them overall. (I wish they would just lower the price of the products instead of spending millions on printing the coupons, buying newspaper space, paying the stores to process them, etc. (Ok, I'll admit it: they're fun to use. They make me feel like.... I *win!*) There are actually more benefits to using coupons than just financial: university researchers found that more than 7 out of 10 users felt a happiness, a boost of ego, personal satisfaction, and a feeling they are smart and savvy shoppers! So, there! When you make your shopping list, mark the items that you have coupons for. Albertson's accepts all other supermarket and drugstore coupons at face value. Online coupons: smartsource.com. To preview next Sunday's coupons so you can make your shopping list early, go to couponpreview.com ., or pick up a copy of Sunday's *San Diego Union* early edition on Saturday afternoon. (Just when you thought you had heard everything.....)

You've probably heard stories of shoppers leaving a supermarket with over $67 in groceries without paying a cent for them; how a woman in New York bought $80 in groceries, paying only 32¢ for them; how another New Yorker bought over $130 worth of food and groceries, for only $7.07; how a New Jersey housewife purchased $32 worth of groceries for only $3.00. Smart shoppers are cashing in. If you use just six coupons a week with an average of 68¢ per coupon, you would save more than $200 per year. However, because almost 300 million are printed and only 2% are actually used, food manufacturers are considering discontinuing coupons in favor of something more people will use. Post and Nabisco now offer a single coupon good for a choice of several brands, reducing their printing costs by as much as 80%. Proctor & Gamble dropped coupons altogether from three markets in New York, and reduced the distribution in the U.S.

Ralph's and Von's will **double coupons** with a value up to $1, so a coupon for $1.50 off will be worth $2.50, not $3. Many shoppers never pay full fare for soap, pain remedies, beauty supplies and other non-food products because coupons are available every Sunday in the *Union-Trib* in the form of two or three supplements. Supermarkets print up their weekly food ads and are available in stacks in the stores and contain several in-store coupons and manufacturer's coupons. Clip, organize and carry your coupons with you in a traveler's check holder, available free from banks, using 3x5 card dividers to create categories. According to a survey by Frankel & Co. marketing services, 81% of grocery shoppers are using coupons at least once a month, and 54% are sending in for refunds or rebates. Look for electronic coupons along shelves in supermarkets for instant savings; and you can download and print coupons on the Web at Super Market Online or America's Coupons at: americascoupons.com..

NOW HEAR THIS: Some people who are really into this couponing deal get trapped into a life of being chained to the kitchen, eating too may prepackaged products and gaining tons of weight. I met a woman who was apparently addicted to couponing. She had about 10 bankers boxes of them (I was absolutely aghast!). She weighed about 575 pounds and was clearly off in another world that revolved only around her stove. Rarely is there a coupon for fresh produce or meats, yet fresh seasonal special buys can cost far less than packaged, frozen or canned goods and are infinitely healthier. Be careful not to fall into the coupon addiction-trap. There are too many other ways to save money that won't hurt your health. Try yard sale-ing. (Now *there's* a healthy addiction!! Ask me if I'm into that one!!)

A caller on a radio talk show said that although she doesn't have a lot of money to give to the needy during the holidays, so she saves the coupons in Sunday's newspaper during the months of October and November, takes them to the store with her teen-aged children and uses them to buy groceries for the less fortunate. She said she can get around $100 worth of groceries for about $25-$30 at a double coupon store, not straining her Christmas budget. And what a nice thing to do for others! And, Goodwill wants your unused coupon supplements! Charitable organizations use them.

The *Refund Express* is a refund bulletin with 350 to 500 new refund offers each month, company toll-free numbers, contests, credits, exchanges, tips. Single issue, $2.50; one year, $21; Send to Refund Express, P. O. B. 10, Allen Park, MI 48101. Say that you were referred by John N. Skuden, Acct. No. 1233. He will get credit (and he gave me this info and deserves credit!). Also, send for sample newsletter from the Refundle Bundle, P. O. Box 140, Yonkers, NY 10710, $3. You've probably read or heard about a few people who have recently been sent to jail for sending in refunds totaling $35,000 and more to a single company. There is usually a limit of 1-3 refunds allowed. Read the find print. A woman in Arizona was jailed for abusing Kodak refunds. She got $35,000 in $5 film rebates, was prosecuted and thrown in the slammer. (I wonder where she got all the film packaging . . . outside their factory?? Hello ? ? (Ohhhh, the great mysteries of life.)

Ralph's, Von's & Albertson's have their own store brands, some of which are pretty good look-a-likes. Albertson's brand baked goods are very similar to Entenmann's; Von's grape nuts are very similar to the big brand name cereal. Von's English muffins seem to stack up pretty well against the more expensive brands; their Von's sour dough bread is GREAT, and their fresh baked sour dough rye baguettes are to die for. Their store brand, Jerseymaid, has great sharp cheese, yogurt, and ice cream.

Go for the **drug store advertised specials** at Long's, Rite Aid, Walgreens and SavOn Drugs. They have unreal prices on their advertised specials: cat food, booze, canned and packaged foods, at a real steal. On Sundays when their ads come out in the *U-T*, the stores are swarming with bargain hunters. Don't forget to ask for a "rain check" is the advertised item is not in stock, and you can come back and get it at the sale price after the sale is over and they have restocked.

Farmers' markets. A *Certified* Farmers' Market is a market for farmers who *personally* grow all their produce, most on 9 acres or less, and *sell* their produce at their stalls on market day. (They do not buy from other suppliers and resell.) They are certified by the State of California that their produce is grown here, sold by owner and meets the state's quality standard. Farmers' markets offer the freshest produce around (usually picked the day of the market), the best tomatoes, seasonal veggies. Other food products are usually sold, too, like homemade jams and jellies, gourmet pickles, baked goods, plus herbs, houseplants, fresh pasta, honey, cheese, flowers, Valencia oranges to die for, and more. Here are some farmers markets, (per the San Diego Farm Bureau, (760) 745-3023, sdfarmbureau.org).

Carlsbad Farmers Market, Roosevelt
  between Carlsbad Village Dr. & Grand,
  Wednesdays, 2-5 p.m.
Chula Vista Farmers Market
  3rd Ave & Center St
  Thursdays, 3-dark
Coronado Farmers Market
  Old Ferry Landing, lst and B Streets,
  Tuesdays, 2:30-6 p.m.
Del Mar Farmers Market
  Camino Del Mar, at 10th, 1-4 p.m.
  Saturdays.
El Cajon Market Place
  Corner of Main & Orange Streets
  Wednesdays, 4-7pm
Escondido Farmers Market
  Grand & Broadway
  Tuesdays, 2-6pm
Pacific Beach (Promenade Mall)
  Mission Blvd. between Reed & Pacific
  Beach Drive, in Pacific Beach
  Saturdays, 8 a.m.-noon.
Encinitas Farmers Market
  Hwy. 101, Lumberyard Shopping Center
  Fridays, 2-5pm.
Hillcrest Farmers Market
  Normal Street & Cleveland
  Sundays, 9-1pm
La Jolla Farmers' Market
  La Jolla Elem. School / Girard & Genter
  Sundays, 9-1pm
La Mesa Farmers Market

Allison St.(East of Spring St.)
  Fridays, 3-6pm
Ocean Beach Farmers Market
  4900 block of Newport ; fruits, baked
  goods, vegetables, plants, fresh
  flowers, fish, more, Wednesdays, 3pm-
  dark
Oceanside Farmers Market
  Pier View and Coast Highway
  Thursdays, 9am-12:30pm
Point Loma Farmers Market
  Liberty Station (Old NTC;) enter on
Barnett, off Rosecrans
  Saturdays 9-1pm.
Poway Farmers Market
  Old Poway Park, Temple & Midland,
  Saturdays, 8-11 a.m.
SDSU area (Faith Presby. Church lot)
  5057 Campanila Dr
  Saturdays, 2-6pm
San Marcos Farmers Market
  San Marcos Blvd (Restaurant Row)
  Thursdays, 3-6pm
Solana Beach Farmers Market
  124 Lomas Santa Fe Dr-SB Plaza
Center; Sundays, 2-5pm
Vista Farmers Market
   Eucalyptus & Escondido Avenue.
  Saturday mornings, 8-11 a.m. Also, on
Vista Way between Santa Fe and Citrus,
   Thursdays, 6-9 p.m.

All swap meets have great fresh produce stands plus vendors who sell gourmet breads, tortas, muffins, Julian Pie, jerky, smoked salmon, pickles, olives, nuts & dried fruits and other specialty foods. (See Swap Meets, this chapter, for locations.)

Food For Less, large warehouse, bulk and regular. The difference here is that Food For Less charges less because there are no baggers.   Hazard Center, (619) 683-7760; Clairemont Mesa, (858) 278-0681; University, (619) 287-6501.

Sav-A-Lot, 46th & University, (619) 584-7721, with five stores in the county (La Mesa, Santee, El Cajon, Imperial Beach). Mainly off-brand names not familiar in San Diego, and some name brands. Buy your bags or bring your own; bag your own groceries. Save a lot. Different.

Bakery Thrift Stores, also known as *Day-Old Bakeries*, are a great find. When a bakery makes its daily delivery to a supermarket, they remove any bread that remains from the previous delivery plus certain cookies and cakes (which can stay on the shelf several days longer than bread because they contain sugar, which is a preservative). These products are returned to the bakery's own "thrift" outlet to be sold at bargain prices. Items include bread, rolls, bagels, buns, cookies, pastries, croissants, and specialty and seasonal items including fruit cakes. Some have frozen pastries, too .Day old bread and rolls are wonderful if you pop them in the microwave for a few seconds. Most stores also carry *"today's"* fresh-baked goods at a discount. Items are usually color coded for different discounts (yellow, 25% off; blue, 50% off, etc.). Quantity purchases are further discounted. Usually there is a special day when you get two-for-one or some other fun gimmick. Try these thrift bakeries:

Millbrook/Bimbo Bakery, 3355 Sandrock Road, of Aero Drive, Kearny Mesa/Serra Mesa, (858) 571-0423; El Cajon, (619) 448-0214; Lemon Grove, (619) 460-1830; Chula Vista, (619) 425-6800; Escondido, (760) 745-6773. Breads and pastries including Roman Meal, Weber, Mrs. Cubbison's stuffing, donuts, sweet rolls, croutons. Millbrook, Roman Meal, $1.15 ($2.49 in store), Weber I lb. white, 49¢; Specials include three loaves of white or wheat bread for $1.47. Fresh and day old. Some stores have senior discounts; every day, 10% off; some stores have a special day that everyone gets 10% off.

Bimbo/Orowheat Entenmann's Thrift Stores, discounts of 30-45% off breads and pastries. Fresh products: 20% discount. Orowheat, Thomas's, Boboli, Old Country, pastries, muffins, chips, croutons, bread sticks, cookies, whole grain cereals. Every day senior discount: 10%. When they have extra stock, they give free bread with $5 minimum purchase. Wednesday special: discount on pies and cookies. Bread days are Wednesday & Sunday with half off retail. Open Monday-Friday; 9-6 p.m.; Saturday, 9-5 p.m.; Sunday, 9-5 p.m. Seasonal goodies and other specials are available at 7051 Clairemont Mesa Blvd., San Diego, (858) 277-6886, 465 C Street, Chula Vista, (619) 427-5030; 1090 E. Washington Avenue, El Cajon, (619) 442-3404; and 800 W. Grand Avenue, Escondido, (760) 741-3773 (no Sundays); Oceanside, (760) 439-1765.

Holsom/Bimbo Store carries day old and fresh Bohemian Hearth breads, cookies, sweet rolls, pastry, crackers, spices, condiments, gravy mixes, noodles, rice mix, syrup, and various store specials. Located at 8926 Carlton Hills Blvd. Santee, (619) 449-2500; North Park (619) 298-8100; El Cajon

Millbrook (was Weber) 1215 N, Cuyamaca, El Cajon, (619) 448-0214 Name brands include Millbrook, Parisian, Roman Meal, Pillsbury, Home style, breads, cakes discounted. Hostess cup cakes. Wednesdays, extra 10% off. North Park (619) 298-8100.

Wonder-Hostess Bakery Thrift Store, 518 Oceanside Blvd., (760) 433-7173; 3510 College Blvd,, Oceanside, (760) 631-0866; 1626 Sweetwater Rd., (619) 477-8230; 1210 E. Plaza, National City, (619) 474-8025, plus stores in El Cajon, San Ysidro, San Marcos, Escondido, Poway and Clairemont ((858) 474-8025. Home Pride, Roman Meal, Wonder Breads, Hostess cupcakes, Tinkles, muffins, snowballs, cakes, cookies, Swiss ice cream, hot dog and hamburger buns, cokes, cereals, Pop Tarts, pancake mix, mashed potatoes, bread sticks. Fresh and day old at a reduced price!

See's Candies has a Quantity Discount Program, available only at the shop at 3751 Rosecrans Street in Point Loma, (619) 291-6086. You or your organization can buy a minimum order for 50 pounds for $450, which is $9.50 per pound, or a $3.80 savings over the regular price of $12.80 a pound. Available only at the above location. Or, if you can get your quantity purchase in gift certificates, which are good any time, any where, with no expiration. Quantity gift certificates are $9.50 per pound box and you can use them in any store. Individuals, or members of organizations or employees of businesses that have purchased a minimum of 50 pounds receive a card entitling them to the discount on purchases made from November lst to October 31st. Holiday wrap is provided at Thanksgiving, Christmas, Valentines Day, Easter and Mother's Day. Sees candy is never marked down; their left over holiday candy is donated to worthy cause except Easter leftovers which are marked down, two for one, or 50% off the day after Easter. Get a free sample with any purchase. Their candy sticks (bag of 30 for $1.20) are great for children's parties and for Halloween goblins.

RiteAid Drugs still has the biggest and best ice cream cone for the price: 99¢ for one scoop; $1.49 for two. Their Chocolate Brownie ice cream is to die for, and their Mango sherbert can't be beat, and you can get it on sale for $1.99 per half gallon. Smart &Final (above)has bulk ice cream for parties in three gallon drums. McDonalds has a great yogurt hot fudge sundae for $1, and a huge yogurt cone for $1, too! No wonder Moms like to take their kids to McDonalds. And, speaking of ice cream, Baskin Robbins and several yogurt shops offer two-for-one coupons in the *Entertainment* coupon book. See chapter on Resources.

Most **Mrs. Field's** and **Blue Chip** cookie stores mark down their remaining cookies about an hour before closing, sometimes two for one. Check with your local bakery or bagel shop to see if they reduce prices on leftovers at the end of the day. My bagel shop does! The French Gourmet in La Jolla always has a basket or two of yesterday's baked goods at great prices. (The microwave does wonders for day-old baked goods.) Ask a bakery if they have any "boo boos" they sell for less. Sam's Cheesecake sells theirs for half off.

I was at **Soup Plantation** one night about an hour before closing. A waiter approached us, gave us plastic bags and said we could go back to the fresh bread bar and help ourselves to all the muffins, pizza, and other bread items that were left! Sometimes when they have a lot left over, they offer it to their patrons. Check about this policy at other soup bars, all-you-can-eat restaurants, etc. The way you ask may be the secret!! Ask (close to closing time): "What do you do with all the left over bread at the end of the day?" Ask about extra fried chicken at the Kentucky Colonel before closing Depending on the time and what's left, and who's manager, you might get extra pieces or two for one!.

Ask the meat manager of your supermarket if and when they mark down meat where the date is about to expire. I have found by asking several employees at the same store that I get different answers, so bear with this one. I've heard: "We don't have any left over meat" or " our beef is turned into hamburger," etc, but a woman told me she buys all her steaks l/2 price when they mark them down at **Ralph's**. I have recently seen marked down steaks at Vons early in the morning.

Healthy Share Program distributes packages of food, value $35, to individuals for $19 per package one day a month at about 325 locations. A small paid staff and a large corps of volunteers package and distribute approximately 4,000 packages of food throughout California every month. The food package varies in content depending on seasonal buys, but a package typically contains about 20 items, pounds of wholesome food including 5 different meats, fresh fruits and vegetables, and 3-5 staple items such as rice, beans, pasta. There are no income qualifications to receive the food, but you are encouraged to contribute volunteer services (in addition to paying the $19). Call (888) 268-8500 for referral to a location near you; register and pay, usually by the first Monday of the month. In San Diego, there are 25 distribution locations at churches and schools.

You can bring back many groceries and food products from Tijuana with these restrictions: only beef (no other meat), lobster (four per person), most vegetables, nuts, some fruits (bananas, blackberries, dates, grapes, melons, pineapples, strawberries). (No potatoes, no avocados, no meat other than beef, no eggs, no citrus fruit.)

Liquor and Wine Here's how to get the best prices on booze for your next party. Comparison shop at the following: Costco and Sam's Club; then check Beverages & More (La Mesa, Encinitas, Carmel Mountain). They offer advice on how much you will need for your crowd. Also check prices at Long's, RiteAid, Walgreens and SavOn Drug liquor departments,; check out supermarket specials; look for specials at Trader Joe's (they have a wine for $1.99 a bottle!); Pier One, S (good wine selections). Purchase six or more bottles and receive a 10% discount. The best price on booze is offered the last couple months of the year during the holidays. Lots of rebate offers then. Wine in a box (5 liters) is the most economical way to go for parties. Home brewing is hot again, with lots of books on the topic, clubs for brewers, and stores specializing in home brewing supplies like Home Brew Mart, 5401 Linda Vista Rd, (619) 295-2337. (Boy, that can be potent stuff. I remember ...been there, done that.) You can only bring back one liter of liquor from Tijuana every 30 days. (Phoo.) TJ has great brandies (El Presidente is one of the world's finest brandies), Kahlua (after all, it is made in Mexico and can be as low as $6.99 a liter, but never that cheap during the summer tourista season), banana liqueur, Tequila (cheap-cheap except Cuervo Gold).

Flowers, Plants & Gardening

North County has the most equable climate in the nation and is a prolific producer of flowers and plants that are sold both nationally and locally. San Diego, therefore, has very reasonable prices on plants and flowers that are easily grown nearby.

Here are the places to check out if you want a *good buy* on plants and flowers for your home or even for weddings and parties, plus buys on garden accessories and ornaments. Also included are some flower shows you shouldn't miss are included here, too, with other good tidbits.

Swap Meets and Farmers Markets are a great place to pick up fresh flowers, cheapo. Go early for the best selection as they'll be pretty well picked over later in the day. Negotiate a discount if you want quantities. If you have a party or special occasion coming up, even a wedding, you can place an order with a swap meet vendor. You can arrange for the flowers to be delivered to you, or you can pick them up, or you can arrange to have them brought to the swap meet or farmers market the following week. Gather a few vendor's business cards when you go and keep them on file for your special occasions. This is also a great place to pick up big and small house plants, and dried and silk flower arrangements, bamboo, cacti, bonzai, yard ornaments, etc. No can beat.

Large bouquets of flowers and roses are available at Costco & Sam's Club. Big bouquets for little bucks. Prices vary with season, but always a definite good buy. From time to time they have huge house plants, trees and flowers at great prices, huge jugs of plant food, insecticides, yard ornaments, giant planters. Also, Albertson's, Von's, Ralph's and other supermarkets can order in flowers to make special arrangements for you. (I love supermarket house plant sales!) A good time to replace the tired ones. I have gotten smart and now have two sets of house plants. For example, I have a few ferns in the dining room, and replace it each week with a second set of ferns that I keep outside in the shade, rotating them. Otherwise, I find ferns don't do that well if kept in the house for several weeks.

Wholesale Flowers & supplies 5328 Metro (Morena Area by Office Depot/Tio Leo's), (619) 295-3444. Public welcome; bulk orders for parties, weddings, 2 dozen roses, always $11! (Love it!) Floral supplies, wrought iron candle holders, decorator items. Wonderful place. So creative.

Today's gardens need bird houses and wind chimes and whimsical metal yard sculptures and weather vanes and old iron gates. And, guess who has come to the rescue to tell us all about it! Martha Stewart, yes the ever energetic Martha, with all her troubles, is now helping us decorate our gardens in style with her new line of garden furniture, accessories and garden tools sold at Kmart. Walmart and Target have garden department with sales all the time and the savings are simply great. They plants, pots, solar lighting, yard ornaments, plant food . . no can beat. **Tuesday Morning** buys huge lots of overstocks of garden statues and accents (when available), 50-80% off. **Big Lots**, too. Some really great finds.

Floral supply stores have an incredible array of vases, baskets, ribbons, florist paper and seasonal decorations to put in floral arrangements. They sell retail to the public, wholesale to dealers. I was amazed at all the things they had at San Diego Floral Supply, 2550 El Cajon Blvd., (619) 260-8080; Carlsbad, (760) 431-8080. Floral Supply Syndicate, 7904 Ronson Road, Kearny Mesa, (858) 268-4611. Catalog available. Web site: fss.com For more supply houses, check the *Yellow Pages* Florists' Supplies.

Wilson's Wedding Flowers, (619) 698-2863. Kathy Wilson does wedding and party flowers from her home. She purchases, designs and delivers customized floral arrangements throughout the county for less than many floral shops. She guarantees personal service because she books only one wedding per day.

Here's an idea: **hire a horticulture student** to do a landscaping project for you. Call Mira Costa, Southwestern, Cuyamaca College horticulture department or Mesa College's nursery & landscape technology program, and ask for what you want. Mesa has an annual plant sale (cheap-cheap prices). Call for date. Some of the colleges also sell mulch, 2 cubic feet $2.75, or free if you fill the bag. (See chapter on Continuing Education for phone numbers.) You can also call any college and ask for their landscape department and see if any of their regular landscapers wants to moonlight.

Smith & Hawkins, E336 Fashion Valley Mall, (619) 298-0441. Pots, stone ornaments, reproductions of European plaques, urns, candle sconces, benches and fountains plus garden tools, clothes, outdoor furniture, umbrellas, wall hangings, bird houses, arches and trellises, pots and planters, bulbs, big reflection balls, yard ornaments, outdoor lighting including solar, and other beautiful things for the garden. Holiday sales; an expensive store, but check the clearance items! Catalog: (800) 981-9888.

Cedros Gardens, 330 S. Cedros Ave, Solana Beach (858) 792-8640. Lots of trellises, statues, unique and colorful decorative stepping stones, tall metal garden sculptures, small to large plants, flowers, lots of bamboo. High quality plants of unusual origins plus everything you need, etc.

The **Bamboo Society** holds a semi annual sale with dozens of varieties at great prices, (619) 453-0334. Bamboo is sooooooooo popular today.

Alan Sculpture Studio & Gift Shop, 3615 Manchester Ave., Encinitas, (760) 753-2705; tons of the latest trend in garden decor: whimsical metal sculptures, some painted; wall hangings, indoor & outdoor stuff.

Tropic World Nursery, 26437 North Centre City Pkwy, Escondido, (760) 746-6108; Beautiful cacti, succulents, bamboo, roses, palms, bougainvilleas fruit trees, perennials, pottery and more. Big place. All kinds of stuff.

You can bring back fresh cut flowers from Tijuana but *no* plants with *soil* (the soil may contain bugs); many people buy flowers for parties and weddings there. You can get small bud roses for about $2 per dozen at street stands. Remember, you can negotiate the price for quantities and arrange for large orders, too. And, Tijuana is famous for terra cotta pots, (get pots that are black-coated inside, or they will just disappear like sugar with time and water), and concrete yard ornaments, wrought iron planters, etc. Prices can be really, really good, and are very negotiable.

More sources for plants and flowers: **Evergreen Nursery, Armstrong Nursery** and Walter Anderson's have great prices on indoor and outdoor plants *during sales*. I like Home Depot, Lowe's, Dixieline, but I don't think you can't beat Target, Walmart and Kmart garden shop sales for potting flowers and house plants, plus they have expanded their lines to include bird baths, sundials, lanterns, fountains, topiaries, etc. **Martha Stewart** is at Kmart, offering us have a "high quality of outdoor living" with her new lines of handcrafted outdoor furniture and patio furnishings including all weather pots and planters, plus Martha-gardening-tools and plants! I understand she is coming out with her own line of designer dirt. (Well.... maybe I didn't hear that. Giggle-Giggle) Walter Anderson has all the above and great sales, plus free classes on seasonal plants, bulbs, wreath making, and more. Inquire about return policies for plants that promptly die.

Free mulch (fresh ground up greenery from the city recycle trucks) is available at the Environmental Services Department at the Miramar Landfill dump (also available at other county dumps). Bring your own boxes, bags (or truck) & shovel your own, or pay $4 per cubic yard for them to load it for you. Compost is rich, aged mulch infused with plant food, and is free for city residents only; for everyone else, it's $8 a cubic yard with bulk discount. Located at 5180 Convoy Street, (858) 573-1420. Check on this, because I *have been told different things about this (like it's all free), so...whatever!*.

Pick up silk flowers, permanent plants and trees at the **San Diego Silk Flower Exchange**, 4620 Alvarado Canyon Rd, #123, (619) 584-8899 and at the **Natural Touch**, 9050 Kenamar Dr., Miramar, (858) 271-7550, over 18,000 sq. ft. warehouse with silk plants and seasonal decor, too.

I get some of my *best* pots and plants at yard sales. People who move don't want to deal with them. And, some of my BEST plants were originally garage sale finds that were half-dead and I resuscitated them in my "hospital." (They were seriously cheap and I can't tell you how wonderful they turned out.) Also, check the *Union-Trib* Thrifties #3190 and Nurseries #3130 and Gardening Supplies #3135 classified ads for plants for sale, large and small. I have seen all kinds of things advertised there. And, I advertised (in the Thrifties) four huge Bird of Paradise plants for one dollar that I wanted removed from my yard because they were taking over the place. I received a LOT of calls. I waited til the rainy season when the ground was soft and easier to dig. The "taker" dug them out! YES! Otherwise, I would have donated them to Balboa Park, after paying someone a fortune to get them out of the ground and carting them off. Now, of course, I wish I had kept *some* of them! I have also bought some great plants from people who advertise them in the Thrifties. I have this AMAZING hanging Easter cactus that is probably 5-6 ft. long with huge blossoms on it in the spring that I bought from the Thrifties for $5. Scored on that one, didn't I? AND, you should see this FERN I got for $2 or $3. Half of it was missing, but somehow I nursed it back to health in a shady spot and it is ENORMOUS and I just love it.

My favorite flower or garden show is at the County Fair in Del Mar the last two weeks in June. Gorgeous gardens are created by designers, and judged, and they offer free classes on how to make succulent wreaths, flower arrangements, etc. And, they sell plants, super cheap there.

If you're a flower lover, you won't want to miss seeing the wildflowers in bloom in the desert in the spring. (That is truly a "don't miss" event.)

See the gorgeous array of ranunculus in bloom in a rainbow of color in March and April at the Carlsbad Ranch flower fields, Interstate 5 at Palomar Airport Road Exit behind the Windmill. Purchase flowers, bulbs, seeds, gifts. Call (760) 431-0352 for recorded information and calendar of events at the Carlsbad Ranch flower fields; over 200,000 attend. Visit their site at theflowerfields.com for more information, dates and admission prices.

From about Thanksgiving through the end of the year, the Carlsbad Ranch (above) exhibits a huge Poinsettia Star in the flower field. Well over 90% of all flowering poinsettia plants produced in the world start in Encinitas.

Annual Flower Celebration: Behind-the-scenes tour of six greenhouses and nurseries in Encinitas area every May-June. Call (760) 753-6041 for info.

Weidner's Gardens is open to the public twice a year: during the spring/summer season from March to September and again for the mid-winter season from November to just before Christmas. See over 20,000 giant flowering tuberous Begonias. Sales in the nursery. Flower shows, too, and special events including speakers. Located at 695 Normandy in Encinitas, (760) 436-2194. Web site: Weidners-Gardens.com

The San Diego Floral Association offers a bimonthly gardening magazine with all the info on gardening here in San Diego. They offer introductory and advanced classes in creative flower arranging, basketry, and more at the Casa Del Prado in Balboa Park. Classes are about $5-7; some slightly more. Phone (619) 232-5762 for more information.

San Diego Home/Garden Lifestyles magazine offers monthly columns on what to plant now, how to maintain what's in bloom, pest control, irrigation, etc. Calendar of gardening, composting, flower arranging classes, annual flower shows and home garden tours, guided tours of public gardens, garden club meetings and special events. Wonderful info for flower show aficionados and the home gardener. Truly a great resource.

There are loads of plant-oriented walking tours in Balboa Park. See Walking Tours in chapter on Things to Do. Balboa Park is also home to the various flower clubs including: orchids, camellias, staghorn ferns, etc. Call (619) 239-0512x0.

The San Diego Museum of Art presents "Art Alive" every April. This is a recreation of 150+ paintings from and sculptures from the permanent collection, done entirely with fresh flowers. Call the museum at (619) 232-7931 for more this year's date and further information. And, don't miss the Pageant of the Masters (paintings) recreated in flowers at the Laguna Arts Festival. (See chapter on Things to Do.)

The University of California Cooperative Extension Home Garden & Pest Control Information Hotline is staffed by master gardeners to answer your questions from 9 a.m.-3 p.m. Monday thru Friday, (858) 694-2860. Wow, are they ever helpful. You can even take your shriveling leaves up to them and they will tell you what the problem is and offer solutions.

Here's a great gardening web site which offers online gardening courses, Q&A section, more: www.garden.org. Links to zillions more sites. Also, good: gardenweb.com; hgtv.com; nationalgardeningassociation.com; gardennet.com, gardenguides.com. Even *I* have become a better gardner, finally.

Formal Wear

Men have always been able to rent their tuxedos and formal wear, and now, women can rent gala ball gowns, prom dresses, short beaded and sequined cocktail wear, and even wedding gowns and attire for the entire bridal party! Here are a few places to check out:

A Nite on the Town, 8650 Genesee Avenue, Costa Verde, (858) 457-1233, rentals $39-$159; wedding gowns, $99-$370. New dresses, rent or buy. Some alterations (take in, shorten, etc., but no cutting.). Sizes 2-24.

Dress To Impress, 4242 Camino del Rio North, Suite 6, (619) 528-9797, rental fee $39-$99, includes beaded bags, shoes and jewelry. Upscale cocktail and formals for rent. Lots of inventory.

Men can purchase **tuxedos** at *real* good prices from tuxedo rental shops when they clear out their old models and buy new ones. Call around and ask when they plan a sale.

Men's tuxedos sell for as little as $15 at the **Rancho Santa Fe Garden Club Rummage Sale**, (760) 756-1554. Also, see **Tuxedo Discount** and **A Better Deal** in Resale/Consignment, this chapter.

For more bridal wear rentals, see Weddings, his chapter.

Frames

I like to pick up *unique* old frames at yard sales, estate sales, antique stores and second hand furniture stores, Goodwill and swapmeets, and I wait for sales on matting, as matting and framing can be shockingly expensive. Get several price quotes by phone before you commit, and find out when their next sale will be, as there is always something coming up. Some framers charge an arm and a leg; some do only the finest and most expensive framing to preserve museum-quality works. Sales can be worth waiting for. The frame can be as good as the artwork inside it and these days, framemakers are so creative. Here are some places to check out for good deals at savings you will love.

Aaron Brothers Art Mart, 2790 Midway, San Diego; 4150 Convoy, Kearny Mesa, 8827 Villa La Jolla Dr.; 8396 Alvarado Road, La Mesa; 2550 Vista Way, Oceanside; 16771 Bernardo Center Drive. With 120 stores in western states, Arron's offers several sales a year, a "1¢ frame sale" (with purchase), 50% off sales on posters, clearance sales, etc. Large supply of ready-made matting. Web: aaronbrothers.com If you just need inexpensive frames, you might do better pricewise, elsewhere.

Michael's Arts & Crafts stores, with nine local outlets to choose from, offers custom framing discount coupons in their advertising supplements in the *U-T* every few weeks Sometimes they are for 33% off, but usually there is a 50% off coupon, so it's worth waiting for. Sometimes, the coupons are only for the frame, sometimes for the whole enchilada, so it's worth the WAIT if you need the matting and glass, too, because those coupons are available probably every 6-8 weeks. I keep an eye on that one because it is such a good savings. They have over 600 frames and 500 colors of mat board. Further, they often guarantee the framing order will be ready within two weeks, or it's free. They also offer classes in Memory Books (how to make fabulous personalized photo albums) See Arts & Crafts for their nine locations.

Frame-It-Yourself, 5523 Clairemont Mesa Bl, (858) 571-3540. Do-it yourself picture framing. They cut all the pieces (mat cutting, dry mounting, frames) and show you how to assemble it. They even have some very nice museum quality stuff.

Cost Plus is a great place for attractive, reasonably priced ready-made picture frames and large selection of framed artwork. Frequent sales, worth waiting for, usually 20% or more off. Downtown, (619) 236-1737; Grossmont Center, (619) 466-2991; La Jolla Village Square, (619) 455-8210. Pier One, too. Even Mervyn's, Ross, TJMaxx have great frames and they get them in at bargain prices. Stein Mart Stores at 2505B Oceanside and 123644 Poway Rd., Poway, (858) 513-9309, too. Hundreds of unique photo frames on display, all at a discount of 25-60% off what they sell in other stores for. Hmmmm. Good one...

Picture Frame Outlet, 1375 N. Cuyamaca, El Cajon, (619) 449-6098; ready-made and custom frames. Warehouse with wide selection; tons of frames.

Gallery Scene, 415 University, (619) 298-3177; Kearny Mesa, 7590 Clairemont Mesa Bl., (858) 569-7511. Big selection of frames and mats; 100's of framed pictures, catalogs of posters, prints and fine art. Framing 10-50% below retail.

World Art, 1120 West Morena Bl., (619) 275-0461; professional framing, good prices. Huge selection of framed posters and graphics.

Tijuana is a great place to get frames. There are many frame stores in the Artisan area just across the border and on Revolucion. A friend had frames made for $11 including glass, stretching and backing at Bernardo's on 5th (towards San Diego) at Revolucion. They would have cost her $25 each for the frame alone in San Diego. I picked up several frames at a nice, large frame shop on 7th street across from the Jai Lai Palace. They have little frames to huge ones. I used them for many years, then sold them at Karen's Consignment (for more than I paid for them).

I bought the most spectacular GOLD leaf, large oval mirror in the world at Goodwill for $88. I am still overwhelmed at it. It was worth at least five times what I paid, but that isn't even the point. The point is: it REALLY makes me happy! I just adore it.

Let me tell you a little story from one of the swap meets. A regular swap meet vendor found a painting in the trash (an oil painting of the Sierras). It was signed, so he called his friend who knows about art, but she wasn't home. The next day, he took it to the swapmeet and a woman asked him how much it was. He said: $175. Immediately he was getting more offers, but he sold it to her for the $175 he had already mentioned. She was offered $10K for it before she left the swapmeet, and a year later, got in touch with an art appraiser who sold it at auction for..........*$187,000!!* That story was in Kobey's Magazine. Now do you know why people are out there scouring the swap meets for "finds"???

Search online at google.com for poster art and picture frames. You can also purchase replicas from museums at their web sites.

Furniture & Home Decor

In this section , you will find unique places to buy new furniture, used furniture, and factory direct furniture from major manufacturers in North Carolina at huge savings. From high end to deluxe bargains, you'll find some amazing opportunities to spruce up the homefront without breaking the family budget.

If you're in the market for new furniture, pick up a copy of the *Union-Tribune* on weekends to see who's having *the big sales*. Furniture stores advertise on weekends to lure shoppers in for their holiday sales, semi-annual, anniversary, annual and clearance sales. There's *always* a sale, so shop around for a few weeks before making that major purchase and see what your opportunities are. I hate it when I buy something and then see it on sale shortly thereafter. Now I usually shop for weeks for a major purchase. Never pay the suggested retail price, as furniture is marked up 200-300% or more. You can see why the stores can afford to have so many "sales" with that kind of markup.

If you want to save a few extra scheckles, see if this works for you: ask if there are any floor models, returns, discontinued, clearance or damaged items. Don't forget that department stores offer a 10% discount if you open an account (Macy's/Robinsons-May) and if you buy and open an account on a weekend when there is a sale, and a 10% or 15% or sometimes 20% discount coupon in the newspaper, start adding up your savings.). Check out the following stores in San Diego to find affordable chic furnishings, and look into the wholesale-by mail opportunities and the "previously owned" market for some real buys.

Robinsons-May and **Macys** have furniture sales every weekend, and I know people who really capitalize on their discount coupons which offer an additional 10-15-20% off the SALE price. I was able to score on a $2300 set of mattresses, marked down to $1200, then they had a weekend sale offering an additional 30% off all sale mattresses, AND they gave me an additional 10% discount coupon, which actually wasn't in effect that day, but was coming up the following Wednesday, so they gave me that discount too! Well, I got this deluxe double-sided pillow mattress set for what anyone would pay for an inexpensive set at a cheapo mattress store!

Ikea, one half mile west of Qualcomm stadium on Friars Road, (619) 563-IKEA. Huge home furnishings warehouse with very affordable prices. Stylish furniture and accessories (many assemble-yourself) for casual lifestyles. Tons of stylish sofas, chairs, room groupings for the whole house. Storage solutions, kitchenware, lighting and lamps, flooring, rugs, vases, lamps, mirrors, curtains, drapery rods. You can get a lot of style on a budget. Similar to Pottery Barn, but more affordable. Save on selected items storewide, discounted up to 50% off, at their twice a year sale, May and after the holidays. Over 129 stores internationally. Call for their huge catalog. Web: ikea-usa.com

Jerome's Furniture, Superstore at 1190 Morena Blvd., plus Scripp's Ranch, El Cajon, Chula Vista, San Marcos. Call (888) 537-6637 for a store directions. Since 1954, Jerome's has been a top retailer in San Diego with medium/moderate priced furniture; over 40 sofas, love seats, chairs; bedroom sets, dining room sets, home office, home theater, children's furniture. Check he clearance room for floor samples, closeouts. Frequent sales. Web: jeromes.com

Wacky Wicker, 8990 Miramar Rd., (858) 547-0487. Name brand wicker furniture with semi-annual sale of top manufacturers in March and September. Other great places for wicker: Cost Plus and Pier One carry great copies of designer wicker at reasonable prices. If you're really into wicker, try these catalogs: Bielecky Brothers (718) 424-4764; Wicker Warehouse, 195 S. River St., Hackensack, NJ 0760, (201)342-6709., or visit their Web site at wickerwarehouse.com.. Discounts on everything.

There are a number of vendors at **swap meets** that sell inexpensive new in-style furniture, futons, sofas, book cases, dining tables, decorator items, lamps, wrought iron, some custom made furniture, contemporary & oriental rugs, wicker, rattan and bamboo furniture & decor. Every weekend. And, don't overlook going to the back area where there are yard sales and people are selling used furniture and antiques. Many real "scores" have been found here. See the $187K painting story, bought for $10, above!!

Metropolis, 1003 University Ave., Hillcrest, (619) 220-0632. Encinitas store: (760) 635-9319. An eclectic collection of California casual furniture, trendy accessories; imports. Wonderful, fun, whimsical designs and beautiful classics. Ask about their WAREHOUSE sales. A couple times a year, they open up the warehouse in Miramar and have a sale with merchandise marked down up to 75% off. Call for next sale date!

Restoration Hardware carries a line of American Arts and Crafts furniture reproductions that mixes well with other casual California style trendy furniture, plus home accessories (and very little hardware!), but a nice collection of drawer pulls and hinges. Fashion Valley Mall: (619) 543-9120; Web: restorationhardware.com Catalog available.

Pier One, Cost Plus and other import stores have young, trendy inexpensive real wood furniture, mainly imported, wicker, wrought iron tables, fabulous decorator items, artwork, shades, pillows, candles and everything you need to create an exotic atmosphere. Imports from the Asia, Africa, Indonesia, Mexico. Not expensive, weekly sales, and always some items for clearance with major markdowns. If I were just starting out and on a small budget, or just relocating from Empty Boot, Nebraska in a major life's change, I would be happy with all new things from Pier One, Cost Plus, Ikea, Pottery Barn and Crate & Barrel, a ton of plants, a few antiques and garage sale finds! People who pay to haul all their stuff across country to move here often with they had just started their new California life over from SCRATCH. You can get all the kitchen things at Target, Ikea, etc.

Pier 1 Imports Clearance Store, 1735 Hancock Street near Washington, (619) 291-9920. Home furnishings and decor at 25% and more off regular store prices. Lots of wicker furniture, love seats, tables, pillows, chairs, pads, tons of candle holders, stemware, posters, lamps, lots of jewelry boxes, baskets and rugs at a discount. Seasonal decorations were 75% off on a recent visit. I know someone who bought a discontinued 6' totem pole for $40 (value $150). She *loves* it. Web: pier1.com.

Z Gallerie, 611 5th downtown, (619) 696-8137; a chain with 60 stores, offers trendy California style casual home decor; big overstuffed furniture, candles, fabulous wrought iron decorator items and accent pieces. Lots of imports, some ornate things, designer furniture, mid-priced. A true fantasy store! I could just move in. Zgallerie.com

Pottery Barn in Fashion Valley Center, (619) 296-8014, offers not only their usual line of china and pottery for the home and garden, they offer contemporary, casual chic overstuffed furniture, wrought iron decorator items, candles galore, drapes, linens, and accessories. Sales. For a delightful catalog, call (800) 922-5507. *Now, when I start over (dream on.)*

Homestead House, 6965 Consolidated Way, off Milch, Miramar, (858) 530-3200; over 100,000 sq. ft. superstore with designer furniture, mainly traditional (+ other styles) solid wood furniture, middle price lines, complimentary design service, discounted from retail, and sales, too. Frequent sales, and a clearance section!

Treasurers Furniture, 7480 Miramar Road near the Pyramid. High end fine name designer brands, Henredon, Century, Drexel Heritage and more. Frequent sales. Upscale, amazing stuff. Large store. Their outlet store is now gone. Once a year they have a Drexel Heritage sale where you can save up to 40% off everything Drexel Heritage makes.

If you're into browsing for furniture, Miramar Road seems to be one of those areas with endless furniture stores, carpet stores, mattress stores, home lighting stores, tile stores, futon stores, wicker furniture stores, mirror stores, etc. I always run out of time, energy or money and have to head for home before getting into all the showrooms along there that are luring me in (like Renaissance, California Closets, & more). For more browsing, visit the Design Center housed in several buildings on Morena Blvd. (around the 4200 block) between Balboa Ave and Costco. Furniture, accessories, mirrors, etc. Morena Blvd is another good area with a cluster of home furnishing stores, down around 1000 - 1400 block with Genghis Khan exotic furniture, several lighting stores, the Oh! Susannah country store, tile stores galore, several carpet stores, etc. Good shopping.

Aspire Furniture, (760 724 2661 2020 Haciena, Vista; Contemporary, Mediterranean, and a mix of furniture. Discounted items, overruns plus custom design. Medium to higher end furniture; carpets & fabrics, too.

Costco and **Sam's** have a selection of quality brand name sample sofas, armoires, end tables, mattresses, computer tables, book cases and other furniture and accessories at great prices that can be ordered and shipped to your home. Patio furniture, umbrellas and accessories, too, in the warehouse..

Ethan Allen, 7341 Clairemont Mesa, Blvd., Clairemont, (858) 560-4404, has a small clearances room with discontinued items, fabrics, floor samples with discounts up to 70%. Desks, sofas, chairs, etc. 325 stores + around the world, traditional furniture. Mid-range priced furniture; good value. Eight sales a year, selected items.

Artifacts International, 9340 Dowdy Drive, (858) 693-6000. This is a warehouse not normally not open to the public, but they have an annual warehouse and showroom clearance sale that is open to the public one day only, with samples, prototypes and overstocks of high end furniture, tables, sofas, stone and iron, armoires, beds, chairs, mirrors, decorator items, planters, all at prices with substantial savings below designer net. The sale is open to decorators only the first two days, and the public is welcome on the third day. Usually in the spring. Call for date. Cash and carry.

South Cedros Avenue Design District in Solana Beach is a dream for shoppers seeking unique furniture and decor, with antique stores, artists, crafts people and furniture retailers. The area is filled with more than 50 shops loaded with decorator items for the home, some reasonable, some pricey, but there is clearance section with markdowns to browse through in every store, and you can try to negotiate the price. The Cedros Trading Co., 307 S. Cedros, (858) 794-9016, houses several dozen vendors with decorator items and antiques. Kern & Co., 143 S. Cedros, has exotic woods, kilims, accessories. Other stores have frames, custom made furniture, paintings, wood, glass, antiques, handcrafts, dried flowers, imports, and more. The Cedros Design District has colorful street fairs and events. Great place to shop, make a day of it and do lunch. So delightful.

This is insider stuff: The public can *browse* at the design centers, which is where professional designers shop for their clients. The nearest one is in Laguna Niguel and the other is in Los Angeles. The **Pacific Design Center in Los Angeles** (8687 Melrose, (310) 657-0800) has 150 show rooms open to the public to explore, and each showroom establishes its own sales policy. If a showroom doesn't sell directly to the public, there are designers on location for you. The **Laguna Design Center**, 23807 Aliso Creek, (949) 643-2929) is also open to the general public to tour, and there are onsite designers if you care to make a purchase. San Diego's big design center folded a few years ago.

American Society of Interior Designers (ASID) (San Diego Chapter) has an annual spring 2-day sale of surplus furnishings from San Diego's finest interior decorator's showrooms at bargain prices. People line up around the block for this event! Everything for the home: floor models, cancellations, custom-made furniture and window coverings that may have been too long or short, antiques, new furniture, accessories, bolts of fabrics and fabric sample books, inventory from model homes, some items consigned or donated by lighting stores, kitchen shops. Call (858) 2274-3345 for this year's date.

Model home furniture from condominiums and new home tracts is advertised in the Furniture & Accessories #3280 section of the *Union-Trib* classified ads. If you are IN a model home and fall in love with the sofa or bedroom set, ask the realtor if you can buy it when they close the model home. I bought a gorgeous high-end sofa for $50 from a model home a few years ago, white raw silk. It had a little stain on the side, but it wasn't a problem because that side went up against an end table!

TIPS: Avoid inexpensive but stylish furniture made of formica over pressboard as it sags with time and absorbs odors. Target, Kmart, Walmart have REAL wood furniture at *really* reasonable prices, and real wood holds up and retains it's value. Beware the "El Cheap-o" furniture stores that advertise ("3 Rooms of Furniture for $300) because the sofa will sag in a short time, will soil quickly due to no Scotchguard, legs break off, etc. It would be better to buy higher quality *used* furniture than to buy "El Cheap-o" new. You can probably resell used furniture for what you paid for it; sometimes, more!

Unfinished furniture stores carry everything from large armoires and entertainment centers, to small end tables, desks, dining room and bedroom furniture. Styles include simple modern, traditional and VERY stylish copies of quality antiques! Visit KrisJon in Oceanside, Haywoods in Kearny Mesa and San Marcos. Finish them yourself. Wait for a sale, because I think the cost of unfinished furniture is a little "pricey."

Catalog furnishings stores are usually fairly small because they carry very few pieces of furniture; however, they have hundreds of catalog sources for you to select your furniture from, samples of fabrics, plus sample displays of Levelors, drapes, shutters, carpeting, wallpaper and items for the whole house and patio. Major brands, 10-70% off. Occasional floor sample sales. Check out: Al Davis, 1601 University, Hillcrest, (619) 296-1221, and see the next listing.

Wholesale-factory direct Why settle for the best deal in town when you can get the best deal in the United States? Here's how to buy furniture at from the furniture manufacturing capital of the U.S., North Carolina. If you're in the market for a big ticket item like a sofa, armoire or dining room set, you can easily shave off 30-80% of the suggested retail prices by ordering over the phone. In North Carolina, there are 600 factories that produce nearly 2/3 of America's furniture, and, there are over 60 showrooms that sell name brands over the phone including Henredon, Drexel, Thomasville, Leathercraft, Pennsylvania House, Martinsville, Brown Jordan, Classic Leather, Design Institute of America, Leathercraft, Sealy, Simmons, Lane, formal pieces, patio furniture, office furniture, clocks, mirrors, lamps (Stiffel,

Wildwood and other lamps) and accessories, plus imported furniture, at a discount. Your job is to locate the furniture, patio furniture, lamp, etc. that you want at a department or furniture store and write down the manufacturer, collection name, model number, wood type and/or fabric style from the sales ticket. Then call one of the following numbers to see if you can get a better deal from a discounter. They look up your item in a catalog of manufacturers they carry and can give you a price quote and estimated freight charge based on weight, and approximate delivery date. There is no sales tax, which can offset some if not all of the freight. Some people order single items, some buy a whole house full! They ship all over the world. It may take 10-12 weeks (sometimes more) for delivery (but it took that long when I custom-ordered a sofa in Mission Valley!) You will order your item(s) directly from the manufacturer's representative who ships it to you. You usually pay about 30-50% down with your credit card, and the balance plus delivery charges when it arrives. There may be no sales tax, which offsets much of the shipping charges. Your order will be unpacked and set up for your inspection. If there is any damage, you can refuse it and it is returned. Otherwise, you better know what you are ordering because there is usually a NO return policy. People all over the East Coast go to this famous area on vacations and shop for furniture, lamps and carpets which they have shipped home! But, all anyone needs to do is call with ordering information! Here are some of the bigger furniture discounters that carry lines from hundreds of manufacturers. Call for quotes and ask for their free brochure which lists available brands and sales policy. Sorry, some manufacturers prohibit the discounters from using a toll free number, (but call anyway):

Boyles, over 100 manufacturers, (336) 998-7712. Since 1949 Web: boyles.com
Rose Furniture Co., 500 manufacturers, (336) 886-6050 Web: rosefurniture.com
Furnitureland South, Inc., more than 400 brands, (336) 841-4328 Web: furniturelandsouth.com
High Point Furniture Sales (800) 334-1875 Over 200 major manufacturers

Blackwelder's Furniture (since 1936), (800) 438-0201; catalog (175 color pages), $l9.95, includes $30 coupon for purchase.
Cherry Hill Interiors, many manufacturers (800) 328-0933
Loftin Black, since 1948, over 200 lines, (800) 334-7398
Henrydon Factory Outlet (336-888-2844 adjacent to Henredon Showroom

Used Furniture & Decor

When you walk out the door of a new furniture store, half the value of your furniture walks out with you. Used furniture is a good investment, as you can usually sell it for a price near what you paid for it. Most antiques retain their value and many will go up! Love of used and antique furniture shopping can be a hobby that becomes a living! It happens, often!

The best deals and steals on furniture of course be found at yard sales. People are moving, getting divorced, or getting remarried and have two sets of everything, and you can pick up marvelous furniture and decorator items for a song. Better neighborhoods often have better quality items and they aren't trying to raise money; they are just getting rid of stuff, cheap. Scan the Garage Sales column #2070 in the classified ad section of the *Union-Trib* for yard sales with furniture. Better hit the deck because there are others out there who are specifically looking for furniture, including pros who will resell it at a profit.

Also check for furniture in the Thrifties Ads #3190 (excellent source for something specific, like twin beds, desks, etc.). Also check Furniture & Accessories #3280, and Estate Sales #2010. Pick up the *Reader* classifieds, too. You'll be surprised what's in them! *Like everything!* Call and inquire about the condition, how old it is, how much they paid for it, etc. This is a good venue for negotiating, as it is sometimes difficult to sell things thru the classified ads since not everyone shops this marketplace.

Check out some of the great furniture consignment stores in San Diego where you can splurge on home decorating without breaking the budget. When rich folks tire of their furnishings and are ready to redecorate, what do they do with them? If they don't give them away to family or charity, they put them on consignment! And, their castoffs are by no means junk. You can really pick up some fabulous quality bargains at consignment stores. Interior decorators are in there everyday, shopping for bargains for their clients. You can sell your excess furniture, mirrors, lamps and do-dads at a consignment shop, too, but call first, as they are selective. Take in photos of large pieces. If you don't have a truck, they can arrange pickups for a nominal charge. You will usually receive about 60% of the agreed upon selling price and the shop gets about 40%. Prices are reduced 10% if the item doesn't sell in 30 days and again in 60 days. If the item doesn't sell in 90 days, you must pick it up, or it is donated to charity. (This varies depending on the store: some actually charge more, some less, and some stores that carry expensive pieces will keep your large items 12-18 months). Small tables and decorator items will sell the quickly. If you're going to sell, pick a store that advertises and gets traffic. Read your contract carefully. The biggest complaint (not often) is that the store goes out of business and doesn't notify you to pick up your furniture. Pick a reputable dealer (call Better Business Bureau to check if there have been any complaints) and keep tabs on your merchandise. Visit it from time to time until contract expires.

Here are some great consignment stores. **Karen's Consignment Gallery**, 4051 Voltaire, Ocean Beach, (619) 225-8585, is a 7500 sq. ft. store with a variety of used furniture and household items ranging from antique to contemporary and simple to exquisite. All furniture is there on consignment which translates to good prices because Karen doesn't have to pay for her inventory until it sells. There is a lot of stock to buy from, and new items arrive daily. Karen advertises a lot and gets good traffic in the store, so things move fast. She gets some beautiful things in from all over the county (including jewelry, both fine & costume). Professionals decorators shop here for their clients. I buy and sell things at Karen's, so say hello to Karen for me! **Two Sisters Consignment Home Furnishing**, 616 Stevens Avenue, Solana Beach, (858) 755-4558. Large store of home furnishings in near-perfect condition at comfortable prices; unique decorator items. Consignments arriving daily. The **Village Consignment**, 1150 Camino Del Mar, (858) 259-0870. Over 4,000 feet of wonderful array of one-of-a-kind decorator items and unique furniture. Oriental, modern, retro, rustic, estate furniture, beautiful linens and artwork. There is a 60 (you)-40 (store) split with a 2-month contract. All quality decor, mainly traditional, with antiques and some contemporary, too. Affordable prices and a friendly store! **Revival,** 3220 Adams Avenue, (619) 284-3999; Since 1989. Over 5000 sq. ft. of constantly changing used furniture and decorator items. The new owner buys whole housefuls/estates of furniture every week for the shop, bringing in lots of antiques, collectibles, decorator items, architectural surplus, unique used furniture, one-of-a-kind-everything. **Antique Cottage**, 2873 Adams Ave, Normal Heights, (619) 281-9663. Mainly older pieces, pre-60's, and a refinishing business, too. **Consignment Classics**, (Formerly Terri's Consign & Design),1895 Hancock St, midtown, (619) 491-0700; 201-D S. El Camino Real, Encinitas, (760) 635-0730. The largest showroom, with over 22,000 sq. ft. of "gently used" unique furniture and accessories from estates and private homes. Fifty-fifty split, 90 day contract. Some new liquidation furniture, some model home, some huge sofas and dining tables, dark pine armoires, iron beds, some doors. Decorator items, mirrors, silver. Always changing. Pick up/deliver. **Country Friends Shop** 6030 El Tordo, Rancho Santa Fe, (858) 756-1192, fax (858) 756-0111. High quality furniture, reproductions and antiques, lighting, crystal bowls and goblets, tables, accessories, and decor, etc. This is a two-building consignment shop with really nice things for the home, and all profits go to charity. You'll have fun shopping here! To sell, you need to make an appointment. **Glorious Antiques**, Girard Ave., La Jolla, (858) 459-2222. Antiques, linens, reproduction, interesting finds. Good prices. Benefits the Humane Society (70% to you/30% to store). **The Ark** (across the street on 7645 Girard also benefits the animals and has beautiful consignments.

More used furniture

Cruise thrift stores like Salvation Army, Goodwill, St. Vincent de Paul, etc. Everyone has a good story to tell about the big score they made on a valuable piece of furniture for a song at a thrift store!! I sure love my gold leaf mirror for $88 from Goodwill that is worth at least 5x more. And, I have a lot more things I could brag about. (A man back East bought an old map for $3 at Salvation Army that turned out to be an original map of Paris commissioned by King Louis, worth MILLIONS. We should be so lucky). The Salvation Army Boutique on Sports Arena gets in some interesting things, and they have frequent sales. Stuff flies out the door.

Fashion Furniture Rental Outlet Center, 8400 Miramar Road, (858) 530-1133. Part of a large furniture rental company, this 10,000 sq. ft. outlet store sells returned rental and vacation home furniture, samples, model home furniture, 40-50% off retail.

Cort Furniture Rental and Clearance Center, 9150 Clairemont Mesa Blvd, (858) 277-8800. Frequent blowout sales where they clear out the warehouse. Ask when one is coming up.

Here's a good one: **free furniture** on trash day (now we'll see who the snobs are!) A student from one of my bargain hunting classes who lives in Ocean Beach said that she has gotten a number of items for her apartment (great things, too) that people were getting rid of. O.B. is a very transient area with many people moving in and out. People either don't want to take things with them or don't have room for something they brought with them, so they put it in the alley or street. Not everything you find is going to be in great condition, so you can pass on those. But keep looking because you'll find items that *are* in good condition. They're out there. If you don't see any, it's because someone else already saw it and took it! I found this huge carpeted cat perch (about $150 at PetSmart) on my street. So, if you want free furniture, drive around beach areas or high density apartment areas like in U.T.C. and Mission Valley where yuppies are on the move. Anything that is placed at a curb is being disposed of. If you don't feel comfortable taking something that isn't yours, then go knock on the door and ask if they are getting rid of whatever it is and would they mind if you took it. My brother who lived in New York for several years had a magnificent old mahogany fireplace mantel in his apartment. When I asked him where he got it, he said it was *in the street*, being thrown away by someone who lived in the same apartments that was moving out! He said people are always carrying off things from the street, that it is a way of life in New York, and that you could furnish the world with all the furniture that you find there! A flight attendant friend in San Francisco says the thing she likes best about living in SFO is trash day! She has found many things when returning from a flight in the middle of the night, so she sets her alarm for 4 a.m. even when not working to see what's been put out in the trash! She raves about antiques, odds and ends, plants galore that she has picked up this way!

Other furniture and design tips

You can take free upholstery and furniture refinishing classes through adult education. See Continuing Education.

Design professionals and individuals are going to Tijuana to get furniture upholstered at really cheap labor prices. Take down the fabric, foam rubber, bindings, etc., and they do the labor. Sofas, $139, chairs, $99, pillows, etc. Aguillar is an upholsterer that many San Diego interior designers use. English is spoken at this shop, just a few minutes from the border. Call 011-52-664-683-1483.

Mi Mexico Curios, on 4th Street just below Revolucion in Tijuana, is a FABULOUS place; tons of unique decorator items made of wrought iron including enormous chandeliers, armoires, lots of trendy patio furniture, candle holders galore plus many currently popular decorator items. Ask for Enrique who is very helpful and speaks English. 011-52-664-683-3361.

Candle Factory Outlet, 3606 Rosecrans; tons of candles, many styles and colors; classes, too. Web: candleworks.com

There are some terrific books and classes at Home Depot, paint stores and The Learning Annex on the magic of paint, and the abracadabra you can perform on furniture to create faux finishes, glazing, graining, stenciling, marbling, lacquering, etc. Videos, too. I'm gearing up for a project, as a novice, soon to be pro (I hope.)

Martha Stewart has a new book, *How to Decorate: A Guide to Creating Comfortable, Stylist Living Spaces*, Clarkson, Potter, $10. Carol Revelli offers the *Revelli Room Design Planner*, a kit containing a grid and furniture symbol sheets to scale for convenient, expert room planning and furniture placement, (800) 738-3554. *Color and Style* books and kits available, too. Another good book is the *Western Guide to Feng Shui*, Hay House, $12.95. Feng shui is the big trend with architects, designers, and celebrities. The goal is to decorate your house in the Chinese "art of placement" to create a balanced living environment so that you live in harmony with nature and the universe. The proper arrangement of furniture promotes better health, wealth and relationships, according to Chinese philosophy. Classes are offered at the Learning Annex, (619) 544-9700.

Interior design classes are offered at Mesa College, (858) 627-2600; The Design Institute of San Diego offers a bachelor of arts degree in interior design, (858) 566-1200. Web: disd.edu

Here's a furniture refinisher recommended to me who does a gorgeous job: **Furniture Hospital**, 7719 El Cajon Blvd, La Mesa, (619) 464-7117.

Web sites for furniture and home decor:

North Carolina Furniture Online . . . . ncnet.com/ncnetworks/furn-onl.html
City of High Point . . . . ncnet.com/ncnetworks/hp-intr.html
Atrium Furniture Mall . . . . webpress.net/furniture
Manufacturer's Direct . . . . romegeorgia.com/cge-bin
Hickory Furniture Mart . . . . webcom.com/ hickory
Interior Classics . . . . classics.com
Furniture . . . . webpress.net/furniture
Access Decorative Market (pillows, fountains, lamps) . . . . accdecmkt.com/admt
Better Homes and Gardens . . . . bhglive.com
Country Sampler's Decorating Ideas . . . . sampler.com
This Old House . . . . pathfinder.com (click Living, then This Old House)

For more furniture and decorator items, see "Resale/Consignment Stores," "Antique Stores" and "Thrift Stores" in this chapter. See chapter on" Things To Do" for a list of fabulous annual home tours.

Garage/Moving/Yard/Estate Sales

San Diego is really a hot area for garage, moving, yard and estate sales. Let's face it, we can sell outdoors all year long. On the East coast, it's a seasonal thing. If you go to enough of them, you'll eventually find everything you could possibly ever want. Literally everything. I've been to sales in the most prestigious areas of the county. It's amazing how many well off people will put out that sign. Maybe not so many older people (it can be a lot of work!), but the aging baby boomers are right out there every weekend, selling off their excess. It's not enough to just drive around and stop at a sale here and there. The people who are totally into this (and it is so addictive!) check Garage Sales #2070 and Estate Sales #2010 in the classified ads of the *Union-Trib* and then storm onto the scene. Some people rely on the *Reader*, the *Pennysaver* and neighborhood newspapers to guide them to the yard sales. I've been converted from a "night person" to a "morning person" because of "Weekend Boutiquing" as we call it! Head for the better areas of town (La Jolla!) where people are just getting rid of things rather than trying to raise money. In upscale areas, you'll find better quality merchandise, mostly in great condition. The possibility of finding an incredible buy is what drives many people to stalk garage sales. At a home that was in the $800K price range, I saw a brand new looking beige mohair sofa for $50; two king-sized bedroom sets with several pieces of furniture for $125 each; a fabulous antique bar for $20 that I wanted so badly but don't have a place for; a huge curved screen TV for $100; enormous framed prints for $10; rattan chair for $4, rattan end table, $1; a junior bed, $25 including mattress; old wooden wall clock $7 (which I bought and love). This stuff disappeared from their yard in a matter of a few minutes. Get organized and go early because there is a regular crowd of garage sale prowlers plus professionals who resell who are sitting in cars and trucks waiting outside long before the sales begin at 7 or 8 a.m. every Saturday. They know what they are doing. I buy lots of things for the home, my adult kids, friends and their kids, everybody. This is a good place to try to negotiate the price. Sometimes a person needs to get rid of something *today* and is in a position to make you a fantastic deal. You can have absolutely *everything* if you do this long enough. I wish I had known about yard sales when my kids were young because I've seen every toy, every sporting good, every bicycle, every book, every educational toy, every musical instrument, every *everything* any kid could possibly want at dirt cheap prices and in great condition, too. And, I find it is simply great entertainment, and probably the best Rx for depression in the world. If I were a doctor I would PRESCRIBE yard sales for patients; then maybe you could deduct your expenses! I bet there isn't one garage "sale-r" on Prozac. I see SMILES and total contentment! P.S. Here's another little tip: Don't take a friend with you. They will buy just what you wanted right out from under your nose, without one sign of guilt. One final word: Never-never-never-never-never EVER pass a yard sale sign. There just might be that one little 25¢ find that will make your day! Hallelulah!

I love the community garage sales where a real estate office sponsors an entire neighborhood sale. ERA, The Property Store, Century 21, etc sponsor huge garage sales at subdivisions like Scripps Ranch in the spring with over 300 homes participating, and they provide a map of participating homes at their office. Watch for them in the *Union-Trib* garage sale ads. Most of these people are just cleaning out and getting rid of their surplus, and will take any and all offers. I love to find a home where this is so beneath them, and they practically GIVE away their stuff and regret having to stand there. Giggles. Shop til you drop, Kiddos. Such a deal. That makes up for the ones I've been to where the seller is anal retentive and wants department store prices for their handmedowns. Funny. I have become an amateur psychologist over observing the separation anxiety levels of sellers. *Just make for more fun, kiddos!*

If you're going to *have* a yard sale, here's some advice: advertise it, post signs at major cross streets, get everything out of boxes and price all your items (unmarked items don't sell as fast as marked ones; prices should be

10%-20% of retail value for used items, up to 50% for new items), cleaned up items sell faster than unclean items, begin early on a Saturday (Sunday sales get less people), start when you say you're starting (not before), have plenty of change. Put bright colored signs up with ARROWS on it heading to your address. If you advertise in the *Union*, you will have hoards sitting in front of your house before the sale begins. Holiday weekends don't get as many people as regular weekends. (Good, that means less competition and more opportunities for ME, the buyer!). Get your neighbors bring over their stuff and join in with you, the more the merrier, but don't let them stand there and yak at you. You're supposed to pay attention to the shoppers! When the sale is over, remove all your signs. Your neighbors will appreciate it. A well planned sale can net several hundred dollars.

Get on the mailing list for estate sales held by Heritage Liquidators (619) 284-8680; James D. McDonald Liquidation Services (858) 454-1218; Bert's Antiques, (619) 239-5531. When you go to an estate sale, ask if they have a mailing list or emailing list. Bert's now sends email notification of their sales. Teri's Estate Sales sends out e-notifications. Get on her list at DTOM715@aol.com

Green Resources

The **Green Store**, 4827-A Voltaire, Ocean Beach, (619) 225-1083. T-shirts, buttons, posters, bumper stickers and information on local, national and global environmental and peace issues and organizations, alternative press magazines, catalogs for environmentally safe products. Lending library, group meetings.

I Love a Clean San Diego, (858) 467-0103, an environmental education organization that coordinates the California Coastal Commission's annual coastal cleanup day and adopt-a-beach programs in San Diego County. Web site: sddt.com/~cleansd.

Home Improvement, Tools & Hardware

Home Depot, 3555 Sports Arena Blvd, (619) 224-9200 (plus 15 other locations throughout San Diego) has become one of my favorite haunts. A fantastic warehouse of everything you need for the home from hardware, tools and paint, to kitchen cabinets, lighting, furniture, carpets, plants and flowers. Their everyday prices are excellent. This is the place to get replacement glass cut for broken window or picture frames, cheap-cheap. They cut wood to make bookshelves, etc., first two cuts are free, then about

50 cents each for additional. If you go to a glass store, look out! I ask my kids for gift certificates from Home Depot for Christmas! (My, how my priorities have changed! This is definitely one of those things Mother *didn't* tell me about!)

Expo Design Center (by Home Depot), located at 7803 Othello near Balboa & Convoy, (858) 569-9600; 1550 Leucdia Boulevard, Encinitas, (760) 479-2600. Expo simply has to be the *Rolls Royce* of home improvement stores! When I saw all the beautiful brass door knobs, cabinets, cabinet pulls, faucets, tile, flooring, mirrors and patio furniture, I wanted to go home and tear the whole house down and start all over. They've got it all, including gourmet quality roof ornaments. Occasional sales with coupons in their mailers.. Call and get on the mailing list.

Lowe's Home Improvement Warehouse, off Friar's Rd. ½ mile East of the Stadium, (619) 584-5500. In the mall with Ikea and Costco, Lowe's is definitely a good place to shop. The environment, wide aisles and colorful displays make it a PLEASANT experience. They have everything, the whole enchilada, from garbage disposals and faucets, tools, cleaning supplies, BBQ's, a complete garden shop, paints, appliances, flooring, custom blinds (some cut on the spot), plus installations for garage doors, flooring, appliances, interior lighting, water heaters, more. Free how-to clinics, demonstrations. Lowe's is often on Home & Garden Channel.

Dixieline Lumber is over 90 years old, with 10 lumber and home centers in San Diego that focus on the needs of contractors and homeowners. They receive large shipments of lumber every 21 days from Oregon. There is a mill center where you can have special cuts made. They made a replica of a small board I needed for one side of a tea cart that was missing. I brought in the other one, and they custom matched the thickness and width. Solved that problem!

San Diego Hardware, 840 5th, in downtown San Diego, (619) 232-7123, is over 100 years old and has all the things you can't find at Home Depot, Lowe's and Dixieline, and they will order anything for you from thousands of sources. It's a great place to get that missing widget, gadget or unusual brass hardware. Restoration, whimsical and elegant details for the home

Costco & Sam's Club have good deals on hand tools, power tools, more.

This site doitbest.com says it's the world's largest hardware store.

Sears **Craftsman** tools offer a lifetime replacement policy on their hand tools. Whadda deal.

Black & Decker, Viejas Outlets,(619) 659-1309; Discontinued, blemished and reconditioned power tools, coffee makers, table saws, can openers, kitchen gadgets, irons, housewares and accessories, all with 2 year new warranties. Some appliances in damaged boxes. They also do Black & Decker repairs. Some new appliances, too.

Builders Trading Company, 202 N. Highway 101, Encinitas, (760) 634-3220. This 5000 sq. ft. place is known as "a candy store for builders." Lots of surplus inventory and job cancellation merchandise from high end manufacturers, sold near ½ price. French doors, bay windows, light fixtures, tubs, faucets, fireplace surrounds, granite countertops, windows, thousands of items from companies like Pella, changing continuously, mostly new and unused. You never know what you will find.

Habitat ReStore, a building materials thrift store located at 3653 Costa Bella St., Lemon Grove, (619) 463-0464. I call it the "Goodwill" of building materials because everything is donated by locals. You may find anything from old kitchen cabinets to electrical parts to exterior and interior doors. People remodel and donate whole kitchens, etc. but the good things go out the door fast. If you need a part to an old window, or old replacement hardware, etc., or to replace an old glass shower door, this might be where you can find it. When I was there, they had just gotten in a fabulous set of large California louvered wooden patio doors, but most everything else was pretty rough. Good stuff flies out the door. People are known to be standing around waiting for the next truck load to come in. This is a non-profit operation, manned mainly by volunteers for Habitat Humanity, which builds houses for those in need. They will pick up your large donations.

Antique Building Materials, (619) 233-1144. Mantels, beveled glass, light fixtures, doors. By appointment. Special stuff.

For good deals on tools, lumber, building supplies, etc., check the classified ads in the *Union-Trib* under #3190 Thrifties and #3040 Tools & Lumber, and you'll find everything. Pick up used doors, bricks, lumber, shutters, cabinets, windows and everything else that's left over from remodeling jobs. Also check #2070 Garage/Moving Sales and #2000 Auctions. Check the *Reader* and PennySaver, too. Many contractors advertise their surplus here, and they also unload their stuff at swap meets.

Scavenger's Paradise in North Hollywood, (323) 877-7945. Boy, I saw this one on Home & Garden TV and I wanna go there. Anyone wanna come along? This is a big warehouse (actually in an old church) that is filled both inside and outside with the most spectacular "architectural" surplus and treasures from fantastic old buildings that were torn down. Garden ornaments, wrought iron gates, fabulous old hardware, doors, unbelievable light fixtures, huge concrete lions, etc. Unique, and a "must do" on my list.

Before you have home repairs or improvements done, call the local office of the State Contractor License Board, (800) 321-2752, for a copy of their 32-page publication, *What You Should Know Before You Hire a Contractor..* Listen to the lengthy menu or go to their Web page at cslb.ca.gov. This is also the number to call to check to see if there are any complaints against a contractor. Before you begin, get three to ten bids, asking for references. Be sure to ask if your contractor is licensed. Unlicensed contractors may not have the skills necessary to do the job if they have not passed state tests. (However, if a repair is under $300, then the contractor doesn't need a license, according to the person I just finished talking to at the above number.) In any case, also check with the Better Business Bureau, (858) 496-2131, or visit their Web page at sandiego.bbb.org to see if there have been any complaints against the contractor. California law limits down payments on home repairs to 10% or $1,000, whichever is lower, so don't be fooled into paying more up front! (Now THERE'S a tip if I ever saw one.) On swimming pools, down payment should not exceed $200 or 2% of the contract price. For real savings, think in terms of specialization: hire individual contractors to get the job done (someone who specializes in wall board, wiring, plumbing, etc.), and save by not hiring a general contractor, who will always cost more. Of course, the whole thing requires nerves of steel, and everyone has their nightmare to report, so the best advice I can toss your way is to get references from satisfied customers. And good luck.

How to Hire A Home Improvement Contractor Without Getting Chiseled by Tom Philbin (can be ordered from book stores if not in stock) says you should make no down payment, pay only for completed work, and hold out 10 to 20% of the fee until 30 days after the job is completed to ensure the contractor will return to fix any problems. According to Tom, if the contractor doesn't pay the supplier, the supplier can get a lien against your property, even though you paid the contractor, so make out a two-party check or make separate checks.

If problems arise, the job does not get done, or it doesn't get done satisfactorily or timely, contact the local State Contractor's License Board and the Better Business Bureau at the numbers above. Also, you can sue in Small Claims Court for amounts up to $5,000, (858) 694-2066. Information is available at the court to assist you in filing your claim. For more information, see chapter on Legal Good Deals.

For inexpensive yard work and some home repairs, use college and high school kids. Call the student placement office of a school near you. Or, call a senior center and hire a senior.

Free classes are offered through continuing education on plumbing, heating, air conditioning, landscape construction, and more. Call (619) 221-6973 for information on the nearest class to you. Free workshops are offered at Home Depot and other home improvement centers on basic wiring, tile, decks, roofs, plumbing, more.

Get good prices on Mexican tile at the Tecate Tile Factory in Tecate, about an hour from here. The factory is near Rancho La Puerta Spa, a few minutes down the road that goes from Tecate to Tijuana. You'll see the tiles stacked in piles on the right side of the road. Be sure you know your prices in the U.S. (Home Depot carries Tecate tiles, too), and prepare to bargain to get a good price down there. Also, Tijuana is loaded with ceramic, unglazed tile, marble and decorative concrete stores, cheap-o.

San Diego Home/Garden Lifestyles magazine is filled with remodel ideas, unique hardware, contractors, how-to's, and has listings of specific local resources for getting the job done. Beautiful ideas from San Diego homes.

Sunset Magazine offers a free catalog of "how-to" books on carpentry, fireplaces, barbecues, children's projects, bookshelves, bathrooms, gardens, indoor and outdoor lighting and dozens more titles. For Southern California living at its best, call (800) 321-0372 and order your catalog.

Lots of "do it yourself" and "fix it" advice is available on the web. Try these: the Do It Yourself Network's site at diynet.com or doityourself.com, or eHow at ehow.com for instructions and advice on plumbing, carpentry, laying carpet, remodels, how to build anything or repair anything. RepairClinic.com. Also, michaelholigan.com of the Discovery Channel. I use google.com to search for instructions and advice on household problems, too, with amazing results. Advice from companies and people who have solved similar problems.

Housing

San Diego is considered to have one of the "least-affordable" housing markets in the nation. Of course, that is all relative. If you move here from San Francisco or Boston, you might think housing is cheap. Actually, the cost of living, *other than housing*, can be very affordable here. After all, you don't need a lot of winter clothing and coats, you don't need heat all winter or air conditioning all summer (unless you live inland), and the Southern California lifestyle is truly casual with some choosing shorts year round, eating less meat which lowers the food bill, and, there are so many free things to do! Utilities and gasoline are going up everywhere; we were just first. Other than housing, many people think San Diego can is actually *cheap!*! It can certainly be a really good deal if you conserve on energy and know where the bargains are! You can live cheaper elsewhere but you won't have all the amenities this area offers, or the no-can-beat weather. Following is a hodgepodge of helpful tips on housing.

CNN/Money Magazine reported that the cost of homes rose in most places during 2002, and San Diego was second among the ten hottest housing markets with a 26.6% increase in price in 2002. Sacramento was #1 with a 26.7% increase. The national average increase was 8%. The cost of housing has caused concern as it becomes less affordable, and San Diego is requiring builders to build more affordable housing. The median price of a home last year was $340,000, and the median price of a resale condo was $250K, but don't let that discourage you because half the homes on the market are below the median and half are priced above the median. So, there are plenty of homes out there on the market under $340K! They go fast, so you need to get informed and make a plan. (I would get a first time home buyer's book below.) A friend recently put in an offer on a 2-BR condo in Escondido for $125K. If you want to browse what's on the market, go to realtor.com or realestate.com, click on California, then San Diego, and you can enter a price range, number of bedrooms, or a zip code, etc, and up will come *hundreds* of listings. This way you won't waste your time or a realtor's while you become familiar with what is out there. Check back frequently. You can get a realtor when you are ready.

If you want to know how much home you can afford, go to the moneymag.com and click on Personal Finance. Everything you want is there. How much house you can afford, the cost of living in other cities compared to San Diego, the best mortgage rates, plus more.

San Diego is one of the cities where renters pay up to 46% of their income on rent. The average rent in San Diego for a studio is $792; 1BR, $942; 2BR, $1147; 3BR, $1437. In San Francisco, rents are about 30-40% higher.

Your goal should be to buy something IMMEDIATELY. Go in with friends and relatives. Get your ego out of the way and go buy the cheapest thing you can get. Plan to keep it five years and sell it, splitting the profits, so don't wait to invest in anything. It will just cost you more down the road.

In the meantime, if you want to reduce your housing costs *temporarily*, here are a few suggestions. These are not life sentences and you don't have to do them forever, but are quick-fix remedies that can bail your out of a high-cost housing situation so you can save some money: 1) Rent a room in someone's home (try a nice mansion in Mission Hills or La Jolla. There are plenty on the market, and you can live well while living economically. Who knows, you might find the ideal situation; 2) Rent out a room in your home or move out and rent the whole place; 3) If you don't own, you can rent a three-bedroom home or apartment and take in roommates or be a host "family" (singles OK) for international students (for pay); 4) Move onto a boat. Go down to the marina area and pick up a free yachting newspaper at any marina store and check the classified ads. Some boat owners need someone to live aboard their fabulous yachts as a caretaker while they live in Arizona or Empty Boot, Nebraska, and only visit San Diego occasionally. Or, consider buying a boat. Many boats on the market are distress sales where the owner needs OUT. Sometimes you can pick up a REALLY good deal. 5) Move to Iraq or Saudi Arabia and work for a couple years and come back and pay cash for a house! You will earn at least three times what you can earn here, and it's tax free after 18 months. Many people are doing this and coming back set for life! Check the classified job ads or ask a librarian for a book on overseas employment. 6) Become a property manager of an apartment complex and get free rent. Some also pay a salary. Check the employment classified ads for opportunities. 7) Shared Housing is a program sponsored by ElderHelp of San Diego, that matches people who have homes with an individual seeking a home. For more information, call (619) 284-9281.

Check out Room Mate Finders, 6110 Friars Road #201, Fashion Valley area, (619) 574-6876.   Hundreds of screened and qualified homes, apartments, condos and pre-screened, pre-qualified referrals.

Home loan rates are published every Sunday in the Home section of the *San Diego Union*. Banks give "A" loans to those with perfect credit histories, good salary/debt ratio. Other financial institutions and private investors offer "B" and "C" and "D" loans. Those who have late or missed payments or have bankruptcies a few years old, but have recent good credit, may be eligible to secure these loans despite being turned down by a bank. Interest rates vary, some are very high, but you can refinance when you are in a better financial situation. Check several sources. Look under "Mortgage Loans" and "Loans" in the *Yellow Pages* or the "Money to Lend" classified column of the *Union-Trib.* Check the Mortgage Mart at mortgagemart.com, bank rates at bankrate.com and Mortgage 101 at mortgage101.com.

To qualify for a home loan from a bank, generally speaking, you need about a 20% down payment. Your house payment cannot exceed 30% of your monthly income before taxes. Your total debt, including other outstanding loans, cannot exceed 38%. Fannie Mae and Freddie Mac are government sponsored enterprises that buy mortgages and package them as investments. They often team with lenders, nonprofits and state and local governments to help people get affordable mortgages. You CAN get financing with less than perfect credit. Then, in a couple years, you can get your credit cleaned up and refinance into an A loan.

For information on how to buy an FHA foreclosed home, contact the Housing and Urban Development office Web site at: hud.org.sdhud. The site includes a listing of homes in San Diego with addresses and prices, and information on how to how to buy one.

Freddie Mac-owned foreclosed properties: for a list, call (800) FREDDIE. And listen to the menu for the list. The list is available on the Web by state and city: homes.freddiemac.com

The Learning Annex and the community colleges offer classes on how to buy your first house, how to buy properties in foreclosure, how to buy investment properties. See "Continuing Education" for telephone numbers.

Home buying on the Net: the San Diego *Union-Tribune* has a database of thousands of existing homes for sale, new home projects and other home-buying resources. Includes photos and detailed information. Web site: signonsandiego and click on "Find a Home."

A brochure of tax-defaulted properties may be purchased over the counter for about $5 from the tax collector's office in Room 162 of the County Administration Building, 1500 Pacific Highway, (619) 531-5708. Maps and assessment information on these properties is available in Room 103, (619) 236-3771. Check this Web site: countyforeclosures.com for updated listing of homes and condos for sale. Posted every Friday afternoon.

If you buy a house, be sure to get a qualified California Real Estate Home Inspector, independent of your realtor, to examine the house for problems. This service costs about $350, and you will receive a report on the condition of plumbing, electrical, roof, etc. Also, get the one year insurance policy to cover anything that may fail in the first year, like furnace, swimming pool, etc. This costs about $600+ or so, depending on the home, but if something fails, it's covered. Ask your realtor about this. People say it is definitely worth it.

The ever popular Dummies books now offers a book entitled, *Home Buying for Dummies,* IDG, $16.99. Nolo Press, (800) 992-6656, offers two or three titles on how to buy or sell a home in California. A must have if you are in the market to buy or sell.

If you're buying a home, make one extra payment per year, and you can pay off your mortgage about 8 years earlier. Or, pay a little extra on your home mortgage every month to pay off your mortgage early. However, financial advisers suggest you invest first in a tax-deductible plan such as a 401(k) at work or a tax deductible individual retirement account first before you consider prepaying your . Second, pay off your high-rate credit card debts before you prepay your mortgage. Paying off your credit cards can earn you up to 17-18%. A 15-year mortgage instead of a 30-year mortgage will save 40% in interest.

For information on being a caretaker for a landowner (caretaker positions may include winterkeepers at lodges, camps, national & state parks, ecological preserves, managers for "gentleman" farmers and ranchers, caretakers of resort properties during off seasons, etc.), send a self-addressed, stamped envelope to: Caretaker Gazette, 1845 NW Deane Street, Pullman, WA 99163-3509.

Homes sell faster if occupied. Home Marketing Associates of Fairfield Connecticut (203) 256-1900 and Showhomes in Dallas (972) 243-1929, arrange for people with tons of fine furniture to move into million dollar homes that are on the market. The homes rent for cheap-cheap, but you must be prepared to move on short notice when the home sells. Call for further information.

Renters Assistance is offered through the San Diego Housing Commission. For further information, call (619) 685-1053.

First time home buyers may receive down payment assistance through Affordable Housing Applications (must meet certain income qualifications). Contact AHA at 9620 Chesapeake Drive, Ste 101, San Diego 92123, (619) 624-2330. Check their programs at ahahousing.com

The California Housing & Community Development program administers more than 20 programs awarding loans and grants related to housing, including the Home Investment Partnership Program. Log on to their web site at hcd.ca.gov/ca/index/html#fac. (They did not list a phone. Sorry.) These programs have many more applicants than they have opportunities for them, but if you persevere ... ...somebody gets them. If it take several years to get them, you'd be better off just trying to get into something NOW, with a friend, relative, co-investor. Property is going up too fast to wait five years to get into a program. It would take much more money to get into one in five years. Act now. ASAP.

Home improvement loans that are either low interest or don't have to be repaid until the house is sold are available from some cities (La Mesa is one) for seniors and/or low income individuals. For more information, call the San Diego Housing Commission at (619) 578-07521. Their web site is: sdhc.net/agencyprograms/housingrehabilitationprograms.

Information for Sale

You've seen those ads telling you to send $10 or so to receive information on how to get a government loan to start up a business, how to buy VA foreclosures, how to buy seized government property, how to buy a government vehicle for $50 . . .blah, blah. Don't do it! Don't be a sucker. What you will get is a page of information retyped from a government publication or just a government address to write to for the information. You can get that information *free* in any library, or call the toll free number for the Federal Consumer Information Center (F.C.I.C.), in Pueblo, CO, (888) 878-3256, and order the **free catalog** of free and low cost government publications, or view all the publications, free, on the web at pueblo.gsa.gov. Subjects include: the student guide to financial aid (grants, loans, work-study), how to buy federal personal property, government sales, public lands for sale, U.S. real property sales list, government medical and social security benefits, foods for lowering your high blood pressure, medical problems from anxiety to urinary problems, financing a home, energy-efficient homes improvements, weatherizing your home, powerSmart tips, living trusts, wills, estate planning, credit info including building better credit, identity theft, retirement planning, travel rights, a Consumer Action Handbook, guide to filing prescriptions online, and more.

For free information on how to do anything, go to findtutorials.com.

Insurance

To get the best deals on any insurance, always check six to 10 sources. They won't all be the same. Many companies offer a 10% discount if you carry more than one type of policy with them (for example, auto insurance + household, life, etc.) Also, the longer you stay with an auto insurance company, the more your rates go down. Be sure and ask for professional discounts and ask if there are other discounts available. For information about various insurance coverage, and to comparison shop for insurance, go to quotesmith.com, or msn.com/money or moneymag.com and click on insurance, or search insurance rates at google.com

To receive information about how insurance works, or if you have a complaint against an auto, health, homeowners, life or accident insurer, call the California Department of Insurance at (800) 927-4357. For an attorney who represents people whose insurance won't pay, call J. Widdecke at (619) 455-6286. If there is no recovery, there is no fee. What do you have to lose? Very often, insurance companies won't pay when they are supposed to and people don't understand that this is a game, and they have to get an attorney to make the insurance company pay. This is COMMON and many people feel they can't afford to sue, but is most cases, you don't pay until you get the insurance company to pay. You can get three free legal opinions. See the chapter on Legal. Also see Chapter 2 for how and where to complain about a consumer issue.

For health insurance, see Health. For auto insurance, see Automobiles.

Internet

About 68% of San Diegans use the internet, but if you haven't joined the Internet crowd yet, there's no time like NOW. It really isn't as intimidating as I thought it was and you can take FREE lessons. I can't believe I can do it, and it really is FUN. The first thing most people want it for is email (electronic-mail.) You can INSTANTLY send mail to your friends and businesses, no postage! Using the Internet, you can look up addresses and phone numbers of businesses and friends all over the U.S. (& world) (just click on Telephone books), pay your bills, do research on genealogy, find information about foreign countries (just type in the name of country you want), look up recipes, apply to colleges, take tours of museums and galleries around the world, look up government documents, find a job locally or anywhere in the world, read academic, scientific, educational, business and recreational web sites. You can shop on it, buy cars, antiques, clothes, books, read today's NYTimes or the Boston Globe, receive breaking news headlines from the top news media of your choice, search for an article you saw five years ago, "talk" to celebrities, sell your boat, sell all your old clothes and housewares on ebay, buy airline tickets, check the weather, make plane reservations, "visit" a foreign country and it's sites, print maps of how to get to a local restaurant or to another city, invest and manage your portfolio online, check the weather in any city, look up literary quotes, access libraries around the world, locate and print government forms, apply for a passport, etc. If you don't own a computer yet, see Computers for affordable new, used and reconditioned machines and free introductory to advanced computer classes, including introduction to the internet, finding things on the internet, how to set up a business on the internet, etc. etc. Some Internet Provider services are free, some cost $10-23 a month for unlimited use, or $29-49 for cable internet. It's sure worth the price. My friend in Florida saves hundreds of dollars EVERY month ordering her prescriptions online! You can learn how to do the internet at learnthenet.com. Can u believe?!

Changing your internet service provider and would like to have your email forwarded? A company called Re-Route.com retreives your email, readdresses it, and sends it to your new e-mail address. Cost is about $10 for one month, $25 for three months. Go to re-route.com

Jewelry

Never-never-never-never-never pay full price for jewelry. Since the markup on jewelry is often 200-500%, you can understand why there are so many 50% off sales!! If you fall in love with a piece that isn't on sale, you can certainly try to negotiate the price. If not, ask when the next sale is. You can be taken advantage of if you have little or no knowledge or experience in buying jewelry, so I've included a mini-course in gold, silver and diamond jewelry. Here are some places to shop for jewelry to fit any budget . . . from shoestring to plush bucks.

Costco Wholesale Warehouse & **Sam's Club** carry some high end diamond earrings to $3,359 and 1.33 carat ring for $4,700, gold jewelry, watches from $78 to $4,000 and appraised at more, all sold at a discount. Beautiful; really good buys. Bracelets, necklaces, rings, earrings. Ask about periodic special jewelry events where they bring in a ton of watches, or gold jewelry, or diamond jewelry. Yum.

Sid Allen Jeweler, 501 W. Broadway, Suite 250 in the Koll Center downtown, (619) 232-8666. Gold, diamonds, pearls, onyx and others. Specializing in ideal cuts and premium cut diamonds. Large selection of wedding bands and engagement rings for about 50% off retail price with documented appraisal.

Fine jewelry sales at major department stores feature diamonds, gold and other fine gems, 25-50%, sometimes up to 70%+ off. Anniversary and holiday sales can be anticipated, so if you can put off your purchase until then, you're better off. Ask a sales associate when the next sale is. Oprah had a guest on her show that said she tracked sale days at Macy's, and only five days in a month were NOT sale days. Ask to be placed on the mailing list and you will receive advance sales information.

Before you plunk out serious bucks for a piece of jewelry, check with the

Better Business Bureau, (858) 496-2131, to see if there are complaints against the store. Find out about the store's return policy. Get in writing that your money is fully refundable if an outside appraisal does not compare (do not use an appraiser recommended by the store). Be sure the seller writes a detailed description of the jewelry (golds, diamond karats, weight, points, color characteristics, etc.) on the sales slip.

Look for the karat mark on gold jewelry (10K, 14K, 18K, 24K.) The mark is usually on the inside or back of a piece. If it doesn't have a marking, it may be less than 10 karat required for an item to be sold as gold in the U.S. Jewelry marked 24K is solid gold, very yellow in color and is soft. European and Asians countries use 22K or 24K in gold jewelry. American made jewelry has alloys added to make it stronger, and the alloy gives the gold its characteristic hues. Jewelry marked 18K contains 75% gold, or 18 parts gold and six parts nickel or other alloy (shown as "750" on European-made gold jewelry). Jewelry marked 14K contains 58.5% gold, or 14 parts gold and 10 parts alloy (shown as "585" on European jewelry). Jewelry marked 10K is 41.7% gold, or 10 parts gold and 14 parts alloy (shown as "417" on European jewelry. Ten karat gold is used for class rings, etc. It is the lowest karatage that can be sold in the U.S. (The lowest in Mexico is 8K). The higher the karat, the deeper and richer (and more beautiful!) the color of the gold is. Jewelry that displays the karat mark must also have the manufacturer's registered trademark. If it doesn't have a trademark, don't buy it, except in cases of some antique pieces. Unfortunately, about 1/3 of the jewelry checked for karats by one of the TV investigative news shows failed to have the full karatage. It was marked 18K but was less than 75% gold, so be sure to use a reputable jeweler and get a guarantee. The retail price of a gold piece is related to the gold karatage and weight, whether it is hollow or solid, machine made or handmade, and the craftsmanship, artistry and design. The clasp should be the same karatage as the jewelry. Compare the karats of the clasp and the jewelry to be sure they are the same. Save your important, *major* jewelry purchases for a store with a solid reputation, and pass on traveling shows, swap meets and mall karts except for lesser expensive items. Gold sells for about $350 or more an ounce, and fluxuates daily with the market.

Gold-filled (or gold-plate) jewelry is made from a metal that has had layers of gold (usually 10K) mechanically bonded. The gold content must be at least 20% of the total weight of the metal. Although gold-filled jewelry usually lasts a long time, the gold eventually wears away with use. Some jewelers can "re-gold" a piece for less than you might imagine. Fast Fix Jewelers is a great place to get jewelry fixed, replated, etc.

Sterling silver jewelry is marked either "Sterling" or "925." This is international. Be sure to check for the number in Mexico, where you can get some very good buys on silver, and you can also be fooled, too.

Diamonds are an investment, and you need to feel confident that you are buying from a reputable store. Department stores and large chain jewelry stores like Zales offer diamonds, but you can often get comparable diamonds for less money at independent jewelers, antique stores, auctions, pawn shops and through the classified ads. You can arrange an appraisal for around $50 or so. The Gemological Institute of America gives a report on most diamonds over one carat, so ask to see it. With your purchase, you will receive a certificate. There are four things that determine the value of a diamond: the cut, color, clarity and weight. The cut determines the capacity to reflect light or sparkle. A well cut diamond reflects light from one facet to another and then disperses it through the top of the stone. "Cut" is not to be confused with "shape" (popular shapes are round, marquis, oval, pear, emerald and heart). As far as color goes, the more colorless, the more valuable; some diamonds have a yellowish or brownish tint. The color grading scale goes from "D" (completely colorless) to "Z" (muddy yellow with gray or brownish tones). The majority of diamonds sold are rated "G" through "J." Clarity is the number of spots or "inclusions" in the diamond. The clearer or more flawless, the more valuable. Clarity is rated from "F1" (flawless) to "I_3" (imperfect with many inclusions). The weight is the size or number of carats. The depth or distance from the top to the bottom should be about 58-61% of the width of the stone. Ask to see the diamond under the jeweler's 10-power magnification after looking at it with your naked eye. For more information on buying diamonds, including photos on how to judge diamond quality, buy the *Diamond Ring Buying Guide* by Renee Newman at major book stores, or send $16.45 to International Jewelry Publications, POBox 13384, Los Angeles, CA 90013-0384. This book describes imitations, flaws, fractures, finding a good buy, the effect of shape on the price, estimating carat weight versus size, color categories, "ideal cuts" and how different cuts affect the price, how to judge brilliance and more. People buy diamonds for pleasure or investment. Quality diamonds have steadily increased in value the past several years. (Renee Newman also has books on buying emeralds, pearls, rubys & sapphires and a gold jewelry buying guide. It pays to know something about how to select your investment piece, or how to identify that fabulous find at the swap meet!)

Now that you have all this knowledge, you can shop for jewelry bargains that are advertised in classified ads. Couples divorce and sell their diamonds and other jewelry. Buy a jeweler's magnifying glass and a couple books on jewelry and you're in biz. You might want to attend/join the San Diego Gem Society (see below) & learn more.

JCPenneys has a "trade-up" policy. If you buy a diamond and later want a larger one, you can trade up, provided you go 50% higher than the price of the original diamond. They issue a certificate upon purchase that never expires. Their diamonds are in the mid-range quality; color: G to J, and clarity, I1 to 3.

Gary Gilmore Goldsmith, 4919 Newport Avenue, Ocean Beach, (619) 225-1137, can test your gold jewelry for under $10 and tell you what karat it is. Or, they can administer an acid test that will determine if an item is gold, but not the karat, for about $3.

Saks Fifth Avenue has a once a year fine jewelry sale the first two weeks of August, 25% off. So nice.

Many department stores offer 10% off on first day purchases when opening an account. Worth looking into if you're shopping for a gem.

Mervyn's has a 50% off jewelry sale about once every other month or so, and a 60-70% off sale a few times a year on Super Weekends. Their styles are limited, but a retired New York professional jeweler told me Mervyn's carries quality jewelry.

Imposters, 110 Horton Plaza, (619) 233-6733 and North County Fair. Imposters has over 30 stores in the U.S., and specializes in copies of Cartier, Tiffany and other fine jewelry by designers like David Yurman, Lagos, Bulgari. Some gold, but mainly gold vermeil (gold plate over silver). They have a look-alike of a Cartier ring ($8,500) for $65; a Cartier necklace ($10,500) for $75. A Tiffany-look alike diamond bracelet made in X's, $95. Replicas of the blue heart necklace from the movie *Titanic*, $65. Lots of large, fashionable fake jewels, etc. A delightful place. I would *love* a Cartier necklace. But, then, I say to myself: "Self, where would you wear it . . . to a garage sale?!?" (The REAL Tiffany store is located in Fashion Valley, but there is a jewelry store across from Imposters that has *real* Cartier jewelry, and the copies are really CLOSE! Check their web site at: premierjewelry.com.

World famous jewelry designer Kenneth J. Lane, who designed for Jackie O, has recreated copies of her famous pearls and sells them on QVC for $76. He also offers replicas of Barbara Bush's famous single strand pearls ($68), Hillary Clinton's inaugural pearl necklace ($45), and copies of 29 jewelry treasures from the Duchess of Windsor's collection, $20 up. All are sold on QVC shopping channel, (800) 345-1515. Call for info. Web: qvc.com.

Pawn Shops have interesting one-of-a-kind jewelry, and judging from what I've seen, some very wealthy ladies sell their very expensive jewelry to pawn brokers! This could be lucky for you. Ask for the manager and negotiate the price. You're dealing with a pro but with perseverance and a little luck, you can do some very good negotiating here. See *Yellow Pages* for pawn shop listings. I love a good pawn shop! Their jewelry is unique, one of a kind and has that "old gold" patina. I love 18K. old gold.

There is a whole building downtown, the Jewelers Exchange building, at 861 6th, (619) 232-9191 with over 80 jewelers. This should keep you busy for a while. Wholesale, retail, jewelry manufacturers. Repairs.

George Carter Jessop Jewelers located in the Emerald Plaza, State and C Streets, offers quality jewelry, new and from estates. They will buy your heirloom pieces. Meet with their certified gemologist appraiser; by appointment only. Appraisals are $75 an hr., with a $50 minimum. Sell the diamond from your ring and replace it with a quality cubic zirconia. (Jessop's said: "That's what they're doing out there.") Cash or consignment. Call (619) 234-4137 for more information.

There are over 300 fine jewelers in the **International Jewelry District** (near the Garment District) in downtown Los Angeles that sell to the public at below retail costs (some say the best prices on the West Coast). I never saw so much jewelry in my life. Well, not since I was in New York. Not all sell to the public, buy many do in the St. Vincent Jewelry Center, "the world's largest jewelry center," 650 S. Hill Street, (213) 629-2124. Ready made, custom design, restoration, repair. The California Jewelry Mart is located at 607 S. Hill Street, (213) 627-2831; over 200 showrooms, but some are exclusively wholesale.

If you're into natural or ethnic jewelry, there are some wonderful buys at swap meets, Cost Plus and Pier One. And, I like the natural jewelry at the gift shops at the Museum of Man and the Museum of Natural History in Balboa Park, and at The Galleria (very pricey) at Bazaar Del Mundo in Old Town. I have a gorgeous turquoise work of art necklace from the Galleria, and I pick up a lot of interesting pieces at garage and estate sales, too. (You betcha I do!)

I love to go to the Gem Faire, (760) 747-9215, which has tons of beads (great buys), mineral, fossils, crystals, antique and estate jewelry, jeweler's supplies, metaphysical items, tools and equipment for making jewelry, demonstrations. They all want to clean your jewelry for free, and if you need a piece repaired, it's a good place to take it; they often fix it on the spot (sometimes free!) or give an estimate for repairs. Classes on beading, wirewrapping, etc. Most shows are held at the Scottish Rite Center, Del Mar Fairgrounds or the convention center. I'm on the mailing list and receive advance notification, which always includes a discount coupon. Web site: gemfaire.com. The International Gems, Beads & Jewelry Show is held at the Del Mar Fairgrounds and is a showplace and marketplace for gems of the world. Free jewelry cleaning. For more info, go to intergem.net. For information on other gem shows, contact the San Diego Gemological Society, (619) 588-0065.

The Gemological Institute of American offers training in the gem and jewelry industry in Carlsbad, (800) 421-7250; www.gia.edu. Call for tours and open house dates. Their site offers information on gemstones. The S.D. Lapidary Society offers jewelry classes, field trips, gem show in June, more, (858) 277-0240.

Design your own engagement ring at diamondisforever.com. Tons of rings to browse through.

Check TV Shopping, this chapter, for more on jewelry from the shopping channels. Good buys on 18K, 14K gold; faux jewelry; designer copies when they have their jewelry "events."

A. L. Jacobs and Sons at 1450 Frazee Rd, #402, (619) 294-7038, evaluates, buys and sells estate jewelry. If you want to sell a piece, you won't get much for it, but you'll get an idea of what it's worth. You might do better selling it on ebay, setting a minimum you'll take for it.

Here are some jewelry web sites for faux jewelry (copies of name brand jewelry by top designers). Earrings, necklaces, rings, watches.

fashion-watches.net	replicaone.com
brilliantalternatives.com	anyknockoff.com
replicasunlimited.com	bluenile.com

Leather & Luggage

The factory outlet malls seem to have the most stores with off-price leather goods. The Carlsbad outlets has the Coach Factory outlet (discounted pricey Coach purses!), Booney & Bourke (pricey handbags at discounted prices), Samsonite Company (large selection of Samsonite and American Tourister luggage, briefcases, computer cases, travel accessories and more) and Wilson's Leather. Viejas Outlets has another Samsonite and Wilson's, and Las Americas Outlets has Samsonite and Wilson's, too.

Every other leather store I had listed in the previous edition is now GONE.

I have purchased **briefcases** at great prices on sale with a discount coupon at Office Depot, from department store ½ price sales, at swap meets and yard sales (which have, of course, the best prices!) In fact, I got a brand new leather faux alligator briefcase for $5. Still had tags on it. It was a gift to a guy who said it wasn't his "thing." Swap meets also have excellent deals on leather luggage, purses, wallets, fanny packs, etc. Really good prices. I have been getting my leather wallets there for years!

People pick up a lot of leather goods in Tijuana at very reasonable prices. Also, the better stores like Sara's have Italian imports, cheaper than in the U.S.

Linens

I do very well at department store sales on linens, sheets, down comforters and towels. I like quality linens but never pay full price for them because there seems to always be a sale going on. Here are a few stores where you don't have to wait for sales and I love them all.

Bed Bath & Beyond Mission Valley Center, (619) 295-9888) and stores in Chula Vista, Mira Mesa, Oceanside, San Diego and Santee. Call (800) 462-3966 for locations. Their large stores have everything from linens to organizers, draperies, decorator pillows, storage containers and so much more. There are frequent 20% off coupons in their ads in the Union-Trib, and they accept competitors' coupons. Their guarantee is that they will not be undersold. **Linens 'n Things** (La Jolla, (858) 452-4348, Carmel Mt. Ranch, (858) 674-1101; Encinitas, (760) 436-9687) is another chain that has huge stores, enormous selections, and frequent sales.

Sales on linens at Macy's and Robinsons-May are frequent, and they offer additional discount coupons in their weekend ads in the *Union-Trib*. Hard to beat. Burlington Coat Factory, Ross, T. J. Maxx, Stein Mart and Nordstrom Rack carry luxury linens at bargain prices. I have been known to truck around to SEVERAL of their stores in order to pull together a set of matching coordinates for a SONG. Tuesday Morning has GREAT sales of linens including sheets, blankets, down comforters, mattress pads, bath towels, etc. with great prices. Polo Ralph Lauren and Versace outlets have some of their designer line of linens. Linens n Things and Bed Bath and Beyond will blow you away with their huge selections and they have frequent sales. Mervyns has fashionable name brand linens on sale all the time. If you're looking for name brand bargains, **Big Lots** gets in some fine quality name brand linens closeouts. Very good prices, Cannon, Springmaid, Wamsutta $50 comforters for $19.

Kmart carries Martha Stewart's new coordinated linens including two lines: Blue Label with 180 threads, and White Label with 200 threads (200 threads are softer, smoother and cost a little more). She offers ten different designs of color coordinated sheets, pillows, bed skirts, comforters, blankets, bathmats and towels that you can mix and match. Shower curtains, bath accessories, too Martha has her own line of color coordinated paint as low as $11.99 when on sale, and window treatments. Kmart's web site is kmart.com, and the troubled Martha's own site is: marthastewart.com.

PROGRAM SPEAKER

Sally Gary, author
The Best Deals & Steals In San Diego

PRESENTATIONS FOR

Brown Bag Lunches	Professional Groups
Staff Appreciation Day	Charities
Professional Growth Day	Social Organizations
Secretary's Week	Church Group
Staff Development	Seniors
	PTAS

Fun and Informative Topic
"It's like a pay raise..."
Sally Gary, (619) 222-8489
Email: Sallygary@cox.net or Sallygary@aol.com

Mattresses

The best quality bed you can afford is worth it's weight in gold. A quality mattress will last longer and some top of the line mattresses will have warranties up to 15 years on sagging. They give better back support. The life expectancy of a mattress is about 10 years, but a cheap mattress will sag earlier and give you a backache. Remember, at 8 hours a day, you spend 1/3 of your life horizontal, so invest in good bedding. It affects not only how you sleep, but how you feel in the morning and throughout your day. It is difficult to comparison shop for mattresses because major bedding manufacturers such as Sealy, Simmons and Serta all make several models for each of the stores they distribute to. The same model will have a different name and different color cover at each store! Ask a sales associate to explain the different features of their mattresses to you. The more coils, the higher the quality and the more the mattress can respond to differing sleep positions. The more padding on the coils, the more comfortable, etc. A good mattress is an investment but a cheap mattress won't last, the cover will tear, it will sag and you'll get a backache. Ask about returns if you get it home and discover you can't sleep on it. A friend and I bought the exact same mattress at a major department store; she paid full price, I got mine on sale, half price, because I watched the newspaper and waited for it to go on sale! I've noticed they're repeatedly on sale for half price! Tips: a down comforter and pillows (on sale, naturally) will make for The Perfect Sleep (get non-allergenic pillow covers if you're allergic to down, available at Mervyns, etc). Buy mattresses from a reputable dealer who will be in business in the future if/when it sags. And, here's a great tip from *Backache Relief* by A. Klein. Put thick plywood between your box springs and mattress, and buy a six inch thick foam rubber mattress (from UFO in Chula Vista) to put on top of your regular mattress. If you have any allergies, get a non-allergenic zip-on mattress cover (from Burlington Coat Factory in Clairemont. I couldn't find one any where else!) Ahh, comfort. Next time, tho, I will get one of those space age memory foam mattress toppers from TechnoScout, (800) 231-3511.

There are endless mattress discounters in San Diego, and they advertise like crazy in the U-T and on TV, with mattresses starting at $75. And, there is always a sale going on. Inquire about unmatched or mismatched pieces for savings. A new mattress might do fine on your old box springs. If you're on a small budget, Salvation Army has used, sanitized mattresses in good condition.

Men's Clothing, Etc.

Men's Wearhouse, Mission Valley (619) 294-6660 plus 8 other locations in San Diego. Call (800) 776-7848 for store near you. Men's Wearhouse carries top quality designer fashions and shoes at 20-30% less than department stores, every day, plus their own styles. Big and tall sizes, also. Big sale once a year after Christmas including tuxes. Free re-tailoring for life. Free pressing for life in between cleanings. Two sales a year, one in mid July, the other around the end of the year. Many Tommy Bahama type styles, but less expensive models.

Men's Fashion Depot, 3730 Sports Arena Blvd, (Sports Arena area), (619) 222-9570; The Men's Fashion Depot buys designer suits that are sold in major department stores directly from the manufacturer. They are discounted about 50%+, with suits priced from $99-$400 and sport coats from $69-$139; silk ties, $9-18/value to $35+. Tuxedos, from $109; tux shirts, 2/$30 ($27 elsewhere). Suits that sell here for $230 are $400 at department stores. Calvin Klein, DKNY, Jones New York suits, $199, sell for $425-650 elsewhere. Personalized service, too. Next door is a men's discount shoe store, with a different owner.

3 Day Suit Broker 2120 Camino Del Rio North, Mission Valley, (619) 293-7555. Large store you can't miss seeing from Interstate 8 in Mission Valley. This store is only open three days a week, Thursdays thru Saturdays, and is part of a chain of 12 other stores, mainly in Orange County and L.A. Prices like: leather jacket $69 (compare at $199); pants $49.90 (compare at $35); dress shirts $9.90 (compare at $22.90); sport coats, $59; (compare at $150); silk ties, $7.99 (compare at $25); tuxedos $79 (compare $225).

Nordstrom Rack in Mission Valley Center, (619) 296-0143, has a good selection of marked down men's clothing from the Nordstrom main stores (plus some items are ordered in just for sales), including pure wool suits ($169-289), sport shirts ($14-19), special purchase silk ties, $5-20; good selection of sweaters, slacks, sport coats, shoes, etc. The Rack has frequent sales with further markdowns.

Polo Ralph Lauren, Carlsbad Company Stores, off Palomar Rd & I5, (760) 929-2898; also at Viejas. This is a large store that carries a lot of casual wear, sweaters, polo shirts, turtlenecks, Oxford shirts, pants, suits, sport coats at 20-50% off. Mostly first quality; some slight irregulars. There is another store in Tijuana at 7th Street and Madero, (Tijuana), 011-52-664-685-13-89, within walking distance to the border. Everything is made in Mexico City but they have the license from Ralph Lauren in New York.

Carlsbad Company Stores, off Interstate 5 & Palomar Airport Rd on Paseo Del Norte, (760) 804-9000; (888) 790-SHOP; **Barney's New York**, (760) 929-9600. Upscale men's clothing, lots of suits at half off original prices of $400-$2000. Barney's private label suits are made at the Armani factory and are knock-offs. Sportswear, golfwear, ties, shirts. Other outlets in the mall include: **Tommy Hilfiger**, **Big Dog Sportswear, FILA, GAP, Polo Ralph Lauren**, **Jones New York Men**, **Banana Republic**, **Brooks Bros.**, and more. See Factory Outlets this chapter.

Las Americas Outlets, Camino del la Plaza, San Ysidro, has a **Van Heusen Factory Store**, (619) 934-7363, with quality current season men's apparel at 30-60% discounts; **Levi's & Dockers by Most**, (619) 690-3218, with jeans, jackets, shirts for men (women and children, too) plus Dockers. **Old Navy** and **Geoffrey Beene** outlets; **Designer Studio**, (619) 662-9571, fashions from Versace, Moscino, Ralph Lauren, Iceberg, all discounted.

Costco carries a number of great buys for men. Designers have included Tommy Hilfiger, Fila, DKNY, Calvin Klein, Polo Ralph Lauren. Jack Nicklaus short sleeve knit shirts, $10.50; Bill Blass knits, $14, Options 100% silk sport coat, $60; J.G. Chappel wool blazer, $99. You won't find these regularly, but you will find the best quality designer they are able to get a good deal from.

Versace, Desert Hills Factory Outlet Mall, (909) 922-9111, and one is coming to Las Americas in the 2004-5. This is a company owned store that carries in-season and past-season men's fashions (women's too.) All items arrive at the store at 50% off the retail price. Jeans that sell in Neiman Marcus and Saks for $160-$325 and suits that sell elsewhere for $1400-2500 come in at half price, and reduced from there, plus additional sales. Fragrances are 20% off. Some home accessories, decorator items and sheets, etc. Call to be on the mailing list for sales, and ask when they are expecting their next BIG shipment!

Watch for the big sales at Macy's (Pre-Season sale in August), the Nordstrom (half yearly sale in June, November) and big sales at other department stores. Call to get on the mailing list to be notified of forthcoming sales. Open an account and you will be automatically advised of future sales. Macy's and other stores offer a 10% on everything you purchase the first day you open an account. So, go to your closet and make separate lists (include colors) of each of the following: all your sport coats, all your suits, all your slacks, all your shirts and all your ties. Make a list of what you need to complete and/or update your wardrobe. Then, wait for Macy's next big men's sale (or call and ask about it). Take in any items you don't have coordinating clothing to wear with and ask a sales associate to match them up for you. You'll get 10% off everything you buy (even if on sale) for opening your account and they frequently have a 10% off coupon in the newspaper. You can use that, too!! Nordstrom also has a free Personal Shopper who will sit down with you and help you create the wardrobe of your dreams or an outfit for a special occasion or on an ongoing basis. Look your best, easily.

Check men's stores: Gentlemen's Resale Clothier, A Better Deal and Tuxedo Discount (used tux shops) plus vintage stores under Resale/Consignment this section. Thrift stores like Goodwill sell all men's jeans for $8.95, slacks & joggers, $6.99; shirts (pullovers) $2.79; dress shirts, $3.29; sport coats, $8.19; plus suits mostly $20, some higher.

For more men's clothing, see Discount/Off-Price Stores, Resale and Consignment and Factory Outlets this chapter.

Office Equipment/Supplies/Furniture/Stationery

Office Depot and **Staples** have hundreds of stores nationally and carry everything you need under one roof including computers, software, equipment, furniture and office supplies. Great specials and sales, and you get 20%+ off coupons in the catalog if you're on their mailing list. Lots of incentives including a discount if you order online the first time.

Costco & Sam's Club have great buys on computers, office supplies and equipment, plus they have an office products catalog offering thousands of additional office supply and furniture items. Free delivery on orders over $250; under $250 order delivery fee is $20 delivery. Walmart, Kmart and Target have great inexpensive file cabinets, plastic storage boxes & office accessories.

Check the *Union-Trib* classified ads #3000 Business Equipment and Business Inventory #3010 and the #3190 Thrifties Many businesses have closed so you have plenty of desks, file cabinets, phone systems, computers, furniture, etc. to choose from for a fraction of the original cost. I picked up a great wrap-around desk and chair for a song. Also, see Auctions 2000 in the classified ads for used office equipment sold by the government and by liquidators.

A-1 Liquidators Inc operates a warehouse with hundreds of pieces of used office furniture, desks, credenzas, conference tables, bookcases, chairs, file cabinets, plus new factory closeouts, 9530 Cabot Drive off Miramar Road, (858) 689-2324. Buy/sell.

PS Business Interiors has tons of used office furniture in a large warehouse with desks, file cabinets, chairs, book cases, tables at 5710 Kearny Villa Rd, Ste. B, Clairemont, (858) 268-0440. Buy/sell.

Here are a few other places to call for office furniture: **Cort Furniture Rental Clearance Center**, 9150 Clairemont Mesa Blvd, (858) 277-6205. **Office Furniture Outlet**, Miramar Rd., new and used, (619) 271-9700; **Office Again Inc,** gently used office furniture, 10,000 sq. ft., at 5750 Kearny Villa Rd, (858) 268-9617.

Gypsy Office Supply, 3409 30th Street, North Park, (619) 295-1553. This place purchases a lot of crates of partially damaged office supplies and sells them for a fraction of the retail price. You can't get everything here, but almost. They often have used copiers, fax machines, sometimes computers. Lots of paper, pens, staplers, files, stickers and the gamut of office supplies, new, used, some slightly damaged boxes, some not. Furniture, file cabinets, etc. Fun place. It won't be around forever because the owner of the property wants to build apartments on the lot in the future.

Check out the vendors at swap meets who sell stationery, office and school supplies. When you buy your ticket, ask for their location. Big savings.

American Stationery Co., mail order only with savings up to 45% off, wide variety of personalized stationery, wedding invitations and accessories, (800) 822-2577. Invitation Hotline, 25% off invitations seen in printers big books, (800) 800-4355x921.

Look under Paper Products in the *Yellow Pages* for good prices on stationery, envelopes, color paper, invitations. I like go to Kelly's Paper, but the cute dude with the amazing green eyes doesn't work there anymore. Phoo.

See Computers and Auctions this chapter for more opportunities to pick up discounted new and used office equipment, furniture and supplies.

Online Shopping

Analysts predict that half of today's retailers may be driven out of business within the next 10 years due to online shopping, as many corporations now offer Web sites for viewing, browsing and ordering. Consumers are opting for the convenience of online shopping, as they are finding stores an increasingly frustrating experience when they go in and can't find what they are looking for, customer service is scant and employees are uninformed. Take a look at consumerworld.org, a non-commercial site which has gathered over 1,700 useful consumer resources on the Internet and categorized them. Go to Compare.net which offers a free online buyer's guide that allows users to compare features on more than 10,000 products. Take a look a Shopping.com and ValueAmerica at VA.com and Internetmall.com. Take a look at bluefly.com, which carries goods from over 400 top designers and is one of the most popular sites for online shopping. Sign up to get email notification of their sales from any or all of them. You can shop at bloomingdales.com, lord&taylor.com, neimanmarcus.com, jcpenney.com, ant top sites that get millions of monthly visitors like The Gap at gap.com, oldnavy.com, fredericks.com, victoriassecret.com, landsend.com, payless.com and more. You can buy airline tickets, perfume, cars, wine, books, jewelry, hardware, shop at museum gift shops, you name it. Millions of new shoppers are giving this a try, and although most are satisfied with delivery, there have been some problems with inventory shortages and items delivered late. Many online sites will search the Web for the product you want and produce a list of retailers in your area. Try shopping.com, buycentral.com, or mysimon.com. Or, you can type in what you want at yahoo.com ("Where can I find designer hand bags?", etc, and up will come a list of sites for you.) You can compare prices at bestdeal.com, ecompare.com, and comsumerworld.com. The web has it's scams, so be sure you are dealing with a reputable firm. Check the online Better Business Bureau at bbb.com. Ebay, the online e-auction leader, has everything under the sun for sale, much is used, but much is also brand new and offered by e-stores with large inventories. Check them out at ebay.com. Andy's Garage sale mixes liquidations, closeouts and clearances with famous names like Rubbermaid, Sanyo and more at andysgarage.com. Goodle.com has added a new search engine for buying merchandise. Go to froogle.com and type in what you are looking for from A to Z. UP will come a gazillion sources, and you refine your search from there. For freebies, go to totallyfreestuff.com, 4freestuff.com, or just type in "free" at a search engine and see what comes up. That'll keep you busy!

Paint

If you can use them, you can't beat the price on "OOPS" paints at Home Depot. "Oops" paints have been custom-blended for a customer and for whatever reason, the customer didn't want the paint, so they mark it down to about 1/3 the regular price. If the color is right for you, you can cash in on the savings. There's everything from pints to quarts of flat or enamel ($1) to gallons for $5 and five-gallon drums of interior and exterior paints ($20 up). Their regular paints are at good prices, too, because of their volume buying, and they have holiday sales with $3 off Behr paints. Home Depot carries Ralph Lauren designer paints in gourmet colors and textures, $20.95 per gallon for flat wall paint; $9.92 per quart for satin finish metallics (his stencils, too). Ask when they will have free classes in paint techniques: color wash, faux glazing, blocking, stenciling.

"Do-it-yourself-from-scratch-Diva Martha Stewart" now has her own line of designer paints carried at Kmart for *only* paints ($16.99 or $12.99 during sales!), which are different from her ultra-designer line, but they are *her* designer colors. Kmart carries her new mid-priced color coordinated linens, too. . . . I understand Martha is off to the Himalayas now . . . . in search of top quality oxygen . . . to make her own line of . . . ...designer water .. (H2O)

There is a paint sale at all paint stores just before every major holiday when people have time off and can tackle a paint project. Why pay $22 a gallon for paint if you can get it on sale for $16 or ? There is a holiday in almost every calendar month, so keep a look out for the sales.

"Better" paint is usually a better buy because cheaper paints drip, fade, don't cover as well, require more coats, don't last as long and don't wash up well. And, remember Murphy's Law: "Any paint will adhere permanently to any surface if applied accidentally!" (Unfortunately.) Check Walmart's paints which were rated excellent in Consumer Reports.

Stencils & Interiors, 973-B Lomas Santa Fe Dr, Solana Beach, (858) 509-1775; has extraordinary stencils from over 25 designers for walls and furniture. Stenciling & faux finishing classes. Bayside Paints, 1228 Knoxville, (near I5 & Sea World Dr., (858) 275-7800, offers faux-finishing instruction and supplies, paint specialties.

Party Supplies

Party City, Pt. Loma, (619) 523-9200; Carmel Mtn., Chula Vista, El Cajon, Encinitas, Mission Valley, National City, Oceanside, Rancho San Diego. Open seven days. Party supplies galore, gift wrap, personalized cards. Really discounted prices, many 50% and more. Greeting cards are always 30-50% off. Special occasion decor; balloons. Michael's has lots of good buys on party supplies and special occasion decor, too. Costco and Smart and Final are great for paper plates, napkins, plastic glasses, etc. in bulk. Get great children's party favors at **Max's 99¢ Stores** or any other 99¢ store. Some party favors are 3/$1. See Clearance Centers.

Check **Florist Supplies** in the *Yellow Pages*. I had a fabulous time at Dave's Displays downtown and the San Diego Florist Supply on El Cajon Boulevard. They have an incredible array of decorations.

Buy special occasion party supplies and cards (St. Patty's Day, Valentine's Day, 4th of July, Christmas, etc.) *on sale* at real savings the day *after* the holiday, for next year. Gift shops, party supply stores, supermarkets, drug stores, Robinsons-May, etc. have 50% or more off seasonal items the day after holidays, sometimes they mark them down on the day *of* the holiday.

Grossmont Nutrition & Gifts in the Grossmont Shopping center has greeting cards, 4/$1, always (619) 465-5225. **Big Lots** carries quite a few greeting cards, for all occasions at a discount. Gift wrap, gift bags, etc. See Clearance Stores for a Big Lots near you.

Oriental Trading Company offers zillions of party decorations & favors for birthdays, holiday decor for all occasions, hats, masks, balloons, flags, banners, hula skirts, theme party stuff, unbeatable prices. You must get this catalog if you need anything for parties, schools, organizations, etc. (800) 228-2269; web: oriental.com. More online party supplies and special occasion decorations and ideas at partyzone.com.

Pawn Shops

Pawn shops have been around since ancient times, and it was during the Middle Ages that the three golden balls became a symbol for them. They sell a lot of very nice gold jewelry, gemstones and watches, plus a number of other things like TV's, silver, china, cameras, stereos, etc. They are usually Mom 'n Pop operations, so you can try to negotiate the price here. All goods are held for police clearance to see if they are stolen prior to selling them. If you want to pawn (or borrow money) on an item for a short period, they will lend about 25% of the value of an item (but probably never more than 50% of its sales value), and hold it in a vault. This "loan" is for a period usually from 30 days to 4 months, with a 60-day grace period. (This varies). Usually the loan can be extended provided the interest is paid; otherwise, if the item is not redeemed or the interest paid, the item is forfeited, and then sold. The interest charges are set by local laws and are very steep, but you can get small loans of a few hundred dollars or so that banks aren't willing to bother with. Pawn shops are a great place to shop for jewelry, but you can get more money by selling your items elsewhere. See *Yellow Pages* for Pawn Shop listings.

Pets

People have told me how WONDERFUL this section is, how helpful it is and how much they appreciate it. Included are listings of places to visit to select your new pet (consider adoptable ones first from Animal Control

Shelters, humane societies or a breed rescuer before you buy one), places to leave off a pet if you can no longer to keep it, a wildlife rescue number to call if you find an injured blue heron in your driveway or a possum family made a home under your shed, what to do if your pet is lost, or if you find one, or need to rent a $4 trap to catch a stray cat, or where to get your pets spayed for about $20, or euthanized if necessary. Lots of goodies follow, as San Diego has many animal rescue, adoption agencies and animal welfare organizations.

Lost or found pets. Department of Animal Control had a telephone line hotline, an automated system, but at this printing, the recording said: Pet Link is currently not in service. Please call animal control at (619) 236-4250 and report your pet." Pet Link may be reinstated, but I don't know at this time. The *Union-Tribune* provides free ads in their Lost & Found classified section. The finder can place a free three-day ad announcing what they found. Another place to check is PetFinder, a national service with local listings on the internet. Check their web site at petfinder.org. Another service devoted to lost, found and adoptable pets is called 1-800-Save-A-Pet and can be reached at (800) SaveaPet. Web site: 1800saveapet.com. If all else fails, call Glorious Antiques or The Ark in La Jolla (see Antiques, earlier this chapter). Their profits benefit animals, and their stores are staffed by volunteers will be happy to help guide you to find your pet or report you have found one.

The County Department of Animal Services (619) 236-4250 does **not** euthanise pets that are considered ready for adoption as was the practice in the past! Yay! The services offered include adoption, licensing, lost and found, shelters, strays, spaying, report animal neglect, abuse or cruelty, dead animal pick-up, report dogs loose, request a patrol officer, and more. They will also euthanize your ill, vicious, (etc) pet upon request for about $5 or more. Adoptions 7 days a week at 5480 Gaines St, Mission Valley, near Friars Rd., Adoption counselor, (619) 236-4250; South County Adoptions, (619) 263-7741; Carlsbad/North County Adoptions, (760) 438-2312; dogs, about $60; cats, about $50, Senior Citizens get a discount to about half price. All animals will be spayed, neutered, have shots, microchips (for identification), leukemia tests before you pick them up. This Shelter will take in stray pet. The web site lists all their services at sddac.com.. If your pet is lost, you can look online to see if it was picked up and report it missing.

Dogs and cats, including purebreds, can be adopted at a nominal cost from the **San Diego Humane Society** (since 1880), 887 Sherman Street, (619) 299-7012x0. Only an "owner" can donate a pet to the humane societies. They do not take strays; therefore, each pet has a history on file. The fee to adopt a puppy or kitten is about $94; adult cat or dog, about $64, which includes spay or neuter, microchip, vaccinations, deworming, feline leukemia testing, a certificate for a free veterinarian exam and two weeks of health guarantee. Pet must be returned to the shelter for medical care within the two weeks. Also receive a bag of freebies, coupons and a video. There is a return policy within two weeks (refund) if the pet doesn't work out, but they will always take the pet back or take in a pet. Purina sponsors a program for 7 seniors (65) per month to receive a free pet. The animals that are brought here are kept until they are adopted. They are not killed. However, they will euthanize a pet that is ill and/or upon request, about $25. Adoptions for guinea pigs, rabbits, horses, goats, too. Obedience training, puppy training, behavior seminars. Obedience class. Abuse investigations. They rent traps to catch stray cats. They will spay lactating mama cats and dogs *free of charge* when you donate the kitties or puppies. The Humane Society is funded by private donations, estates, fundraising, etc. Web: Sdhumane.org. They are building and will be moving to new quarters next door to the Dept. Of Animal Services on Gaines Street.

For a free list of all the humane societies, shelters and places where you can adopt or relinquish a pet, see the "San Diego Pet Lovers Handbook" (a free publication) below. The Humane Societies have a new web site to assist pet owners challenged with finding pet-friendly rental housing and help owners identify responsible pet owners. Web site: rentwithpets.org and Pet Friendly Rentals at (619) 295-8940 or pet-friently-rentals.com; Email to: petrent@san.rr.com

F.O.C.A.S. (Friends of County Animal Shelters), (619) 685-3536, offers pet adoptions, Afghan to Siamese, mixed and purebred, cats and dogs once a month at their adoption event in Balboa Park, PetCo, etc. Cats, about $60; about $75 for dogs; purebreds a little more. They can help you find a specific pet or breed. Web site: focas-sandiego.org

Cats can be donated or adopted at the **Cat Protection Society**, 9031 Birch in Spring Valley, (619) 469-8771. Founded in 1968, this is a good place to adopt a cat or kitty. Kitties go fast. Old cats welcome, too. I adopted a beautiful grown cat here.

Breed Rescue maintains a list of purebred dogs, cats and other pets including horses that are available for adoption. You may also donate one. Call the Humane Society and ask for the current contact number for this organization.

Pet web sites: Pets / Vets, sandiegopetandvet.com. Information to provide for the well-being of your pets and animals, vetcentric.com. Pet pharmacy site, petmedexpress.com, or (888) 925-2799. The American Veterinary Medical Association offers information about pet ailments, advice and pet safety tips at: avma.org/care4pets. Site by the American Veterinary Medical

Association offering information about specific animal ailments, advice on selecting a veterinarian and pet safety tips.

You can search on google.com for pet medications for less. I bought Advantage cat flea stuff on Ebay for about half price ($8 for $40).

Pet Insurance VPI (Veterinary Pet Insurance) Insurance Group of Anaheim insures about 800,000+ pets (dogs and cats); from about $121 for $7,500 benefits to about $206 for $12,000 benefits a year, (800) 872-7387. Ask about 2-year plan discount.

Birds, purebred cats and pedigreed dogs, guinea pigs, bats, mice, fish, goats, ponies, horses and you-name-it are advertised in the Thrifties #3190 classified ads in the *Union-Trib*. Good prices, too; often free to good homes. Also, check the Pet Adoptions #3340 classifieds. For more pets, look in the *Reader* classified ads.

Pet Assistance Foundation, spay & neutering, (619) 544-1222; North County, (760) 745-7986. Cat neutering for around $20 through the County program! More than 12,000 referrals a year (since 1976).

Pet medical assistance, Mercy Crusade, (858) 278-1745 from 9- 5pm; For volunteer information, call (858) 693-1933. Emergency wildlife rescue, Project Wildlife (619) 225-9453; Wildlife Rehab, (619) 443-3692 or (858) 653-7300 or (760) 789-5033. Also, see Veterinarian Hospitals, (24 hours), in the *Yellow Pages*.

San Diego Pet Lovers Handbook (FREE), wonderful little annual handbook of animal resource information for the county, all adoption locations where you can get ALL varieties of pets or relinquish them, including emergency information, calendar of pet events, contests, fundraising events, contact numbers for volunteering. Available free at local shelters. The other publication is the "San Diego Guide to Dog Walks, Beaches and Pet Services" including pet-friendly restaurants where you can dine out with your pet, a map with 97 places to walk your dog in the county, and over $250 in coupons and free items. Available at local pet stores for $2.50, or call (760) 631-7886. Also available for LA, Orange and Houston. Web site: petloverspublications.com.

More Pet Information

Fleas: It takes a three-pronged attack to control fleas: lawn, carpet and pet. Experts say spray malathion, Dursban or Vapona on the lawn. On carpet, use Dursban or Precor. Treat the pet with Petcor or Advantage which has Precor in it. Precor has an insect growth regulator in it that tampers with the bug's hormones so it can't reproduce. (I want to find a source for Advantage in Tijuana!) I found a good place to but it on EBAY. Search for Advantage Flea. You'll find several sellers of pet medications & supplies.

ABC Veterinary Clinic comes to pet stores and administers **low cost shots**. Call (800) PET-8297. I think it's hard on a pet to get all four shots at once. I am going to spread this into two visits in the future. My cat didn't feel so hot after getting four in one day. The Web site is abcvet.com, and offers coupons for **free vet exam ($29 value)**.

Free dog runs on Dog Beach in Ocean Beach, Fiesta Island, Morely Field, Nates Point, Grape Street Park. No leash required.

Swap meet vendors sell pet supplies, collars, tags, leashes, medications, flea treatments, shampoos, etc., at affordable prices. Some birds and pets, too. (Think I'll check here for Advantage, too.)

Photography

Glamour Shots, Mission Valley across from Macy's (619) 299-5665; and North County Fair; Las Americas Outlets, (619) 662-1090.   Frequent advertised specials as low as $19.95, normally $29.95; includes makeover and a 16 pose session. Plus portraits from $40; their $99 package includes an 8x10, 5x7 and 8 wallets. Many people who need business photos go here because they make you look *good*. Specials: "Bring a friend free." Web: glamourshots.com

Some of the larger Target, Kmart, Walmart, Sears & JCPenney stores have portrait studios with frequent sales with good prices, even better around the holidays. Walmart has a package for $3.95 that includes a 10x13, 8x10's, wallets, portraits for PC's and more. Call (800) 599-4343.

Digital cameras are the rage, and can be pricey. Check Fry's, Costco, Walmart and Ebay. I have a good one, but I took a class on how to buy and sell on ebay, and the instructor said you can get a reasonably good digital camera, suitable for selling one bay, for about $40 on the ebay site. You don't need an expensive one if you need one for selling on ebay. That's the good news. The bad news is you will probably end up wanting a much better one.

To save money on photo developing, watch for discount coupons in the newspapers for SavOn, RiteAid, Longs, Von's, Ralph's and Albertsons, Dean's & Fox. You get real savings on free duplicate sets, enlargements, reprints and discounts on video transfer service. (Put your home movies and slides on video tape for TV viewing!) Costco & Sam's photo centers have REALLY great prices on photo processing, and offer larger prints, cheapo. Fox offers a club membership with discounts on enlargements, film and accessories.

Kinko's will make a poster size blow-up (18"x24") of your photo for $15+

Go to kodak.com for free tips on how to take photos, lighting tips, and other free publications or check this Web site on tips for non-professionals on how to take great pictures, angles, weddings, travel, digital. How to capture the moment. Web: takegreatpictures.com

Plumbing

Budget Heating and Plumbing, (619) 563-1400, charges about $55 for the first hour, and every half hour thereafter, plus equipment used. Try to get an estimate by phone.

Don't call a plumber for stopped up drains, call **Baird's Drain Service** at (619) 462-8229. They clear drains for about $20, main sewer lines for about $40. I've had them out several times, find them very timely (come when they say they will), very friendly and work fast. All work is guaranteed for 30 days. No can beat.

You can get plumbing (and electrical) work done by a licensed *handyman* for probably $15-25 an hour. They are qualified to do jobs up to $300 without having a specific plumber's or electrician's license. It's best to get a referral from someone who has used the handyman, or check with the Better Business Bureau.

Public Libraries

Public libraries have to be one of the best bargains known to man with their endless resources and services. All the San Diego City libraries and County Libraries are listed in the government pages in the front of the White pages telephone directory. Librarians can help you find anything you need, even over the telephone, and can get things for you, even if in another *state*. Here are some of the special features of San Diego's public library system: more than 2.5 million volumes, books in 23 foreign languages, books and tapes to learn languages, travel guides, maps, U.S. patents, government documents, cook books, auto repair manuals, income tax, Kelly Blue Books (auto-pricing), college catalogs, electronic schematics, genealogy room, major city newspapers (about 80 current subscriptions) and complete holdings of local newspapers, index to the San Diego Union, index to California periodicals with San Diego info, job and career information/resources, college catalogs, sheet music, song books, records, CD's, audio cassettes, video cassettes, videodiscs, personal investing books, ethnic information, imports & exports info, foundations & grants, Pacific Rim info, government regulations, NAFTA info, trademark search, patent search, career books, business reference including Dunn & Bradstreet, large print books, picture file, San Diego telephone books, plus computer homework centers, inter-library loan service, art displays, films, chamber music concerts series (free), opera preview, traveling exhibits, children's programs, story hours, rare book room, criss-cross directory available in person or through a 900 number, (900) 225-5223, special services to the blind and hearing impaired, shut-in service to the homebound, literacy program for adults, computer room for public use with Internet access, CD ROMs and typewriters. Many branches have a meeting room. The main library at 830 E Street downtown offers a free Internet demonstration once a month; call (619) 238-6621 for date; You can access the library's web site at: sannet.gov/public-library/index.html. There are several beautiful new libraries in the county, and a new world-class $130 million dollar Main Library is planned for, downtown near the ballpark. Soon!

Records, Tapes, CD's, Videos, DVD's

Public libraries have records, tapes, CD's and videos and DVD's that can be checked out. A current movie or an educational or travel video rents for about 50¢ a day. Some libraries are better stocked than others (Carlsbad and Chula Vista libraries have lots.) Some libraries have free rentals.

Long's Drugs has video rentals for 99¢ .**Music Trader** with over 500,000 used CD's at their 12 stores in San Diego County. Trade in two CDS and get one used CD. **Kobey's Swap Meet** has several vendors that sell used and new videos. **Movies 2 Sell (Used)**, 4718 Clairemont Mesa Blvd. Near Ross, (858) 274-3456. Over 15,000 used movies to choose from, classics, foreign, largest Disney selection in San Diego. Most videos sell for about $6 up; some double sets. Buy, sell, trade. Wants to buy out-of-print older movies. They buy for about 1/3 the selling price. **Reel Inc**. is the "planet's biggest movie store,"featuring 35,000 titles for rent and 80,000 for sale through it's Web Site: reel.com. I have bought some used CDs at Ebay for only a couple dollars plus about $2 shipping.

Ebay blew me away with their offerings in this area. I bought a CD of Yanni in "near perfect" condition for a dollar and change, and less than $2 to shop it. It came packaged beautifully. No can beat. Check out their stuff. Well, we just lost YOU for a few days on that one. Now, don't stay up all night.

Recycle for Cash (& for the Environment)

Plastic containers, aluminum cans and glass bottles that have the CCR (California Cash Refund) or CRV (California Redemption Value) stamped on the bottoms have a cash value. Take them to a recycler and receive about 40¢ to 50¢ a pound for plastic; about 90¢ to $1.05 for aluminum, and about 5¢ a pound for glass. The price fluxuates according to market changes. An organization called **20-20 Recycle Centers** will buy your plastic, aluminum and glass for the California redemption price paid at purchase point, plus a little more. They in turn sell to scrap merchandiser who recycle it into new aluminum cans, bottles, etc. Call (800) 883-CASH for a location near you. **Recycle auto waste**: used oil, oil filters, antifreeze and auto batteries. Call the City of San Diego, (619) 235-2105 for location near you (funded by the California Integrated Waste Management Board). For other toxic and hazardous materials, call **I Love a Clean San Diego** County Hotline at (800) 237-2583; **Household Hazardous Materials** Hotline at (619) 235-2111; **TCR (Toner Cartridge Recycling**) 5466 Complex Drive, Kearny Mesa, (858) 279-0322, will pay $3+ for your old laser printer toner cartridge; they sell recycled and refurbished toner cartridges, plus cleaning and repairing of printers.

Resale/Consignment Shops

There all different kinds of resale and consignment shops. Some specialize in children's clothing or women's fashions or men's wear. Some specialize in furniture or appliances or sporting equipment or videos/records, etc. Some particularly good buys can be found in children's clothing, formal wear, exercise equipment, sporting goods and furniture.

Clothing consignment shops carry "previously owned" apparel that is in perfectly good, next-to-new condition. A resale shop may or may not buy from customers; but a consignment shop always buys from customers (but may have other inventory also).

Recycling has been popular for many years, and the "used" market is thriving. Today people clean out their closets and find things they simply don't wear any more, things that never fit in the first place, things that simply don't flatter, things they can no longer squeeze into and things they have dieted out of. They may donate some of the things to a charity thrift store and take the better items to a privately owned consignment shop where they can retrieve some of their original outlay. A price is established by the consignor and the consignee. You will earn about 60% of the selling price and the store will get 40% when the item sells. Some pay cash up-front, but a smaller percentage goes to you if they pay you on the spot. Consignment is usually for a 90 day period, with the selling price reduced 10% every 30 days until it is sold. (A pitfall here is that some women say they never get paid, so be sure to keep your receipt and check back before 90 days to see if your items have sold.) There are shops that specialize: women, men, tuxedos, bridal, children, big women, vintage, maternity You see upscale fashions for women, bargains in designer clothing, casual wear, formal wear and things for the household. You'll see women drive up in their big Mercedes to add to their wardrobes or sell their excess. Consignment shops carry everything: casual, formal, suits, lingerie, you-name-it and are a great place to pick up belts, purses, jewelry and outfits for costume parties. If you haven't been shopping at a resale or consignment shop, now is the time to investigate them. We have lots of new shops, and buying and selling at resale stores is definitely a hot trend. I have a friend in Jacksonville who owns a successful antique store, and she says she shops resale stores in upscale neighborhoods for Chanel purses, especially when she travels, and has quite a collection of them!

Here's a success story: a friend was invited to a very yuppie wedding in Chicago and she didn't want to pay for a designer dress she'd never wear again. I suggested she try one of the better resale shops that carry designer clothing in La Jolla (rich ladies live there, right?) not thinking she'd ever do it. Well, she did, and she called to report she had found THE PERFECT DRESS to take to Chicago. She went to the wedding and had a fabulous time because she knew she was wearing something spectacularly competitive (when you have *that* feeling--it really makes a world of difference in the fun you can have). When she got home, she sold the dress right back to the store! So, it only cost her a few dollars to have a *fabulous* outfit to wear for a very special occasion! You can do it, too.

If you want to sell your clothing or other merchandise, call and tell them what you have and see if there is interest. Then make an appointment. Find out before going what the percentage is that they will pay you as some only pay 35-40%. Sometimes you won't like the experience because they may try to bargain you down on the price so it will sell quickly, or they will refuse your merchandise. But, you will learn what they want and can anticipate a better experience next time. Things need to be clean and in great condition. Browse through some of the following stores for today's styles at yesterday's prices:

A Better Deal (used tuxedos & new)
369 Bird Rock Ave
La Jolla (858) 551-6044

Act II (Women's)
6195 Lake Murray Blvd.
(619) 698-8636

Act II (Women's)
8243 La Mesa Blvd.,
La Mesa, (619) 698-2392

Always Fabulous
1217 Camino Del Mar
Del Mar, (858) 481-8866

Atomic Trading Co.
1036 Garnet
Pacific Beach, (858) 272-8822

Buff (The) (Vintage/Resale/Costumes)
1061 Garnet
Pacific Beach, (858) 581-2833

Buffalo Exchange (Women's & Men's)
1007 Garnet (Casual clothing_
Pacific Beach, (858) 273-6227
Used, plus some new clothing. Nearly
new, natural fibers. Sell your clothes for
35% of ticket price and receive cash, or
receive 50% in store credit.

Buffalo Exchange Hillcrest
3852 5thAve., (619) 298-4411

Carolyn's Such a Deal (Ladies)
920 Hwy. 101 Street
Encinitas, (760) 943-1556

Carolyn's (Ladies)
13th & Camino Del Mar
(858) 481-3843

Carolyn's
1310 Camino Del Mar
Del Mar 481-3843

Cherry Pickers Vintage
4230 Adams Ave
Kensington, (619) 281-2821

Clothing Cottage
620 Grand Ave, Suite A,
Carlsbad, (760) 720-5219.

Creme de la Creme
10330 Friars Rd
Mission Gorge, (619) 282-5778

Cream of the Crop (women's)
4683 Cass Street
Pacific Beach, (858) 272-6601

Daily Exchange (women's & men's)
628 First Ave.
Encinitas, (760) 753-4000

Deborah's Next To New (Everything)
1624 E. Valley Parkway,
Escondido, (760) 743-8980

Denimville, U.S.A.
166B N El Camino Real,
Encinitas (760) 635-7777

Designer Consigner (Women's designer)
7660 Ste. D Fay St.
La Jolla, (858) 459-1737

Discovery Shop (everything)
3651-B Midway Drive
Point Loma,(619) 224-4336

Discovery Shop
11972 Bernardo Plaza Drive
Rancho Bernardo, (858) 385-0479

Down on the Corner (women's casual)
3572 Mount Acadia Blvd.
Clairemont, (858) 279-9649

Dress to Impress (women's rentals/resale)
4242 Camino del Rio North
Mission Valley, (619) 528-9797

Double Take (ladies)
2931 Roosevelt
Carlsbad, (760) 434-0101

Double Take
731 South Hwy 101
Solana Beach (858) 794-54511

Double Take
509 South Coast Hwy.
Encinitas, (760) 479-2501

Echoes Boutique
7705 Fay Ave (ladies)
La Jolla, (858) 459-6588

Encore (women's designer)
7655 Girard
La Jolla, (858) 454-7540

Fellini's Vintage Warehouse (packed!)
Features upscale & designer vintage and
more, for men, women, children. Voted
the best Vintage Shop in San Diego!
1940 California St.,
Little Italy (619) 230-1930

Fine Feathers Resale
8376 La Mesa Blvd
La Mesa (619) 466-8131

Flashbacks
3847 Fifth Ave (Vintage, retro)
Hillcrest, (619) 291-4200

Garment Gourmet
(women's clothing & bridal)
831 Williamston
Vista, (760) 630-6630

Gentlemen Resale Clothier
4695 Date Ave
La Mesa, (619) 466-4560

Great Curves (larger women's)
2810 Lytton
Midway area, (619) 224-9174

Indigo Way (used Levis)
437 Market (Gaslamp), (619)338-0173
LeChauvanist Consignment for Men
7709 Fay Ave
La Jolla (858) 456-0117
Memories
1916 Cable
Ocean Beach, (619) 224-8828
My Sister's Closet (benefits Y.W.C.A.)
3590 Fifth, downtown, (619) 299-1474
Pacific Beach/ Garnet Ave are
one resale   shop after another . . . have
fun!
R.A.G.S. Fashion Exchange
534 University
Hillcrest, (619) 297-6988
Rave Review
120 W. Grand
Escondido, (760) 743-0056
Retro
4879 Newport
Ocean Beach, (619) 222-0220
Rodeo Drive (women's designer)

3707 Avacado,
La Mesa, (619) 660-7787
Second Act (women's)
7449 Girard Avenue
La Jolla, (858) 454-6096
Sentimental Values (juniors, women)
1077 Broadway
El Cajon, (619) 442-3231
Shake Rag (Mostly men's)
440 F Street
Gaslamp, (619) 237-4955
Sparkle Plenty Boutique
1816 Oceanside Blvd.
Oceanside, (760) 757-8804
Tuxedo Discount
989 Fifth Avenue, downtown
(619) 239-7027
Wear It Again Sam (vintage men's
& women's), (619) 299-0185
3823 Fifth Ave., Hillcrest
Whatever
6495 El Cajon Blvd
College Area (619) 582-2006

For more stores that sell slightly used clothing, see Thrift Stores this chapter. Some thrift stores have boutiques for their better merchandise. For consignment stores that sell furniture and decorator items, appliances and electronics. sporting equipment, see other sections of this book.

There are over 50 consignment shops in **Palm Springs** (rich folks' used goodies) including a store called Celebrity Seconds at 333 N. Palm Canyon Dr., (760) 416-2072. Many shops are on the north end of town on Palm Canyon Drive at Tamarisk. Should make for a fun day. Cathedral City's Resale Row has some really great stores with bargains from the local fabulously rich folks. For more info, call the Palm Springs Visitors Bureau at (800) 347-7746. They faxed me a short list of resale shops. You can also visit their web site at palmsprings.com. In the summer, you can book SUPER DELUXE hotel rooms, for cheap, because it's 105+ degrees! The shopping is great, tho, with LOTS of sales. I also enjoy shopping the resale shops in Laguna Beach, too. Ah, yes, with lunch above the Pacific . . . are we having fun yet?!

Rummage Sales

There is nothing like the news of a *good* rummage sale coming up to get the heart pounding and blood rushing! I hadn't been to one in years and years, so when I was dragged off to one, I didn't expect much. Ho! HO! Was I ever pleasantly surprised! Now I wouldn't miss a good one for the world.

Tips: Go prepared. Bring tote bags, plastic grocery bags, boxes or crates with you to put things in and carry around with you. Go early and stand in line so you can be one of the first in the building because the very best buys are always scooped up within the first hour. Here are some of the best annual rummage sales. I call them the Rolls Royces of rummage sales. You will see phones numbers below, so call to find out the exact date for this year's events and mark them on your calendar.

Rancho Santa Fe Garden Club Rummage Sale, corner of La Granada & Avenida de Acacias, Rancho Santa Fe, (858) 756-1554. Held every May, usually the first weekend in May. This is a three-day event, with all items reduced to half price the third day. Some fine designers in the French Room, regular clothing, china, jewelry, furniture, some of everything. Also, all year long you can buy some items like stereos, typewriters, refrigerators and furniture on Wednesday mornings, 9-11:30a.m, excluding summers. However, most of the things are sent into storage for the next rummage sale. **Thursday Club Annual Rummage Sale** (every year since 1921!), This one is held every March in the Municipal Gym Balboa Park. Over $60,000 in proceeds benefit 22 local community agencies and four Balboa Park organizations. This is a Big One. Computers and electronics, art, antiques, household, clothing, books. Half price on Sunday. In the spring, call the Thursday club (619) 224-5264 for exact date. **Social Service League of La Jolla**, Darlington House, 7441 Olivetas Ave, La Jolla, (858) 454-7625; Two rummage sales! One in spring, one in fall with collectibles, near-new items, quality clothing, low prices. Call for dates. **American Society of Interior Designers (ASID)** (San Diego Chapter) has an annual spring or summer 2-day sale of surplus furnishings from San Diego's finest interior decorator's showrooms at bargain prices. People line up around the block for this event! Everything for the home: floor models, cancellations, custom-made furniture and window coverings that may have been too long or short, antiques, new furniture, accessories, bolts of fabrics and fabric sample books, inventory from model homes, some items consigned or donated by lighting stores, kitchen shops, some bloopers. Second day, some items reduced. Proceeds benefit ASID education programs and various charities. Call the Society at (858) 2274-3345 for this year's date. **St. James By The Sea Episcopal Church**, 743 Prospect, (858) 459-3421. There is an annual two-day rummage sale every September with some pricey antiques, household items, electronics, books, more. Call for exact date. A woman told me she buys all of her clothes at this rummage sale because there is such good quality clothing (designer labels) hardly worn!! (Rich La Jolla ladies get rid of clothing that is perfectly new or in great condition!) She said that by purchasing her wardrobe at rummage sales, she can save her money for travel! **La Jolla Congregational Church Rummage Sale**, 1216 Cave St., La Jolla, (858) 459-5045. Every October, since 1947. Call for this year's date and put in on your calendar. Indoor and outdoor sale of furniture, some antiques, household, collectibles, china, jewelry, art, books, clothing, more. Some lavish items priced by appraisers, but a lot of affordable stuff is at this sale, too. **La Jolla Lutheran Church**, 7111 La Jolla Blvd., annual sale in the fall, (858) 454-6459; **St. James By The Sea,** 743 Prospect St. (858) 459-3421; good event every September, since 1934! Some "choice-y" stuff. Sidewalk presale a few days before with large items. First Night pre-sale, $5 admission + 25% premium over the price tag. Worth it! Call for date. **Torrey Pines Christian Church**, 8320 La Jolla Scenic Dr, La Jolla, (858) 453-3550. Every March, call for this year's date. Boutique, furniture, outdoor, clothing, more. **Mission Hills Congregational Church**, 4070 Jackdaw, Mission Hills, (619) 296-1601. Every May, with a presale the night before. Call for this year's date. Good one. Sometimes they have a pre-sale the night before and you pay $1 or so to get in. It's worth it, for sure. **St. Andrews Episcopal Church Rummage Sale**, 4816 Glen St., La Mesa, (619) 460-7272. Held in October. Call for date. **La Jolla United Methodist Church**, 6063 La Jolla Blvd., (858) 454-7108. Every March, usually the first weekend, since 1964. Call for date. Quality items, furniture, clothing, plants, household, more. **United Methodist Church**, 1702 South Ditmar, Oceanside, has their annual rummage sale every October; (760) 439-8311. **St. Patrick's**, 3585 30th Street, North Park, (619) 295-2157; every October. **Pacific Beach Presbyterian Church**, 1675 Garnet, (858) 273-9312; Held in October, since about 1972. **Kensington Community Church**, 4773 Marlborough, (619) 284-1129; Usually in October or November. Stuff from those wonderful Kensington homes. As with ANY sale, whether it's Nordstrom's or Big Lots, it's the early bird that gets the worm, so suit up and show up early and plan to stand in line. It's DEFINITELY worth it. If you go at the end, it's usually all leftovers which often looks like debris! BUT, you could get lucky and score something that didn't sell, for half price. The smart ones go early. I can't emphasize this enough. Of course, if you can't go early, go anyway, but it's not the same experience as racing for the cream of the crop.

There are numerous other church rummage sales, too many to list. They are usually advertised in the Union-Trib Garage Sales #2070. There are two churches near me and I KNOW to go to those early, as they are small. One year I got a crystal chandelier with LARGE crystals on it for $3. It was missing a few crystals, but wouldn't you know, I went to another yard sale one day where a lady was selling this bag of 25 crystals in three sizes, which MATCH my crystals! And, I can sell the rest on Ebay when I get my act together there. Just remember to go early, wait in line before opening (I stop at McDonalds and get my 37 cent senior coffee and stand in line), and those in the better neighborhoods will most likely have better rummage. Wanna know how to get the best deals at a rummage sale? Volunteer to help in the organizing of it!! Sometimes helpers are allowed to make early purchases.

Shoes

Major department stores including Nordstrom, Neiman's, Saks, Macy's, Robinsons-May regularly schedule their anniversary sales, semi-annual and end-of-season shoe sales where you will get the BEST names in the shoe biz. Scoop up designer labels at discounts up to 50% and more. If you and Imelda Marcos have something in common and you're really on a roll with shoes, ask the shoe department manager to put your name on their mailing list and you'll be notified by mail (or called) about their future sales. You can have the finest quality designer shoes in every color at a fraction of the original cost. Buy the best quality shoes you can, and your feet will love you for it. Here are some other great places to shop for shoes.

Famous Footwear, over a dozen locations in San Diego, plus factory outlet stores in Carlsbad and Viejas. Call (800) 403-2668 for store or outlet near you. Shoes and boots for the whole family: L.A. Gear, Reebok, Keds, Naturalizer, Florsheim, Nunn Bush, Bare Traps, Sketchers, Nike, Adidas, Cherokee, K-Swiss, Ipanema, I.e.i. Not their latest styles, but all on sale.

DSW , over 40,000 pairs of shoes. This is a new store to San Diego, part of a national chain in many major cities. Everything from boots to dress shoes to sneakers and sandals, clogs, Reebok's and more. Men's and women's. Mission Valley West Shopping Center by Gateway and Marshall's, (619) 296-4079.

Just For Feet, Mission Valley (619) 293-7463;Vista, (760) 806-3338 ; Las Americas Outlets in San Ysidro, (619) 690-3338. Thousands of styles of athletic shoes and sandals, golf shoes. Nike, Jordan, Adidas, Reebok, OP Gauley, Open Country, OP's, Fila, and many more. Regular sales with half off second pair.

Skechers Outlet, 4475 Mission Blvd, (858) 581-6010; These are Skechers shoes, last season's merchandise, 3-6 months old. The Skechers store in Horton Plaza has all the newest styles. The outlet sells last season's at a discount.

Walking Co. Fashion Valley mall, (619) 291-8926, carries comfortable shoes for anyone who is working on their feet a lot, plus walking shoes for exercise, too. Prices range from $59-$300, and there are sales. Website: walkingcompany.com.

SAS Comfort Shoes, Mission Valley (619) 220-6818; Escondido, (760) 741-9848 Carlsbad. Specializes in narrow to double wide, 4000 pairs .

Payless ShoeSource stores has over 4600 locations internationally. They carry only their own brands, and the most expensive women's shoe is $20; the most expensive men's boot is $40. Frequent Buy Two/Get One Free sales. Good return policy. Over 70 stores in San Diego. Baby's first pair of shoes free. Web: payless.com. Visit their web site and print discount coupons, order online, no shipping deals available, etc.

Shoe Pavillion, 4240 Kearny Mesa Rd., (by Comp USA), (858) 492-9833; 304 E. H Street, Chula Vista, 691-0640; Pt. Loma, (619) 222-6787; Carmel Mountain and Mira Mesa; large stores with stacks and stacks of name brand shoes like Easy Spirit $39 (retail $85); Sperry Topsiders $19 (retail $38); Esprit sandals $10 (retail $36); women's Rockport, $49 (retail $89) plus Keds, Amalfi, Adidas, Naturalizer and more. Special sales: Reebok Princess, $19.99; Boot sales, buy one, second pair, ½ off.

La Sandale, 3761 Mission Boulevard, Mission Beach, (858) 488-1134, has Birkenstock "look alikes" for less than the real thing costs. They are outrageously comfortable and good for the legs.

Banister Factory Outlet, Carlsbad Company Stores, (760) 438-0034 . Over 40 famous brands of shoes for men and women including dress, casual, Easy Spirit, and athletic shoes.

Bass Outlet, Viejas Outlets (619) 445-9616 and San Diego Factory Outlet Mall, (619) 690-6029. Fashion footwear for men and women including casual, boots, dress shoes, range: women's, $19-59; men's $29-69. All are Bass labels, sold in Macy's and Robinson's (you may not see the current models, though.) Lots of overruns.

Nike Factory Outlet, Las Americas Outlets, (619) 428-8849 and Viejas Outlets, (619) 659-3460; Nike casual shoes, apparel and accessories (discontinued styles of all sport shoes including running, walking, basketball, aerobic and more.) None of the latest styles, only closeouts, at about 30% off. Tights, t-shirts, more. Clearance rack with discounts up to 70%. This is the busiest Nike Factory Outlet in the U.S.

Reebok Factory Outlet, Viejas, (619) 659-8160 and Carlsbad Company Stores, (760) 804-0200.; San Ysidro, (619)690-9006; Polo, Reebok, Rockport discontinued styles. Web site: reebok.com has all their current shoes styles. You can get a 20% discount here with your AAA card!

Nine West Factory Outlet, San Diego Factory Outlet Mall, (619) 428-8838; Carlsbad Company Stores, (760) 930-8955. Popular shoes sold at many department stores; many styles, frequent sales.

Van's Shoes Factory Outlet, at Viejas Outlets and Carlsbad Company Stores (below). Their shoes include: walking, skating, tennis shoes, canvas shoes found at department stores. Men's, women's, children's

Athletic and active wear shoes: Big 5 sales are hard to beat and are frequent. Name brand shoes often at clearance prices where a whole groups of shoes will be on sale for $19, with values to $59. Road Runner's Sports is a big San Diego-based catalog company with an outlet store at 5553 Copeley Drive, off Convoy in Clairemont, (858) 974-4455; discount prices, some clearance items. Costco & Sam's have great buys on leisure shoes. No need to pay full price for them, ever! Plus you've got the Reebok & Nike factory stores to check out (below.)

Shoes for Less, 3730 Sports Arena, (619) 222-1177; They buy bankruptcies, close-out inventories of men's shoes. Shoes are on racks and sell at good prices. Famous brand shoes from $29-$495. Crocodile and alligator shoes, $295-495, at least 30% less than stores.

Foot Solutions, 1347 Encinitas Blvd, Encinitas, (760) 634-1600. Custom made removable orthotic shoe inserts for foot comfort. Great for runners and people with special needs. Custom inserts can relieve leg and foot pain which often affects the whole body. They sell comfort shoes, too.

Jon's Wide Shoes, 273 Third Avenue, Chula Vista, (619) 422-1464. Clairemont Mesa, (619) 277-2064. Mainly women's wide and extra wide; whole line for children, some men's.

Factory Outlets If you want designer shoes for less, check out the **Carlsbad Company Stores** for shoe outlets including Adidas, Barney's New York, Cole-Haan, Easy Spirit, Etnies, Factory Brand shoes, G.H. Bass, Hush Puppies, Kenneth Cole, Nine West, Puma, Reebok Outlet, Rockport Outlet, Skechers outlet, Stride Rite, Timberland and Vans. The **Viejas Outlet Center** has these stores: Aerosoles, Bass, Naturalizer, Nike, Reebok and Vans. Las Americas Outlets has the following outlets: Adidas, Bass, Hush Puppies, Magic Step, Nike Outlet, Payless, Skechers, and Strideright. See the Section on Factory Outlets for addresses and phone numbers.

Swapmeets have shoe vendors who sell dress shoes, street wear, dress sandals, wedges, tennis shoes & leisure, mules, more.

Singles

If you're single in San Diego, check out the "Possibilities" column (the personal ads) on Thursdays in the "Night & Day" section of the *Union-Tribune,* and also in the Sunday edition. Also, check out the telephone dating service in the *Reader* entitled "Phone Matches" and look for singles activities under Notices and Personals. For other networking organizations, head for the library and thumb through the *San Diego Source Book,* which lists hundreds of clubs and organizations: political, ethnic, social, professional, etc., where you can meet people with a common interest. Or, go to google.com and search for "San Diego singles" and you will find a number of them, including Sierra Singles, Jewish Singles, Catholic Singles, Christian Singles, Over 30 Club, Over 50 Club, Single Parent, New York & East Coast Singles, Singles In San Diego Dancing on Tuesdays and Saturday nights, and more. Also, the Learning Annex is known as a good "you-meet-'em" place. Pick a class that you think will be attracting more of the opposite sex, and sign up. They have big registration parties a few times a year with hundreds of people and a great place to meet other singles. Otherwise, check some of these Web sites for singles like one2onemag.com, americansingles.com, match.com, which has over 2.5 million registered; kiss.com which has over 40K hits a week, including more than 1,000 San Diegans; Webwoo.com; people2people.com, dateable.com, and Datingfaces.com; memberships run around $20 a month and some offer free trial periods.

Sports & Fitness Gear

San Diego is loaded with sporting goods stores, so this can work to your advantage in scoring anything you want by comparison shopping for that good deal. Big 5, one of the leading sporting goods chains in California with 10 stores in San Diego carries a huge selection of seasonal clothing, gear and accessories. Their enormous buying volume allows them to discount merchandise 20 to 50% & more below retail. Gear for running, tennis, golf, fishing, bowling, skiing, camping, hunting, workout wear, and much more are sold here. Great full page sale ads in the *Union-Trib* featuring incredible sale prices. Check their Web at Big5sportinggoods.com. And, you take note of the sales at SportMart or Sports Chalet for end of season clearance sales. With these great opportunities for shopping, you can let your fingers do the walking and call around. Here are some other sports and fitness stores to check:

Total Gym You've seen the infomercial on TV starring Christy Brinkley and

Chuck Norris, right? Well, Total Gym is a San Diego based company, in business over 20 years, and has moved to a new location at 7755 Arjons, Miramar, (858) 586-6080. You can buy directly from their warehouse, and compare models, see demonstrations. There is an exercise physiologist on staff to answer your questions. Total Gym is used by hundreds of hospitals for rehabilitation in their physical therapy clinics. Save on reconditioned gyms, returned equipment. Negotiate a deal!

Road Runner, a San Diego-based, enormously successful, national name brand running shoes and apparel catalog company. They sell their overstocks and accessories, returns, once worn clothing (cheapo), etc. plus new catalog items at their retail/outlet center at 5553 Copley Drive, off Convoy in Clairemont, (858) 974-4455) They also have 3-4 big warehouse blowout sales a year. Club membership gives additional guarantee plus discounts. For a catalog, call (800) 551-5558. Web site: roadrunner.com

Buck Knives has an annual clearance sale in November with up to 70% off discontinued and overstock items. Hunting & fishing knives; outdoor and tool knives; everyday knives. Other occasional sales, free knife sharpening demos and over $1000 in product giveaways. Located at 1900 Weld Blvd., El Cajon (619) 449-1100, or visit their website at buckknives.com.

Just For Feet claims to be the largest athletic shoe store in the world; located in Mission Valley ((619) 293-7463; Vista, (760) 726-3338; Las Americas Outlets, San Ysidro,(619) 690-3338. Regular prices, but always some on sale. Buy 12 pair, get free pair. Web site: feet.com

prAna in Vista holds an annual warehouse sale of yoga and climbing gear that is sold at REI and Adventures 16. Call (760) 566-8015 for date. See their line of clothing and shop online at prana.com.

Climax Manufacturing holds a "clean out the warehouse" sale for casual wear and skateboarding hardgoods (trucks, wheels, decks, hardware) and soft goods (T-shirts, shirts, shorts, pants, boxers, jackets, backpacks and accessories). Held twice a year, around February and August, at 3210-B Production Avenue, Oceanside, (760) 722-1455.

No Fear, Carlsbad Company Stores, (760) 603-8643. This is not an outlet store with discount prices, but they have the whole line of No Fear merchandise that is in department stores, with frequent sales. Men's and boy's casual clothing: surfing, shorts, denim shorts, button shirts, Tshirts, sweats, jackets, pants, wallets, belts, etc. Good selection. Check their whole line at nofear.com.

Jet Pilot, the San Diego manufacturer of wet suits and life vests sells their overstocks through a liquidator at Kobey's Swap Meet. Samples, one-of-a-kind, prototypes, seconds, of all kinds of surf shop stuff: gear for water sports, wetsuits, life vests, gloves, booties, some rashguards, personal watercraft gear, shorts, Tshirts, casual wear, kids to adults. Now sold at Kobey's swap meet. When you enter, ask where their booth is.

Golf Mart, discount golf supermart, Mission Valley Superstore with indoor putting green, (619) 298-9571; Del Mar, (760) 794-9676; Encinitas, (760) 944-1534; San Marcos, (760) 741-0441. Large inventory, computerized club fitting system, on-site repairs, components, apparel, shoes. Ask about their occasional parking lot sales.

San Diego Divers Supply Discount Outlet has an annual consignment sale in July. Good time to pick up some bargains, or bring in your old gear and sell it.

The **Aventine Sporting Club** is free for a day if you book one of their services (massage, etc). You will have full use of the club, both floors, pools, 80 degree outdoor pool. For services and amenities, call (858) 552-8000 or go to aventine.com. *Don'tcha love it?*

Used Sporting Goods: Resale/consignment sports stores are a great relatively new concept, and there are some particularly good deals. All sorts of sporting gear, exercise equipment, balls of every description, surf boards, skis, etc. You can shop there for your surfboard or skis, and sell 'em back when you tire of 'em. New and used surf boards, skis, ski boots, skate boards, bicycles, motorcycle helmets, inline skates, balls, wet suits (long and short), diving equipment, fishing equipment, hockey, lacrosse gear, tennis rackets, snorkels, fins, tents, camping equipment and exercise equipment. Buy, sell, trade, consign. Antique sporting gear is hot! Here are a few around town: **Second Chance Sports**, 4811 W. Point Loma, Ocean Beach, (619) 224-9524. **Play It Again Sports**, Pacific Beach, (858) 490-0222; Mira Mesa, (858) 695-3030.; Encinitas (760) 633-3966; Oceanside (760) 630-6156; Escondido, (760) 489-1644; La Mesa (619) 667-9499. Chula Vista, too. **Retro Sports**, La Mesa, (619) 465-9000; Poway, (858) 486-8989.

Fitness Direct, 7590 Miramar Road, (858) 653-3600. New and some used fitness equipment, recumbent bikes, treadmills, cycles, stairclimbers, home gyms, free weights, benches and racks. Web: efitnessdirect.com

Fitness sells home gyms and fitness equipment, big floor model clearance sales. Ask when one is coming up. San Diego, (858) 560-9599; Escondido

(760) 738-1538; Del Mar (619) 793-1010; La Mesa (619) 667-8778. Encinitas, Mission Valley, too. **Fitness Outlet**, El Camino Real, (760) 634-2124

If you're interested in fitness equipment or sports gear, look in the Thrifties #3190 classified ads of the *Union-Trib*. You'll find every thing that is manufacturer if you look long enough. Inquire about the condition and age of the equipment, where they got it and how much they paid for it. This is a good place to get that first pair of skis, first surf board or any kind of fitness equipment, camping gear, etc.

Swap Meets have a number of vendors that sell new sports gear and clothing, from surf and snow wear to gloves for sailing, skiing. Used gear, too.

Buy or sell sports gear on **Ebay**. One woman told me her husband decided to sell his old snowboard on Ebay. He thought it would sell for probably $200, but the bidding went up to over $1200! Drag out your stuff you are no longer into and see what you can get for it on ebay. Remember, the buyer pays for shipping. Not a problem.

Your kids can have *every* kind of sporting gear if you go to yard sales. Skis, tennis rackets, skateboards, surfboards, golf clubs, even boats, etc.

Students (Employ One)

Use a college or high school student to clean your house, do yard work, childcare, run errands, do your personal or professional bookkeeping, office work, set up your computer files, detail your car, serve at parties, wash windows, create your web page, etc. Call the student employment office at a school near you. Use a horticulture student for yard work, get a childcare major at a community college to care for your kids, get a catering school student to help at your party, a bartenders college student for your party, a graphic arts student for your church flyers . . *Get my drift?* .

Sunglasses

In my next lifetime, I am going to sell sunglasses. That, my friends, is because I read somewhere that the average Californian has at least four pairs. What a market we have here! (Let's see, now. That's four times 35+ million........Yup . . I could probably live on that!!)

Sunglass City, 1478 Garnet, Pacific Beach, (858) 272-6041. Major brands at discount prices, Hot right now: Maui Jim, $140-200 (value over $200); Revo, $145 up. Gucci's, $128 (Reg. $160); Guess, Black Fly, $40-90; two-toned colors, $60. Big rack of designer knockoffs, $60; everything discounted. Good lenses; repairs, too. Web: sunglasscityonline.com

Costco & Sam's Club have great prices on moderate to very expensive sunglasses. Maui, Hobie, Guess, Serengeti, Gargoyles. Big discounts.

Sunglass & Optical Warehouse, 3450 Kurtz St., Ste D, behind Sports Arena, (619) 291-4810; thousands of stylish frames, all 15-50% off (except 4 brands). Everything from Dragon, Oakley, Arnette to Maui Jim's ($100 up) to Raybans (always a big seller) to Serengeti, Dior, Armani, DKNY, Fendi, Gucci, Quiksilver, Bolle, Carrera, etc. At Kobey's swap meet. Web: sunglassoptical.com Occasional sale: "Buy one, get 2nd pair for $1"

Sunglass outlet stores are in all factory outlet malls with good prices and selections. Liz Claiborne, Anne Klein, Donna Karan have sunglasses at their factory outlets. (For more information, see Factory Outlets, this chapter)

Swap meets have hot sunglasses plus lots of inexpensive brands, and department store sales are great for designer sunglasses.

Swap Meets/Flea Markets/Bazaars

Swap meets are phenomenally popular in Southern California where the weather lends itself to year-round outdoor shopping. They've become tourist attractions and people come from miles away with advance knowledge of our famous swapmeets. Shoppers are mostly educated and middle class. Vendors are supplementing social security or retirement, maybe they have a large family, are supplementing their businesses or starting new ones and some are there for the social aspect of it -- they don't care if they sell 50¢ or $50. It only takes a few thousand dollars to get started in a swap meet business. Vendors buy bankruptcy lots, factory close-outs, etc., offering their wares at a savings of 40-50¢ or more on the dollar. They are smart business people: it's easy money and a good place to work for yourself. They have to buy smart, sell cheap and treat people right, which makes the swap meet a great place to shop. About 70% of merchandise is *new* merchandise, 30% used, everything under the sun from A-Z, every weekend. Whatever you're looking for, you'll probably find it for less at a swap meet. Acres and acres of bargains, domestic and imports, including art, arts and crafts, artwear, automotive accessories, clothes and shoes for the entire family, baskets, beauty supplies, belts, bicycles, cellular phones, dance and exercise wear, eelskin and leather goods, flowers, furniture, gifts, hardware and tools, fine jewelry, natural stone and ethnic jewelry, photo supplies and equipment, plants, sheets and linens, sporting goods, sunglasses and more. Flowers are $2-3 a bunch (value $7 up), telephone and accessories, good buys on imported pots and decorator items, futons, wicker, and more. You'll find garage sales at swap meets, too, usually in the back. Many people head for the swapmeet for recreation or to get that $5 item that's worth $500; others go routinely every Saturday morning to scoop up the little or big "finds" either for themselves, or to resell. I have several sets of bar wine glasses for parties in all sizes accumulated piece by piece at garage sales at the swap meet for 25-50¢. This is a good place to find second hand gourmet kitchenware. It's a great place to browse for "therapy." San Diego's swap meets draw large crowds. They are becoming more and more fair-like, with entertainment and food. If you are interested in becoming a vendor, the office has free information on how to start your swap meet business and where to find wholesale suppliers. Here are the ones around the County and nearby:

Kobey's Swap Meet, parking lot of the Sports Arena, 3500 Sports Arena Boulevard, in Point Loma,(619) 226-0650, is open Friday-Sunday, 7-3 p.m.; 50 cents on Fridays, $1 on weekends, 75 cents for seniors. Free parking. Kobey's Swap Meet is the biggest swap meets in the area, over 1200 regular vendors every weekend, with an entire array of goods, both new and used. The weekends draw crowds of over 20,000. A must on your list: pick up a copy of *Kobey's Magazine & Directory* which lists their many vendors and what they sell (antiques, arts & crafts supplies, audio/video, automotive supplies, beauty supplies, books, clothing (adult & children) computers, electronics, engraving, food specialties, furniture, gift items, health & fitness, home furnishings, home improvements, jewelry, keys, household/housewares, pagers, incense, insurance, knives, luggage, miscellaneous, music, optical goods, perfumes & colognes, pets & pet supplies, pictures, frames & art, plants & flowers, pools & spas, produce, psychics, real estate, restaurants, services, shoes, signs, sporting goods, stationery & office supplies, sunglasses, swap meet supplies, T-shirts, tarot cards, tools, toys, used merchandise, videos and watches). Their magazine is free of charge at the swapmeet. Check Kobey's Web site: kobeyswap.com

Santee Drive-In Swap Meet, 10990 Woodside Avenue North, just off Hwy. 67, (619) 449-7927. Open every Saturday and Sunday, 6:30 a.m.-2 p.m. Acres and acres of bargains and garage sellers. lst & 3rd Saturdays; ham radio & electronic swapmeet next door; 4th Saturday, fishing gear and sporting goods swapmeet. **Spring Valley Swap Meet**, 6377 Quarry Road, east end of Hwy. 54, adults, 50¢, 463-1194. Saturday and Sunday 7-3 p.m. **Escondido Drive-In Swap Meet**, 635 W.

Mission Avenue, 7-4 p.m. Wednesday, Sunday, (760) 745-3100. Lots of good bargains., lots of food concessions, really good farmers' market, indoor and outdoor, 50¢ Wed & Thurs., Fri., and 75¢ Sat & Sun **South Bay Drive In Swap Meet**, 2170 Coronado, Imperial Beach, Wed., Sat., Sun., (619) 423-9676. **National City Swap Meet**, 3200 D Ave, National City, Sat. & Sun., (619) 477-2203. Farmer's market! **San Ysidro Swapmeet**, Wed.-Sun., very busy! (619) 690-6756. **Seaside Bazaar**, (760) 753-1611, one block South of Encinitas Boulevard on South Coast Hwy. 101 Street in downtown Encinitas next to the La Paloma Theater. Every weekend year round plus holidays, 50 vendors sell an ever-changing eclectic collection of antiques, collectibles, ethnic imports, arts and crafts, candles, incense, wrought iron, unusual clothing, children's clothing, pottery, jewelry, CD's and tapes, plants and flowers, home decor, imports from direct importers who travel the world and much more. Written up in *Sunset Magazine* as" the secret find along the coast." **Orange County Swap Meet**, held at the Orange County Fairgrounds, (949) 723-6616, is the largest weekly swapmeet on the West Coast (huge) with 1000+ vendors, Sat & Sun, $2,

free parking, mostly new bargains, few garage sale items, big name manufacturer's outlets selling overstocks from big-rigs, street performers, great food, good bathrooms, 40-60,000 people a weekend. Check their web site at: ocmarketplace.com **Rose Bowl Flea Market** in Pasadena, the "Mother of All Swap Meets" is held the second Sunday of each month, from 9-3 p.m., since 1968, (323) 560-SHOWx99, then 11. This is the largest flea market in the U.S. with over 2,200 dealers from all over the West and Midwest. Art Nouveau & Art Deco are strong sellers here. Admission, $6 admission at 9a.m.; early admissions, 7:30a.m., $10; 6a.m., $15. Located at 1001 Rosebowl Dr., near the 210 Fwy., 134 Ventura Fwy., 110 Pasadena Fwy. Check their web site at: RCGShows.com. For bus tours from San Diego to the Rose Bowl Flea Market, call DayTripper Tours, (619) 299-5777.

The **Paris Flea Market** is considered to be the leading shopping experience in the world, according to Weissmann Travel Reports, with over 3,000 sidewalk stands and permanent stalls. Kowloon, Hong Kong is second, and the Sunday Market in Kashgar, China is third, in case you kids get around!

Telephone & Services

Compare local land phone telephone rates at UCAN (Utility Consumers Action Network) at ucan.org. Check long distance calling plans at trac.org and click on long distance. They compare for billing increments (some charge by the minute, others every 6 seconds), monthly fees, in-state rates, out of state, and local long distance rate plans. A company usually offers more than one PLAN, so find out which plan is for you. TRAC is a non-profit organization that compares long distances rates. Compare rates at their web site: trac.org Also check teleconsumer.org for comparisons of telephones, mobile phones, telephone cards, etc.

Many people are opting for cell phones only which include local and long distance plans. If you're in the market for a new cell phone, check the *Reader*, which is loaded with cell phone ads for you to compare.

Kobey's Swapmeet (and others) have about a half dozen vendors that sell portable phones, telephones, answering machines, phone cords, cell phones, etc. And, Big Lots always has new phones from under $10 and up. Target, Kmart, Walmart, Fry's, Office Depot, Best Buys, etc dozens of instruments. Compare prices and save.

Out-of-town phone directories including the *Tijuana Yellow Pages* are available from Pacific Bell (ask for out of town editions), or at the downtown library. Past editions of San Diego directories are available in libraries too. Anywho.com is a good online phone directory, and also has a reverse directory (look up by address or phone number).

If you are dissatisfied with the service from a **900 number**, you can ask for a refund. You can block calls from your phone to all 900 and 976 numbers. Blocking is a free service for residential customers.

Have your phone listed in a different name (such as your middle name) instead of paying extra for an unlisted number. Not only is it cheaper, but it helps to sort out phone calls. If a caller asks for the different name, it's probably a salesman.

If you are troubled by repeated anonymous hangups, the phone company will put a trap on your phone, and the harasser will be identified. A free service. Call your telephone company.

It costs about $35-50 to have a phone extension installed. Do it yourself. Radio Shack has the stuff, and they can tell you how to do it. Even I think I can do it since I saw some do it!

Thrift Shops & Boutiques

Altho some thrift shops are privately owned, most are sponsored by charitable organizations that sell donated merchandise. All profits go to good human causes to assist those in need. Some thrift shops are owned by entrepreneurs, but most are run by hospitals or Disabled American Vets, Purple Heart, Amvets, American Cancer Society, Salvation Army, GoodWill, YWCA, St. Vincent de Paul, Assistance League, Children's Hospital, organizations for the disabled, underprivileged, abused, etc. There's nothing more fun than rummaging around in a good thrift shop. I am not always in the mood for this, but when I am, it's like potato chips: sometimes I can't stop with just one....I have to keep going from one store to the next until they close the very last one! I know other bargain hunters who have gone on organized campaigns to hit every thrift store in town, one in search of old silk ties to add to her one-of-a-kind silk and velvet patchwork quilt, an award winner in-the-making to be sure. Another said she wears only silk blouses, and she goes from one thrift store to another in search of more colors for her never-ending collection of beautiful silk blouses. I saw a woman recently in Goodwill who bought up most of the jewelry to sell at a swapmeet.

Here's a thrift store story that'll get your attention: a man found an old map of Paris in nine pieces in a Salvation Army Store in Indianapolis that he thought, after rubbing the dust off of it, was *not* a reproduction but had actually been hand-painted. He bought it for $3 thinking he could possibly sell it for $30-$40 to a dealer. He took it to the local university and had the head of the Geography Department take a look at it. The professor recognized it from a book he had read and sent him to an auction house in New York to have it appraised. Guess what! It was one of the few surviving copies of a map commissioned by King Louis XIV in 1671 valued at $12 MILLION!!!! It had probably come to America in the drawer of a shipment of French antiques, and the new owner tossed it into the Salvation Army collection.

All thrift stores price their clothing about the same. Here is the price list of clothing from the downtown Goodwill store: women's clothing. Fresh clothing hits the floor each week. All items are *one* price, regardless of whether they are silk or linen or velvet or cotton or denim): all blouses, $3.09; blazers, $4.99; all sweaters, $4.29; all blouses/vests, $3.09; all dresses, $5.99; all skirts, $3.79; all jumpsuits, $5.99; all jackets & coats, $8.99; all slacks/joggers, $4.29; all jeans, $6.59. Men's clothing: all sport-coats, $6.19; all jeans, $6.59; all slacks, $4.99; all suits, individual prices up to $20; all men's short sleeve pullover shirts, $2.79; all button, short & long sleeve, $3.29; sweaters, $4.29; jackets & coats, $10.29, belts & ties, $1.29. Children's (boys & girls): shirts & blouses, $2.19; jackets & coats, $4.99; pants & joggers, $3.09; sweaters, $3.09; shorts, $2.09; girls dresses, $3.59, skirts, $3.09; sleepwear, $1.89. Some items in stock are new, complete with original store price tags, and many things look nearly new! (Please note: all sales are final! No returns!!)

Here are some of the larger chains of thrift shops with multiple locations. Some have boutiques with their more valuable items.

Goodwill Industries, 4359 Home Ave., (largest store) (619) 262-6596; downtown, (boutique, too) (619) 232-2083; San Ysidro, (619) 690-1795; El Cajon, (619) 444-8370; Pacific Beach, (858) 274-4960;Tierrasanta Boutique, (858) 278-7120; Rosecrans, (619) 225-5600; Oceanside, (760) 722-2874; Escondido, (760) 745-0501

Disabled American Veterans, 881 Broadway at L, Chula Vista (largest store), unlisted phone; Downtown, (619) 232-0141, and Oceanside, (760) 433-5404.

St. Vincent de Paul, 1550 Market Street, Downtown (largest store), (619) 233-1800. Specialty Shop: 3137 El Cajon Blvd., San Diego, (619) 293-3098.

Army, new store at 3240 Sports Arena with boutique, (619) 758-1716; 901 12th Avenue, downtown (619) 232-1378; with several other locations: Pacific Beach, Mission Bay, (619) 272-6541.

AmVets, Sutherland, (619) 297-4213; Spring Valley, (619) 697-6008; Escondido, (760) 747-2793.

Fabulous Finds, 114 El Camino Real, Encinitas, is an upscale thrift store sponsored by the Assistance League.
Purple Heart Thrifts are in Chula Vista, Santee and Escondido.

There are dozens and dozens of thrift shops, too many to list, so check the *Yellow Pages* under "Thrift Stores" and head out for an afternoon of fun.

Thrift Store Boutiques: Salvation Army has a boutique with antiques and collectibles, jewelry, and other upscale items at 3240 Sports Arena and at their Oceanside, Santee and Poway stores. The Sports Arena store has a calendar of events flyer you can take home (the other stores may have this, too), with days marked on the calender when books are 50% off, Senior day for half off on clothing, upholstered furniture sales 10-25% off; early bird sales, boutique sale of items in the store over 30 days, Manager specials, 25% off storewide sales, plus a monthly Moonlight Madness sale with 25-5-% off various departments on a select Friday of the month from 6-9pm only. Check their web site at thriftstoreonline.com and they also sell things online at salarmy.net; Goodwill has a boutique upstairs at their downtown store at 16th & Broadway and in Tierrasanta at 10601 Tierrasanta Blvd.. St. Vincent dePaul has a specialty store at 3137 El Cajon Blvd, (619) 298-3098.

Tijuana

U.S. residents can bring back $400 of merchandise per person per month; non-residents, $200. You can bring back many groceries and food products from Tijuana with these restrictions: only beef (no other meat), lobster (four per person), most vegetables, some fruits (bananas, blackberries, dates, grapes, melons, pineapples, strawberries), nuts. (No potatoes, no avocados, no meat other than beef, no eggs, no citrus fruit.) You can bring in one liter of booze every 30 days. Americans like to bring back baked goods, hand crafted furniture, clothing, cut flowers (no plants with soil), medications, pottery, leather purses, coats, jackets and luggage, wrought iron, stain glass, silver jewelry, tile, planters, yard ornaments. Tijuana is a freeport, meaning you can buy imported articles (French perfumes, Italian leather shoes, imported sunglasses, etc.) duty free, which translates to: less than you'd pay for them in the U.S. where import taxes have been levied.

If you're headed south, stop at the Customs Office. Take the *last U-turn*, head back north, park on the street and enter the U.S. Customs office and ask for their publication that covers what you can and can not bring back into the U.S. They told me they are really only looking for illegal items (illegal drugs and things forbidden by the U.S. Department of Agriculture because they do not meet our standards of safety), and purchases over the monetary limit on which you need to pay duty.

Many Americans are lining up to buy prescription drugs in Tijuana, and many are heading down there for doctor and dental appointments at prices below those in the U.S., and to play golf (cheap), have massages, spa treatments, enjoy lunch, or head farther south for the weekend. Remember to get Mexican insurance if you're driving as they require it, and it will keep you out of jail if you have a fender bender.

TV Shopping Channels

QVC, the Home Shopping Network, ValueVision and the NBC Shopping Channel offer couch-potatoes the opportunity to shop *after* you drop, 24-hours a day. Prices are considered to be competitive, and the convenience is unbeatable. Just pick up the phone and order, saving a trip to the mall. QVC offers celebrity designer clothing and products including Delta Burke (Plus sizes), and big **fashion designers** like Bob Mackie, Princess Mirah, Susan Graver, Jessica Holbrooke and many more. Other products from stars include TV's Susan Lucci (hair care products), Joan Rivers (jewelry), Victoria Principal (cosmetics), and world famous jewelry designer Kenneth J. Lane who designed for Jackie and has recreated copies of Jackie O's famous pearls, ($76), replicas of Barbara Bush's famous single strand pearls ($68), Hillary Clinton's inaugural pearl necklace ($45), and copies of 29 jewelry treasures of the Duchess of Windsor, $20 up. QVC also sponsors Martha Stewart and Peter Max designs, (800) 345-1515. You can also shop on their Web site at qvc.com. The Home Shopping Network and ValueVision are also on 24 hours a day. The Home Shopping Network (hsn.com) carries clothing lines by Suzanne Sommers, Connie Stevens, and shoes by Vanna White, plus fashions from the world famous designer Diane Von Furstenberg. ValueVision (vvtv.com) has 9 West leather coats, jackets and shoes, Oleg Casini watches, Pierre Cardin luggage, Charles Winston jewelry (major N.Y. jewelry designer), Rolex, Movado, Cartier watches at a discount! And, you can purchase all the products you see on infomercials on TV at productsontelevision.com

Weddings & Parties (Do-It-Yourself!)

You can put together your own fabulous wedding (or party) on a shoe string budget if you are willing to do a lot of the work yourself rather than pay someone to plan, buy, fix, serve and clean up everything for you. Pick up a good do-it-yourself party or wedding planner book from a bookstore, used bookstore, library (or yard sale). Party goods stores have party and wedding planners, too, which outline what you need to do and how to plan for your size event, including a time schedule. Have the event at home, or you can obtain a permit ($32.50, on a lottery basis/30 days in advance) from the Parks & Recreation Department, (619) 221-8900, and have your event outdoors, at the beach, Mission Bay, La Jolla Cove, Mount Soledad, Torrey Pines, Sunset Cliffs, the Presidio, Silver Strand or anywhere in the outdoors including the Carlsbad Flower Fields, (760) 930-9123. Each public park has its own rules to adhere to, including number of guests, glass containers, etc. Or, you can rent the Bahia Belle sternwheeler and have your reception on the bay. The Heritage Park Bed & Breakfast Inn in Old Town is a wonderfully romantic site you can rent for a wedding and reception. Or, you can tie the knot at the outdoor arch by the bay at the County Administration Center for $50, and have it Webcast for $25 more. Then, check Smart & Final for their wedding/party menu suggestions which tell how many containers of bulk salads, etc. you will need to feed "X" number of people. Their prices are great, too. Costco & Sam's Club do great party trays with 5 lbs. meat & cheese, about $23; or veggie tray (6 lbs veggies and dip, about $18; Shrimp ($39), sushi, sandwich & antipasto trays, too. Order in advance. Their gourmet frozen hors d'oeuvres are fabulous (mini-quiches, egg rolls, stuffed phyllo, fried stuffed jalapenos) and serve 18-50. Honey Baked Hams and Golden Baked Hams have not only hams, but turkey and roast beef, cheeses, salads, olives, pickles, honey mustard, etc. Pt. Loma Seafoods will whip up a bowl of ceviche, platter of shrimp, mountain of crab legs, etc for you. Almost every restaurant will do catering (which is as simple as just supplying the food), even an Oriental all-you-can-eat restaurant or an Italian or Mexican food restaurant or Rubio's Baja Grill. Buying your own beer, wine and champagne at a discount warehouse is going to be 70-80% cheaper than what a hotel will charge you. A wedding lunch or brunch is usually less expensive than dinner. For a complete selection of wedding or party supplies including invitations, cake and candy supplies, wedding accessories, guests books, invitations, rentals, and more, check Michael's Crafts Stores and Party City. Costco and Smart & Final have the best prices on paper plates, napkins and plastic glasses in bulk. Party rental stores rent tents, champagne fountains, huge bowls, chairs, tables and cloths, arches, and everything you need. Check flower prices at the swap meet (go several weeks early and make arrangements with a flower vender), or go to Tijuana florists. The *Reader* has a wedding and party section in the classifieds where you can get various services. Sample the locally famous and very popular Black Forest wedding cake at the European Bakery, 3361 Voltaire, (619) 222-3377, not cheap, but fabulous. For personalized service and a quality affordable cake, call Shirley Resnick, the Cake Lady, (619) 561-9377, an independent wedding cake baker who bakes beautiful, delicious, yummy, affordable cakes (the chocolate cake with chocolate/raspberry filling and decorated with white shaved chocolate and fresh flowers is a beaut) and she delivers the fresh cake on your big day. Or, you can check Tijuana bakeries for wedding cakes at real savings; most major local supermarket bakeries and Costco make sheet cakes that serves 30-48, or hire a student at a culinary school or cake decorating class. Some churches have a parishioner who specializes in making wedding cakes which is worth checking into (usually a senior citizen who is thrilled to have the opportunity to make it for you, at a great price.) Then gather up the friends and relatives and put them to work for you. It's recommended that you have a few paid employees at the event -- call San Diego State University's job listing board and get a student or two who do catering work for a few hours for you. For **music,** check under Musicians in the *Reader* classifieds for bands to rent, or call the award winning UCSD jazz ensemble, SDSU's jazz ensemble or SDSU's Faculty Trio, (619) 594-6031. If you need a bartender, call a bartender's school (National School has built careers in bartending and the culinary arts for 20 years, (619) 283-0200). Get at least two friends to run around with their cameras and videos capturing you and the guests on film. (The candid shots are my favorite.) The bottom line is: with a little imagination and creativity, you can put on a wedding nothing short of a coronation, or have a fabulous party ala the lifestyles of the rich and famous for a very small percentage of what it would cost to have someone do it all for you.

You can get big samples of **wedding cakes** at bakeries to take home for the mother of the bride, groom, etc. to taste.

Affordable Garden Gate Florals, Donna Treadway, (619) 443-9383. Lovely customized wedding flowers for all budgets from her home office. Savings, here!

The average price of a wedding gown is about $800+. .**Rent a wedding gown** from A Nite On The Town, 8650 Genesee, (858) 457-1233. The **Garment Gourmet** has used **bridal** and wedding party dresses at 831 Williamston, Vista, (760) 630-6630.

In Mexico, they really go in *big time* for weddings, and good buys on wedding gowns and tuxedos can be found all over **Tijuana**. Stores called

Novias (Sweethearts)are loaded with wedding gear, veils, garters, all the trimmings and there is one in every block!

Check the Thrifties #3190 classified column in the *Union-Trib* for used (some new!!) wedding gowns, usually at great prices, including some dirt cheap. Some are unworn but had been altered and couldn't be returned (hmmm . . .let's not go there). Ask about the value, condition, where it was bought. You can negotiate the price on this one, for sure. See the *Reader* classified ads, too. There are always several wedding gowns advertised! Keep watching .. .

I have seen spectacular wedding gowns at the **Salvation Army Thrift Store Boutique** next to Pier One on Sports Arena. They also had gotten in a shipment of new sample mother of the bride dresses in silks with price tags (retail, $150; Salvation Army price, $30!) **Goodwill** boutique has wedding gowns, too. And, I've seen many, many wedding gowns at yard In fact, just last weekend a lady had TWO wedding dresses . . and they were both hers. Husband #3 was helping her with the sale. Giggles. There was an absolutely gorgeous one I almost bought just because it was only $10! It was such an incredible buy I had a really hard time leaving it there, even though I don't know anyone who is a size 8 who is getting married! Now I wish I had bought it to donate to the costume department at the Old Globe . .or SDSU drama dept . . or the local highschool. That way, I wouldn't still be thinking about it! *Grrrrr.*

Here are two Web sites (many more available) where you can view gowns and select invitations, complete wedding planners, honeymoons, :weddingnetwork.com and weddingchannel.com

Martha Stewart publishes her own do-it-yourself Wedding Planner available at bookstores or directly from Martha at (800) 950-7130. I gasp at the thought of doing one her way.

Party City (9 locations in San Diego Co.) has personalized wedding invitations, several choices, and all the bridal paper goods you need at 40% off manufacturer's list price. Michael's Crafts has them, too.

Window Coverings & Wallpaper

A lot of savings can be had here. Find what you want at any decorator shop or wallpaper and paint store, get the book pattern and number and then call a wholesale company to see if they carry it for less. Most companies have free UPS shipping and no sales tax. Compare prices. Try these:

Wholesale wallpaper & window companies, 40-80% off, Design Place Direct, (800) 627-0400; American, (800) 346-0608 (up to 82%) with scores of suppliers. Most orders ship in 48 hours.

Home Depot, Lowe's and Expo carry a full line of wallpaper, shutters, blinds and other window coverings. Good selection and good prices. **Costco** now offers custom window coverings; order from samples.

Wallpapers to Go, 4647 Kearny Mesa, (858) 565-4550. Semi-annual sale, lot of wallpaper in stock, lots of order books.

Costs Plus, **Pier One** and **Ikea** have great, trendy and reasonably priced window coverings made from fabrics plus heavy canvas, rice paper, matchsticks, etc., and wait for a sale, usually less than a few weeks away.

JCPenney has custom decorating and there is usually a 25-50% off sale every couple months. Ask a sales associate when the last sale was, and when the next will be. Ask about catalog returns and cancellations of custom orders (maybe the color was too light or dark, or the length was too long or short) etc. You can get some REAL good buys here.

Check the Thrifty classified ads. Often there are draperies that you might be able to use. Some were in model homes, canceled custom orders from decorators, etc.

Chapter 2

$MONEY-SAVING TIPS &
CONSUMER SAVVY / HOW TO COMPLAIN

Whatever it takes to get more for my money, I am usually willing to do. (Even if I won the lottery, I'd never abandon this philosophy.) Here are a few tips I've picked up along the way that enable me to inevitably get more bang for the buck.

Money-Saving Tips

KNOW THY PRICES How else will you know you've found a bargain? You gotta do your homework here. Jot down prices as you shop for items you're interested in purchasing. Keep a record of them. I keep track of prices in the back of my check register (they're free) whether I'm shopping for a computer, sofa or comparing prices of laundry detergent. I also keep a record of ATM withdrawals there. **COMPARISON SHOP** Check at least six to ten sources before you make a major purchase. You'd be surprised at the difference in prices you'll be quoted and chances are someone is always willing to sell "it" to you for less if you keep looking. Let your fingers do the walking and use the phone. (There are a *lot* of phone numbers provided in this book.) Always deal with the manager or person at the top who can give you the best price, and tell them you are getting quotes. **KEEP RECEIPTS** Keep all receipts for your personal purchases in a file, bowl or drawer. I just toss all receipts for purchases in together. Many stores refund the difference if you buy an item that goes on sale within two weeks, and at least I know where the receipt is! **LOW PRICE GUARANTEE** Many stores offer to meet or beat any advertised price on an identical item in stock. And, many offer a "30-day price guarantee" and will refund the difference + 10% if you find your purchase for less elsewhere within 30 days. **RAIN CHECKS** If a retailer advertises a special which is not stipulated to be in "limited quantities," and you make a trip to the store to buy it and it is not on the shelf, ask for a "rain check." This will allow you to buy the item later at the advertised price when they restock. When I went to Long's Drugs to buy L'EGGS hosiery (advertised at half price), they were out. The manager offered me a "rain check," a little form he filled in with the date, number of pairs I wanted, advertised price and an expiration date. He told me when to check back to see if the rack has been restocked and gave me the phone number to call to see when they were in! I almost fainted!! *This* is a store that believes in customer satisfaction!! Here's another "rain check" tale: a friend went to Sears expressly to get some 100% cotton underwear for her allergic daughter. They were out. She asked the clerk for a "rain check." She was told they didn't give "rain checks." She went home and called the manager who *mailed* her a "rain check" and ordered in the merchandise she wanted from another store! Another friend went to Target to get an advertised toaster oven. Target had sold out but offered her a "rain check" and told her to come back in a week. When she went back seven days later, they were still out, so they let her have a more expensive model at no additional charge! In 1971, the Federal Trade Commission issued the Retail Food Store Advertising and Marketing Practices Rule which provides that you receive a "rain check," or a substitute or comparable item, or compensation, if an advertised special isn't in stock and the ad did not stipulate "limited quantities. Always ask to speak with the department manager or store manager about "rain checks" because many employees do not know of this policy. WHEN A STORE OVERCHARGES If a store overcharges you for an item, point this out to the manager. I was overcharged for some cantaloupes at Von's. They didn't charge the advertised price and I paid over $3 more than I should have, but didn't catch it until I got home and thought about it. I called the manager who suggested I come down. He refunded the whole amount I paid for the cantaloupes AND gave me two $1 Von's coupons! They appreciate customer loyalty and want to make amends for situations that really shouldn't occur. IMPULSE BUYING Walk away from impulse buying and wait 24 hours. Chances are you won't still want it. Make a shopping list and stick to it. Only buy what you NEED. Carry only enough cash to make your purchases, and avoid carrying credit cards. Spend smart. If you're not a smart spender, you're going to always be in bondage to your creditors. MAKE FINANCIAL GOALS Make a plan. Lack of priority to save (for a house or car) *causes* impulse buying. Always have a savings plan (10% or more should go into savings.) If you're only planning to make ends meet, you're only going to make ends meet. Saving is the way most Americans get ahead. BARGAIN HUNTING Bargain hunting can involve a lot of trade-off's. Don't expect all the niceties of a department store when shopping discounters. Many off-price stores offer a "no-frills" environment, some with communal dressing rooms or no dressing room! Remember, you're not paying for all those niceties that drive prices up, either. You're saving MONEY!! CLEARANCE Many stores have specific days for sorting out items for clearance. Ask the manager of your favorite store about dates. PERSONAL SHOPPERS "Better" department stores offer FREE personal shoppers who will put together an outfit or a complete wardrobe for you on your budget. You can even finance your new wardrobe on a long term contract. They'll tell you if they know an item is going on sale soon. Also, the "pricier" stores offer bigger markdowns on sale merchandise! **SALES** Hit the department store sales to save 25% or more. They have a great selection and the sale price is as good as outlet prices. Watch for pre-season sales, clearance sales, end of the month sales, end of season sales, red tag sales and other specials at major department stores who advertise in the Union-Trib. Weekend newspapers are loaded with sales. Wait for major sales like Columbus Day, Memorial Day, Labor Day, anniversary sales, customer appreciation days, etc. to make a major purchase like carpeting or furniture. No point in buying just before a big sale and there's *always* a sale just around the corner. Do your research, then wait for the sale. **MAILING LIST** Get on the mailing list of your favorite stores. Even if you don't want to open an account, you can ask to be placed on the mailing list to receive advance notice of sales. Some department stores have private sales for their "special" customers with drawings, entertainment, refreshments and giveaways you wouldn't believe. I won a Waterford crystal clock at a drawing, a large package of potpourri, and a collection of fine perfume samples!! **OPEN AN ACCOUNT** Many stores offer a 10-15% discount on purchases made the day you open an account, and this can really add up when you make major purchases. **SHOP EARLY ON A SALE DAY** Be there when the store opens for the best selection. If possible, shop the day before and ask the sales person to hold items for you until the sale begins. Most stores will hold for 24 hours. **RETURNS** Don't assume you can return items. Some sales are "Final." Carefully examine items before you buy, and always ask a reliable sales person or the manager for information on returns, refunds and credits. Return policies should be posted. **NEGOTIATE THE PRICE** Attempt to negotiate the price. Independent stores (Mom & Pop stores) almost expect it. If you're new at it, start honing your skills at yard sales. You can make an offer, quietly and in private, and never take "no" for a final answer, Keep going. Say: *What'll you take for this?* or *Will you take X-amount for this?* or *Can you take anything more off the price?* or *That's a little above my price range. Will you take $___ for it?* Or you can say: *I'd buy it today if you could reduce the price by $___.* Hey, whaddaya have to lose? Then, learn the fine art of shutting ye ole mouth and waiting a moment for their response. Chances are they *will* lower their asking price if you give them a moment to think about it. Most yard sales are for "getting rid of" rather than raising money, so never buy at the first price offered. Say you're on a tight budget. Find something wrong with the item. Make an offer and counter offer. Don't take "no" for a final answer. And, all the while, be gracious, and do this where others can't hear. Remember what Grandma used to say: *You get more flies with honey than you do with vinegar*, so *charm* your way into getting a better price!! Make it fun! Say: *Let's play "Let's Make A Deal"* or *How about letting me make you an offer you can't refuse?* Make it a win-win situation. No one wants to deal with a person who's out to screw 'em. Negotiating is a skill; you have to practice the art to have confidence and be good at it. You should always negotiate the price of a new or used car. Furniture and jewelry at "Mom & Pop" shops or antiques shops are negotiable. Even attorney or doctor fees! Even your funeral! Always negotiate the price of hotel rooms and car rentals (they have several deals they can offer you. **REASON TO USE A CREDIT CARD** A good reason to charge auto repairs, appliance repairs, airline tickets, etc. is: if you car doesn't work properly or the bargain airline trip didn't materialize, your credit card company will credit your account if you provide proper documentation. Keep good records, receipts, agreements, etc. Check the back of your credit card statement for their policy regarding credits.) **BEWARE** Nothing is a bargain if it doesn't fit and just sits in your closet. Just because an item is marked down to 10% of its original value doesn't mean that it's for you. Don't be seduced into buying something you won't wear or use just because it is an incredible bargain. We've all fallen into that trap. Ahhh yes, live and learn. **GENERIC** Sometimes generic brand cleaning supplies or products with the lowest price require more product to do the job, making them far more expensive than name brands. **CONSIDER TIME SPENT** If you're spending an extra two hours to save $5, you're putting a very low value on your time. If, however, you spend 60 hours painting the exterior or your house when the bid is $2000 and the paint and materials cost less than $200, you've "earned" $30 an hour and saved $1800 doing the work yourself. **PUTTING OFF REPAIRS CAN BE COSTLY** Failure to recaulk the tub for a few cents can do damage to the wall, which can cost 1000 times more to repair. A toilet that needs the ball replaced can add hundreds to your water bill. You can replace it yourself. Ask a sales associate at a home improvement center to show you how. **BEING TOO THRIFTY** Scrimping on little things like using less toothpaste or washing and reusing coffee filters can cause more stress and illness than it's worth. Being too thrifty can end up costing you. And, there's not too much point in scrimping and saving unless you're able to enjoy spending when the right occasion comes along. **LITTLE LUXURIES** Treat yourself to the little luxuries that make life wonderful: a cup of gourmet coffee, a new plant or colorful new towels (on sale, of course). Show a healthy sense of self-love and reward yourself for all the money you've been able to save! **PAY A COMPLIMENT** Write or call a company on their 800-toll free line and pay a compliment. They may send you products, discount coupons, etc. A woman told me she sent a letter to a cat food company saying theirs was the only cat food her cat would eat, and a few days later, she got several cases of cat food delivered to her door, and tons of discount coupons. Another woman paid AT&T a compliment for their service, and they asked if they could use her testimonial in their ads, and paid her $28,000 for royalties, and she doesn't think they even used her name!

Avoid Fraud / Be Consumer Savvy

Avoid "get rich" and "work-at-home" schemes. Con artists bilk $100 billion a year out of Americans, mainly in telemarketing, followed by mail order, credit repair, health insurance, investments, maintenance and auto repair. BE SUSPICIOUS of unsolicited calls. Never answer the door unless you know who is there. Con-men are hoping you will foolishly open the door, and if you do, they know they have a fool. Don't cash the free money" check in the mail scheme. You'd probably be signing up for something costly. See the small print. Avoid doing business about which you know nothing. Say "NO" to high pressure tactics. Beware of "testimonials." If it looks too good to be true, it probably ISN"T true. Check out individuals and companies before opening your wallet or check book. Never spend money to claim a prize. Keep your bank account number and social security number a secret. Don't be fooled by a money-back guarantee. Check out contractors with the City Attorney's office before hiring one. Be wary of 900 & 976 telephone numbers. For a free copy of "Too Good To Be True! A Guide To Consumer Fraud" write to the Consumer Information Center, No. 640Z, Pueblo, CO 91009, or go to pueblo.gsa.gov and search for scams. The **San Diego County District Attorney Fraud Division** has a hotline with recorded information, (619) 531-3507. That feeling of being ripped-off or treated unfairly and not knowing where to turn is devastating, and we have all experienced it. Seek resolution and justice, and help prevent others from the same misfortune by bringing the matter before the appropriate authorities. An effective complaint letter can produce surprising results: replacements, refunds, gift certificates, free samples and customer appreciation gifts. *YES!!*

How & Where to Make a Complaint

Here's what you do if you need to take action against someone or a company has given you poor service, inferior products, etc. First, sit down and write a vicious, hateful, mean, nasty, bitter letter of complaint. Ventilate. Get into it. Say horrible things. Use disgusting language. Get it out of your system. Then, wad it up in a ball and throw it away because no one on the other end will read it if you send it! They'll think you're just another "crazy" and simply throw your letter in the trash. Now, after you've gotten that off your chest, sit down and write a coherent, specific, detailed letter outlining your complaint. Include dates, copies of invoices, warranties, receipts and other appropriate documentation. Make copies of everything before mailing it off. What else can you do? Check the list that follows for the appropriate agency to contact.

San Diego Mediation Center, (619) 238-2400, will give advice and/or assistance, including letter writing (a free service). Report the problem to the **Better Business**

Bureau, (858) 496-2131, or file a complaint at sd.bbb.org. Contact Marty Emerald, Troubleshooter, Channel 10 KGTV, (619) 237-1010 or online at kgtv.com. Contact **Consumer Bob** at Channel 7/39, (858-571-8888, or online at nbc739.com. Call **Turko** at KUSI, (858) 571-5151. Call the **California Dept. of Consumer Affairs**, (800) 952-5210. They offer live operators and recorded information. Call the San Diego City Attorney General's Office **Consumer Protection Division**, (619) 533-5600, 525 B Street, Suite 2100, San Diego, CA 92101. Write to: **Bureau of Consumer Protection**, Federal Trade Commission, Washington, DC 20580, or online at www.ftc.gov, and ask for a recommendation on how to pursue your complaint, or file your complaint online at ftc.gov. Send for the free **Consumer Resource Handbook** which lists contacts to help with consumer complaints. Send request to the Consumer Information Center,

Dept. 21, Pueblo, CO 81009, or view it online at pueblo.gsa.gov. Resolve disputes with **mail-order companies** by writing to Direct Marketing Association Mail Order Action Line, 6 E. 43rd Street, NY, NY 10017-4646. For **automobile dealer complaints**, get the address of the district offices and/or the factory (available in your owner's manual), or call the corporate offices, using the toll free number, and find out to whom you should address your letter. Founded in 1999, as a free-of-charge public service, the UCAN Fraud Squad offers non-legal dispute resolution advice to San Diego consumers and UCAN members. While the Fraud Squad's focus is on dealing with complaints regarding abusive utilities, the staff is also trained to offer advice and information on over 300 of the most commonly reported consumer complaints. Complaints are recorded and are frequently used as evidence in legal proceedings Web: ucan.org.

Check "Consumer Complaint & Protection Coordinators" in the White Pages for complaint against any of the following:

Accountants
Advertising
Alarms (Burglar)
Athletics
Automobile Repair
Banks
Barbers
Beauty Salons
Cemeteries
Collection Agencies/Debt Collection
Contractors
Cosmetologists
Credit Practices (Excessive Charges)
Credit Unions
Dance Studios
Dental Examiners
Dental Auxiliary
Doctors
Employment Agencies
Engineers (Professional)
Escrow Companies
Finance Companies
Food-drug-cosmetic-hazardous
 Household-chemical

Franchise Industries
Funeral Directors/embalmers
Guarantees (Deceptive or Unhonored)
Health Professions
Home Furnishings
Home Improvement
Insurance
Investment Fraud
Loans
Family Counselors
Nursing Home Complaints
Optometrists
Pest Control Operators
Pharmacy
Physicians-surgeons
Podiatry
Private Investigators & Private Security
Real Estate
Repair Services
Savings & Loan, Structural Pests
Tax Preparers, Tv Repair
Transportation (Moving, Busses)
Veterinarians
Warranties

Chapter 3
101+ FREE & BARGAIN
THINGS TO DO

There are many, many, many things to do in San Diego that are free or low cost and the selection to choose from is absolutely fabulous. We live in a county filled with unique leisure opportunities: bays and an ocean full of water activities to the West, mountains and a desert to the East, a major metropolis to the North (with Laguna and Newport en route) and a foreign country to the South! And nearly perfect weather year round! What more could you ask for? No wonder this place is known as a little piece of paradise!

If you want to save money on the high price of entertainment and things to do, there are special money-saving membership subscription packages with a 10-30% discount, plus priority seating, on series tickets to music, dance and theater performances, or you can buy half-price day-of-performance tickets at Arts Tix at Horton Plaza. Annual memberships to museums and attractions entitle you to unlimited usage for 12 months which can be a huge bargain for a whole year of entertainment. From time to time, attractions like Sea World, Disneyland, Universal Studios and Knott's Berry Farm offer discounts for those with a Southern California zip code on their driver's licenses. Wild Animal Park offers free admission on it's anniversary every year. The zoo offers discounts from time to time for those living within the city limits, a free admission day every year on their anniversary, free admission for children two weeks before Christmas, etc etc. And, you can get senior, student and military discounts. There are also organizational discounts (AAA, AARP, Boy Scouts, etc.) and professional organization discounts. Call ahead and ask if there are any discount coupons you should know about, or any organizational or corporate discounts, etc. and group rates. The Entertainment Book offers half-off coupons for many museums in Balboa Park, cruises on the bay, roller skating and much more. With all these opportunities for you to take advantage of, why pay full fare if you don't have to?

Even if you're on the tightest budget, you can have a fabulous social life by volunteering and getting into many museums, theaters and events, free. And, there are enough *free* things to do to in San Diego to keep you busy for the next three lifetimes! So, if you are a San Diego "go-*er* & do-*er*," here are some great things to check out and put on your calendar.

Free & Bargain Things to Do

Free Days at Balboa Park Museums One of the best freebies in San Diego has got to be the free admission on Tuesdays to specified museums in Balboa Park. You could truly spend many a memorable day exploring this spectacularly gorgeous park containing ornamental Spanish revival architecture, courtyards and fountains. The park is known for it's massive trees, colorful seasonal flowers in bloom everywhere, lush tropical and formal gardens. Rare and unusual fauna span the hills and canyons of the park. On weekends, there are street musicians to entertain you while you sit and "people watch." You can participate in sports, have a picnic on the endless green lawns, go on a guided walking tour or participate in educational activities. Pick up a $1 park map and schedule of activities at the Information Center in the Casa de Balboa near the Space Center. Call (619) 239-0512 for recording of hours of operation and directions to park. Web: .balboapark.org

Tuesday is FREE DAY at specified museums. Free admission entitles you to see the *permanent collections* (traveling exhibits have their own entrance fee). Going on free days only saves you about $70 per person!

FREE ON THE FIRST TUESDAY
San Diego Natural History The Museum of Natural History contains exhibits from the natural environment of our planet with emphasis on the plant and animal life in the Southwest; Desert Diorama; gems, minerals and crystals; Shore Ecology Diorama; dinosaurs, Antarctica; free on 1st Tues., 9:30 a.m.-4:30 p.m.; (619) 232-3821. Web: sdnhm.org

Model Railroad Museum North America's largest operating model railroad exhibit with four permanent giant scale model railroads, toy train gallery, hands on exhibits and railroad artifacts; free on 1st Tues., 11 a.m.-4 p.m.; (619) 696-0199. Web: sdrm.org

Science Center of Reuben H. Fleet Center a hands-on science center with over 50 exhibits; free on 1st Tues., 9:30 a.m.-6 p.m.; (619) 238-1233. Web: rhfleet.org Check out the Imax Theater's deal ($5 after 5pm).

FREE ON THE SECOND TUESDAY
Museum of Photographic Arts contemporary and historic photographic exhibits of nationally and internationally known photographers; free on 2nd Tues., 10 a.m.-5 p.m.; (619) 238-7559. Web: mopa.org

Museum of San Diego History local history and American cultural history from 1850 to present; free on 2nd Tues., 10 a.m.-4:30 p.m.; (619) 232-6203. Web: sandiegohistory.org

FREE ON THE THIRD TUESDAY

Museum of Man an anthropological museum with emphasis on American Indians, Pre-Columbian Mayas and Early Man. Permanent exhibits include "Life Cycles and Ceremonies" and Egyptian artifacts; free on 3rd Tues., 10 a.m.-4:30 p.m.; (619) 239-2001. Web: museumofman.org

San Diego Museum of Art Elegant collection of Italian Renaissance and Spanish Old Masters, American Art, 19th century European paintings and 20th century paintings and sculpture plus the Frederick R. Weisman Gallery for California Art; free on 3rd Tues., 10 a.m.-4:30 p.m.; (619) 232-7931. Do lunch in the Sculpture Garden. Web: sddt.com/~sdma

Japanese Friendship Garden Small Japanese meditation garden in the Zen style with bamboo and rock surroundings, symbolically conveying harmonic oneness between man and nature. Includes an Exhibit House with Japanese cultural displays. Free the 3rd Tuesday., 10 a.m.-4 p.m.; (619) 232-2780. Web: niwa.org

Mingei International Folk Art Museum Arts of people from all cultures of the world. Free 3rd Tues.,10-4pm, (619) 239-0003.

San Diego Art Institute New exhibitions of works by SanDiego artists opens every six weeks. Open 10 a.m. - 4p.m., T-Sat; noon to 4pm on Sundays. Gift shop with jewelry and gift items made by locals artisans. (619) 236-0011.

FREE ON THE FOURTH TUESDAY

Aerospace Museum Originals and replicas of historic planes and spacecraft from the Wright Brothers to the Space Shuttle. Highlights include a replica Spirit of St. Louis, an A-12 Blackbird, WWII SPDA and an F4 Phantom. Includes the International Hall of Fame with portraits and plaques honoring aviation heroes; free on 4th Tues., 10 a.m.-4:30 p.m.; (619) 234-8291. Web: aerospacemuseum.org

Automotive Museum Over 60+ automobiles make up the museum's core collection, featuring historic, elegant, luxurious and power motor vehicles from a bygone era to present. Traveling exhibits; free on 4th Tues., 10 a.m.-4:30 p.m.; (619) 231-2886.

San Diego Hall of Champions Sports Museum, new location in Federal

Building, showcases over 40 sports, making the museum one of three multi-sports museums in the nation; AFC Championship Ring, Superbowl memorabilia, Olympic pins, new Bass Fishing Exhibit with live bass. Free on 2nd Tues., 10 a.m.-4:30 p.m.; (619) 234-2544.

Hall of Nations Film at the House of Pacific Relations is free on the fourth Tuesday.

FREE ON THE FIFTH TUESDAY

Normal museum prices are in effect on the Fifth Tuesday, but the Timken Museum, below, is always free.

The Balboa Park Tram is always free, and pick up every 8-10 minutes from the parking lot at Inspiration Point and deposit you in the heart of Balboa Park.

Now, to really experience San Diego like royalty without emptying your pockets, after you've visited all the free museums on Tuesday, drop by Bertrand at Mr. A's (619) 239-1377) on the top floor at 5th & Laurel. This will cost you the price of a drink, which is pricey here (Chardonnay starts at $6 a glass; coffee, $4.50, but the view from Mr. A's will knock your socks off. There is no longer a Happy Hour here with special drink prices, BUT, you can see the breathtaking view of bay, ocean, Point Loma and Mexico Watch the planes land at Lindberg Field from the outdoor deck or at a window seat inside and wave to the pilots as they fly by. . . you can practically see the whites of their eyes. A sunset is really special here if you can catch one, and the city lights are spectacular after dark. I love to have my annual toddy at Mr. A's during the holidays when the downtown buildings are decorated (gorgeous site). Web: BertrandatMisterAs.com

ALWAYS FREE IN BALBOA PARK

Timken Gallery features the Putnam Foundation collection of Old Masters from Spanish, French, Venetian, Flemish and American schools (one of the best west of the Mississippi) and a world famous collection of Russian icons; free daily, 10-4:30 p.m., Tues-Sat; 1:30-4:30 p.m. Sun.; 1:30-4:30pm; (619) 239-5548. Web: gort.ucsd.edu/sj/timken Always free.

House of Pacific Relations A cluster of small cottages exhibiting the culture, traditions and history of 31 national groups. The International Resource Center at the United Nations Building offers a computerized library that includes books, periodicals, reports and videos. Open house with cultural displays, outdoor activities, ethnic son, dance and refreshments on Sunday afternoons. Entertainment March-October. Also open the fourth Tuesday with free Hall of Nation's films. Free when open, Sun., 12:30 p.m.-5 p.m., and on the 4th Tues., 11:30 a.m.-3 p.m. with continuous films;

international ethnic clubs; (619) 292-8592. Always free.

Spanish Village Art Center consists of 41 studios feature works of local artists for display and sale; 11 a.m.-4 p.m. daily, free; (619) 233-9050. Always free.

Botanical Building This redwood lath arboretum houses nearly 1200 permanent plants and seasonal color displays tropical and subtropical plants. Exhibits are changed seasonally. Picturesquely framed by flower beds and a lily pond; great place for a photo; free, Fri.-Wed., 10 a.m.-4 p.m.; closed on Thursday; (619) 234-8901. Always free.

Centro Cultural de la Raza a multi-disciplinary arts and cultural organization with exhibits and events that promote native American, Mexican and Chicano cultures; gallery hours: Thursday through Sunday, 12 noon- 5 p.m.; free; (619) 235-6135. Always free.

Free concerts at the gorgeous Spreckles Organ Pavilion in Balboa Park, featuring the largest organ in the world, with 4,445 pipes. Every Sunday, rain or shine, from 2-3 p.m., 52 weeks a year. Free concerts on Monday evenings at 8 p.m. from June through August. Twilight concerts from late June through August from 6:15-7:15 p.m. on Tuesdays, Wednesdays and Thursdays, (619) 235-1105.

Free walking tours of Balboa Park. Explore the gardens, architecture and history of the park. **Spanish Colonial Architecture tours**, lst Wed;. Meet at Visitor's Center, House of Hospitality, 9:30 a.m.(619) 223-6566. Web: balboapark.org Click on tours. **Balboa Birders Guided Walks,** monthly, lst Thursday, 7:30am-p:30am (619) 232-3821x7 **Offshoot Tours** of Balboa Park. Explore the gardens, architecture and history of the park. Weekly tours on Saturday, 10a.m. Meet in front of the Visitor Center. (619) 232-1122. **Ranger-led Tours**, historical and botanical treasures of the part; every Tuesday and Sunday from 1-2pm. Meet in front of the House of Hospitality, (619) 232-1122.

Balboa Park Passport You can purchase a Balboa Park Passport which entitles you to visit the 12 major museums and attractions in the park for one week for $30 ($70 value). **Passport/Deluxe Zoo Pass Combo** This passport includes a one-day zoo pass for about $55. Value over $100.

Holidays on the Prado The museums in Balboa Park are free the first Friday and Saturday of December, from 5-9 p.m. during the annual Holidays on the Prado, with live entertainment in the Organ Pavillion.

Stars in the Park is a 50 minute program offered at the Reuben Fleet Space Theater on the first Wednesday of the month. You'll be seeing the stars, constellations and planets that will be visable in the San Diego sky over the next month. A panel of experts in on hand to answer your questions. Afterwards, you may view the stars outside through telescopes provided by the San Diego Astronomy Association, (619) 645-8940. Web site: sdaa.org. Adults, $3; juniors, $1.75. Memberships start at $35 and include many benefits including free space theater tickets. Call (619) 238-1233 for further information. For more information on the stars in San Diego, see the Star Gazer every Wednesday in the Quest section of the *San Diego Union-Tribune.*

The **Museum of Contemporary Art**, 700 Prospect St., La Jolla, (858) 454-3542 is free the first Sunday of the month and the third Tuesday. The downtown museum at 1001 Kettner at Broadway, (619) 234-1001, is free daily. Closed Wednesdays, and is open the first Thursday evening of the month with music, art and dance, $3 donation. Web: mcasd.org

Money-saving Memberships Join any of the museums, galleries, zoos, major attractions, etc. listed herein and get many freebies including *unlimited* entrance, classes, special admission to exhibits, passes for your friends and relatives, invitations to special events, openings. Participate with others with the same interests, etc.

Museum Gift Shops All the museums above have great gift shops with unique and unusual items including beautiful photographs, art cards, books, space gadgets, natural jewelry, shells, rocks, t-shirts, etc.

Learn **folk dancing** with the International Dance Association of San Diego County, (619) 222-7645. Dance to the music of 35 different countries every Sunday from 12:30-5 p.m. in the Balboa Park Club Building, and on Friday at 9:30-noon at the Casa del Prado. Folk dancing lessons Monday through Thursday at 7 p.m., about $1-2; Call (619) 422-5540. Annual folk dance festival in July is free with vendors and food.

Ballroom dancing at the Balboa Park Club Building at 7 p.m. on Fridays and Sundays, 6:30 p.m., 297-4363. See the *Reader's* "Events" and the *Union-Trib's* "Night &Day" section for more on dancing (country western dancing, swing dancing, jitterbug, etc.) Free dance lessons,.

Suspension Bridge Cross the Spruce Street suspension bridge at First Street near Balboa Park. It crosses high above Highway 163 below. This is for thrill seekers. Don't look down!

***Entertainment* coupon book** The *Entertainment coupon book* has "two-for-one" coupons for most of the museums in Balboa Park.   (See Resources.)

Tour the Globe Theater at 11 a.m. most Saturdays, $3; seniors and students, $1; (619) 231-1941.

San Diego Zoo   Admission to the zoo is free one day a year, on its anniversary, celebrated on the *first Monday* in October. Go early in order to get parking. Regular adult $19.50, children 3-11 $11.75, under 2 and military in uniform free. Senior passes for I year, $35. Membership entitles you to *unlimited* entrance to the zoo *and* the Wild Animal Park ($19.95), two guest passes, 6 discount coupons, Zoo Nooz Magazine, 4 two-for-one Zoo bus tour coupons, monthly membership specials, free zoo Skyfari. One membership, $68; dual membership, $86; Koala Kids Club, age 3-11, $21; 12-17, $25. Membership is a great gift for a family on a budget because it provides 365 days of wholesome family entertainment. You'll never see all of it! Children are free the whole month of October. Children are admitted free with a toy donation for the needy, from about mid-December to December 24. The *Entertainment* coupon book has 20% off coupons for the deluxe ticket package at the Zoo.   (See Resources.)   Discounts are available with memberships to AAA, credit unions , etc. Call (619) 231-0251 for more information. Web: sandiegozoo.org.

Wild Animal Park is free on Founder's Day, *second Wednesday* in May. Visit Wild Animal Park during a full moon. Take the tram and see the animals feeding. Or, get in free with zoo membership which entitles you to unlimited use of Wild Animal Park, (800)628-3066. And, the *Entertainment* book has $4 off coupons for the deluxe admission to the Zoo and Wild Animal Park. (See chapter on Resources.)

Serra Museum at Presidio Park above Old Town offers exhibits, photographs and artifacts from the American Indian, Spanish mission and Mexican periods of California history. Archaeological excavations are ongoing to unearth evidence of the first European settlements on the Pacific Coast, comparable to the establishment of Jamestown and Plymouth on the East Coast. The grounds are beautiful and the site of many weddings). Free the second Tuesday of the month (regularly $5 for adults; $2 for children), (619) 297-3258. The *Entertainment* book has discount coupons.

Visit the **Mission San Diego de Alcala,** the first of 21 California Missions founded by Franciscan Missionaries from Spain in 1769 by Father Junipero Serra. This mission was originally on the Presidio, and was moved to it's present site by the stadium, (619) 281-8449.

Old Town State Historic Museums including Casa de Estudillo, a home belonging to one of San Diego's early families. Adults $2, children $1. Seely Stables has a collection of wagons, carriages and other western memorabilia. Adults, $1, children $1, 619) 220-5422. Johnson House, a reconstructed historic building and Casa de Machado y Stewart, (619) 220-5422. Free. Black Spanish Heritage Museum, (619) 515-4578. Thomas Whaley Museum (ghosts!), Southern California's first brick building, at one time San Diego's seat of government. Located at 2482 San Diego Avenue, $4 adults, (619) 298-2482. Free Old Town tours daily, (619) 298-2482.

Maritime Museum Three ships to explore. The 1863 sailing ship Star of India is the oldest active ship in the world. She still sails from time to time and is a beautiful sight to see with her sails billowing. The Star has been in the Embarcadero since 1927. The Star recently received the American and World Ship Trust Maritime Heritage Award, the greatest award given for preservation of maritime history. Tour the 1898 ferryboat Berkeley from the San Francisco Bay area with its beautiful filigreed moldings, handcrafted teak and stained glass windows, and the 1904 European steam yacht Medea. Adults $6; juniors $2; under 5, free. Call (619) 234-9153 for more information. Free during Fleet Week in August, (619) 544-1340. Web: sdmaritime.com

Tall Ship Californian is a full-scale recreation of an 1848 cutter that today is used as a training vessel for young students the forgotten art of sailing tallships. Adults can participate in special single-day or multi-day cruises a few times a year for about $75 per person, 12-4 p.m, always a sell-out. The ship is owned and operated by the Nautical Heritage Society and is funded through private donations and grants. Call (800) 432-2201 for availability and reservations.

Fleet Week, every August. Visit Navy ships at the Broadway Pier, tour the Maritime museums, enjoy the free performance of the San Diego Symphony, see the Blue Angels fly-over, hear the Navy Band, see the Parade of Ships, sponsored by the San Diego Chamber of Commerce. (619) 544-1338. Web: sdchanmber.org

Children's Museum/Museo de los Ninos of San Diego is an interactive museum; special exhibits, workshops; and more, is being built at their old location at 200 W. Island Avenue; (619) 233-5437. Will open in 2005.

Chinese Historical Museum Originally built in 1927 to house the Chinese Mission. Exhibits include the photographic history of the Chinese in San Diego, writing instruments, tea sets, opera face paintings/masks and archaeological artifacts. Downtown at Third & J St., (619) 338-9888.

Free Trolley Tour of downtown San Diego is offered by the Center City Development Corporation, 10-12noon and 12-2pm on first & third Saturdays. Reservations required, (619) 235-2222.

San Diego Convention & Visitors Bureau offers from time to time a discount coupon book for San Diego attractions. Call (888)4-SAN-DIEGO or go to sandiego.org.

Scenic Drive Drive the 59-mile San Diego Scenic Drive. Start at the foot of Broadway downtown and continue up Harbor Drive to Harbor Island, Shelter Island, Cabrillo Monument, Sunset Cliffs, Mission Bay, Pacific Beach, La Jolla, Old Town, Balboa Park and more. Follow the blue and yellow Scenic Drive signs with a white seagull located every quarter mile. Great places to stop and take photos. I am so glad I discovered this within a few months of moving to San Diego. I was, and still am, captivated!

Discover all the different beaches (San Diego has 70 miles of them, and they are all different.) The most popular is Mission/Pacific Beach area with all the shops and restaurants, but don't miss Torrey Pines State Park and Beach with the enormous cliffs. Black's Beach is for the nude sunbather, but the rest are family beaches.

Great Views Take in the great view from the top floor at the Hyatt Regency, Harbor Drive at Market Street. You'll see.Pt. Loma, downtown, coastline to Mexico. Check out more great views from the top floor of Bertrand's at Mr. A's at 5th and Laurel; Del Mar Plaza sun deck at 1555 Camino Del Mar; Presidio Park above Old Town; Sea World Sky Tower (280 feet high); Mt. Soledad Park at the top of Soledad Mountain Road in La Jolla; Mt. Helix. Gorgeous views and the price is right: they're all free.

Tour a navy ship Call for schedule, (619) 532-1432; 545-1141; The Midway Naval History museum may be coming to San Diego, midway.org

Firehouse Museum Memorabilia of firefighting including a hand drawn fire engine, 1841 Rumsey hand pump and a 1903 horse-drawn Metropolitan steamer, $2 adults; $1 for juniors, seniors and military; under 12, free.. Open Thurs.-Sun. Located at Columbia & Cedar, downtown, (619) 232-3473.

Marine Corps Recruit Depot Museum Visit the Command Museum at MCRD and view the artifacts (including a tank) from 1846 to Kuwait. Enter Gate 4, Pacific Highway, 10-4 p.m., Tue-Sun. (619) 524-4426; Web: www.usmchistory.com. Anyone can attend the graduating parade ceremony for Marine recruits, free, (619) 524-8727.

Sea World adult admission is $42 includes 5 shows and all attractions, fireworks and more; 2-day ticket is $45; children 3-11, $31 (2-day, $35); and 2 and under are free; (619) 226-3901. Discount coupons are frequently offered at Von's, McDonald's and AAA. Student, military and senior discounts available. When the economy slumps, Seaworld has offered $10 off deals for Southern California residents, and in the past has offered unlimited visits with the purchase of one ticket for a few months, and a visit-twice-on-one-ticket deal. Be sure to ask if there are any current specials. They are currently offering many different ticket plans with unlimited visits, including a two-week pass which includes Universal Studios and Seaworld, and the "pay for one day, come back until December lst" deal. Wow. Don't expect these to be permanent, so I don't know what will be available when you inquire. I know families who ask grandma for membership for Christmas so they can go often. Shamu Club cards are available through some credit unions, good for 20% discount on admission, 10% on merchandise. Group rates for 15 or more, 10% discount, call (619) 226-3844. Sea World Summer Camp, one week with overnights; day camp rate varies with age of child. Field trips for school groups, October-May. They also offer Dolphin interaction program, walking tours, education department, birthday parties. Call the education program at 222-6363x. 3273. Residents with Southern California zip codes often are offered discounts at certain times of the year (usually off season). The web site has all the different ticket prices and plans, and a lot more. Buy tickets on line and save. Web: Seaworld.com.

Go to any hotel lobby or Visitor's Center (see list of Visitor's Centers later in this chapter) and pick up a copy of *San Diego This Week*, which usually has a discount coupon for Sea World (and a "2-for-1" coupon for the Kobey's swapmeet (which may be where you end up going!)

Legoland in Carlsbad, (760) 918-LEGO, offers 40 rides and attractions, interactive displays made of Lego bricks that invite participation, three-dimensional shows, many animated life-size replicas of dinosaurs and animals made out of Lego bricks. Mainly for kids to age 2-12. One day Admission: $41.95 for adults, $35 for kids 3-16 and seniors 60+. Two day admission, $49 adults and $43 for kids; Legoland has offered special discounts for Southern California residents from time to time, so call and ask if there are any specials. Parking $6 for cars. Annual passes available. The first park of it's kind in the U.S., with sister parks in Denmark and England. *Entertainment* book has $4 off coupons for 6 persons; AAA discount, 10%. Web: legoland.com

Book store events Many chain book stores have a calendar of special events including lectures, demonstrations, major authors on tour, local author signings, children's events. Bay Books in Coronado and Warwick's in La Jolla have many free book events with national touring authors, as does Barnes & Noble, Borders, Bookstar. Ask about their events calendar.

Half-price tickets to *tonight's* performances at theater, symphony, ballet and more are available downtown at Arts Tix in Horton Plaza. Call (619) 497-5000 for recorded information on tickets available. (See chapter on Cultural Arts.)

San Diego Opera holds five free lunch time concerts in front of the Civic Theater with world renown stars during the opera season. Call (619) 236-6510 or (619) 232-7636 for dates.

Cabrillo National Park offers one of the most incredible view points in San Diego, plus trails, nature walks, tidepools,education program, etc; Slide shows and lectures on the gray whale, sculpture and photo exhibits. Park entrance is $5 per car, good for 7 days. You can get an annual pass for Cabrillo Park for $15, (619) 557-5450, good for one year. This is where I fell in love with San Diego shortly after moving here. Whadda view of the city and coastline down to Mexico. I was completely breathtaken. When I saw that huge expanse of blue water, I felt like Balboa discovering the Pacific! Go on a sunny day. You don't want the fog to cloud your view. Santa Ana days are absolutely gorgeous. Whale watching from December to March. More than 15,000 whales journey from Alaska to Baja. About 200 a day have been seen during mid-January. **Golden Eagle Passport** if $50 and you can get into all national parks free for one year including Cabrillo. It's good for everyone in the car. **Golden Age Passport** is for residents **age 62** and over; get in free to all national parks for $10 for lifetime including Cabrillo National Park, good for all in the vehicle. Available at Cabrillo National Park, (619) 557-5450, or get one at the ticket booth on your way in. **Golden Access** pass for handicapped is free.

Whales See the gray whales off the San Diego coast during their migration South from January to March, free, from Sunset Cliffs Natural Park or Point Loma Nazarene University, 3900 Lomaland, Point Loma. Ask the guard at the entrance where the public area is (drive through the beautiful campus to the public parking lot above the ocean).

Whale Watching One of the best short vacations I can think of is a 2 ½ hour boat ride out to see the whales, especially on a warm Santa Ana day during whale watching season. The boats take you out near the Coronado Islands and guarantee sighting whales or you get to do it again! Trips cost about $15 per person, and "two-for-one" coupons are in the newspapers and the *Entertainment* coupon book. (Call H&M Landing and ask if they have any coupons.) If you take a boat from Point Loma, first have the best fried fish or fresh tuna sandwich in the world at the Point Loma Seafood Market, 2805 Emerson Street at the wharf, (619) 223-1109. Seafood lovers: you'll adore this place! They used to have the best cole slaw in town, but now my favorite is the Cambodian salad at Saffron on India.

Entertainment **coupon book** has "two-for-one" coupons for the Harbor Excursion, Old Town Trolley, Knotts Berry Farm, Ice Chalet, more. (See chapter on Resources.)

ARCO Olympic Training Center in Otay Lakes is one of three Olympic Committee training facilities in the U.S. Every year, over 20,000 Olympic-caliber athletes train, live and eat at the facility and participate in medical and sports science testing. There are free daily tours from the Copley Visitor Center seven days a week from 9 a.m. to 5 p.m. The tour begins with a six-minute image film about the Olympic movement and then continues with a one-hour walking tour of the 150-acre site. On the tour, visitors will see four beautifully maintained soccer fields, a field hockey pitch, the cycling criterium, the largest archery range in North America, a dynamically designed track and field venue, tennis courts, and the lake where rowers and canoe/kayak athletes train. Experience the Olympic dream. Watch top athletes train for international competition on state-of-the-art, outdoor sport venues. Athletes who trained here for the 1996 Centennial Olympics include the Gold Medal Men's Archery team including individual gold medalist Justin Huish, Men's and Women's Soccer team, Gold Medal Decathlete Dan O'Brien, Men's and Women's Rowing team and the U.S. Cycling team. Shop for unique gifts in the Olympic Spirit Store which sells official Olympic merchandise and support the Olympic movement. Located West of Otay Lakes with a view of the Chocolate Mountains at 1750 Wueste Road, Chula Vista, CA 91915, (619) 656-1500; web: usoc.org

Walking tours are a great way to get to know your city, and a good way to get some outdoor exercise. On a glorious day in San Diego what could be a better combination? All the following walks are free unless other wise indicated: Also, all are area code (619) unless indicated.

Walking Tours/Walkabout International . . . . (619) 231-7463
Walkabout sponsors over 150 walks a month, several per day, morning and evening, theme walks (historical walks, view walks, beach walks, Christmas Lights walks and walks before or after special events downtown, etc.) A great way to see and learn more about your county and beyond. This organization encourages people of all ages to walk their way to greater neighborhood awareness while exercising, socializing and learning more about local history. They also sponsor out of town trips with walking tours in Julian, J. Paul Getty Center, Palm Springs, Scotland, Canada, Santa

Barbara, New York, Chicago, Denver, Hawaii, Ireland, Washington, DC, San Francisco, L.A., Chinatown, Amish country, etc. Also, fly to Vancouver for 3 days of walks, then board a cruise ship to Los Angeles with stops and walks in Astoria and San Francisco. Great newsletter, $15 per year. Over 800 subscribers. Call for a sample or email your request to: walkabout-int@bigfoot.com.

Balboa Park tours .... See Balboa Park listing (above)
Cabrillo Monument .... (619) 557-5450
   Tidepool explorations fall and winter, great during low tide, $4
   Bird walks, plant walks, military walks
   Call for dates of mini-seminars on whales, the harbor, etc.
Coronado Historical Walking Tours, $5 .... (619) 435-5993
Gaslamp Quarter (2 hours) .... (619) 233-4682
   Walking tours every Saturday, Sundays, $8, ($6 seniors) at 410
Island Ave.
Old Town walks, 2 p.m. daily, free 11am, 2pm, ... (619) 220-5422
Quail Botanical Gardens, tours Saturday, 10 a.m. .... (760) 436-3036
SD Natural History Museum walks .... (619) 232-3821x203
Bird Walks . ... 619) 409-5900
Salk Institute tour .... 453-4100 x 1200
Sierra Club walks .... (619) 299-1744
Desert Hikes .... (619) 227-3719 or 565-0548
(See the *Reader* and/or *Union-Trib*/Night and Day for more walks)

For a list of bird and nature walks throughout the county, contact the **Chula Vista Nature Center**, (619) 422-2964. Bird workshops, field trips and special events.

Sierra Club and Sierra Singles Club A not-for-profit, all volunteer organization involved in the protection of the environment. They offer an inexpensive outings program with day hikes and over night camping trips in the mountains, desert, wilderness, forests and San Diego urban and coastal area. Local hikes almost daily. The newsletter contains nine pages of outings for two month period. Free orientation meeting once a month for anyone interested in exploring and protecting the environment. Introductory membership, about $30;seniors/students discounts. Call (619) 299-1743.

Daley Ranch is a 3,058-acre former cattle ranch north of Dixon Lake that has opened to the public as a nature preserve in Escondido (enter the ranch on La Honda Drive off El Norte Parkway.) Guided hikes, bike trails, horses and tours of the historic Daley Ranch House. Robert Daley settled on the land in 1869. The property remained in the family after his death until 1980 when it was sold to Mobil Oil. Mobil sold it to Shea Homes in the 1990's and it almost became the site of 3,200 homes until it was rescued by conservationists and purchased by the city of Escondido for $21 million. There are more than 20 miles of trails with gorgeous views to the ocean, flowers, birds. For more information, call (760) 743-6115.

Visit **Grape Day Park** which includes an old Victorian house, a blacksmith shop, train station, and museum of the history of Escondido, (760) 741-4691. Next to the California Center for the Arts in Escondido,

Visit the **Battlefield at San Pasqual** near Wild Animal Park. Re-enactments of the Mexican-American War are held in December, (619) 220-5340.

Women's History Reclamation Project is located in the Union Arts Building, 2323 Broadway, Ste. 107, Golden Hill, (619) 233-7963. The feminist archives include rare books, photographs, news clippings and other memorabilia about women of note locally, nationally and internationally.

Kite flying Take a picnic lunch and watch the free kite flying near the Hilton Hotel on Mission Bay, South of the Visitor's Center, or at Seaport Village. Some of these colorful and unique kites cost hundred of dollars.

Salk Institute Take the half-hour free guided tour around Salk Institute for Biological Studies, Louis Kahn's most famous work in the West, while Nobel Prize winners labor inside, (619) 453-4100 x 1200.

Tour the Union-Tribune Building, complete with a film covering the history of the paper and a guided tour of the building from the editor's office to where they tie up the newspapers. Call (619) 299-3131 for next tour.

Tour KGTV Channel 10 and find out what goes on behind the scenes. Call (619) 237-1010x474 for further information. Form your own group of not more than 30, or ask to join a group that is booked.

Free bicycle maps, routes and information are available at CalTrans, (619) 231-BIKE.

Family History Library Get free assistance is checking out your genealogy through the Family History Library, 4195 Camino del Rio South, Mission Valley, (619) 584-7668; Genealogy Home Page web site at genhomepage.com or contact the National Genealogical Society, 4527 17th Street N., Arlington, VA 22207. Web: genealogy.org/ngs/

Sailing and power boat lessons The Coast Guard Auxiliary offers free sailing and power boat lessons (not hands on; only boating laws, etc) for beginning, intermediate, advanced, plus navigation, seamanship, more. Classes are held throughout the County. Call the Auxiliary for class locations at (619) 683-6307. Then, you can rent a boat using two-for-one coupons *Entertainment* coupon book (see chapter on Resources.)

Sally's Favorite View Here's how you get to Sally's favorite view of San Diego Bay, the view that is on promotional literature for San Diego that shows the San Diego Yacht Club, the bay, sailboats, downtown and more. This view is mind-bogglingly gorgeous. Take Rosecrans South past Shelter Island Drive, right on Talbot Street for two blocks, left on Harbor View Drive, right on Harbor View Place, left on Bangor, left on Lucinda to Golden Park and stop! A breathtaking view. Check out the lovely homes in the area which are really something to see. You must take all your guests to see this view, then drop down to Pt. Loma-Shelter Island Pharmacy and let them pick up postcards to send home with that view on them! They'll love this! Truly " Eye Candy."

Mexican dinners anywhere are a bargain, and Old Town is a favorite place to dine. In San Diego, generally speaking, inexpensive dinners are under $10; medium priced dinners are $10-$20; expensive dinners are $20-$30 and deluxe dinners are over $30. Compare that with NY or LA! Old Town is a great place to take visiting friends and relatives, particularly in January when you can eat outdoors at the colorful Casa de Pico in the Bazaar Del Mundo, (619) 296-3267, or the Casa de Bandini, (619) 297-8211; or El Fandango, (619) 298-2860 (most items under $10 the menu). Dine in shirtsleeves year round in this historic setting with lush foliage, flowers and birds everywhere. On weekends, there is entertainment including mariachis and flamenco dancers from 1-4 p.m. Definitely a favorite spot. Enjoy a huge Margarita (tequila with lime, strawberries, etc.) the national drink of San Diego (ok, did you get the joke?) or a Virgin Margarita (fruit juice without the tequila). Go into the Bazaar Del Mundo office and ask to be placed on their mailing list and receive their Passport, which contains a calendar of events for the year, and discount coupons for dining and shops.

Mormon Battalion Visitor Center, 2510 Juan Street, Old Town, (619) 298-3317, is open 9 a.m.-9 p.m., daily. Photos, videos, artifacts from the famous Mormon Battalion in Old Town dating from 1847.

Ferry boat Take the ferry boat ride from foot of Broadway at Harbor Drive to Coronado Landing for about $2 per person and roam the shopping center, have lunch, or board the Coronado Trolley and head for Hotel Del Coronado. Take your bicycle, a buck extra. Ferry boats leave every hour on the hour, (619) 234-4111. Water taxi's operate from 10am-10pm to all points in San Diego Bay including South Bay, Coronado, Harbor Island and Shelter Island, $5 one way, (619) 235-8294. Call ahead.

Hotel Del Coronado Spend the day at the Hotel Del Coronado and take the tour of the hotel at 1 p.m., or go on a self-guided tour using a tape available at the gift shop. Find out about the ghost of Kate Morgan, the 12 presidents who have stayed there and what films have used the Del as a back drop. Lounge out back in the sun on their deck or walk on the beach. I go there for a stress break and play "Bring Me: . . .". *You know: "Bring me a Blood Mary" . . . "Bring me a Club Sandwich."* Just crossing the bridge makes me feel I have left town. It's a nice little vacation. The beach is the best in town if you ask me, but windy. Fabulous on a Santa Ana day.

Coronado Historical Assn. and Museum of History and Art. Visit the Coronado Beach Historical Museum located at 1100 Orange Avenue, Coronado, (619) 435-7242; $4 suggested donation, $3 for military and children; Call for current exhibits. Photographs showing early Coronado from its establishment, Tent City, the ferry boats, the beginning of North Island. Find out where Frank Baum, author of the *Wizard of Oz* and *Emerald City* lived and wrote in Coronado, and how the Hotel Del Coronado inspired his works.

Visit the **Inn Suites Hotel** San Diego Balboa Park Resort at 2223 El Cajon Blvd., (6`9) 296-2101; the recently remodeled hotel was a grand Hollywood hideaway in it's early days: Ava Gardner, Harry James & Betty Grable were guests. Johnny Weismueller designed the pool, and San Diegan Florence Chadwick trained in it before she swam the English Channel in the 50's.

Volunteer! You'll have a great time and meet lots of new people. The opportunities to volunteer are endless. You can volunteer at the Mayor's office, Super Bowl, golf tournaments, Chargers, Padres, San Diego Historical Society's Designer Showcase, home tours, and any event that is going on in San Diego. Television stations need volunteers to work at the station, as do radio stations. Museums in Balboa Park, theaters, events at the Convention Center -- they all need volunteers. Call and ask about their volunteer program. The benefits of volunteering are many fold: not just an opportunity to do good, but an opportunity to co-mingle with those of similar interests and make new friends. And, you get lots of freebies. If you volunteer to be an usher at a play, you see the play for free. If you volunteer at the Department of Parks and Recreation in Old Town to be a docent (they provide training to be their tour guide) you receive a card entitling you entrance to all California State Parks free! You can volunteer at Humphrey's and see the concerts. Volunteers at Palomar Hospital, you get discount tickets to movies and use of their gym! Get free lunch at Grossmont Hospital (& others). Volunteer for the Mainly Mozart Festival and get in free. Volunteer for any event at the Convention Center and get in free (pass out brochures for a couple hours; then get in free.) Many of the events co-sponsored by the City of San Diego require thousands of volunteers: Superbowl, America's Cup, GOP Convention, Russian Arts Festival, presidential and dignitary arrivals, etc. Meet fabulous people. Singles can meet quality others through volunteer organizations such as anything in support of animals, abused or underprivileged children, Special Olympics, etc. For more information on opportunities to volunteer, see the listings in the *Union-Tribune* every Thursday (subject to change) in the Currents section. And, call the KGTV Channel 10 Volunteer Line for service organizations that need volunteers, (619) 237-1010. Or directly contact any organization or event you would like to volunteer for. Make your contact well in advance, not the day before an event. Many volunteer programs require an orientation meeting. San Diego Cares, (619) 232-CARE, web: cerfnet.com/sdcares; Volunteer connection: www.servenet.org and type in your zip code. Other opportunities for volunteering include: Retired Seniors Volunteer Program (R.S.V.P.), (619) 505-6399; United Way Volunteer Center, (619) 636-4131; Youth Volunteer Center, (619) 636-4125. Volunteer to help a youth to read. Be a tutor or mentor. Call San Diego Council on Literacy, (619) 232-9921; San Diego City Library Project Read for Adults, (619) 527-5475. For information on organizations and opportunities for service, call the "America's Promise -- the Alliance for Youth" toll-free number at (888) 55-YOUTH.

Antiques Browse through the antique districts in Ocean Beach, or Adams Avenue in Kensington, La Mesa, Carlsbad, the Gaslamp Quarter. Don't miss South Cedros Ave. For more information, see Antiques.

Heritage Park Village Walk through Heritage Park Village on Juan Street at Haney, in Old Town , (619) 565-3600, and see the old Victorian homes that were about to be torn down, but were saved and moved here thanks to the Save Our Heritage Organization and the San Diego Historical Society. Be sure to stop at Ye Old Doll House located in the Sherman-Gillman House, then have tea at the Heritage Park Bed & Breakfast, (619) 295-7088. This is a very peaceful setting with NO cars, great for weddings

Visit the **San Diego Historical Society**, Villa Montezuma, 1925 K Street, (619) and browse through old photos of San Diego. I want one of Mission Valley when there were COWS there, in the late 60's when I arrived. There was a dairy farm across from the new stadium. I swear. No one believes me when I tell them that! I must get a picture of those cows before I leave this planet. You can view some photos at their site at sandiegohistory.org

Marine Room Check out a sunset from the Marine Room on the ocean at 2000 Spindrift Dr., off Torrey Pines Rd., La Jolla, (858) 459-7222; or during storm season when the waves are pounding on the windows! Beautifully lit at night. No happy hour, but one of the most spectacular views right on the ocean and rated one of the most romantic restaurants in San Diego. The highest tides are in December and January; lowest tides are then, too!

Grunion Hunting Don't miss a chance to go grunion hunting at midnight on a full moon night at high tide. (You must have these three conditions for the grunion to run.) Best place to see them: the beach at the foot of South Mission Blvd. There'll be a big grunion party going on!

Have you seen the **Green Flash**, the rarely seen magical phenomenon that occurs precisely when the last speck of the sun drops into the ocean at sunset on a clear night? There are those who say it doesn't exist, probably because coastal fog often sits on the horizon, blocking the sun. The Green Flash truly exists and has something to do with light refraction. Many people have seen it, and the best viewing is during a Santa Ana condition. People sit and wait for it every night, even in the fog, at the Green Flash bar on the boardwalk in Pacific Beach! Definitely a beach thing; check it out any where along the coast. OK, now, if you have gone grunion hunting and checked out the Green Flash, well, you are now a real San Diego insider..

Check out the **tide pools** at Cabrillo Monument or below the Ocean Beach Pier during a super low tides. December and January have very low (and high) tides. These special high and low tides are mentioned on weather reports, the Union Trib weather page and in the Farmer's Almanac. Don't miss seeing these tides. Definitely worth driving to the beach to see the high frothy waves and watch the surfers or the low tide expanse of beach.

San Diego Trolley Take the San Diego Trolley from downtown to the border for about $1.75, (619) 233-3004; schedules, (619) 685-4900.

San Diego Transit . One day bus/trolley pass, $5; two day, $8; three day, $10; four-day pass, $12. The pass is good for unlimited access to buses, the trolley . Bus fare is usually around $1.50-$3.50. Direct line for personal trip planning in Southern San Diego County is (619) 233-3004. Northern County, call (800) 266-6883. Unlimited monthly bus and trolley passes, $54 for adults age 18-60. One ride, $1.50 up. Seniors, disabled: $13.50 a month; youth pass, $24.50; half-month passes available. Located at lst & Broadway, (619) 234-1060. Inquire about Super Saver fares, "3-for-1" weekend cheap seats, airport shuttle bus, Coaster train, etc. Check their Web site at sdcommute.com for routes, time schedules, prices.

Coaster Take the Coaster train, up the coast as far as Oceanside. Stops are in downtown, Old Town, Sorrento Valley, Solana Beach, Encinitas, Carlsbad Poinsettia, Carlsbad Village and Oceanside; $4.75 maximum fare round trip, depending on where you get on. Monthly pass, $130, unlimited travel, Monday thru Saturday. Call (619) 233-3004 or 685-4900 (recorded). (800) COMMUTE.

Take **The Wave,** the new hydrofoil that commutes from Oceanside to San Diego, leaving Oceanside at 5:30a.m. and returning at 4:45pm. The ride takes a little over an hour. It's only $5 and sounds like it sure beats the traffic jams for commuters in that area. I would like to just do it some day on a Friday from San Diego at 4:45pm, because the last train on Fridays from Oceanside to San Diego is at 8:26pm. That would work! And the Coaster is only a block or so away (so the Coaster told me), so this leaves time to play on the Pier, if that's where the Wave arrives! For more information, call toll free (866) 928-3929. Web site: takethewave.com

Sing along with Karaoke A dozen or so bars that offer Karaoke are listed in the *Reader* Events and *Union-Trib* Night & Day section. Fun, fun, fun.

San Diego County Parks & Recreation publishes a great $2 brochure describing all the County's parks & facilities, tennis courts, (619) 694-3049. **San Diego Park and Recreation**, (619) 235-1100. Ask about tennis, golf, dance, etc. **San Diego City Swimming Pool Hotline,**(619) 685-1322. Locate a swimming pool near you.

Torrey Pines Hiking Trail is free, parking $4 . . . . . . (619) 755-2063
   Mission Trails Regional Park . . . . (619) 668-2375
   Las Penosquitas Canyon Reserve . . . . (619) 484-7504
   Tecolote Canyon . . . . (619) 581-9952

Cowles Mountain Hike up Cowles Mountain, a 1.7 mile trail that leads to the top of the peak. Great view to the ocean. Spectacular at sunset. Take flashlights for after dark, and be careful! Don't do what I did: I broke my ankle in the dark coming down, but limped my way off. Park at Navajo Road and Golfcrest.

Chargers Watch the San Diego Chargers practice at summer training camp during July and August, every day, two times a day, 9:30 a.m. and 8:30 p.m. Call (858) 874-4500 for further information and dates. I hope they won't be practicing up in L.A.

UCSD Take a walking tour of UCSD on the 2nd, 4th and 5th Sundays at 2 p.m.; a 90-minute walking tour of the campus; view the Stuart Collection of sculpture. Call (619) 434-4414 for information and directions. Tour the UCSD SuperComputer center on Fridays, (619) 544-5000; see free previews of their music, dance and theater productions. Call the departments.

San Diego State University Tour the grounds of San Diego State University and visit the new glass domed futuristic entrance to the library. SDSU was founded over a 100 years ago, in 1897 (and, I graduated from there, but, it was a couple years after it was founded.) Tour the University of San Diego (USD) and it's the beautiful Spanish architecture on Fridays, (619) 260-4659.

High Tea at the Rancho Bernardo Inn, (858) 675-8500, is a bargain at $5 per person, from 4 p.m. to 5 p.m. on Wednesdays. A tea cart magically appears with coffee, tea, wine, finger sandwiches, scones, pastries and fancy cookies dipped in chocolate., cheeses, crackers. The U.S. Grant, Westgate, Le Meridien, Hotel Del Coronado, Horton Grand and the Heritage Park Bed & Breakfast have high tea for about $15 per person. No bargain, but don't miss high tea at the Five-Star Ritz Carlton Hotel in Laguna, for about $20. What a view of the ocean from the lounge! Get a window seat. This is a must-do afternoon on the California Riviera.

Paul Ecke Poinsettia Ranch in Encinitas offers a limited number of tours of their grounds during the holidays when the poinsettias are in bloom. Call for dates, (760) 753-1134. Reserve early.

Del Mar Race Track There is no admission charge at the Del Mar race track after the fith race, about 5 p.m. or so. Many people head for the track right after work! Web: dmtc.com. (858) 755-1141.

Stephen Birch Aquarium-Museum Tour the aquarium-museum at Scripps Institute of Oceanography, 2300 Expedition Way, La Jolla near Scripps Pier; (858) 534-3474. Open 9-5 p.m. Admission: $9.50 for adults; seniors, $6.50; students, $6.50. Discount coupons ($1 off) are in their brochures in hotel lobbies everywhere and also in *San Diego This Week*. One-day scholarships for those who can't afford to pay. Membership includes unlimited usage, guest passes, discount at the gift shop and invitation to special member events. Memberships range from $45 for students to $66 for families. Web: aquarium.ucsd.edu

Holiday Home Tours Point Loma Home Tour is held every year the first Saturday in December, (619) 223-6394. Del Mar Holiday Home Preview, first weekend in December, (619) 574-5911. San Diego Historical Society's Holiday Homes Tour, (619) 232-6203. See fabulous Xmas decor in fabulous homes in fabulous neighborhoods. Check San Diego Magazine and San Diego Home & Garden Magazine for schedules of other home tours.

San Diego Historical Society's Showcase The SDHS works with a group of interior designers to transform an empty estate in San Diego County into a masterpiece of interior design for public viewing every spring. Each room is decorated by a different designer. The event, a tradition since 1973, is awaited by everyone interested in design, interior design, art, architecture and history. For this year's location and other home tours, call (619) 232-6203x110.

American Society of Interior Decorators (A.S.I.D.) holds their annual showcase in the fall, (619) 687-1313. Another fabulous event that benefits a worthy causes. Ask about volunteering to be a host and get in free!

Coronado Home Tour; For tickets & information, call (619) 522-8969.

The **Tour d'Elegance** is the self-guided tour through four or five new posh estates; tickets, $12. For more information, call (619) 835-9003 or log on to tourluxuryhomes.com..

Oceanside Pier Browse around the Oceanside Pier, the longest pier on the West Coast, stretching 1,940 feet out to sea. Beautiful panoramic view at the end of the pier from Fisherman's Restaurant and Oyster Bar.

Continuing education Many courses are free. I have been taking *free* computer and word processing courses at the Pt. Loma campus of West-City Center, 3249 Fordham Sheet in the Sports Arena area, (619) 221-6973, for a several years, and the San Diego Career Center. I was a computer dwid, but I hung in with it because I felt that if three-year olds can do it, there was hope for me. See Continuing Education for free classes.

Community Colleges The California community college system is one of the seven wonder of the world, as far as I am concerned, and still one of the best bargains on the planet at only $11 per credit. Shortly after moving here from the East coast many years ago, I discovered Grossmont College and called immediately to see if it was affordable. It was FREE at that time, and trust me, I was the first one in line at registration that year! Nothing was free on the East Coast! I went from wife and mother (with two years of college) to part time student at Grossmont College, to full time student at SDSU, to high school teacher to what I am doing now. The moral of this story is, of course: *If I can do it, you can do it, too!* For more information on the cost of education in San Diego, and free money for college, see Continuing Education.

Palomar College offers free planetarium shows and programs for the public the first Wednesday of each month during the school year. Often overcrowded, reservations recommended, (760) 744-1150.

Palomar Observatory To get to Palomar Observatory, 35899 Canfield Road, Palomar Road, take Interstate 15 North to 76 East to County Road S6, home of a 200-inch reflecting telescope, the world's second largest, used since 1949 to probe the mysteries of deep space. FREE admission, (760) 742-2119. A small museum next to the observatory has a replica of the scope and other displays. Open daily, during day, except Christmas.

Observatory at SDSU Visit the observatory of San Diego State University at Mt. Laguna from Memorial Day through Labor Day for their free summer program. See a slide show and view the sky through telescopes. Call (619) 594-6182 for more information or go to mintaka.sdsu.edu

County Fair (formerly Del Mar Fair) Don't miss the Fair every summer during the last two weeks in June, ending the Fourth of July. About $7.50 admission, and discount coupons are usually available at Albertson's supermarket. It's the roast corn that gets me up there every year or so, not to mention the free concerts with big name entertainment. Go online and attend more than once on your ticket at delmarfair.com

Hang Gliders Watch the hang gliders strapped to their apparatus take off from the edge of the 300-foot high cliffs at Torrey Pines on weekends near UCSD above Black's Beach.

Sunrise For the best view of a sunrise, take County Road S-1 to the top of the Laguna Mountains eastern edge to a designated viewpoint. You'll see the forest above and the desert below. Nice. Also, try a sunrise from Shelter Island or from the intersection of Trumbull & Bangor on Point Loma. Wow! Good lookin' sunrise with the sun coming up over the bay and downtown.

Quail's Inn Walk around the Quail's Inn, 1035 La Bonita Dr., (760)744-0120, at Lake San Marcos. Rent boats and go for a spin around the lake or stroll the beautiful gardens along the trails and feed the ducks and birds. The bar has a good happy hour, 4-6:30pm.

Tour **Hollandia Dairy** in San Marcos with it's 1000 cows, milk barn and maternity ward, (760) 744-3222.

Self-Realization Fellowship Tour the Self-Realization Fellowship grounds and gardens on Highway 101 (215 K Street, Encinitas), (760) 753-2888. The Center on Sunset Boulevard in Los Angeles is 10 times larger than the one here and very interesting to browse, too. Lectures and teaching of a blend of Christianity and Hinduism. Free. Peaceful. Retreat facility, too.
Flower Fields See the ranuncula fields in bloom in March and early April behind the Windmill at Palomar Airport Road and Interstate 5 in Carlsbad,

(760) 930-9123. Web: theflowerfields.com. You can wander through the rainbow of blooms and purchase bulbs and blooms. Wow. This area is the flower capital of the world. Visit the **Grisby Cactus Garden** and nursery with over 2,000 varieties of cacti and succulents, 2354 Belle Vista Drive, Vista, (760)727-1323. **Bates Nut Farm**, 15954 Woods Valley Road, Valley Center has a picnic area, farm zoo, gift boutique with gourmet honey, olives, etc; pumpkins in October. Open 9-5 p.m., (760) 749-3333.

Art district Stroll around the art district between about 4th to12th in the Gaslamp District downtown or around Italy and visit local galleries. Attend the annual Art Walk and open house every April. Free. Call (619) 232-4395 for dates.

Art Alive   Don't miss the Art Alive exhibit in the spring at the San Diego Museum of Art. Paintings and artwork are recreated with fresh flowers Very special. Call museum for the date, (619) 232-793. You get free entrance with museum membership, which doesn't cost much more than a ticket to see this, yet you get to go all year and attend events, free, plus receive free guest passes, etc.

See the memorabilia and have breakfast at the **Big Kitchen**, the restaurant where Whoopi Goldberg used to wash dishes before being discovered. Located at 3003 Grape Street at 30th, (619) 234-5789. (Great made-from-scratch food, famous people's pictures on the wall including Whoopi's.)

Get your photo taken at **Kansas City Barbeque** restaurant beside the big photos of Tom Cruise. A scene from the movie *Top Gun* was filmed here, 610 West Market, across from Seaport Village, (619) 231-9680.

Walk around **Seaport Village** and window shop, or picnic along the bay in the big park and watch the sailboats and Navy ships go by. There's tons of free family entertainment, with clowns and mimes. Pick up a discount coupon booklet at the office.

Tour **Calloway Golf** in North County to see how clubs are made, (760) 931-1771; tour **Taylor Guitars** in El Cajon to see how guitars are made, (619) 258-1207.

Mission San Luis Rey Visit the Mission, or stay over night for a Retreat, (760) 757-3659.   About $50 a day, with special rates for Family week; Holistic week (integrating mind, body and spirit); Senior week.   Rates include private room, two beds, retreat activities, lodging and meals, depending on number of days of the retreat. Everyone welcome.

Wineries. Visit the San Diego area's wineries and tasting rooms.

Bellfleur Restaurant (wine tastings from their winery in Fallbrook) (760) 603-1919
Located in the Carlsbad Company Stores Mall, 5610 Paseo Del Norte. Wine tastings every other Thursday; $6-8 samples for $20+ hors d'oeuvres

Bernardo Winery .... (858) 487-1866
Tasting room is open daily, 9-5 p.m. Specialty shop with gift items. Located at 13330 Paseo Del Verano Norte.

Deer-Park Winery .... (760) 488-1666
Tasting room is open daily, 10 a.m. to 5 p.m. Classic auto museum with 49 restored antique cars, open from 1-5 p.m. every day. Located at 29013 Champagne Blvd, Escondido.

Ferrara Winery .... (760) 745-7632
Tasting rooms open daily, 10 a.m. to 5 p.m. Self-guided tours available. Located at 1120 W. 15th St., Escondido.

Orfila Vineyards .... (760) 738-6500
13455 San Pasqual Rd., Escondido

Menghini Winery .... (760) 765-2072
Tasting rooms open Friday through Monday, 10 a.m. to 4 p.m.; a picnic area is available. Located at 1150 Julian Orchards Drive, Julian.

Wilson Creek Winery .... (909) 699-9463
Tasting room open daily, 10 a.m. to 5 p.m. Sample six wines for $2.50. Located at 2608 B Street, Julian.

Thornton Winery .... (909) 699-0099
Free tours every Saturday and Sunday from 11 a.m. to 9 p.m.; tasting is $6; award-winning sparkling wines produced here. Their Cuvee de Frontignan was served at two state dinners at The White House. Wine tasting rooms, gold medal restaurant, gifts shop, case discounts. Located at 32575 Rancho California Road, Temecula. The Temecula Valley has about a dozen more wineries.

Hot air balloons Watch the hot air balloons take off and land around sunset from several points in the San Dieguite Valley. Try El Camino Real and Manchester or next door to the polo fields on Camino Real and San Dieguito Road, or by the Doubletree Hotel at Camino Real and Carmel Valley. Watch while they are blowing them up, too. Sunset Balloons says to give them a call at (858) 481-9122 and they will tell you where they are going to launch that day, depending on the winds. Pick up a discount coupon for a ride on Sunset Balloons in their brochures in hotel lobbies. The International Balloon Fiesta is held in Albuquerque and is quite a spectacular sight, (505) 821-1000.

Birds See the birds sitting on the telephone wires on Jimmy Durante Boulevard in Del Mar. Also, on the wires to the right of Interstate 8 West near Sports Arena exit. Tons of birds are always there. Wish I knew why. Maybe they enjoy the view??!!

Arts and Crafts exhibits are held every weekend at several locations: at the end of Shelter Island; near the Hilton Hotel at Interstate 5 below Clairemont Drive; in Spreckle's Park on Orange Avenue in Coronado and Balboa Park.

Bahia Belle Take a ride on the Bahia Belle sternwheeler around Mission Bay on a Friday or Saturday. Adults, $6; children and seniors, $3. The *Entertainment* coupon book usually offers a "two-for-one" coupon. Music, dancing and cocktails on board after 9pm. Stop off at the Catamaran Hotel or the Bahia Hotel, and get picked up on the next trip around. Great observation deck. Fun to do at sunset, (858) 488-0551.

Be an extra in movies, or on TV! Call Background San Diego's hotline if you want to be in productions filmed here, or call Tina Real Casting, For a list of casting agencies, call the San Diego Film Commission. For more information on this and telephone numbers, see the chapter on How to Raise Quick Cash.

Produce your own TV show, free, on Southwestern Cable, Daniels or Cox Cable. Call the cable company and ask to be placed on the list for the next class on how to produce a TV show. The FCC requires that the public be allowed access to television programming. The class is free and you'll meet others who will be your camera crew for your production

Time Shares Listen to a time share pitch and receive gifts or trips. I listened to Riviera Resorts pitch at the Carlsbad Inn and received a free weekend at a Marriott and dinner for two at Fidel's restaurant at the Inn. I have been invited to the Lawrence Welk Resort in Palm Springs for a weekend (value $250 a night), and toured the Coronado Beach Club, and received brunch for two at the Hotel Del. I got a free trip to San Francisco, too, for listening to the pitch at the Gaslamp Suites. Friends got free tickets to Puerta Vallarta to see a time share. TWICE!

Chula Vista Nature Interpretive Center The CVNIC offers a unique opportunity to experience the vanishing salt marsh environment of San Diego Bay. Observation platforms overlook the Sweetwater Marsh, one of the last remaining habitats in the United States for some rare species of birds. Over 175 species in the marsh. Petting pools and interactive displays. Park at E Street and Bay Blvd., just off Interstate 5. Busses run from the foot of E Street to the center for 50¢; admission is about $3.50 for adults; $2.50 for seniors, $1 for children. Call (619) 422-BIRD for further information.

Buena Vista Lagoon The lagoon is off Interstate 5 between Carlsbad and Oceanside, another good ecological reserve and haven for birds and bird watchers.

Silverwood Wildlife Sanctuary (Audubon Society) At the Society's Silverwood Wildlife Sanctuary, you'll find over 152 species of birds at this nature preserve at 13003 Wildcat Canyon Road, Lakeside. Over 10 miles of trails on 725 acres, hiking trails, picnic areas. Nature walks are held on Sundays at 10 and 1:30 p.m. Call (619) 443-2998 for more information on bird walks and events. Also, Wild Birds Unlimited in Santee carries a wide variety array of bird houses, feeders, books, laminated charts of local birds, etc. There are more than 475 varieties of birds in the county due to our geography from ocean to desert. Web: americanbirding.org

Antique aircraft is available for viewing from 1-2 p.m. the first Sunday of each month in front of the airport administration building at Gillespie Field, 1960 Joe Crosson Drive, El Cajon, (619) 596-3900.

Bancroft Ranch House Museum of the Spring Valley Historical Society is located at 9050 Memory Lane, Spring Valley, (619) 469-1480. This is a national landmark built in 1863, with artifacts and memorabilia. Free. Call for hours of operation.

Bonita Historical Museum, 4035 Bonita Road, Bonita, (619) 267-5141, is located in an old fire station with a collection of old California artifacts. Free, open Th-Fri, 10-3 p.m., Sa-Su, 12-3 p.m.

California Surf Museum, 223 North Coast Hwy., (760) 721-6876. Vintage films and videos of surfing, historic photos, displays of boards, free. Open 10 a.m. to 4 p.m., Thursday thru Monday; closed holidays.

Chula Vista Heritage Museum, 360 Third Avenue, Chula Vista, (619) 420-6916, contains photos of big old homes, the old Otay watch factory, artifacts, free; call for hours open.

Heritage Walk Museum, 321 North Broadway, Escondido, (760) 743-8207. Free, features Escondido's first library from 1894, a Victorian house beautifully furnished, a blacksmith shop (with classes!), paintings, etc. Call for hours it is open.

Julian Take a drive to Julian in the fall and have a slice of their famous apple pie for about $2 during the Apple Festival, (760) 765-1857.

Poker and bingo Try your hand at poker and bingo at the **Sycuan** Indian Reservation Casino, 5409 Dehesa Road, El Cajon, 445-6066; or **Barona** Bingo, 1000 Wildcat Canyon Road, Lakeside, 443-2300. **Viejas**, (619) 445-5400. Three casinos offering 24-hour Las Vegas-style action. Video machines, 21, poker and other card games, off-track betting, bingo. The **Rincon** Casino, 33750 Valley Center Rd. Call (877) 777-2457 for free bus. Casino, off Interstate 76 in Pauma Valley, toll free (877) 68-PAUMA.

Casino Pauma offers free bus transportation from your area, seven days a week. Buy $10 and get a $10 bonus. Call toll free (866) 271-7770 for pick up points and more.

Go Fishin' at one of San Diego's many freshwater lakes: Lake Poway, a 60-acre trout-filled lake; for bass, try Lake Hodges. Call the Lakes Fish Line, (619) 465-3474, for recorded information on this week's big catches at the lakes, plus information on when the lakes will be restocked with fish. Go deep-sea fishing on a half-day or all day trip with an *Entertainment* "two-for-one" coupon. **Go clamming** at Black's Beach in the winter when tides are lowest. Fishing license is required. Catch your own lobster and abalone off the coast during the certain months when it is allowed. There was a moratorium on this for several years. Find out more about this at any marine supply store or diving center.

OUT OF THE AREA (but not far)

The Laguna Arts Festival is held every July and August with many art shows and artists selling their hand made creations. The highlight of the festival is the Pageant of the Masters, a re-creation of great works of art using live models and props which are presented in a frame to portray the original work of art, thanks to highly technical lighting effects, makeup, costuming and backgrounds. An orchestra and narration round out the presentation. This event has been a sell-out for decades, so get your tickets early. Call (714) 496-7050 for ticket information. See the *Union-Trib* classified ads, Travel Agencies #1690 for tours to the pageant. Call the Laguna Beach Visitor's Bureau, (800) 877-1115 for information on the pageant, the Sawdust festival, shopping, resale, restaurants & hotels.

Hear renowned speakers like Wayne Dyer speak at the **Crystal Cathedral in Garden Grove**. Drive up or take a tour bus. See tour info in previous listing.

Visit the new **J. Paul Getty Center** near Interstate 405 and Interstate 10. Huge collection of art and antiquities. The museum is free, but parking is $5 and requires a reservation (310) 440-7300. Web site: getty.edu

Call the **L.A. Convention & Visitor's Bureau** for visitor guide, (213) 624-7300, which contains info on special events and discount coupons.

Los Angeles County Museum of Art is free the second Wednesday of the month. (213) 857-6000.

Take the self-guided scenic auto tour through the **Borrego Springs** area, with its spectacular views of the badlands. Dirt roads, deep canyons, 6,000 foot mountain, campgrounds. Information is available from the Borrego Springs Chamber of Commerce or at the Desert Park headquarters in Borrego Springs.

Drive to the **Anza-Borrego Desert State Park** and stop at the underground Visitor Center to see an amazingly beautiful computer-run slide show of the 660,000-acre desert park's changing seasons. Park Headquarters, Palm Canyon Drive, two miles west of Borrego Springs, (760) 767-5311.

Disneyland .... (714) 781-4565
Discounts to Disneyland are hard to come by unless you are military, a college student whose school participates, a senior, employed by a major corporation or going on a group rate. However, a Magic Kingdom Club Card is offered through certain major employers, credit unions, and professional associations which entitles you to a $2-$8 discount on admission. In the off-peak season in the fall through December 15th, and in the spring from about February through mid-May, Disneyland *usually* offers a discount Passport for Southern California residents with a 90000-93599 zip code and proof of residence; two-day passes available, too. This may not be continued, but it has been available the past few years during a downward swing in the economy. A regular Disneyland one day adult pass is about $43; children under 10, about $33; three and four day passes available, too, for about $111 and about $137. They offer three levels of *annual passes* for Southern Californians from about $89-$139 which could be worth considering if the blackout dates work for you since they cost the same as the three-day passes at this time. In October, the Disneyland Hotel offers reduced-price package deals that include tickets. For more information on Disney Vacation Packages, call (714) 956-MICKEY. Sometimes it's better to stay at Disney for the convenience rather than trying to save a few bucks at a nearby hotel. You lose the savings by having to pay parking, you lose *time* and end up standing in longer lines. Web site: disneyland.com **Disney's California Adventure** is the Disney theme park where kids participate in activities at Paradise Pier, Hollywood Pictures Backlot, and explore California cultures. Tickets cost the same as Disneyland, and similar discounts are available. They lower the cost from time to time, so you might get lucky. **Downtown Disney** is entertainment, dining and shopping.

Club Disney is the new 24,500 square foot playsite located in the Promenade shopping mall in Thousand Oaks, Ventura County, an hour's drive West from downtown Los Angeles. For the price of a movie ticket (about $8 per family member), kids can play alongside Goofy, Winnie the Pooh and Tigger, create "mouseterpieces" in art classes or climb a jungle chamber. Lots of Disney stuff for sale. Group birthday parties available.

Six Flags Magic Mountain in Valencia has the tallest and fastest stand-up coaster with speeds of 65 mph and a height of 156 ft. Day pass, about $35. Inquire at Ralph's about discount coupons for the park. Ralph's and Food For Less have offered about $17 off Knott's Berry Farms admission, (714) 827-1775. Inquire about discount coupons or if they give a California resident discount, etc.

Join the lottery to **win a liquor license**. I know someone who won! You put $5,000 in the lottery which is fully refunded if you don't win. The State has use of your money for the year. You won't earn interest on the money, and it costs $25 to join, but if you win, you get a liquor license worth many thousands which you must keep and use for two years, then you can sell it, which is what my friend did. You can't lose, if you win. Giggles.

Get on **Who Wants To Be A Millionaire** . . . . (212) 838-5910

For **tickets to see a Hollywood TV show** while it is being taped, call Audiences Unlimited, (818) 506-0043x1 and listen to the recorded information for shows this week, next week, two weeks from now, etc. They have offer tickets to many shows including Drew Carey, City Guys, Ellen, Everybody Loves Raymond, King of Queens, Just Shoot Me, Spin City, Three Sisters and more. Call to see the current offerings, or check their web for more info: tvtickets.com. On-camera Audiences seeks people for the audiences of a variety of shows. Log on to ocatv.com.

Get free tickets to the **Jay Leno Show** by writing at least four weeks ahead of time to the Jay Leno Show, 30000 West Alameda, Burbank, CA 91523. Also, if you're up in the L.A. area, you can stand in line on the day of the show at the NBC ticket office in Burbank where passes are given out on a first-come, first-served basis. They beginning giving them out at 8am.in the morning, so be there. The show tapes at 5pm and you must be there at 4pm. You might get lucky and show up just before 4pm and see if someone who has tickets didn't show up. For further information, call Guest Relations at (818) 840-4444. **Tour NBC Studios** in Burbank, (818) 840-4444. Web: tvtickets.com.

Tijuana Convention and Tourist Bureau. . . . Toll free (888) 775-2417 Call for a tourist information packet. Good web site: mexonline.com

Drive down to **Rosarito Beach** and have a Ramos Fizz at the famous Rosarito Beach Hotel. Movie stars including Kim Novak, Lana Turner, Orson Welles, Vincent Price, Rita Hayworth and Mickey Rooney were guests of the hotel. Paulette Goddard and Burgess Meredith were married there, according to owner Hugo Torres, whose aunt married into the family in 1937. Winter and off-season room rates are less than half the summer rate and my favorite time to go because you'll have the place to yourselves with your own private virgin beach view from your ocean front balcony. Senior discount available at age 45! Weekdays are cheaper than weekends, (800) 343-8582. Ask about specials. I went there on their 75th anniversary when they rolled back the rates to the first year open: $4! Check their site at rosaritohtl.com and sign up for email notification of room rate sales, etc. A few blocks South on the left is a great Mexican open market area that goes on and on for blocks. In the winter, after tourist season, you can get some real steals on garden decor, Mexican artifacts, etc.

Foxploration of Fox Studios Baja is a new movie theme park a few minutes south of the Rosarito Beach Hotel. Some of the remaining props, sets and costumes are on display from the filming of the movie **Titanic** on location in Rosarito Beach. Other films shot here are "Pearl Harbor" and the James Bond film, "Tomorrow Never Dies." Props from other movies, too. Create sound and visual effects. Admission is $12 for adults, $9 for seniors and children 3-11. Web: foxploration.com

About six miles past the Rosarito Beach Hotel is the **Las Rocas Hotel**, newer, and on a wonderful site on the ocean. Go on a Santa Ana day in January or February, and you'll love it. A great place for lunch outside with a view of the ocean and coastline. Fabulous sunset happy hour in the palapa. The amazing thing is you'll have the place to yourselves (in winter, that is!) For more information and directions, call (800) 733-6394.

Tour the Tecate Brewery Monday through Friday at 9, 10, and 11am and 3 and 4pm. The beer garden is open Monday thru Friday, 10-6pm. Saturday tours by appointment.

Baja California Tours offers day trips, overnights, art tours, fishing tours, busses to Baja for sightseeing along the Mexican coastline, tours to see the whales, the caves of Baja, more. Call (858) 454-7166.

Discover Baja Travel Club, everything you need to know about Baja, (858) 275-4225.

Leisure Resources

If you like to go and do, here's how to keep up with what's happening. These resources will keep you entertained in more ways than one:

The **Reader** is a free newspaper published every Thursday. It contains a

"Guide to Local Events" for the week, including major events and *free* things to do. Many people in the know rely on this source for their weekend leisure activities. What I like about it is it lists outdoor things: what stars are in the sky, extreme high and low tides, the seasonal flowers in bloom along the freeways and in the desert, and other little things worth noticing that are unique to San Diego and make it such a fabulous place to live in. Then, there is the section on upcoming Lectures, Drama, Music, Film, In Person, Sports, and Special Events, and of course, Night Life. You'll always find a number of "two-for-one" coupons for restaurants, too. The *Reader* is distributed free of charge throughout San Diego County at libraries, liquor stores, convenience stores and other locations and if you don't get one by 3 p.m., you may not get one this week. For a drop-off point near you, call (619) 235-3000.

The "Night and Day" section of the Thursday *Union-Tribune* contains info on what's going on in San Diego: special events, water sports, arts, theaters and night life, in addition to concerts in town and what's playing at the movies. Still a bargain at about $13 a month delivered; longer periods are cheaper per month; first time subscribers receive a substantial discount. Ask about current specials. Call (619) 299-3131 for delivery.

San Diego Magazine has a column of forthcoming special events and happenings in town called "What's Doing," which is especially helpful because it comes out on the 21st of the preceding month so you have more advance notice of events. The August issue contains their special *Annual Guide to Dining and Night Life*. Back issues are available while supply lasts. Special introductory subscription offer, around $12 for 12 issues, (619) 230-9292. Ask about specials, especially near year's end, and a subscription is a great gift for a friend. Web: sandiego-online.com.

Visitor Information Centers Pick up **free maps** and brochures at visitor information centers, and a Quarterly Calendar of Events, if you can get one! They go fast.

Visitor Information Center, I-5 & Clairemont Dr.	(619) 276-8200
Cabrillo National Monument	(619) 293-5450
Downtown Information Center	(619) 235-2222
Gaslamp Information Center	(619) 233-5227
International Visitor Info Center, Ist & F Street	(619) 236-1212
Balboa Park Information Center	(619) 239-0512 or 235-1100
Carlsbad Convention & Visitor Center	(800) 227-5722
Encinitas Visitor Center	(760) 753-6046
Escondido Convention & Visitor	(760) 745-4751/
Coronado Visitors Bureau	(800) 622-8300
Oceanside Convention & Visitor's Bureau	(760) 721-1101
East County Visitor Center	(619) 463-1166

San Diego Convention Center The San Diego Convention Center monthly schedule of events is available in the office at end of the first floor toward the Marriott. They are free of charge, or to subscribe, send $10 to the San Diego Convention Center, ATTN: Subscription, 111 W. Harbor Drive, San Diego, CA 92101.

For a free 200-page travel guide and a picture map of California, call the **California Office of Tourism**, 1-800-TO-CALIF. They send an amazing amount of information. Same for L.A. Convention & Visitors, (213) 624-7300.

My **favorite map of San Diego County** is a colorful 20" x 30" *pictorial* map with darling artwork showing all the points of interest in the county: Cabrillo Monument, whales, sailboats, Old Town, the Tecate Border, the Desert View Tower on Sunrise Highway, all the lakes, the Cleveland National Forest, Mt. Laguna, Julian apple country, all the Missions, Mt. Laguna, Palomar Observatory, mountains, lakes, beaches, the coast line highlights and much more. It's an *"at a glance view"* of everything in the whole county. Produced by Unique Media, it's available at Cabrillo Monument, some Visitor's Centers and many drug stores for about $5. I bought the laminated one for about $15. But you could get it laminated at Staples or Teacher's Pet for about a few bucks. It's a great reminder to go see things you've heard about and always wanted to see. On the back of the map is all the pertinent information about the places, including phone numbers to contact! This is a great gift idea, too, especially for someone who likes to scratch around and familiarize themselves with every crack and crevice in San Diego. I adore my copy and have bought several over the years.

Cultural/Ethnic Heritage/Social/Political Groups Get in touch with your cultural or ethnic community. Most ethnic groups have a local organization that meets for social gatherings and special events, etc. For example, the United Italian American Association has monthly meetings and sponsors the annual Columbus Day Parade, (619) 469-0795. Other organizations are listed in the *Yellow Pages* under Associations, Organizations, Clubs and, the *San Diego Source Book*, lists hundreds of political, professional and social clubs and organizations in San Diego, available at libraries.

Books on San Diego There are dozens of books about San Diego, mostly written by San Diegans who are experts on local fishing, boating, walking, hiking, birds, shells, rocks, gems, wild-flowers, mountains, national parks, hot springs, history, architecture, casinos, ghosts, deserts, biking trails, etc. Check local book stores. They make great gifts, too.

Chapter 4

CULTURAL ARTS FOR LESS

You know how expensive good tickets to *live* performances can be. But, did you know that you can attend practically every cultural event in town at a discount? or for half price? Sometimes for just a few dollars? Or even for totally *free*? There are some fabulous performing arts ticket bargains, so get set for many nights on the town. Theater, dance and music. Take your pick. San Diego has it all. Enjoy more events this year . . .and pay less than ever!

San Diego Performing Arts League . . . . (619) 497-5000
The San Diego Performing Arts League is a coalition of more than 130 San Diego theater, music and dance companies. SDPAL offers a number of programs for San Diego residents and visitors who are interested in substantial savings on tickets to insure affordability to anyone interested in the arts. The League sponsors ARTS TIX (half-price tickets),Arts Tix OnLine (electronic half-price tickets), "What's Playing" (a print guide to the performing arts) and an E-newsletter emailed to you containing performances that are available for half price. Visit their web site at sandiegoperforms.com. More information on their services follows this list of members:

Aardvark Alley Productions
Academy of Performing Arts
Actors Alliance of S. D.
Actor's Asylum Productions
Advocates/Classical Music
Alpha Omega Dance
Allegro
Appel Presents
Asian American Repertory
  Theater
Asian Story Theater
Athenaeum Music & Arts
  Library
Balboa Theatre Foundation
Beacon Theatre
Broadway/San Diego
Butterworth Dance Co.
California Ballet Company
California Center for the

Arts, Escondido
Camarada
Carlsbad Community
  Theatre
Carlsbad Playhouse
Center for Creative History
Centro Cultural De La Raza
Christian Community
  Theater
Chula Vista School for the
  Creative&Performing Arts
Cinema Society/Visual
  Arts Foundation
City Ballet
City College Performing Arts
City Heights Perf. Annex
Civic Youth Orchestra
Classics For Kids
Coast Kids Theatre

Community Actors Theatre
Coronado Playhouse
Coronado School
  of the Arts
Creative History Consortium
Culture Shock San Diego
Dance Troupe
Culy Theater
Cygnet Theater Company
Diversionary Theatre
East County
  Performing Arts Center
Eveoke Dance Theatre
Fern Street Theater
The Fritz Theater
Gay Men's Chorus of S.D.
Grossmont College
  Theater Arts Dept.
Grossmont Symphony

Orchestra & Master Chorale
H.I.T. Productions
Icarus Puppet Company
In aChord Men's Ensemble
J*Company Youth Theatre
Jazz Xpress
Jean Isaacs' San Diego
Dance Theater
Korbett Kompany Production
La Jolla Music Society
La Jolla Playhouse
La Jolla Stage Co.
La Jolla Symphony &
Chorus
Lamb's Players Theatre
Lamplighters Community
Theatre
Lower Lert Performance
Collective
Lyric Opera San Diego
Mainly Mozart Festival
Malashock Dance & Co.
McCaleb Dance
Mesa College Theatre Co.
Metropolitan Educational
Theatre Network
Mira Costa College Theatre
Moonlight Stage Productions
The Muse Theatre
Musical Merit Foundation
Mystery Café Dinner Theatre
National Comedy Theatre
New Village Arts
North Coast Repertory
Theatre
North County Productions
Old Globe
OnStage Productions
Palomar College
Performing Arts Dept.

PASACAT Asian Pacific
Arts Company
Patio Playhouse
Community Theatre
Patricia Rincon Dance
Collective
Pig's Eye Puppet Theater
Planned Parenthood's
IMAGES: Theater for
Young Hearts & Minds
Playwrights Project
Poway Center for the
Performing Arts
Poway Performing Arts Co.
Renaissance Theatre Co.
Salomon Theatre
SAMAHAN Filipino
American Performing Arts
San Diego Actors Theatre
San Diego's Balboa Park
Puppet Guild
San Diego Ballet
San Diego Black
Ensemble Theatre
S.D. Center for Jewish
Culture
San Diego Chamber
Orchestra
San Diego Children's Choir
San Diego Civic Dance Assn.
San Diego Civic Theatre
San Diego Civic Youth Ballet
San Diego Civic Youth
Orchestra
San Diego Early Music
Society
San Diego Junior Theatre
San Diego Master Chorale
San Diego Men's Chorus
San Diego Mini-Concerts

San Diego Museum of Art
San Diego Opera
San Diego Repertory
Theatre
San Diego School of Crea-
tive & Performing Arts
SDSU Theatre Department
SDSU School/Music&Dance
San Diego Sun Harbor
Chorus
San Diego Symphony
San Diego TheatreSports
San Diego Youth Symphony
Scripps Ranch Theatre
Seagate Concerts, Inc.
Second Avenue Klezmer
Ensemble
Sixth @ Penn Theatre
Sledgehammer Theatre
So. California Youth Ballet
Southwestern College
Speckels Organ Society
Speckels Theatre
Starlight Musical Theatre
Super Sonic Samba School
Sushi Performance &
Visual Arts
The Theatre in Old Town
Triple Espresso, LLC
UCSD Theatre & Dance
UCSD Univ. Events Office
USD Theatre Arts Dept.
Vantage Theatre
Welk Resort Theatre
Westminster Theater
Westwind Brass
Women's Repertory Theatre
Young Audiences of SD

Times Arts Tix (half-price tickets) . . . . (619) 497-5000
Times Arts Tix is a public service sponsored by the San Diego Performing Arts League. Since 1986, Times Arts Tix has offered *day-of-performance* tickets (for half price plus a surcharge) to theater, music and dance events throughout San Diego County. Half-price tickets for Monday's performances are available on Sunday. Call (619) 497-5000, listen to the recorded daily listing of what is available for *tonight*, and hurry down to pay, or you can pay *online* at their website by credit card. Tickets are sold on a first come/first served basis. (A word of caution: call early in the morning, and pick more than one performance because by the time you get down to pay for your tickets, the show you want may be sold out. The recording is not updated

during the day.) They are located on Broadway Circle by Horton Plaza. Hours are Tuesday through Thursday, 11a.m.-6p.m.; Friday and Saturday, 10 a.m.-6 p.m, Sunday 10-5pm. Parking is available in the green area (15 minutes) in front of City Bank or in the Horton Plaza parking building on Fourth Avenue, and Arts Tix will validate parking for three hours. It is usually easier to get tickets for matinees and early-in-the-week performances than for weekends. Full price advance tickets to Ticketmaster events are also available. You can now check the daily half-price ticket availability on the web at sandiegoperforms.com or you can receive Arts-Tix Today, a daily e-mail listing of half price shows. See next listing.

ArtsTIX Today (Online tickets) . . . . sandiegoperforms.com The San Diego Performing Arts League has inaugurated the Arts-Tix internet program. Log on to the League's site at sandiegoperforms.com and click on Arts-Tix Today to sign up. After 6pm, Tuesday through Saturday, you will receive a list of unsold seats available for the next day's performance! Pay by credit card online. (See chapter on Travel for half price ticket booths in NYC, Boston, Washington DC, and London.

"What's Playing" (Print guide to what's playing) . . . . . . (619) 238-0700 "What's Playing" is the complete guide to the performing arts. For $12, you will receive a bi-monthly subscription for a year by mail. Pick up a free sample at ArtsTix above.

How to see performances for free! Volunteer to usher at plays, concerts and dance performances and get in free! Most arts organizations use a team of volunteer ushers at their events. Call any of the theaters, music or dance groups that interest you and inquire about their volunteer usher program, or offer to help with mail-outs, answer phones, work on costumes or sets; offer printing, bookkeeping, public relations, fundraising, etc. Volunteers usually have an opportunity to see performances whenever there are empty seats. I have volunteered at the Old Globe, handed out programs before the performance, shut the door when the lights were dimmed, then sat down and watched the performance! When the lights went up, I opened the doors and stood there until the lights dimmed again, etc. I have a friend, a librarian and a cultural arts junkie, who said: "Let me tell you *my* schedule of volunteering: I'll be at the San Diego Repertory Theater tomorrow night, then the symphony the following. Next week I'm at the ballet and the Old Globe." She sees almost everything that comes to San Diego . . . and rarely has to pay because she ushers! (The Old Globe has a waiting list of volunteers a mile long, and the opera uses professional ushers, but most other performing arts are in need of ushers and other volunteers. It's best to sign up before the beginning of the season and attend volunteer usher "training," but calling a few weeks ahead can work, too. Even last minute, sometimes.)

Tickets to **preview performances** (dress rehearsals) are usually offered at a very low price, sometimes only $5 or $10 or half the regular price, and sometimes FREE. Call one of the Performing Arts Members listed above, and listen to their recorded upcoming schedule, then call the office and find out when the preview performance will be! (You clever devil!)

The *Entertainment* book offers **"two-for-one" coupons** for the La Jolla Music Society, Poway Performing Arts Company, San Diego Symphony and more. For more on *Entertainment* books, see Chapter on Resources."

Old Globe . . . . (619) 23-GLOBE
The crown jewel of San Diego theatre for over 60 years, The Old Globe is a Tony® Award-winning theatre that produces 14 shows on its three stages every year. The Old Globe features new works, beloved classics, musicals, and of course, Shakespeare. Their annual holiday show How the Grinch Stole Christmas has become a San Diego tradition. Regular tickets in the A section run $25-$52, with $19 B section seats available for every performance. Series tickets are available at a savings, but that is not the real advantage of buying a subscription to the series: the real advantage is selecting the same seating for performances, a chance to upgrade those seats the next season and an opportunity to be a part of the theater arts community and its special receptions, dinners and events. Half-price tickets are available at ArtsTix, above. Seniors, students and military can also get Globe Tix—50% off at the Globe ticket office on the day of performance (must have ID). There are additional discounts available for groups of 15 or more; call (619) 231-1941 x2408 for more details. Tickets and information on tours, preview performances, education programs, purchasing costumes, donating costumes and more are available online at theoldglobe.org. The Old Globe has survived two major fires since 1978, but was promptly rebuilt with an outpouring of community donations.

Broadway/San Diego . . . . (619) 231-8995
For over 25 years, the Broadway/San Diego has been responsible for getting major touring Broadway blockbuster musicals and plays to San Diego like Evita, Footloose, Fosse, Tap Dogs, A Chorus Line, Cabaret, Titanic, Cats, Phantom of the Opera, Sunset Boulevard, Riverdance, The Producers. Artists have included Faye Dunaway, Katharine Hepburn, Lena Horne, Yul Brynner, Bette Davis, Richard Chamberlain, Eartha Kitt, Carol Channing, Jerry Lewis, Tony Bennett, Johnny Mathis, Enrique Iglesias, and Robin Williams. Broadway/San Diego is a part of Nederlander, the largest theater organization in the world. All performances are held at the 3,000-

seat Civic Theatre. Individual tickets range from about $25 to $50/$60, and are sold at the Civic Theater, (619) 570-1100 or (619) 615-4178, and Ticketmaster, (619) 220-TIXS. A subscription series offers up to about a 35% savings, but the advantage of series tickets is seating and an opportunity to upgrade seating the next season, and an association with the theater community, post-performance actor chatbacks, receptions, lectures and special events. Student, senior, military and group discounts. Web site: broadwaysd.com

La Jolla Playhouse .... (858) 550-1010
La Jolla Playhouse was founded in 1947 by movie stars Gregory Peck, Dorothy McGuire and Mel Ferrer so that Hollywood actors could explore their craft on the stage (originally in the auditorium at La Jolla High). It has become a world-class theater, the recipient of over 250 major awards including the Tony Award, and has been acclaimed by the *Village Voice*. Such shows as *Big River*, *The Who's Tommy*, *How To Succeed in Business Without Really Trying* and *A Walk in the Woods* previewed here and moved on to Broadway to receive numerous Tony Awards. La Jolla Playhouse shares a facility with the UCSD Department of Theatre and Dance. Home of the nation's first "pay-what-you-can" program, La Jolla playhouse offers several discounted ticket programs including under age 25, seniors, and subscriptions including "Meet The Artist" series. Call for details. This is a very popular playhouse with many season ticket subscribers. Web site: lajollaplayhouse.com

Starlight Musical Theater .... (619) 544-7827
San Diego Civic Light Opera Assn. offers a half dozen musical theater performances indoors and outdoors. *My Fair Lady, Annie, A Chorus Line, Hot, South Pacific, Music Man, Hello Dolly, Fiddler on the* Roof and more have played here. Since 1946, the summer tradition has continued under the stars at the historic Starlight Bowl amphitheater in Balboa Park. Kids 12 and under are free Thursdays & Sundays all summer when accompanied by an adult. Discounts for military and dependents, seniors over 60 and full time students. See what's coming and order tickets at starlighttheater.org.

San Diego Symphony .... (619) 235-0804
A musical landmark of San Diego, the Symphony has brought years of artistic excellence to America's Finest City. During the winter and spring, there is concert series with six performances including classical music, classic film music, a Holiday Pops Festival and a Family Festival. Winter/spring performances are held at beautiful Copley Symphony Hall (which seats 2000) in Symphony Towers, 750 B Street, downtown, and at the California Center for the Arts in Escondido. Summer Pops concerts are held at the Navy Pier on Harbor Drive, just South of Broadway, and include

classical, show tunes and patriotic music. Subscriptions for the season offer a 20% discount off regular prices. Students, seniors 60+ and military may get a $3 discount per ticket available the Monday prior to each event. Student Rush tickets can be purchased 45 minutes prior to the concerts and are $10 with a student ID. Group discounts for 15 or more. The Symphony also offers educational events for students and a Kid's Concerts priced at $5. Web site: sandiegosymphony.com

San Diego Opera . . . . (619) 232-7636
The San Diego Opera, Southern California's longest-established opera company (since 1965), has achieved top ten status in America. Five main stage productions are held each season (January-May) at the 3,000 seat Civic Theater with tickets ranging from around $20-$150. Some tickets turned over to ARTS TIX. *However*, in an attempt to make opera affordable to everyone, one hour before the performance, "rush" tickets (unsold seats) are available for $20. People will stand in line for two hours to get these $20 tickets, so plan to go early if you want one. Other opera bargains include: seniors and students receive a 20% discount on Tuesday subscriptions; groups tickets of 20 or more, 20% discount. The Pre-opera Lecture Series is under $5. Freebies include performances at schools and five lunchtime concerts in front of the Civic Theater with world renowned stars. Students may attend dress rehearsals through the Opera Education Program for $5 each; $7.50 for their chaperon, with a minimum of 10 students. Subscription benefits include a chance of better seating and advance notification of special events and recitals. Past performances have included *Falstaff, The Magic Flute, Marriage of Figaro, Romeo and Juliet, Madama Butterfly, Salome, the Barber of Seville, Aida, Streetcar Named Desire, Fidelio* and *Lohengrin*. For more information, tickets, subscriptions, or to be on the mailing list or be notified of free performances, call (619) 232-7636. The San Diego Opera will send "Update" reminders of free concerts, lectures, parties, etc. by email: sdostaff@sdopera.com. Visit the Opera's site at sdopera.com The San Diego Opera radio program is heard on 89.5 KPBS at 7pm every Sunday night from December through May.

Lyric Opera San Diego (formerly SD Comic Opera) . . . (619) 231-5714
Lyric Opera San Diego has offered accessible, affordable opera and musical theatre productions in San Diego since 1979. The company performs operas and musicals from the European and American tradition, in English, presenting the fine musical talent with full orchestra and chorus accompaniment. Performances are at the historic Casa del Prado Theater in Balboa Park from March through October. The lyric opera incorporates a combination of both music and spoken dialogue, a tradition that dates back to balladeers and troubadours who criss-crossed Europe as far back as the Middle Ages. They have a loyal following with nearly 20,000 tickets

sold annually. All performers are local, many of whom have moved on to principal status with the San Diego Opera, the San Diego Symphony as well as other national and international companies. Subscribers enjoy a major savings over regular ticket buyers, up to 33%. Performances have included Gilbert and Sullivan operettas, Gershwin, the Mikado, The Beggar's Opera and more. Regular single ticket prices are about $17-$27. Student, senior and military discounts are available. Final dress-First Views for students, military and social service organizations for a nominal fee. Part of the Education & Outreach program is touring schools. There is a focus lecture before matinee audiences allowing an up-close look at the show they will be seeing. For more, se their web site at lyricoperasandiego.com.

La Jolla Music Society . . . . (858) 459-3728
The La Jolla Music Society is the most comprehensive classical music presenter in San Diego, showcasing the finest symphonies, soloists, chamber ensembles, and dance companies in three series plus an annual three-week summer festival, SummerFest La Jolla. Concerts take place in Sherwood Auditorium in La Jolla, and in the San Diego Civic Theatre and Copley Symph9ony Hall downtown. Individual performances range from $25 to $105. Series prices range from $99 to $1,500. Millitary and student discounts available.

Mainly Mozart, the annual concert series, usually held in May or June with performances throughout the county and Baja by an all-star orchestra of concertmasters and principal players from orchestras such as those of Boston, Los Angeles, Pittsburgh and San Francisco, with internationally-known musicians from the most accomplished chamber ensembles and music institutes. (610) 239- 0100. Web: mainlymozart.org.

California Ballet Company . . . . (858) 560-6741
Since 1968, the California Ballet has offered traditional ballets such as the Swan Lake, Coppelia, Romeo & Julie and Giselle, plus an annual performance of the Nutcracker during the holidays. Single seat tickets range from about $20-$45, and subscription prices are offered at a considerable savings. Subscribers get priority seating, a newsletter, invitations to dinners and receptions. Seniors, military, college student and group discounts available. Students may attend dress rehearsals for nominal fee. Call for more information or go to site at caiforniaballet.org

If you travel and want to take in a play or concert in other cities, take a look at **Culture Finder** on the web at culturefinder.com. Or, go to **Theatre Finder** at theatrefinder.com for theater listings all over the world. You can click an online booking service, too.

Humphrey's Concerts By The Bay .... (619) 523-1010
Humphrey's has name entertainment at their 1200 seat outdoor theater,
featuring jazz, rock, pop and country music stars, plus comedians, from
May to October. Performers have included: Christopher Cross, B-52's,
Buddy James, Boss Scaggs, Hiroshima, Whitney Houston, Jimmy
Buffett, Linda Ronstadt, Chicago, Sergio Mendes & Brazil 99, Crosby
Stills & Nash, Harry Belafonte, Ray Charles, Johnny Cash, Pointer
Sisters, Willie Nelson, Tom Jones, Hootie & the Blowfish, Moody Blues,
Taj Mahal and Peter Frampton to name a few! Tickets from $35 to over
$100. Call early in the season to volunteer to usher (and get in free!)
The schedule is printed in April or online earlier at humphreysconcerts.com.

Spreckels Organ Pavilion hosts free concerts in Balboa Park every
Sunday, 52 weeks a year, from 2-3 p.m. Seating for 2,000. Free
concerts on Monday evenings at 8 p.m. from June-August. Movies, too.

Summer concert series: Many neighborhoods have free weekly outdoor
concerts all summer. One of the best is the **La Jolla Concerts by the
Sea** series which has been held since 1983 at Scripps Memorial Park at
the Cove every Sunday from 2-4 p.m. during June, July and August and
are extremely popular. Go early. Money to pay the musicians is donated
by local businesses, organizations and town residents. Attendance
ranges from 600 to 1,000 weekly, and the Fourth of July evening concert
performance attracts over 2,000 spectators to the village. Call (619) 645-
8115 for a recorded schedule, or visit their site at ljconcertsbythesea.org.
Coronado Concerts summer series. Somewhat similar to the above.
For more information and schedule, call the Coronado Visitors Center at
(619) 437-8788. The *Reader* usually lists the schedule of concerts by
neighborhood in their calendar of events.

Carlsbad Arts Events Info Line (free concerts). ...... (760) 434-2904

To request good seats, check the **theater and stadium seating charts**
in the front section of the *Yellow Pages* telephone directory.   It has the
Old Globe, La Jolla Playhouse, Starlight, Lyceum, Civic Theater and
more. You can view the seating charts online at their web sites (and
order tickets, too.)

Ticket tips: Ticketmaster offers tickets to major performances, concerts
and appearances throughout San Diego and So. California including Los
Angeles, Orange County plus Las Vegas, (619) 220-8497. Web site:
ticketmaster.com. Also, Check the *Union-Tribune* Tickets &
Entertainment #1430 classified column for tickets agencies.

Great for you and the kids: If you live in an area near a college or university, call the drama and music departments and ask to be placed on the mailing list to receive notification of performances. (Very inexpensive.)

Bus tours: Every semester, Mira Costa, Palomar and Grossmont Community Colleges offer bus tours to major cultural events in Los Angeles. Most offer tours to the Laguna Arts Festival, the Getty Museum, art galleries in L.A., etc. Because of early planning, they usually get very good seats. You know you're in good hands when you travel with the colleges. Call the colleges listed in chapter on Continuing Education. Also, check the *Union-Tribune* classified ads section on Travel Agencies #1690 for bus tours to theaters and events in Los Angeles, etc.

Keep an eye on free events listed in the Calendar of Events column in the *Reader*, *San Diego Magazine*, *San Diego Home/Garden* and the *Union-Tribune's* Night & Day section.

Many concerts, performances and other cultural events including Baroque Chamber Ensemble, solo pianists and cellists, are held at the **Athenaeum** in La Jolla, (858) 454-5872. Call for schedule.

Get on the mailing list for upcoming performances at the California Center for the Arts in Escondido (760) 738-4100; the Poway Center for Performing Arts (858) 440-2277; East County Performing Arts Center, (619) 440-2277.

Movies: Most independent and big chain movie theaters including Mann, United Artists, AMC and Edwards Theaters charge around $5.75 for their early bird shows prior to 5 p.m., sometimes as late as 6 p.m. It's too expensive to pay full fare! The *Entertainment* coupon book (See Resources) contains **discount coupons** for AMC, UltraStar, United Artists, Regal Cinemas and Edwards Theaters for about $5.50 each. For **classic, foreign and off-beat films**, check the *Reader's* "Guide to Local Events," (Films). UCSD, SDSU and other colleges and community colleges, libraries, museums and art galleries offer **art films** usually at a very low cost. The **Cinema Society** is a cultural arts organization that premiers sophisticated commercial and art films once or more a month during its season, from fall to spring. Other activities include cocktail parties, celebrity salutes, discounts to film festival trips, special receptions, discussions, Oscar Night Party, and a trip to the Palm Springs Film Festival. About 750 members, membership fee is approximately $200 per membership for the season, and tickets are transferrable.

Newsletter before each program. For more information, call (619) 280-1600. **Visual Arts Foundation** offers the annual Cox Communications Film Festival. Every August, they show about 15 free family-oriented films under the stars in parks throughout San Diego County. For dates, call (619) 280-1600. You can still rent **videos for 99¢** at Long's Drugs. Many public libraries also offer video rentals $1 or less. Chula Vista and Carlsbad libraries have an excellent selection of video rentals, cheap! **Movies 2 Sell**, 4724 Clairemont Mesa Blvd., (858) 27-FILM, offers thousands of used videos selling mostly for $6-7. Good place to take your unwanted classic, horror, old favorites and Disney videos and cash or trade them in for around $3. Check their web at movies2sell.com.

Chapter 5
FREE & BARGAIN TRAVEL

Ok, Globetrotters, fasten your seatbelts. Here are some fascinating travel bargains for you to consider. If you are a little bit flexible and are willing to do some extra planning, you'll be able to see a whole lot more of the world. There are some real travel addicts out there who manage to feed their addictions on a shoe string budget. I've discovered some of their secrets and am sharing them with you. In this "soft" travel market today, there are some *real* travel bargains! To find the best fares, there is simply no substitute for shopping around. Let your fingers to the walking . . .

Air Travel & Cruises

Be a **courier** and fly free or up to 70% discount, but most are about half off. Every year, about 35,000 people travel the world as a courier. I *know* people who are doing it: college professors, retired people, students, and even those who only have a two-week annual vacation. A professor friend took a flight to London with a 30 day return, then took a London courier flight to Africa, then India, back to London, and back to San Diego. CHEAP.

A courier is a person who escorts "cargo" on a passenger flight. The "cargo" may be a document, parcel or freight. The Federal Aviation Agency dictates that cargo sent on a *passenger* plane must be accompanied by a passenger. Many international corporations and businesses need important cargo or documents delivered *immediately,* in person, and checked through customs. Regular freight can sit for days before being cleared. It may not be economically feasible for a corporation to send an employee who has other responsibilities. Why should they pay an employee *and* his round-trip ticket when they know you and I are willing to travel for them as a courier for just the price of the ticket? Courier companies have sprung up to meet this modern need; they act as brokers between the corporation that needs the personal escort and the individual who wishes to act as the courier. The courier broker charges you a percentage of the ticket price as a commission, unless the company agrees to pay for your ticket *and* the commission to the courier, too, which sometimes happens. Many companies have a need for daily flights to another country. Therefore, you can sign up for one two or three months away. The super cheap ticket bargains are when a company needs someone on short notice; then the price of your ticket can be as low as $50 or even free. Sometimes hotels get thrown in if they are desperate for someone to take a flight. Trips to the orient originate from mostly Los Angeles and San Francisco. Trips to Europe originate mostly from New York, and trips to South America from New York or Miami. The down side is: you can't take luggage. You sacrifice that for the cargo you are escorting. But, you know, I can jam a lot of things into my carry-on luggage for a free (or seriously discounted) ticket to a destination I want to go to! The flight might be canceled, but that is fairly rare. Courier Flights are on regular scheduled airline, not charters. Your documents state the contents of each bag you accompany, and the freight has been inspected or xrayed by the courier company prior to being manifested. A courier representative meets you at departure and at arrival at each end of the trip and takes care of the paperwork. You receive a one way ticket for each leg of the trip, an envelope of documents (cargo manifests) and a letter of instruction for the return flight. Each deal is different; some allow you to stay a few days, others allow you to stay up to 6 months. No alcohol on flight, before or during. Cost: You pay a percentage of the regular fare plus departure taxes. Some courier companies charge a registration fee of $20 to $50 a year. Some require a deposit of $100 to $500, refundable on return; if you miss the return flight, your deposit is forfeited. You must be 21 years of age, have a valid passport, have conservative looks, be self-assured and wear business clothing. Each company and each flight will have it's own advantages and restrictions. This works only for one person traveling; the second person pays, or in ideal circumstances, you plan it so that you go today, your partner goes tomorrow on the same flight, as only one courier is allowed per flight due to FAA regulations. The Learning Annex offers a three hour workshop on how to be a courier, (619) 544-9700. Or you can pick up a copy of "The Insider's Guide To Air Courier Bargains," by Kelly Monaghan, 200+ pages, soft cover, $17.95, at book stores and local libraries. Several courier services are listed. The **International Association of Air Travel Couriers** of Keystone Heights, Florida offers free information on how travelers can get involved and a newsletter containing 30 courier companies, etc., $45 per year, (352) 475-1584. Web Site: courier.org. You can join on the web site and get a password that will enable you to click onto their web site and check the listing of courier opportunities, updated twice daily. Do it! They deal with a company that has daily flights abroad, with frequent flights to London. Yup! The **Air Courier Association** offers members ($29 a year; $99 for life) a schedule of courier flights on it's Web site. Departures from New York, Los Angeles and San Francisco, incredibly cheap, even free. Last-minute flights are posted on the Web site and go to the first taker. For more information, call (800) 282-1202 or log on to aircourier.org. If you go to their sites, you will see links to all sorts of great travel opportunities.

Volunteer to be bumped and get a voucher for $$ off your next flight or a free round trip airline ticket to anywhere the airline flies within the continental limits of the United States. Airlines are allowed to book more than 100% of their seats, knowing that a percentage of passengers will be "no shows." However, if all show up, some won't be able to board. They will be "bumped" off the flight, so to speak. To compensate them for this inconvenience, and to insure good will, the airline offers the bumped passenger a voucher, or a ticket to anywhere the airline flies, or cash, and sometimes all, and books them on the next flight out. If the flight isn't until the next day, the airline frequently gives vouchers or cash for hotel rooms and meals until their budget for doing so has expired. The airline asks people on board if they are willing to give up their seat in exchange for tickets when overbooked. You want to volunteer to get off the plane and let someone else have your seat. Fast. They may only need ONE person to get off, although I know of an instance when they were overbooked and needed SIXTEEN people to give up their seats. They ended up giving each person who volunteered TWO round trip tickets to get off! Don't you wish that happened on YOUR flight?! Why hasn't that happened to me??

Here's how to get bumped: Plan it!! Reserve on the busiest flights...Sunday nights, Monday mornings, Friday evenings when the business people travel and before or after a major holiday. Business people have to get where they are going, but if you are on a leisure trip and it really doesn't make any difference to you when you get there, you can volunteer to be bumped. Check in early. Be among the first in line to present your ticket. Ask if the plane if full, because if it isn't, no point in getting your hopes up. If it's full, tell them you want to volunteer to be bumped. Some airlines keep a list of those volunteering, some don't. They might tell you to get on board and they will call you if needed. They might tell you not to board, to sit and wait to see if the plane fills. If they need your seat, you can negotiate your benefits. Remember, your luggage has already been placed on board and will arrive ahead of you. If you're getting on the next flight, who cares? For further information on being bumped, call the library and ask if they have the U.S. Department of Transportation's free guidebook, *Fly Rights*. How they made such a fascinating topic so boring is absolutely beyond me! This is probably available at the government's consumer information site: pueblo.gsa.gov.

A Saratoga man volunteered to give up his seat on an overbooked San Jose/Seattle flight, and in exchange, American Airlines gave him a ticket with a $900 value, and he continued on to Seattle on the next available flight. A Los Angeles frequent-flyer scooped up between $4,000 and $5,000 in tickets over the past few years by being bumped. A woman and her daughter, returning to San Diego from Boston, volunteered to be bumped, received round trip tickets to anywhere the airline flies, booked the next flight out, volunteered to be bumped again, and they now have four round trip tickets to anywhere Continental flies! Approximately 130,000 people are bumped a year, and 80% of those are *volunteers*. I have been bumped several times returning from Orlando and Washington, DC. I like to fly on Northwest and rack up frequent flyer miles. Their flights go thru their hub in Minneapolis/St. Paul. The flights I take are almost ALWAYS booked from Minneapolis to San Diego, and I just volunteer to get off and get my round trip ticket voucher or cash or whatever they are giving that day, and then get booked on the next flight out! I love it. This can work very well for you if you plan it!

If you're taking a flight, always join the airline's **"Frequent Flyer"** program even if you don't think you'll ever use the airline again. Many people think the Frequent Flyer Program is for business travelers only. Not at all true...it's for you and me! The reservationist will give you a number to call and they will assign you a member number right then and there, at no cost to you. As a frequent flyer, you will be placed on the e-mailing list (some still have snail-mailing lists too) to receive their newsletters outlining air fare specials, double mile offers, your accrued mileage, etc. When you accumulate 25,000 miles, the airline will give you a free ticket to anywhere in the Continental U.S. I am a Northwest frequent flyer. With one trip to Washington, DC (receiving double miles for flying into National Airport), a trip to Hawaii, plus my MCI long distance miles, I earned enough miles for another free ticket! I volunteered to be bumped on a Washington trip, so *I've already gotten one free ticket!* Whadda deal!! There are several ways to accumulate miles: miles actually flown and bonus miles offered on special deals, miles for hotel and restaurant charges (1 mile for every $1 spent), long distance service (5 miles for every $1 spent) and credit card charges (1 mile for every $1 charged on your airline Visa or Master Card.) I know a retired couple who charge *everything* they can on their Citibank card through American Airlines to get AA frequent flyer miles. They use their credit card for the dentist, groceries at Vons, all department stores, newspaper subscriptions, gas, dentist, vet, doctors, airline tickets, hotels, restaurants, rental cars (anything where they will take plastic), and they have gone to Europe, free, more than once, on their frequent flyer miles!! They pay their Visa bill monthly, so there is no accumulated interest. They're enjoying their retirement freebies. I know another woman who said she charged a $15,000 AUTO on her credit card to get the miles; then refinanced through her credit union. I read in today's paper that a man charges everything to get mileage, and he just paid his daughter's college tuition on his credit card so he can get mileage. He pays his off monthly.

Airline Web sites Internet usage by travelers continues to soar. Some airlines are charging more if you don't get an eticket. Airlines are offering deep discounts only available on the internet. Also, last-minute deals. And weekend special fares you won't believe that are booked at the last minute. Get on the emailing list of the airlines that serve your most visited cities, or the city you want to visit. Some allow online ticket auctions (make your offer). Sign up for email notification of sales. Some airlines allow discount travel to originate only in selected cities. Here are a few web sites, and it's easy to find any airline online. Go to Ask.com and type in the airline.

Continental COOL fares	flycontinental.com
TWA (Wednesdays)	twa.com
Northwest	nwa.com
American	american.com
United	ual.com
Cathay Pacific (fares to Hong Kong from $499 incl. hotel	cathay-usa.com
Digital City	digitalcity.com
Southwest Airlines	swa.com

Southwest Airlines has sales-sales-sales on fares with frequent $99 fares each way, coast to coast. Also frequent sales where you can fly to their California airports for $35 each way. Awesome. I went to Orlando for $99.

Travel Agent Web Sites You can perform one search for the lowest air fares, hotel prices, car rentals, make travel plans, reservations, purchases. Enter a departure date and city, and it will search every airline for their lowest travel fares. Travel information, virtual tours of destinations. The biggest web sites for booking world wide travel are:

Expedia	expedia.com
Travelocity	travelocity.com
Preview Travel	previewtravel.com
Internet Travel Network	itn.com
TravelWeb	travelweb.com
American Express	americanexpress.com
Deals Watch (last minute cyber deals available)	webflyer.com
Priceline (bid what you want to pay)	priceline.com
Digital Datebook	digitaldiscounts.com/datebook.html
Frequent Flyer buy/sell	frugalflyer.com
Frugal Traveler Travel News	.ftns.com
Cheaptickets.com	Cheaptickets.com
Flights for Less	flightsforless.com

At **Priceline.com**, the popular site, you can enter a city you want to fly to, and you can name the price you are willing to pay for the tickets. They will confirm within three hours whether your bid is accepted. This is true for hotels, too. Click on hotels, neighborhood you want to stay in, whether you want economy to deluxe and the price you want to pay. Also, if you join SmarterLiving.com, you receive $5 added to your bid. This can work great for you. Hotels are rarely filled. You can stay in deluxe rooms for economy room rates! Be prepared to commit, as once you give your credit card, you are committed. So, be SURE you are ready to commit if you bid 'cause it's a done deal if it goes through. Go to Travelocity first, as they compare prices for you to see. You don't want to do what a friend did . . He paid more on priceline because he didn't know what his top price should be. So, do your homework first, then put in lowball bid at priceline. If you don't get it, so what. Just bid up to just below the next lowest fare you found.

The new low-cost airline **Jet Blue** now offers two non-stop flights daily to New York for under $300 round trip for tickets purchased on the internet. The airline, which serves 22 U.S. cities and San Juan, Puerto Rico, will be adding more flights, including San Diego. Their planes are new and offer large leather seats and individual satellite TV's for each passenger. See jetblue.com for more information.

Bid4Vacations.com World Class Vacations Auctioned Daily: bid on cruises, travel packages to Hawaii, Florida, more at bid4vacations.com. Another bid site for all inclusive travel is bid4travel.com

Trading Spaces You can bid on time shares that people don't want to use themselves this year. Real good deals. Visit tradingspaces.com and see the deals waiting for you at timeshares in Mexico, ski resorts, beaches, etc. Another site for timeshares at bargain prices is tug2.net.

Discount Fares/Travel Brokers/Consolidators I first found out about discount travel when I was aboard a cruise in the Mediterranean en route to see the Pyramids in Egypt. A lady standing behind me in line waiting for dinner one night mentioned in passing that she was on the same trip, *half* fare! *Needless to say, this ruined my whole trip!* She told me she belonged to three discount travel clubs. A few months later, I saw a list of several in travel magazine. Here's the way they work. Airlines and hotels, tour operators and cruise lines all suffer from an abundance of unsold tickets on almost every trip. Since they can't have a "clearance sale" and risk offending traditional travel agents who sell their offerings at full price, these travel suppliers turn to clearinghouses or brokers or consolidators who buy their unsold seats in huge lots at huge savings, and resell them at discounts ranging from $100 to $2,000+ per person off the published retail price. The only catch is that these special savings are secret. Clubs are strictly prohibited from advertising the original supplier of their offerings; only their members receive this highly confidential information. After paying a membership fee, you receive a telephone *hotline* (web site, too) which is updated with the latest offerings. Verify the seat confirmation with the airline you will be using and check their rates to see what you're saving. Longer trips are usually available about four weeks in advance, short trips may be available only 10 days or a week in advance. Many cruises are put on the hotline up to six months in advance. The key here is to be flexible. The lady I referred to had gotten her call about availability about 48 hours before the trip left. But, she says she does this all the time, and usually she gets more notice. She always keeps her suitcase packed with essentials; tosses in a few wearables and she's off. Check out available fares through these travel discounters: Remember, you could search the net all day and not find these prices on regular travel web sites. They are only available through consolidators. Check these out.

Moments Notice . . . . Web: moments-notice.com   (888) 241-3366
   Tours, packages, flights.
UNI-Travel   Web: Unitravel.com . . . . (800) 325-2222
   Consolidator. Specializing in Europe.
Council Travel . . . . (858) 270-6401
   Specializing in travel for students, everyone. Hawaii/$199
Last Minute Travel (good prices) . . . . (617)-267-9800
Cendant Traveler Service (20 years) . . . . (800) 255-0200
   Membership/3 mo. trial, $1; 24 hr. bookings, lowest fares, no booking fee, 5% cash bonus + hotels worldwide at ½ price. Good deals
Smarter Living Last minute airfares/Unpupublished fares . . . smarterliving.com

I went to google.com and searched for "travel consolidators" and up came many, many. Try it.

Best Fares (Magazine & Travel Club) . . . . (800) 635-3033
   $58 for 12 issues; coupons, 64 pages. Travel deals galore. Web site: bestfares.com   Tom Parsons is on TV a lot telling us about the best fares.

 If a deal seems too good to be true, the deal may not fly. Those ads that read tickets to "Hong Kong $299, "Paris $199" may not be available. The consolidators may only have one seat available at the advertised price.

Strangely enough, some presumed "cheap fares" are actually higher than you'd pay elsewhere. There is simply no substitute for shopping around if you want to save money. The web has the cheapest fares.

British Airways flies non-stop from San Diego to London. Fares have been published in the newspaper around Thanksgiving as low as $198 round trip to London with specials including hotels, $49 per person per night and cars, $19 per day. Call toll free (877) 428-2228. I noticed a similar ad for $198 in the spring that said they will be offering the same deal again next November lst. They may continue this pattern. Then, you can plan. Who can just drop everything and go because the fare is $198RT? As travel is down at those times of year, they probably will offer these fares again. Web tickets have been as low as $160 *round trip* to London in winter (but it's COLD in London in the winter, and rainy and snowy) and $249 round trip in summer. Check their web site at: ba.com. You can sign up to receive their e-newsletters. Or, call and ask to be a member of their Frequent Flyer Club and they will send you specials which have included a two-for-one deal, or a "book by _____(date) and receive two coach tickets free." If you plan to visit London, call the British Tourist Assn. for free information at (800) 462-2748 or log on to visitbritain.com.

While you're in London, go to the half-price ticket booth in Leicester Square. London offers a cornucopia of stage entertainment that no city on earth can match. Sign up to receive a free emailed "London theater magazine" at theatrenow.com. This site also has theater info for all over the world, including Broadway. Another good site: londonconnection.com.

Pay for your travel tickets on a credit card, and if the trip does not go, you can get the charge backed off your credit card. You won't have to hassle with getting your money refunded.

Order **special meals** on board flights with one day's notice. The dairy vegetarian is absolutely exquisite gourmet food! Everyone around me was lusting after my fresh looking meal. Also available, low fat, low calorie, non-dairy, low salt. Kosher meals require longer notice. Be sure to check to see if the airline will be serving meals, and if so, when, so you'll know whether to bring your own food. Some airlines are switching to selling meals and snacks to help resolve their financial woes.

The **week's best airfares** to major cities in the U.S. and world are published weekly on Sundays in the Travel section of the *Union-Tribune*.

If you are traveling because of an **emergency or bereavement**, say so. Many airlines have discontinued the policy of giving you the lowest rate available as a gesture of good will, but check around. Policies change from time to time, so check with several airlines. Northwest as of this writing offers 70% off the no-notice fare, which is very good, but no doubt temporary. Some airlines evaluate on a case by case basis, so hone up on your "sweet talk" skills. You may do better with a consolidator or Last Minute or Moment's Notice, mentioned above; or look in the Travel classified ads of the *U-T* for individuals who are selling tickets, coupons.

You can re-book your non-refundable ticket (for the same date) if the fare is lowered after your purchase, and lower fare seats are available. And, you can get a refund on your non-refundable ticket with a doctor's excuse, or apply it to your next flight.

Some long distance phone companies offer frequent flyer miles. **MCI and AT&T** give five miles for every $1 spent on long distance, which can add up! It costs you nothing to switch. Other companies are now doing this, too. I already had MCI, so I called and got 1000 miles for re-signing up through Northwest Airlines!

Check the **Air Travel #1710 classified ads** for travel opportunities in the *Union-Tribune.* Also, check the *Reader and Los Angeles Times.* People sell tickets they have won and frequent traveler coupons and more. Always try to negotiate the price. You can ask: "Will you take $__ for the tickets?" or "How much will you take for them?" as it is sometimes difficult to sell tickets through the classifieds. Not everyone is aware of this marketplace, and it might be your chance to score. Make sure the tickets are transferable. Call the airline and check. Airlines tend to "look the other way," but this would be a good negotiating point for a lower price.

When booking a ticket, always ask for the least expensive fare; otherwise, you will only be asked: "Do you want first class or coach?" Frequently there are other fares far less expensive than coach, so you have to ask for the least expensive way to get where you are going and then see if what they have fits your needs.

For complaints against travel agencies, airlines, etc., see Ch. 2, Consumer Complaints.

Entertainment publishes coupon books for 115 U.S. cities including Los Angeles, San Francisco, Orlando, Manhattan, plus several European cities (London, Amsterdam, etc.) with ½ off hotels, entertainment, food. They also have a book for just hotels all over Europe, about $50 each. Hawaii, $46. If you have a San Diego *Entertainment* book, there is a discount coupon in the back, half off. Call (800) 374-4464.

If you're looking for **bargains under the warm Mexican sun**, consider traveling the first two weeks of January when it is less crowded and many hotels offer special rates. High season in Mexico is mid-January to mid-April, low season is mid-April to December 15th, with a sur-charge for Thanksgiving. The Christmas rate is higher than high season because of a sur-charge. **Baja Expeditions**, (619) 581-3311. **Mexican Government**

Tourist Office, free information, (800) 262-8900. The Mexican Ministry of Tourism has set up a web site devoted to safe travel in Mexico at safemexico.com.

Good money-saving travel advice: Check consolidator fares for lower priced international travel. Negotiate the price of a hotel room, or book into lower priced facilities like college dorms, hostels, pensions. Do occasional picnics from local supermarkets, delis, bakeries. Use public transportation instead of taxis. Book car rentals and make train reservations from the U.S. prior to departure. Find walking tours through tourist offices. Pack clothing that is hand washable and do your own laundry in the room. Pack light so you don't need porters. Make copies of your passport, ticket, hotel phone numbers, travelers checks, etc. and keep in your suitcase.

Cruises

If you've never taken a cruise, this is your chance for a "real" cruise for just a few hundred dollars. The Viking Serenade is a 1,500 passenger cruise ship that offers short cruises out of the port at San Pedro, about an hour and a half up Interstate 5. Four-day cruises with departures on Mondays start at about $435 per person; Friday departures are for the 3 day trips which start at about $396 per person, based on double occupancy. Fares are also based on the time of year, with the lowest fares in November. This is a very popular cruise, usually sailing with 98% occupancy. Stops in Catalina, San Diego (don't laugh -- it's fun to be a tourist in San Diego) and Ensenada. Be sure to ask for any current specials. Specials sometimes include rates of about $299 for persons over age 55; third and fourth passengers in a single cabin, $49 per person; children under 12 free as third and fourth passengers, etc. Specials vary throughout the year. For rates and reservations, call Royal Caribbean Cruise Line at (800) 327-6700; for brochure, call (800) 659-7225 or go to their web at royalcaribbean.com. (No stand-by fares available in advance, but you can show up at the dock at the last minute.) Friends in Florida won this trip and I visited them on board when they docked in San Diego. It was very nice! It was a REAL cruise ship! They are selling this ship in January 2002 and it is not known if this trip will continue afterward, but I would think that if it's a near sell-out each trip, they will get another one to replace it. Web site: rccl.com

Always ask for the least expensive cabin, then ask for the guaranteed room rate (for an upgrade to better quarters.) In the event they sell out all the least expensive cabins. This policy is basic to the industry, although the language may differ somewhat. My travel agent suggested this on my first cruise and we ended up being upgraded two price levels in accommodations (yet paid the lowest fare!) You have to book early to get the least expensive cabins because they always sell out fast.

Many cruise lines have a **standby fare** which is discounted 40-60%. You pay for your ticket in advance and three weeks before the cruise, you are notified whether you are on. You have to be flexible for this one, but most cruises DON"T sell out, so your chances are good. Even sell-outs have cancellations at the last minute. When booking, ask about a standby fare.

Check the schedule of cruise ship arrivals in San Diego on the web at portofsandiego.org. (Recorded port information is available at (619) 686-6342.) Then, call the cruise line on their toll free number, and ask if they offer a standby fare from San Diego. Then, keep your bag packed. If you're in a London, drop by the port and see when a ship is due in. You might be taking an unexpected cruise!

Repositioning Cruises can be a deal. After a cruise ship has cruised the Mediterranean all summer, it will cruise across the Atlantic and reposition for the winter season in the Caribbean. This long sail across the ocean can be a great vacation, but many people don't want to pay to be at sea, so prices can plummet. Ask a cruise line when the repositioning cruises are. The same is true for Hawaii or Mexico cruise ships that reposition for Alaska tours in the summer, etc etc. Some real nice prices on trips going to or returning from Hawaii if you like to relax.

Cruise Only Lowest Rates, (800) 327-3021. If you find lower price, they will beat it. Cruise specialists sites to check out: cristatum and cruisenet.com. Also check with smarterliving.com

Ocean Liner Queen Elizabeth II offers a standby fare. A real bargain is a minimum cabin in one direction during low season. Early December and early April have the lowest fares. Call (800) 221-4770 for schedule of rates and departures. Incredible specials are offered from time to time, including one way on the Concorde for 600 bucks a few years ago (a $3000 value!!).

If you really want to be up on cruises, pick up a copy of the *Complete Idiot's Guide to Cruise Vacations* or a similar title in a book store. Great tips that can save you plenty. The more you know in advance, the better prepared you are for the unexpected, and the more enjoyable your trip is.
The internet is a great place for getting people's opinions of cruises, tips, and things to avoid.

Cutting costs on a cruise: Don't book shore excursions. Get your own group together and take a taxi for the day. Much more personalized. Or, take public transportation, or local tours. Those helicopter rides are pricy if you pay in advance on board, but there is usually a discount coupon for rides in the free tourist newspapers that are usually sitting on the ground near the dock. More cheapo tricks: bring a bottle or two of your favorite "cheer" on board. Buy one drink in the bar and go to your room for a refill. They will catch you if you use room glasses, which are usually different!

Free Cruises for Single Men Over Age 50 (Here's one that the ladies throw tomatoes at me for when I speak before groups.) Single men over the age of 50 can go free on some cruise lines as a Cruise Host. Because there are so many more single women on cruises than single men, the owner of Royal Cruises, who has received a great deal of publicity for his creative idea, decided to supply the ladies on board with dancing partners called Cruise Hosts. The bottom line is: women would rather have someone to dance with on their vacations than not have someone to dance with; in fact, the program has been phenomenally successful. The deal is: men of average or better height who are fairly good dancers with reasonable social skills are provided free passage *and* a bar tab....in exchange for dancing and socializing with the ladies. It's a tough job, but somebody's got to do it, *right?* There are conditions, of course...the host cannot fall in love and sit in the corner sipping wine with Ms. *Right* all through the cruise or he may find himself swimming home. For further information, contact about Cruise Host Programs, contact Lauretta Blake's Working Vacation, (708) 301-7535. They recruit hosts for the Delta Queen, Holland American, Orient Lines, World Explorer, Radisson and Silver Sea. Some cruises that feature big bands need as many as 10 hosts. Check their web site at: theworkingvacation.com

Get a **free cruise** (or about 75% off) for two if you can teach a seminar aboard a cruise ship. Or teach aerobics, bridge, give dance lessons, a tax seminar, do handwriting analysis, read auras, teach massage, etc. Write to the individual cruise lines and offer your services or contact the Lauretta Blake Agency above.

Crew on a yacht. Go down to the marina areas (Shelter Island, Harbor Island, Mission Bay, Chula Vista, Oceanside) and pick up a copy of the many free marine publications that are available in yacht sales offices and marine supply stores. Look in the "Crew Wanted" classified section. Many captains are looking for compatible people for a long trip and do not require that you have experience. Can you scramble an egg? Also, there is a "Crew Announcement Board" in many marine supply stores. Place your ad, or respond to one. If you're really interested in this, check the library or bookstore or online bookstore for a copy of *Work and Sail Your Way Around the World* (Writer's Digest) which has boocoo opportunities.

Other Travel Information & Tips

Low Cost Trips and Tours are available through most of the local community colleges. One of the good things about traveling with the community college system is that you have the security of knowing you are under their insurance coverage. Their schedules contain day trips to L.A. museums, major theater and/or to special events like the Laguna Arts Festival (at least two buses!) **Gadabout Travel Club** has a newsletter of **tours for senior citizens** for about $5 per year with trips galore. You don't have to be a senior to travel with them, (619) 291-3402; and **Day Tripper Tours**, (619) 299-5777, offer many local tours to regional attractions including Laughlin, Crystal Cathedral, Rosarito, Ensenada, Hollywood, Julian, Tahoe, San Francisco, more. Call for calendar of events. San Diego **Trailsetters Travel Club**, (619) 231-5999; membership about $5 per person 45 years or older. Call for monthly schedule of trips and benefits. Also, check bus tours listed in travel classified ads, Travel Agencies #1690, in the *Union-Trib.*

Las Vegas If you're calling to make air reservations to **Las Vegas**, be sure to ask if there are any specials as airlines frequently throw in the hotel room. Southwest Airlines specials often include two-for-one fares to Vegas or fares sometimes as low as $19 per person, with 21 day advance purchase.

Las Vegas "Turnaround" for about $15, available through Carlsbad and La Mesa Park & Recreation. A "turnaround" is a 24 hour trip. You leave about 7a.m., get to Vegas by about 2pm, you are dropped off at a Casino and are picked up about midnight; sleep on the way home, and get back to San Diego by about 6am. See the *Union-Tribune* classified ad section Travel Agencies #1690 for more turnaround trips to Vegas. I've met many crazy people who LOVE to do this. Some like to return home Monday morning just in time to go straight to work, tired, but with a smile on their faces. (It would KILL me.)

Check the Las Vegas Web site at lasvegas.com. And, here's one for ya: *The Cheapskates Guide to Las Vegas*, $9.95, Citadel Press. And, the **Las Vegas Advisor** monthly newsletter is the ultimate source of all the bargains, coupons, deals. Call (800) 224-2224 or visit their Web site at lasvegasadvisor.com. This guy offers some great info on hotel rooms, show deals, cheapo buffets, bargain shopping and all kinds of deals.

Las Vegas half-price "day of performance" tickets for shows, including Celine's, are available through **Tickets2Nite** outlet on the Strip near the giant Coke bottle, just north of the MGM Grand or go to their web at tickets2nite.com.

Half price theater tickets for day of performance are available in **New York City** for Broadway shows at Duffy Square on 47th between Broadway and 7th Ave and at South Seaport St. Call (212) 221-0013 or go to tds.org. A similar deal is available in **Washington, DC** at 1100 Pennsylvania Avenue, cultural-alliance.org/tickets. **Boston** also offers half price tickets at bostix.org.

Rental Car Insurance Many credit card companies offer auto rental insurance automatically when you use their credit card to charge your auto rental. Check with your credit card company. You may also be covered under your own auto insurance policy, but if the value of your car is less than the value of the rental car, you may come up short. Call your insurance company.

Attend travel shows and traipse around, dropping your card in the bowl of cruise lines, travel agents, etc. Who knows, you might win the trip of your dreams. Someone will! Cruise Holidays has frequent travel shows, (619) 576-2299 or (800) 869-8321. I won a cruise for two on American-Hawaii Cruise Line at the AAA travel show! A $3800 value. Loved it.

Traveling solo? Check "108 Resources for Solo Travelers" by Sharon B. Wingler, for tours and cruises that charge a low single supplement or none, or will match you with a roommate. For more info, go to travelaloneandloveit.com. There are many single travel organizations: Singles Travel International (877) SOLO-TRIP, Solo Flights (800) 266-1566. Or, search the internet for "single travel" or "solo travel" for tons of organizations for single travel.

Costco offers travel discounts on several cruises, hotels, car rentals and vacation packages for Costco members only. Good savings. See their travel brochure available at warehouse locations or check their travel Web site at: costcotravel.com.

Passports To apply for a passport, take proof of citizenship (birth certificate or naturalization certificate) and proof of identity (drivers license or state ID card) to one of the post offices on Midway Drive, (619) 221-3121. Cost:

about $75 for adults, about $50 under 18. If you have a passport issued within the past 12 years and after your 18th birthday, you can renew it by mail with a form the post office. If it has been more than 12 years since your passport was issued, apply in person at the post office. The process takes about five weeks, but you can pay additional to expedite the process. Also, some travel agencies can get passports within 48 hours for a fee. Also, you can download passport applications at travel.state.gov. For 24-hour Visa/passports, go to travisa.com

Hotel Rooms for less if you ask! Questions to ask: Are there special promotions? Does it make a difference if you're there on a week day or weekend? A room with vs. without a view? Do they use a "frequent flyer" program (earn mileage)? Do they give senior, student or military discount? Are there are any two-for-one coupons available? Do they honor AAA membership? Do they give a discount for professional, employment, organizational, credit union or other membership? Do they accept *Entertainment* book coupons? (Vons Club card will get you a 25% discount at Outrigger hotels in Hawaii.) Are there any cheaper rooms? Call for rates on their 800 toll free number, then call directly and see if there is a difference in room rate. According to a national publication, many hotels quote a higher rate over the toll free line! For deep discounts at hotels, negotiate-negotiate-negotiate. You'll do best with advance reservations, advance purchase and a minimum stay. Keep asking questions about discounts, and add one final question: "Is that your lowest rate?" They will tell you. Ultimately, ask "Who gets the lowest rate?" (if you think they won't throw you out!!) Here's a little morsel for what it's worth: You can *ask* for the corporate rate even if you don't work for a corporation! Off-season rates are very negotiable. And, you can ask for an upgrade when you get there (a room with a view!), etc.

Discounted hotel rooms good deals, hoteldiscount.com. Everyone is saying tho that priceline.com is the place to book, AFTER you do your homework and find the lowest price elsewhere. You can book $400 rooms for $75 on priceline, just as an example. There are even better deals, too. Remember, hotels are normally booked only about 70% full (except when they have conventions or Super Bowl or some other huge event), so your chances of getting deep discounts on a hotel room are really great. Check these Web sites: 1travel.com, hotelrooms.com, priceline.com

Stay in **regional hotels** at 50% off with your San Diego *Entertainment* coupon book. Use coupons for hotel rooms all over California: San Francisco, Carmel, Hollywood, Universal City, Beverly Hills, Long Beach, Costa Mesa, Orange County, Laguna, Pine Valley, Palm Springs, Dana

Point, San Clemente, more. Or, put your visiting friends and relatives up in San Diego, half price, at some of the best hotels. Don't forget to ask about specials as maybe you can beat half price!

Travel Insurance Travel Guard International (800) 826-1300) offers an insurance package with $15,000 cancellation insurance, $20,000 of evacuation coverage, $10,000 medical, and more. Travel Assistance International (800) 821-2828) offers a full-year policy for frequent travelers with $15,000. This may sound unnecessary, but what if you break a leg and have to leave the cruise you spent your life savings on. People who travel a lot want this coverage. Also, when you pay for your tour by credit card, you may be automatically insured for travel *accidents* on a common carrier (airline, train, etc.). Check with your credit card company. Certain limitations would apply.

Useful Web Sites:
Track flights/get an estimated time of arrival, T. . . . . thetrip.com
Money conversion . . . . xe.net/currency
How to say hello in another language . . . . travlang.com
Travel Medicine/Disease . . . . cdc.gov
Fodor's Travel Guides . . . . fodors.com
Arthur Frommer Travel Encyclopedia . . . . frommers.com
Rand McNally-Online Maps & Info . . . . randmcnally.com

The Web has everything you can imagine on travel from booking your flight to information about customs in various countries

Whether you're heading to Tijuana or Timbuktoo, head for the library or bookstore and check out the Travel books available for every major city and country in the world plus special books on cruises, freighter travel, camping, etc. Contact the Chamber of Commerce and Visitor's Bureau in any city you plan to visit before going and they will send you tons of free info. All this is available on the Web, too.

NationalParks.com is your site for U.S. National Parks & Monuments information and accommodations. Featured parks range from Acadia National Park to Zion National Park. National Parks are also listed by State. A Golden Eagle Passport, $39, will get you into ALL national parks, and everyone in the car for one year. A Golden Age Passport will get Seniors into national parks free for life, $10. Passports are available at the Cabrillo Monument or online at the above site.

Friendship Force, an adult international travel program. Stay in homes around the world. Over 130 U.S. chapters and 180 clubs in 45 countries.

The local chapter (over 100 members) meets monthly on the 3rd Sunday at Joyce Beers Center, (619) 698-0833 or (619) 465-8969. Over 20 years old. Two outbound and two inbound trips a year. The last few trips were to Romania, Ireland, Turkey, England and Australia. **Foundation for International Cooperation** is an exchange program with foreign families, cultural exchange, group travel, 20 local members, (619) 463-8084, (800) 890-3543. In existence 40 years with recent trips to Cuba and Equador.

Return a rental car to its city of origin. Call any rental agency and as if they have any cars they want returned. You pay gas. A major credit car is required. Check the opportunities to drive someone's personal car across country for pay in the Travel & Transportation #1700 classified ad column in the *Union-Tribune*. For more opportunities, check the *Yellow Pages* under "Automobile Transporters & Drive Away Companies." A good opportunity. I told a young Australian this, and he got a car immediately to St. Louis; then got another one to Boston. He LOVED driving across the country with a couple friends sharing gas expenses. Oh, my, did he love it.

Summer prices drop by degrees at warm resorts. Palm Springs has room rates in the summer you won't believe. You can have a hotel room fit for a king for a song with use of the spas. Your chance to get away for a day, escape in the air conditioning where the rich and famous frolic and play. Oh course, it's 114 degrees outside but . . .Great bargains at Mexican resorts in the heat of summer, too. I don't think you can beat just being in San Diego in August . ...it's finally warm enough for me along the coast!

Go to work for an airline, railroad, travel agency or cruise line. Airline/travel employees **receive free travel benefits** for themselves and certain relatives, and some award a limited number of passes for friends!

You can always *ask* for a **free upgrade** on planes, trains, in hotels, etc. The way you ask has a lot of influence on whether you get it. Use that charm. If you are a frequent flyer on their airline, it can "help."

This is a little sophisticated, but when you purchase your ticket, you can say: "I wanna fly non-rev." Think about it. Giggles.

Walkabout International's local chapter offers group travel to various destinations in the U.S., sometimes Hawaii or Europe, with guided walking tours. For more information, call (619) 231-SHOE.

San Francisco Walking Tours, free, (415) 557-4266. San Francisco Convention. & Visitors Bureau offers several visitor kits. Log on to sfvisitor.org or phone (415) 391-2000.

Washington, DC has the most freebies. Almost every museum is free making it a great cheap vacation spot! Most sights are open seven days.

Sears, Auto Club of Southern California and American Association of Retired Persons (AARP) have **travel clubs** that offer group rates on trips and will give you maps, and map out your driving trips.

Home Exchanges Trade homes with people from all over the world. See *Frommer's Swap & Go: Home Exchanging Made Easy;* Intervac International home exchange network, over 40 years, (800) 756-4663; Home Link, (800) 638-384; homelink.org. International Home Exchange Web site: homexchange.com

University Campus Accommodations, (all ages), a guidebook with over 300 listings in the U.S. or abroad, available for an average price of $20 a night, lower if you are a student, with access to cultural and recreational offerings, and inexpensive meals to boot. Check libraries for similar titles.

YMCA has more than 28,000 beds around the world, including Hawaii, Australia, Israel, Hong Kong, Finland and Yugoslavia, many with spas an swimming pools. Most rooms cost less than $30 per night. Travel packages are available to many U.S. cities and to Europe. Mainly for students and young people, but older people frequently use their services. The Y's Way International, a 24 page catalog describing accommodations and travel packages, can be obtained by sending a legal-size envelope with 66¢ stamp to: Y's Way International, 356 W. 34th Street, NY, NY 10001. Web: ymca.org (800) usaymca

If you are planning a trip or tour, pick up a copy of the Sunday **Los Angeles Times.** The travel section is huge; lots of deals & steals, bargain basement fares through consolidators, etc etc etc.

Travel Store, 739 4th, (619) 544-0005, downtown, is the "ultimate store for travelers." Travel tips, books, maps, luggage, travel accessories, translators, money-converters, money belts, security belts.

If you **put together your own travel group of 15 people,** sometimes only 10, contact your travel agent, and *you go free.* And, everyone in the party gets a 20% discount (with some agencies).

Hostels International-American Youth Hostels are not by any stretch for youth only. Anyone can and everyone does use them. San Diego AYH Council, 655 Fourth Ave., downtown, (619) 338-9981; Point Loma Youth Hostel, 3790 Udall, (619) 223-4778. For a free 24 page booklet "AYH Discovery Tours," write to AYH, POBox 37613, Washington, DC 20013; (202) 783-6161. Web: hiayh.org

Inter Hostel, travel programs for those over age 50, (800) 733-9573.

Elder Hostel travel program for seniors. Stay in college dorms, 1 week of special classes, food and lodging for as little as around $350 each. Write to: 80 Boylston St., Boston, MA 02116, 96170, (617) 425-8351or (617) 426-8056. There is an elder hostel group through Grossmont College Community Education, 465-1700, x650. Another chapter at SDSU. Web site: elderhostel.org. My cousin goes from Elder Hostel to Elder Hostel in major cities in the U.S. and Canada. She says it's a great cheap vacation and the classes are always on something interesting like the history of music, how to negotiate, discount travel, etc.

SERVAS This club is over 50 years old and it's members say free in the homes of other members, both in the U.S. and abroad. It does not have to be reciprocal. The goal of the non-profit organization is "world peace" through people-to-people contacts. Call (212) 267-0252 for more information or visit their Web site at servas.org.

For a free train travel planner and information for an **Amtrak vacation**, (800) USA-RAIL. Web: amtrak.com. Amtrak has frequent half-off sales. Get on the emailing list.

For information on **freighter travel**, contact Freighter World Cruises, Inc, Pasadena, CA (800) 531-7774, or pick up Ford's *Freighter Travel*.

Travel/Study Programs If you are 18 to 70+, you are eligible to take advantage of travel opportunities provided by the extensions of the colleges. You don't have to be a an enrolled student, or you can enroll and earn credit if you desire. Travel/study tours are different from other tours available, as academic tour leaders avoid the tourist routes and show you the real culture of the area. Travel to Mexico, Ancient Egypt, Greece, the Holy Land, Italy and other exotic lands. For a brochure of travel study programs, call UCSD at (858) 534-0406x60 or SDSU at (619) 594-5152. Travel/Study programs are also available through the Museum of Man, the Smithsonian Institute and other museums throughout the country. See ancient cave paintings, archeological finds, etc. that are not available to the general public by touring with a museum. Call a museum of choice to ask about their travel programs or visit the web site.

Travel for Those With Disabilities Tours featuring wheelchair accessible transportation, lodgings and sightseeing are available for those able to care for their personal needs or who are accompanied by someone who can help. Write for publication to Consumer Information Center, Pueblo, CO 81009.

Rand McNally-Online Maps and travel info web site: randmcnally.com

The Web has everything you can imagine on travel from booking your flight to information about customs in various countries.

Chapter 6
HEALTH & MEDICAL BARGAINS

This chapter contains important money-saving information on health care services (some free), discount prescription drugs, medical insurance that won't cost you an arm and a leg, dental services and insurance for less, medical research centers where qualified persons can get free medical care *and* get paid for it, plastic surgery deals, deluxe spas at a discount and other joyful tidbits. About 47% of San Diego's population is covered by employer-paid health care, and about 25% of San Diegans are uninsured. Here are some great resources you should know about whether insured or not, but especially if you aren't.

Health Services & Tips

Urgent Care, ("The ER Alternative,") 3434 Midway, Sports Arena area, (619) 225-6200. You can come here with flu, abdominal pain, for suturing or a broken arm, but not by ambulance. The law says an ambulance must take you to a hospital. The costs for being seen here are about 1/3 that of a hospital emergency room. The minimum office visit is $150 and they will bill the patient for additional charges. Insured or uninsured. Xrays are about $50-$100; total cost for broken arm including initial office visit, xrays and plaster cast is about $300 (less for velcro cast). Urgent care for adults and pediatrics; no surgeries. See index in the front of the *Yellow Pages* for more urgent care facilities, clinics, etc.

The San Diego Info Line .... (619) 230-0997
The San Diego Info Line is a free service sponsored by United Way which successfully puts thousands of callers in touch with San Diego County Health and Human Care services and other health related services. Most of the services are free or low-cost, based on a sliding scale according to income. More than 1000 medical, psychological, bioterrorism alerts, emergency, suicide, crisis counseling, birth control, abortion, shelter, abuse, elderly, personal, child care, family and other organizations are in their database. The Info Line exists to help you quickly locate an appropriate organization for assistance, some of which are difficult to find on your own.

262

The Info Line also has a Rolodex file chocked full of self-help and support groups for everything from loneliness, depression and grief, to various illnesses. For information and assistance, call between 8 a.m. and 8 p.m. weekdays, 11 a.m. to 6 p.m. Saturdays, Sundays and holidays.

Dial 211 is a new service coming to San Diego County that will be manned by a trained, multi-lingual staff seven days a week, 24 hours a day to refer you to health and human services and organizations, including those in the San Diego Info Line (above), Childcare Resource Service, Access and Crisis Line, Aging and Independence Services. Being able to dial 211 will put these services into a more accessible arena with a number no one will have to look up, and will remove some unnecessary calls to 911. This service is already in 20 states. For more info, go to 211sandiego.org.

Free medical care/hospitalization . . . . (800) 587-8118 858-514-6888 If your income falls below approximately $697 per month (for one person), you are eligible for free urgent/serious medical care at UCSD Hospital through County Medical Services (CMS). Call for income requirements for additional family members. Legal residents age 21-64 without medical insurance can apply for medical care through County Medical Services. You must be able to verify that you earned less than approximately $600 (for single) a month income in the previous month. UCSD treats over 625,000 uninsured residents, one-fourth of them children. Medi-Cal coverage for children, no-cost, (888) 747-1222. You may qualify even if you are working, married, own a car or home or are homeless.

San Diego Council of Community Medical Clinic . . . . (619) 265-2100 San Diego County has 21 community medical clinics which offer free and low cost comprehensive primary care services. Call for clinic nearest you.

After Hours Nurse Advice Service for the Council of Community Clinics, (800) 995-4200.

Scripps Memorial Hospital Chula Vista, 435 H Street, Chula Vista, (619) 691-7000, provides **examinations to all people** in the community who present to their emergency department to determine if they have an emergency medical condition. This examination will be provided without undue delay, regardless of a person's ability to pay or type of insurance, including Medicare and Medicaid. Scripps also offers **free health seminars** on substance abuse assessment, intervention programs, weight loss, heart disease detection, skin cancer detection, how to get a good night's sleep, and more. For a free quarterly calendar of events, call (800) SCRIPPS or go to scripps.org.

Obtain free or low-cost health insurance for children by calling the national toll free telephone number, (877) KIDS-NOW or (877) 543-7669, (8am-8pm) which will automatically connect you to the agency where you can enroll children in Medicaid and a new program for people under age 19. Health, dental and vision care for children.

The **County of San Diego Department of Health Services** offers a variety of services and clinics, free or low cost, as follows:

General Information . . . . (619) 515-6770
Immunizations for children . . . . (619) 692-6600/692-8661
Sexually transmitted diseases clinic . . . . (619) 692-8550
Tuberculosis control and testing . . . . (619) 692-8600
Child health & disability prevention . . . . (619) 692-8428

Middle income families who are not insured can apply for free **pregnancy health care** under Proposition 99, (800) 675-2229.

Planned Parenthood . . . . (619) 683-7526; (760) 634-8333
Provides examinations, birth control, "morning after" pills, pregnancy counseling and options, plus services and education. Planned Parenthood is **free** or fees are based on a **sliding scale** according to income. There are several clinics throughout the County. Web Site: ppfa.org/ppfa

Facts of Life Line . . . . (619) 683-7543
A 24-hour recording, sponsored by Planned Parenthood, with selections including information on where to get help, pregnancy counseling, sexually transmitted diseases and legislative updates.
   Pregnancy counseling, parenting & adoption services . . . . . (619) 231-2828
   Door of Hope (under age 18 pregnancy housing) . . . . (858) 279-1100

Asthma Hotline, (800) 727-5400.

If you're **sick all the time**, check for mold, mildew or lack of direct sunshine in your house. If you house gets little or no sun exposure during the day or your bathroom has a problem with mildew and mold, this can be the source of your ill health. If you can't move to another location because you own your house, consider skylights, cutting back trees that prevent sunshine from entering the windows, adding glass doors and more windows to let sunlight in, punching out walls to catch sunshine, etc.

More than 90% of women survive who have their breast cancers detected through regular mammography. October is Breast Cancer Month, so call the American Cancer Society at (800) 227-2345 and see who is offering

free mammograms during this time. If you have no insurance, you can contact the state Breast Cancer Early Detection Program at (800) 511-2300 or the National Breast Cancer Early Detection Program at (888) 842-6355x7 for information on where to get free or low cost mammograms. Also, Scripps Hospital in Chula Vista, (619) 425-1780, offers free or reduced cost mammograms.

New blood test can **predict heart attacks** (costs less than $100), measures body levels of renin, a natural hormone produced by the kidneys that helps regulates blood pressure, according to Dr. Michael Alderman, New York Hospital-Cornell Medical Center. Also, a blood test for a substance called C-reactive protein (CRP) indicates if arteries are inflamed. Ask for these tests when you get your cholesterol checked. Also, for a blood test can determine **ovarian cancer**, ask for CA-125 test as part of your annual physical.

Cardia Salt Alternative tastes exactly like salt, but it can lower your **blood pressure** up to 13 diastolic points and 8 systolic points after six months use. It contains potassium and magnesium and 54% of the sodium found in standard table salt, costs about $4.50 for 50 packets sold over-the-counter in pharmacies.

Henry's Marketplace sponsors **low cost screening** for blood cholesterol, osteoporosis, heart function, etc., in their stores. They occasionally offer a non-dominant hand DEXA scan for osteo for $25 (costs much more in medical offices). Call (858) 679-5544 for upcoming dates and locations. (For future dates and locations of blood screenings, check fingerstick.com.) Henry's also offers free in-store lectures on homeopathic remedies for a variety of ailments. There is a nutritionist on duty always to advise you on natural remedies!! Don't miss Henry's **Wellness Fair** at the Scottish Rites Center in Mission Valley in the spring and fall ($10) with numerous health screenings, testing; lectures, exhibits. Call a Henry's Market for exact date and mark your calendar. Also, Longs Drugs, SavOn and other pharmacies offer free and low cost health screening tests and flu shots. And, even if you're not a senior, read the FYI and Senior columns in the *Union-Trib* for listings of **free medical screenings** including blood pressure, cholesterol, blood sugar, hearing, etc. These services are usually not just for seniors.

Kaiser Permanente offers a **Health Risk Analysis** for non-members under age 40, which includes blood pressure, vision screening, lung function screening, lab tests for infection, anemia, diabetes, cholesterol and kidney function, for about $150. A report is sent to your home following the visit, and you will receive a call if there are any cardiac risk factors. Women may include a PAP smear and breast exam for an additional $40. Call (858) 573-1885 for additional information or appointment.

Alzheimer Disease Education/Referral Center, (800) 438-4380. Report on gene mutation may be responsible for nerve cell death. Common anti-inflammatory drugs shrink tissue, and research shows, which reduces onset of Alzheimer's disease. Web: alzheimers.org

Ever wonder what's in your **public record medical record file**, and who put it in? Write to: Medical Information Bureau, P.O. Box 105, Essex Station, Boston, MA 02112, or call (617) 426-3660, or download the form at mib.com

Become an **organ donor**. Talk to you family and let them know your wishes. Your next of kin must give consent upon your death. Contact the Living Bank, (800) 528-2971, the only national organ registry in the United States. Ask for information and a registration packet. As recently as 2002, 80,000 individuals were waiting for transplants; of those, 53,000 were waiting for kidneys. Over 28,000 potential recipients died waiting for kidneys. About 14,000 kidney transplants were performed with 8,200 from cadaver donors and 5,.900 from living donors. Living donations are growing by 12% over the pervious year. For full body donation, call UCSD Medical School donor program in La Jolla, (858) 534-4536.

Great health books: *Prescription for Nutritional Healing*, James F. Balch, M.D.-Phyllis A. Balch, C.N.C., Avery Publishing Group. A practical A-Z reference to drug-free remedies using vitamins, minerals, herbs and food supplements, $29.95. (This book is great!) *Spontaneous Healing* (How to Discover and Enhance Your Body;'s Natural Ability to Maintain and Heal Itself) and *8 Weeks to Optimum Health* (A Proven Program for Taking Full Advantage of Your Body;'s Natural Healing Power) by Andrew Weil, M.D. Pick up used copies at used bookstores or online bookstores.

Surgical Fees Can Be Negotiated. Here's how! Contrary to popular opinion, surgical fees are not fixed in stone. You can save money by bargaining with your doctor. First, determine the lowest prices available for your surgery by checking with surgeons in your area. Then find out what your insurance company says is a reasonable charge. Armed with this information, ask if your surgeon will accept the insurance payment as full payment. Or, explain to your physician that you can only afford to pay so much, and that your insurance will cover only so much. Then tell him/her that other doctors are charging less for the surgery. Your physician may direct you to speak to his office manager about the fees, or state that the fees are fixed and non-negotiable. Most will accept a lump sum payment of less. As a last resort, you may tell the surgeon you will be forced to go elsewhere if he will not lower his fee.

Quit Smoking, free, UCSD Free Smokers Helpline, (800) 7 NO BUTTS

Do-It-Yourself Medical Kits are available at local pharmacies. There are at least 35 or more on the market that test for pregnancy, gum disease, colorectal, cancer (blood in stools), diabetes, marijuana use, HIV, Lyme disease, Hepatitis C, urinary tract infection and others. Inquire at Long's, SavOn, Rite Aid, Walgreen's, Vons (Vons delivers!)and other pharmacies. Some of these pharmacies have "Do -it-yourself" blood pressure machines. Sit in a chair, put your arm in a cuff and press start. Do the test several times to see how your blood pressure varies. These pharmacies also put on occasional low cost health screening events (very popular). Some Costco pharmacies, too.

The world famous **Mayo Clinic** has medical information galore at their site, and online specialists to answer your questions. Web: mayoclinic.com.

Health Info Online with Dr. Koop. Web: drkoop.com. Dietary supplements, nutrition. Consumerlab.com

Harvard Medical School site provides a ton of information, plus information on diagnostic testing procedures What do you have to do to prepare for a MRI? Will having a liver biopsy be painful? Will I need to do anything special afterward? How soon will it be safe to go home after a cardiac catheterization and what are the risks? How soon will the results of an antibody test be back? Web: health.harvard.edu

Optimum Health Institute of San Diego . . . . (619) 464-3346 6970 Central, Lemon Grove. The OHI offers one to four week sessions for detoxification from diet, illness, stress, or substance abuse. Classes, meals (all raw foods and wheatgrass juice) and room: $575 a week/shared; $750 private. Commuter (no room) $400. People attend from all over the world and rave about what this program does for them (cleanses the system). Open house every Sunday at 4:00p.m. Tour the grounds and have a meal with the guests ($4 donation). Web: optimumhealthinstitute.com

Free Programs at the famous Deepak Chopra Center (mind-body-spirit) located at La Costa Resort & Spa include an introduction to meditation class on Friday afternoons from 2:30-3:30pm, and 30-minute meditation sessions to support you in creating more balance, creativity and energy in your life, Monday-Friday at 5:00pm. They also offer free "Satsangs, which are gatherings to listen to dialog of some of the most inspiring philosophers and authors of our time. These are offered free to the community on a regular basis. Seating is first-come first-served. For more information check their web site at: deepakchopra.com. Additionally, they offer a free Seven Spiritual Laws of Success Study Group every 2nd and 4th Monday of each month with a facilitated reading and discussion of the Seven Laws and their day-to-day application into your life. Introductions, guided group meditations and small group exercises. This study group is at a private residence in La Jolla,. For further information, contact Irene at (858) 453-5648. Cost is free, donations accepted. Refreshments served.

Self-Heal School of Herbal Studies and Healing .... (619) 224-1268 One-hour consultation with 3rd year students, $20; recommendations for herbal tinctures and teas. Classes in herbal medicine, nutrition, energy healing; $170 for 6 week course. Weekend retreats.

Vital Imaging is a relatively new technology that can determine the amount of plak build up on your heart and coronary arteries, and detect scars, lesions, aneurisms and masses throughout your body from the shoulders to the pelvis. Head and neck MRI's are also available to detect blockages in these areas. Non-invasive. No preparation. No fasting before and no drink is required. The test is about $725, takes 10 minutes, and within 20 minutes, your test results are available. (Ask when the next sale is as they often offer two for one or 30% off.) A radiologist examines the results, and a nurse practitioner will discuss them with you. Other tests include colon, brain. Oprah had the body test done, and I saw the show where she shared the results with us on TV. This testing has become controversial as many "spots" which may be totally unimportant show up on the test causing alarm, and further and often unnecessary testing will follow. For more info, call Vital*Imaging* at (858) 848-2511, or check their web at vitalimaging.com.

Get a **free chiropractic adjustment** at health fairs, street fairs and the swap meets where there is a chiropractor booth. I know people who attend street fairs just to get the adjustments!

Here is a comparison of a **generic pain reliever** and a name brand pain reliever: Tylenol, 100 count, acetaminophen 500mg, $8.^{99}; Von's Pain Reliever, 100 count, acetaminophen, 500mg, $5.^{25} (with occasional two-for-one sales!). Costco & Sam's have an even better deal! Gel caps, too.

Get a **massage (for less!)** at massage training schools:
    Student massage $35/hr., School of Healing Arts, 7 days .. (858) 490-2560
    IPSB Massage School, $30/hr. (by student) .... (858) 490-1154
    Mueller College of Holistic Studies, $25/hr. (by student) .... (619) 299-8680
    Body Mind College, $25/hr (relax)or $30hr (tension) (student)(858) 453-3290
    Beauty School student facial massages are about $10- See *Yellow Pages*

Public libraries have a **shut-in service** which brings books to the homebound. For more information call your local branch. There are also large print books, books on tape, plus special services for the blind and hard of hearing. Tell your Aunt Minnie in Empty Boot, Nebraska, that these services could be available there, as they are available in almost every city.

Buy **no-frills vitamins**. Designer versions and heavily advertised brand names are no more effective than "Brand X" varieties.

Many people think that **doctors** are like "gods" and place them on undeserved pedestals. Doctors are human, and, just like in every other profession, there are those who graduated at the top of their class with honors, good ones, mediocre ones, bottom of the class graduates, unethical ones, criminal ones, psychologically-off ones, addicted ones, incompetent ones, etc., etc. In the last few years, a doctor cut off the wrong leg of a patient, another removed the wrong breast, many have disfigured patients, many have told patients they have diseases including A.I.D.S. when they didn't, and one even disconnected the wrong patient from life support resulting in death. Call the San Diego County Medical Association and inquire about your doctor's recorded disciplinary actions. (Unfortunately, most law suits get settled out of court, therefore they have no verdict, and are thus, not recorded. However, you can go to the downtown court house information desk and ask about checking to see if/how many *suits have been filed against the doctor for wrongdoing*. Or, call a law library and pay a law student to do it for you.) The New England Journal of Medicine reported 1,500 instruments are left in patients each year. The researchers checked insurance records from about 800,000 operations in Massachusetts for 16 years ending in 2001. They counted 61 forgotten pieces of surgical equipment in 54 patients. From that, they calculated a national estimate of 1,500 cases yearly. A total of $3 million was paid out in the Massachusetts cases, mostly in settlements. Two-thirds of the mistakes happened even though the equipment was counted before and after the procedure, in keeping with the standard practice. Most lost objects were sponges, but also included were metal clamps and electrodes. In two cases, 11-inch retractors (metal strips used to hold back tissue) were forgotten inside patients. In another operation, four sponges were left inside someone. Check your doctor's record at .docboard.org/ca/df/casesearch.

HealthGate offers access to National Institutes of Health library system, healthgate.com.

On Tuesdays, RiteAid pharmacy offers **seniors** (55 years or older) a 20% discount on any of their private label items (always cheaper than name brands), including hydrogen peroxide, eye wash, diet pills with the same formula as name brand pills, bandaids, toothpaste, pain relievers, cough syrup, cotton balls, and many other products including their brand ice cream!

On the first Tuesday of the month, Gold Card members ($10 fee) save 20% on GNC brands at RiteAid stores, even on sale-priced items. GNC Gold card members save 20% all week at GNC stores the first week of the month.

Prescription Drugs

To get the **best prices on prescription drugs,** let your fingers do the walking and comparison-price shop as drug prices vary daily like the Dow Jones Industrial. Shop around to see which is the cheapest. And, always ask if there is a generic substitute. Why pay more for a name brand if the generic is the same drug, only cheaper. The savings can be substantial. Here are some stores to call to **compare prices**: Costco & Sam's (you don't have to be a member to buy prescriptions at Costco and Sam's; however, you must pay cash). Check SavOn, RiteAid, Long's, Walgreen's, WalMart, Kmart, Target, Drug Emporium, Von's, SavMart Drugs and Tijuana drug stores (see below). If retired, call AARP. Make a page called "Pharmacies" in your personal telephone book; then look up the phone numbers in your area of the pharmacies above and list them on your page for handy reference so you can call and compare prices easily. Online pharmacies reportedly offer little savings, but, heck, might as well check online sites like drugstore.com; healthquick.com; healthcentral.com; vitamins.com. Also, longs.com. You can order over-the-counter items, too. Good sale prices.

I have a nurse friend in Florida who emailed me that she is now ordering her $700 a month meds from Canada for $400 a month including shipping. Check prices at canadiandrugstore.com She said she went to google.com and searched for Canadian Drugstores, and up came a zillion. She shopped several til she found one that had most of the meds she needs. They required a picture ID and a fax of the prescriptions. Bill to your credit card. No controlled substances. The government in Canada dictates the prices of meds. This is a great find. I checked a price here on their site and it was about 35% off U.S. prices. She said she also uses drugstore.com for nonprescription things, heating pads, cosmetics, all dirt cheap, she says. hy in the world are meds so expensive in the U.S. ? ? ? ? ? Congress MUST do something about this. The bottom line is: there's basically no substitute for shopping around and comparison price shopping, and the internet sure makes it easy for you. Go for it.

Many **prescription drugs** can be purchased for less in Tijuana at pharmacies (farmacias), and there is one on every corner. Because of the high cost of medical care and low wages in Mexico, many drugs are dispensed in Mexico without prescriptions. There are several drug stores just as you cross the border if you are walking, and they are loaded with Americans down there buying stacks of prescriptions. (I have a friend in Florida who flies in to get the Mexican version of Prozac; another from Colorado who has made a "relationship" with one of the pharmacists so she can call in her requests, and they mail the medications to her. I think they enter the U.S. to mail them.) Many of the drugs are made in Mexico (some by American companies in Mexico). Bring your prescriptions and any literature you might have to compare ingredients. Be sure to check to see if the dosage and milligrams are the same. Pharmacies on side streets away from the business area may have the best prices. I like Gusher Farmacia (Tel: 011-52-664-684-0235) in the Plaza Rio shopping mall because it is minutes from the border, they speak English, will show you the drug book in English, and because they have frequent sales (22% off) and because they have two fresh fruit bars with delicious fruit drinks and fruit salads! I also like Gusher because the supermarket, Commercial Mexicana, is steps away with interesting stuff, a good bakery, and more. In the mall, there is a large department store, several duty-free import stores, an upscale leather shop and a number of boutiques. Electronics shops offer duty-free Japanese imports of all kinds, including watches. I am working on a book about bargains in Tijuana, so stay in touch if this interests you. Back to prescriptions: prescription drugs that are available in Tijuana without a prescription include blood pressure and heart medications, birth control pills, antibiotics, inhalers, hormones, antidepressants and more. You can buy controlled substances (pain killers, tranquilizers and many diet pills) *only* with a Mexican doctor's prescription (they will not honor U.S. doctor's prescriptions). You can bring back a 90-day supply for personal use, and you must declare them at customs. Retin-A, both the Mexican and the American versions, are available without a prescription. The Mexican version is selling for anywhere from $3 up for the small tube. The American version, which sells in the U.S. for about $16 for the small size, sells down there for varying prices, both lower and higher.

If you are taking an expensive drug that you feel you can't afford, write to the drug company (your pharmacist can supply you with the address), and tell them it is a hardship. Some companies will send the prescription to you, free. HONEST! Over 5.5 million patients are served. You can ask your doctor for assistance on this one. You can also write to the Pharmaceutical Manufacturer's Assn, 1100 15th St., NW, Washington, DC 20005 and ask for a copy of the directory for patients of prescriptions drugs and drug companies that offer assistance, complete with toll-free numbers. You can call and request a copy at (202) 835-3400, or request a copy at their web site: phrma.org. Requirements must be met. Another site is: rxassist.org

Medical Insurance

Medical insurance plans differ dramatically in terms of what they cover, co-payments and monthly premiums. If you aren't insured through our job, join an organization such as a trade association or alumni or fraternal group that offers members group insurance rates, or check into health maintenance organizations.

Health maintenance organizations (HMO's) or preferred provider organizations (PPO'S) are typically cheaper than traditional reimbursement policies, and some carry no deductible or high co-payment. If you need special care, be sure they have staff members who are trained to treat your condition.

Kaiser Permanente . . . . (800) 245-3181
Kaiser, with over 9 million members nationwide and 5.5 million in California, offers about the most reasonably priced medical insurance around, although it keeps going up every year. Their preventative medicine program is excellent; they want you to stay healthy. I've had their coverage for years. No complaints. The Kaiser plan includes all preventative care with $20 doctor appointments, $10 copayment for most generic prescriptions, and full hospitalization with no deductible. Call for current rates and no-obligation information packet, or get an instant quote at: kp.org/individuals. Their pharmacy prices are usually very good, some coverage includes free prescriptions, some coverage requires you pay all your meds, and some plans have nominal copay. It's best to comparison shop for savings on prescriptions.

Kaiser Permanente offers a Health Risk Analysis to non-members for anyone 14 to 40 years old.

Health Net, affordable individual and family health coverage. Call for free information kit, (800) 909-3447x249; or apply at healthnet.com.

National Association of Self-Employed . . . . (800) 827-9990
Health insurance for the self-employed.

Costco offers small-business health insurance to businesses with two or more employees for Executive members, (800) 235-5300 or costco.com.

California HealthQuote Insurance Services . . . . (800) 788-4678
Since 1986, this Carlsbad company has offered over 200 medical programs including major carriers such as Blue Cross, Blue Shield, CalFarm, Cigna, HealthNet, Kaiser, Pacificare, Prudential. For individuals, self-employed, single parents, groups from 2-50. Dental plans, too. Also check their web site at ca.healthquoteins.com for free online quotes.

AARP (Association of Retired Persons) . . . . (800) 523-5800
Supplemental hospital plans for persons age 50-64, and over 65, starting at around $10-20 for one plan at any age; another plan is around $100-135 per month for under 65. Ten medicare supplemental plans.

 If you have a **pre-existing condition** and can't get health insurance, here's a tip that was shared with me: go to work for any company that has group insurance. Usually after about one to six months, you will qualify for their group health plan. Most *group* insurance companies take pre-existing conditions, excepting certain major health problems. When you leave, you can opt to pay to continue coverage, depending on insurer. Some allow you to continue for one year only. Kaiser allows you to continue coverage. The federal government is the only employer I unearthed who will allow *any* pre-existing medical condition.

 If you have difficulty getting insurance, consider enrolling in a college to get college student medical coverage. Check the age limit, although there may be none. Contact student services for information at any college. You must carry a minimum number of credits. (See "College Fees" for insurance companies.)

Terminal Illness (Read this NOW!)

    Hang with me on this one. It is better for you to read about this NOW so that if you or a friend ever needs this info, it won't be all new to you and more difficult to understand. Death is a subject that, traditionally, this society has preferred to avoid discussing. However, it will happen to us all inevitably. A dear friend who cared for her dying husband at home suggested I include something on this subject, and I am happy to. I am glad to desensitize myself to this subject, learn more about options and plan my affairs for that event, right down to the release of the helium balloons after I'm gone. Here are some things I looked in to:

You (or a family member) have the right to check yourself out of the hospital and die at home or in a hospice. **You have the right** to refuse a respirator and IV's. Hospitals can keep you alive on machines although there is no chance for your recovery, at a huge expense and trauma for the family, and probably a huge profit for doctors and hospitals. You have the right to have your own physician and/or a hospice physician administer pain control medications at home, including morphine. Or, you can choose the environment of a hospice rather than a hospital if you are terminal.

San Diego Hospice is a 28-year old independent, not-for-profit community based health care organization that provides quality physical, emotional and spiritual care for the terminally ill and ongoing support for their loved ones. An important part of the program is their complete at-home care (doctors, social workers, visiting nurses and more) as an alternative to hospitalization. They also maintain a 24-bed home-like care facility. Hospice services include information on choices and options for the patients and their families. Terminal pain differs from the pain in a healing injury, and the San Diego Hospice is able to provide leading-edge terminal pain control due to their extensive involvement in research in this area. The hospice also offers free classes every third Thursday on dealing with grief from the loss of a loved one, friend, loss of a child or parent. Classes are offered on communicating with the seriously ill, the holistic approach to the end of life, how to help someone who is grieving, taking control of your future, the durable power of attorney for health care, and more. There is also a Speakers Bureau, and a variety of bereavement support groups for adults and children. The hospice receives millions in charitable contributions, and has served over 2000 terminally ill patients and thousands of survivors. There are 375 volunteers. San Diego Hospice is located at 4311 Third Avenue, Hillcrest, (619) 688-1600; web: sandiegohospice.com. See "Hospices" in the *Yellow Pages* for several other hospices in the county. A dear friend who died of cancer had Kaiser home-hospice care, and she couldn't say enough good things about them.

Hemlock Society, (619) 233-4418. This is the San Diego chapter of Hemlock USA, founded in 1980 by Derek Humphrey, author of *Final Exit* and new book, *Freedom to Die.* They offer support for those who are terminally ill, their caregivers and family members; are working on CA bill AB 1592 for the right to die. There is an advocacy group to ensure implementation of members' living will and durable power of attorney for healthy care. Caring Friends counselors will come to your aid. Bi-monthly meetings, Sundays at 1:30pm, at the Joyce Beers Hall, Vermont & 10th Ave. Web: hemlock.org.

The **"Durable Power of Attorney for Health Care"** form includes clauses such "do not resuscitate" and other options. They are available from doctors or hospitals and the Hemlock Society. These forms enable you to make specific decisions about your health care in the event you should face death or there is no hope for no recovery, and provides for another individual to take over in the event you are incapacitated. Make it a part of your personal documents and give one to your doctor.

Medical Research (Clinical Trials)
Get Tests, Treatments, Earn $$$

In recent years, San Diego has become an acclaimed center for **medical research**. Local universities, research institutes and doctor's offices receive over $400 million a year in funds from the National Institute of Health and pharmaceutical firms, making San Diego the third largest recipient city in the nation. And, over 100 bio-medical related companies have sprung up, making San Diego possibly the city with the highest concentration of biotechnology companies in the world.

Research leads to better prevention, diagnosis and treatment of a disease. Some of the advantages of participating in medical studies are: free medical evaluation and treatment by experts in their fields, the opportunity to take advantage of the latest developments in diagnosis, treatment and pharmaceuticals for a variety of medical problems, and financial compensation for participation. A study lasts anywhere from one day to several months. The longer the study, the more you get paid. In some studies, you may or may not be taking a placebo or a drug; you won't know. Either way, they won't let you suffer if you need medication. You can drop out; and they won't allow you to stay if you aren't doing well. Check with your doctor before participating. Of course, your doctor may not want you to participate because he might lose you as a paying client. I always ask how many patients have already participated and if there have been any negative results.

Over 8.3 million Americans participate in over 80,000 clinical trials a year. Clinical trials are scientific studies of a new treatment or medicine for humans, or a new way of administering conventional therapeutics, or the use of an existing medication for a medical condition other than the one it is currently being used for. The Federal Drug Administration (FDA) has strict requirements for determining if a treatment is safe for humans. This may take from one to 10 years for approval. There are four phases a drug must go through before it is approved. In Phase I, new treatments are tried on volunteers for whom other remedies have not worked. Few are enrolled. They start with a low dose and scrutinize the side affects, establish the best dose, etc. If that goes well, the new drug goes to Phase II, where there are more people, more chance to observe effectiveness and uncommon side affects. If the treatment works, it moves to Phase III. Treatment in Phase III is compared to other treatments. Large numbers enroll, and there is a control group that takes conventional treatments or a placebo (sugar pill) and the treatment group that gets the new drug. This phase can be skipped if there is compelling reason to believe the new therapeutic is superior to conventional treatments or clearly better than no treatment at all if no conventional treatment exists. Phase IV studies continue investigating for toxicity and effectiveness in large numbers of people. When you enter a study, inquire about the history of the medication you'll be taking and the known or potential risks. You will have a lot of information to read about the study before they accept you, and you must sign a consent form. You can drop at any time, and they won't let you stay in a study if you aren't doing well. Many people sign up for studies to get the state-of-the-art testing, free medications, excellent monitoring and follow-up, and compensation for their time and travel.

I learned a lot when I participated in a 12-week asthma study at the Clinical Research Institute (see below). I became a happy, asthma-free camper and gained a better understanding of what asthma is. My breathing went from 62% of capacity for my sex, height, etc., to 114%!! I was the only one in my group who did so well, *and* I was the only one taking "Km," a natural potassium concentrate which helps with respiratory ailments in addition to the medication!! *Hmmmm!!!* (See White Pages for a "Km" distributor near you). We had EKGs, blood work, breathed into a tube connected to a computer, received medication, underwent some allergy testing, received a meter to blow into at home and a form to record the meter results on, and we were paid $350 at the end of the study!! (Many asthma studies pay up to $800-$1000 today. I haven't had an asthma attack since! But, I also learned a lot from reading a book I bought entitled *Asthma and Hay Fever* by Leon Chaitow, N.D.,D.O., Thorsons Publishing Group, which offered proven drug-free methods to combat the causes of asthma. I learned to avoid milk and milk products like the plague; mold and dust, too, and removed carpeting which traps dust, removed the HEATER, put non-allergenic covers on mattresses and down pillows. I also learned to stay tuned to my breathing. Have had the wheezing pretty much under control by eliminating the irritants. According to a doctor I talked with since, I may have had "worms or bugs" in my lungs that were killed by the medication! Who knows?! I think it was eliminating all milk, carpeting, dust and down (new down pillows & comforter are non-allergenic, thank heavens), removing all heat and avoiding air-conditioning. And, taking "Km," which does wonders for anything respiratory-related.

The following institutions are engaged in clinical research. Call and inquire about their *current* studies and compensation, as new research studies are continually being offered. Some of the larger research institutes have as many as thirty different studies going on at the same time. Most offer compensation to participate, although certain studies may only offer medical care. Compensation varies from under $50 for travel expenses to several hundred dollars. A 30-day sleep study paid $3000! (Too bad we missed that one, right?)

University of California San Diego (UCSD) Medical Center ranks in the nation's top 10 for research funding received from the National Institutes of Health. The National Cancer Institute recently designated UCSD Cancer Center as a Comprehensive Cancer Center, the highest distinction awarded to a cancer center by the federal government. Many UCSD studies are done in conjunction with the VA Hospital. Their web site, health.ucsd.edu/NTRIALS/index.htm lists dozens of studies. Call (619) 543-6163 for *current* studies and compensation. Studies have included:

Alzheimer's disease	Colitis	Osteoporosis
Arthritis	Diabetes	Panic attacks
Asthma	Leukemia	Post traumatic stress
Autism	Genital herpes	disorder
Brain imaging sleep study	High blood pressure	Shingles
Breast cancer	Insomnia	Smoking
Cancers	Kidney disorder	Social phobia
Chronic back pain	Migraine	Tinnitus
Chronic pain	Obsessive-compulsive	Tourette's syndrome
Cold sores/fever blisters		Vertigo

> Check these sites for all clinical trials in the U.S. (by city or by disorder or subject): centerwatch.com, clinicaltrials.gov and clinicaltrials.com. You can get on the list to be notified when studies come up for dozens of health related issues.

Following is a list of medical research organizations and the type of clinical trials they receive funding for from the government and pharmaceutical companies. I have participated in several, and I know others who have, too. I can't say enough good things about them. You can always drop out if or when you want. Many say they can't get their doctors to give them the tests or treatment that the researchers provide at no cost. You will also receive compensation.

Allergy Associates Medical Group .... (619) 229-2355
Studies allergies and asthma, pulmonary disease, sinus, Hives and eczema. Call for current studies and compensation. Web: allergyassociates.net

Allergy Medical Group .... (619) 291-2321
Studies have included eczema, atopic dermatitis, ulcer, prostate, ear infection, sinusitis, cholesterol, arthritis, heartburn, diabetes, menopausal, osteopenia, irritable bowel. Call for current studies and compensation.

Allergy & Asthma Research Center .... (858) 292-1144
Studies have included hay fever, asthma, allergy, pediatric flu. Call for current studies and compensation.

Behavioral & Medical Research .... (858) 571-1188
Studies have included post traumatic stress disorder, paranoia, panic attack, ADD, worry, memory, PMS, sleep disorders, depression, fear, bronchitis, pneumonia, more. Call for current studies and compensation.

California Research Foundation .... (619) 291-2321
Digestive and stomach disorders, cold, flu, bronchitis, weight loss, more

California Skin Research Institute .... (866) 857-SKIN
Many skin research studies. Compensation. Web: calskin.com

Children's Hospital San Diego .... (858) 576-5832x5934
Call for current studies and compensation. Web: chsd.org Click Research.

Dermatology Associates .... (760) 753-1027
Studies have included skin problems, eczema, cold sores, psoriasis, acne, antifungal, laser, cosmetic, facial hair. Call for current studies and compensation

EyeCare of San Diego .... (619) 296-8585x128
Studies have included dry eyes; eye devices; glaucoma; compensation.

Encompass Clinical Research .... (619) 660-9068
Studies have included postmenopausal, blood pressure, diabetes, cholesterol, more. Call for current studies and compensation.

Feighner Research Institute .... (858) 554-0100
Studies have included depression, anxiety, migraine, Alzheimer's disease, schizophrenia, central nervous system studies. Call for current studies.

HealthQuest .... (858) 5712-1199

Institute of Healthcare Assessment .... (619) 582-5564
Pediatric asthma
Depression, bi-polar, schizophrenia, memory. Call for current studies

Manchester Clinic .... (858) 622-1000x500
    Studies have included saline filled mammary implants, laser skin resurfacing.
    Call for current studies.
Medical Associates Research Group .... colds, more (858) 277-7177
Medical Center for Women's Clinical Research .... (619) 299-1105
    Studies have included osteo, menopausal, more. Call for current studies &
    compensation.
Neurology Center .... (760) 732-0557x7
    Chronic fatigue; chronic low back pain. Call for other studies and compensation.
Radiant Research .... (760) 436-3988
    Studies have included asthma, allergies, hypertension, sinusitis. Call for current
    studies and compensation.
Research Studies VA Hospital .... (858) 552-8585x4346
    Located at the Veterans Administration Hospital. About 600 research studies,
    mainly sleep studies, depression, etc. Call and inquire about current studies.
San Diego Arthritis/Osteoporosis Medical Clinic .... (619) 287-1966
    Studies have included osteoporosis. Call for current studies.
San Diego Sports Medicine .... (619) 229-3909
    Chronic shoulder pain, more.
San Diego State Univ. Center for Eating and Weight Disorders .. (619) 594-2895
San Diego Uro-Research .... (619) 236-0045
    Men and women with urinary problems; prostate, incontinentence, impotence.
    Call and inquire about current studies.
Research Eye Clinic .... (858) 554-9611 or 554-6726
    Eye studies, allergies. Call for current studies.
Scripps Clinic (High cholesterol studies) .... (858) 592-1144
Scripps Clinic Weight Loss studies .... (858) 794-1247
Scripps diabetes clinical trials .... (800) SCRIPPS
Sharp Healthcare .... 858) 499-3139
    Studies have included cardiac, heartburn, blood pressure, arthritis, heart flutter.
Sharp Rees-Stealy .... (858) 794-3838
    Weight control studies; facial hair for women. Call for current studies.
Sidney Kimmel Cancer Center .... (858) 452-7344
    Cancer research; call for current studies
Synergy Research Center .... (6129) 426-7272
    Anxiety, panic, worry Email: synergycrc@msn.com
Therapeutics Inc Dermatology research .... (858) 638-SKIN
    Sun damage; Acne for 12 yrs or older, examinations, medications, compensation
VA Medical Center/UCSan Diego .... (858) 552-8585x3830
 Chronic low back pain

The following numbers are at the **National Institute of Health** in Bethesda, Md.
This is the CENTRAL site for dissemination of free government information
throughout the U.S. Call for STUDIES that you can participate in locally:

Nation Cancer Institute .... (800) 422-6237,
    NCI can refer you to studies in San Diego. Web: nci.nih.gov;
    NCI recently designated UCSD Cancer Center as a Comprehensive Cancer
    Center, the highest distinction awarded to a cancer center by the
    federal government.
Osteoporosis studies .... (800) 624-2663;
 Arthritis studies .... (800) 283-7800.

Medical Web Sites

Here are some helpful medical web sites to check out. Chatrooms for support are available on the net for every conceivable problem with valuable sharing.

All Clinical Trials (Government site) .... http://clinicaltrials.gov
    Created by Congress. Includes all life-threatening illnesses (gov.. & private)

National Institutes of Health .... nih.gov
    The world's foremost biomedical research centers and the focal point for biomedical research in the U.S. Contains a guide to diseases under investigation and connections to health resources.

American Medical Colleges .... aamc.org
    Information about human testing in clinical research

Healthfinder .... healthfinder.gov
    550 sites created by the government including info on cl web sites, databases, support and self-help groups, frequently asked questions, as well as the government agencies and not-for-profit organizations

Mayo Clinic .... mayo.edu
    Information on research programs and services plus links to reputable health sites.

American Medical Association .... ama~assn.org
    Databases of more than 650,000 physicians, a medical society directory and links to other medical sites.

National Mental Health Association .... nmha.org
    News, prevention information, outreach programs.

National Library of Medicine .... nlm.nih.gov

Medical Dictionary .... graylab.ac.uk/omd/index.html

Medical Advice .... housecall.com
    Medical advice from doctors re: 350 diseases

MedQue Medical Help, ... medque.com
    Medical supplies & photos .... freemedicaljournals.com

Medical Journals (free access, online .... www.free

Prescription Drug Side Effects .... rxlist.com
    Over 4000 drugs

Cancer Med ...., ... cancermed.com/bri.htm

Meet the Patients .... burzynskipatientgroup.org
    Cancer Med and Meet the Patients are from the famous cancer institute known for successful treatments in Houston run by S. R. Burzynski, Phone: (713) 335-5697/Fax: (713) 335-5699

Dental Services & Insurance

Preventative maintenance, including regular cleaning and flossing, is the key to keeping dental costs low in the long run.

If you don't have dental insurance through your employer, the American Dental Association doesn't recommend that individuals try to purchase dental *insurance* on their own. Nearly all dental insurance companies once offered coverage to individuals, but by 2001, only 10% of companies did so. Most of the coverage available is restricted to "referral" plans which offer members a discount on dental procedures from participating dentists. For a fee of about $10 a month, these plans give you access to a network of dentists who charge you a discounted set fee for each procedure, sometimes as much as 50% off some procedures. Get a list of member dentists before you send any money. Call a few dentists to make sure they are still with the plan. Check with the Better Business Bureau for complaints against the dental plan and the dentist you intend to use. Usually the dentist pays to be a member of the plan and receive referrals.

The *Reader's Digest,* February 1997 issue, has a cover story: **"How Dentists Rip Us Off."** It is an investigative report that uncovers disturbing news about the dental profession. Web Site: readersdigest.com Read and be informed.

According to Harold Slavkin, dean at the University of Southern California School of Dentistry, in the future, cavities and gum disease can be prevented by using gene therapy to modify the bacteria in a person's mouth that cause dental disease.

SmileSaver . . . . (800) 445-8119. SmileSaver is one of California's largest dental plans. Two plans for individuals: $7.15 a month; or $17.15 a month, includes routine cleanings and xrays. Call for family rates. Savings up to 30-50% on other services including cosmetic procedures. Choose from list of dentists. Coverage must be in effect 30 days before it can be used. Optional **orthodontic coverage** available for children or adults. Web: smilesaver.com.

California HealthQuote Insurance (dental plans, +) . . . . . (800) 788-4678

Dentalplans.com offers plans from about $79 a year; family, $99

USC School of Dentistry . . . . (toll free) (888) USC-DENT The University of Southern California School of Dentistry Clinic, located in downtown Los Angeles, offers everything from low-cost teeth cleaning, fillings and root canals to braces, oral surgery and implants. For anyone of all ages. And, it's a great place to go for a second opinion if you are considering extensive repairs to your mouth. Your first visit is on a walk-in basis, Monday, Wednesday, Thursday or Friday from 8:15 a.m. - 10:00 a.m. or Monday-Friday, 12:30 p.m. - 2:00 p.m. You will receive a full mouth examination, pan-xrays and evaluation for about $50. Check, cash, Mastercard, Visa. Within two weeks, you will be assigned a dental student who will call you and make an appointment. USC has one of the top dental schools in the country, and an outstanding staff. All work is pre-approved by the staff but the work is basically done by students at a big savings. USC is highly recommended by their patients who say it's worth the drive (about 2 hours from downtown San Diego.)

They say their fees will save you about 50%. Root canals are around $300, porcelain crowns are around $350, full mouth braces are between $1800 and $2600. An orthodontic evaluation is $20. For information and an appointment, call their toll free number above. USC is located a few minutes off Interstate 5. Take Interstate 5 to Interstate 10 (Santa Monica Freeway), exit Vermont, left on Vermont, left on Jefferson. Park in Gate 8 for $4 per day.

UCLA Dental School . . . . (310) 206-3904.
The University of California at Los Angeles Dental School has a full service dental clinic for anyone of all ages. Open daily from 7:30am-4:30pm when school is in session. The clinic is located on campus at 10833 Le Conte Avenue in Westwood off Interstate 405. Visa, Master Card welcome.

I am sorry to report "not good" things about the American Dental Clinic in Tijuana. Two highly reliable people had root canals there that were improperly done, resulting in the loss of a tooth; another was told he had 11 cavities. He went to another dentist in San Diego who said he had NONE. The dentist in Tijuana gave him a crown that had to be redone in the U.S., and neglected to diagnose a dead tooth that had been involved in an accident. Their standards of care are different and a crown done there has no margins, which allows leaks into the roots which decay at the roots which can cause the tooth to die. A bridge was improper and caused jaw joint aches, etc., etc. Also, a Dr. Marco A. Valle Ibarra on Constitution is not recommended due to a patient having to have all the work redone. His work included crowns that were too small which allowed food in between teeth (which will destroy gums), he made a crown too short so he didn't have to adjust it to fit the tooth above, made a crown that leaked, etc. Long on "jive" but short on quality work.

Regular brushing of your gums with a paste of baking soda and hydrogen peroxide can do wonders for the health of your gums. Before having periodontal surgery on your gums, be sure to get a second opinion. Many people are told they need the surgery who don't. (Sad, but true.) See the Reader's Digest article referred to above.

Bargains at Spas

Most spas have reduced rates during the summer months, and some offer the summer rate during most weeks that have a major holiday. Remember to ask if there are any specials, or if any discount coupons are available! Here are some spas in area /region worth visiting! **Rancho La Puerta Health Spa**, in Tecate, is the sister spa to the ultra deluxe Golden Door spa in San Marcos. The ranch is located a few minutes South of the border in Tecate, about an hour's drive from downtown San Diego, on 3,000 acres. They offer over 50 exercise classes a day, swimming, running, hikes, pampering. Single rate,

Saturday to Saturday, $2,374 a week; double rate starts at $2,000 per person. The summer rate is 12% less, during July and August. Call for brochure, (800) 443-7565. Web site: rancholapuerta.com. (The sister spa Golden Door, (800) 424-0777 is $5725 a week.) **Carlsbad Mineral Water Spa** is located at Carlsbad Boulevard at Christiansen Way, Carlsbad, on the site where two wells were dug more than 100 years ago. They were named after the Karlsbad, Bohemia mineral springs, which gave the city it's name. Three rooms offering mineral baths, massage, facials and package deals, (760) 434-1887, web: carlsbadmineralspa.com. **Cal A Vie Spa** in Vista offers a $400 discount during the summer, the rates are about $4450-$4750 depending on treatments, and the regular rates are $4850-$5150. There is a $400 discount during holiday weeks; all single rooms. This is the spa that Oprah went to (and found her chef, Rosie); (760) 945-2055. The **Desert Hot Springs Hotel & Spa** offers day use passes for $5 on weekdays, $6 on weekends. Admission entitles guests to use the eight spring-fed pools, dressing rooms with lockers and showers and the sauna, from 8 a.m. til 10 p.m. Bring towel and lock (or rent them). On Tuesdays, a pass is only $3, and after 3 pm everyday, it is only $3, $4 on weekends! Call (800) 843-6053 for further information and directions (about 2-2 ½ hours from San Diego airport). This is a full service spa with 80 services offered. **The Palms Spa** in Palm Springs, (800) 753-7256 offers 14 optional fitness classes, three low-calorie meals, pools, saunas and spas, and accommodations. Rates from $300 for a two night stay, (share) or $1050 for a 7 night stay (share). Ask about specials. Summer savings: 25% off from June til end of August. Here are the **least expensive spas** I found: **Glen Ivy Hot Springs**, Corona, CA, This is a **day spa** (no overnights) less than two hours from downtown San Diego, near Lake Elsinore. For $30, you get to use the 17 mineral pools, red clay bath, sauna & steam rooms, (909) 277-3529, web: glenivy.com. Daily admission including use of outdoor mineral baths, outdoor therapy pools, red clay mud bath, outdoor hot spas, olympic-size swimming pool, sunning deck and sauna, aqua aerobics; Monday-Thursday, $25; Fridays-Sundays and holidays, $35, no reservations required. **Agua Caliente Valparaiso Thermal Mineral Spa** in Tijuana offers hot mineral baths, massage, rooms, a restaurant with divine fruit drinks and more. Valparaiso means "on your way to paradise" and it provides a very relaxing environment only minutes from the Tijuana border. Moderate prices. Special package deals. Great nearby getaway. Call 011-52-664-624-0786, web: valparaisobc.com. **Rancho Los Chabacanos** (ranch of apricot trees) is a low cost facility for healing mind, body and spirit in Tecate, about an hour from downtown San Diego. You can bring your own food to this low cost holistic/spiritual retreat. Hiking, Aztec traditional healing/detoxifying sweat lodge (temazcal), mud treatments, holistic classes, feng shui classes, cold spring waters, hot pools, massages ($40/40 minutes), rooms for two (casitas), $90; meals, $40 a day ea., or their day package includes transportation from Tijuana border, three meals, a massage and use of a casita for $135 per person. For more information, call 011-52-665-665-1624 or web: rancholoschabacanos.com. **Red Mountain Adventure Spa**, (800) 407-3002.

Located in Ivins, Utah, near Zion National Park. Rates from $995 a week dorm style, 4 in a room. includes meals, lodging, exercise, nutrition lectures and use of all facilities. (This place is a real deal! I have a couple friends who go there for a month or two every few years.) An ultra-cheap spa is the **Tennessee Fitness Spa**, located in Waynesboro, TN where you can get accommodations for as low as $645 a week (quad), $750 (double) and up. Call (800) 235-8365 or check it out on the web at ftspa.com. *For additional information on* **major spas**, *including current rates and brochures, call the Spa Finder toll-free number, (800)-ALL-SPAS*, or check their website at spafinder.com.

Medical Care in Tijuana

People who live in border towns across the U.S. are heading to Mexico for medical treatments and prescriptions. *I am not advocating this nor am I NOT advocating this*, but I will say that Mexicans go to Mexican doctors all the time, even rich Mexicans, and I know many Americans who have told me they go to Tijuana for xrays, tests, prescriptions, examinations, alternative therapies for terminal diseases, orthodontia, and even deliver their babies there (in order to have dual citizenship which entitles the parents to purchase Mexican land). There are doctors who have nice offices near the Zona del Rio (River Zone) Shopping Area, and those that have medical offices you probably wouldn't want to walk into. Many speak English; some speak perfect English. Ask the doctor where he got his medical degree and how much training he has had before making your decision. Many have done graduate work in the United States. Some may be charlatans. Check him/her out. Doctors in Mexico report that Americans comprise one in four patients. They go down for prescription drugs, physicals, allergies, ear aches and other medical treatment. People who go there say they are happy with the service. Although most would prefer getting care in the U.S., health insurance or care here is sometimes unaffordable or their insurance excludes coverage, or has such a high co-payment that it is cheaper to go to a border town. Doctor visits average about $25-$35. In the U.S., a first visit to a pediatrician is about $65+; a surgeon, $125+; family practice visit, $55+, twice the price you pay in Mexico.

Plastic Surgery

UCSD Medical Center Plastic Surgery . . . . (619) 294-3746
Plastic surgery performed by an intern or resident (a medical school graduate from who is specializing in plastic surgery) at UCSD Medical Center can cost less than elsewhere, depending on the procedure. You might be surprised at their prices. All services are completely supervised by Board Certified Plastic Surgeons.

Call the American Society of Plastic and Reconstructive Surgeons at (800) 635-0635 and (800) 332-FACE and request **free brochures** on procedures, and check the library or book store for information on plastic surgery.

In one of my bargain hunting workshops at Mesa College, a young woman jumped up and announced that she had her thighs "vacuumed" in Tijuana by a plastic surgeon, and she said that I should let everyone know that this procedure can be done down there for much less than up here. I know some people will read this and scream, but I am not advising you *to* or *not to* do this: I am telling you that Californians are having plastic surgery in Tijuana for less than they can in San Diego (facelift with neck, about $3500; nose, about $1800). Always inquire about credentials. Get all the information you can from plastic surgeons here and be knowledgeable about the procedure, the dangers, etc. before inquiring in Tijuana. Dr. Alejandro Quiroz, an English-speaking Tijuana plastic surgeon, was featured on Channel 10 news. Dr. Quiroz is a Board Certified plastic surgeon, licensed to practice in both the United States and Mexico. He is a member of the San Diego Plastic Surgery Society (verified), American Medical Association, Professional Associate of the American Society of Plastic and Reconstructive Surgery, as well as an active member of the International Society of Aesthetic Plastic Surgery and the Lipolysis Society of North America. After finishing his medical training and three years of Plastic Surgery Residency in Mexico City, he spent an additional year in training at the University of California, Irvine. For several years, he practiced cosmetic surgery at a clinic in Orange County. His CosMed offices in Tijuana are within minutes of the border in a modern medical building in the Rio Zona. Some staff members speak English. Procedures offered include body contouring (lipo-suction), breast enlargement, reduction and lift, cheek and chin enhancement, ear modifications, face, neck, forehead and eyebrow lifts, nose and eyelid surgery, tummy tucks, Paris lips, chemical peels, laser peels, wrinkle and scar improvements, and a complete range of re-constructive surgery and dermatology. The majority of their patients are from Southern California. Brochures and/or references from satisfied clients are available upon request. CosMed has a local telephone number for California clients. Call (619) 428-4803 for more information and directions to the office.

Chapter 7

JOB INFORMATION

About 95% of job openings are *not* listed in the classified ads. And, if you are applying for an advertised position, you may be competing with hundreds of applicants for the same job!! This chapter is devoted to information and resources that may make the job hunt easier.

The annual publication, "San Diego County Occupational Outlook," contains valuable information on the present status and future outlook for 34 occupations, including salary range from entry level to 3 years+ experience, the current number of people employed in the occupation, the number of new job openings anticipated in the next few years.

The leading industries in San Diego are: telecommunications, software development, health care products and services, business and financial services, tourism and hospitality, recreational goods and electronics. "Occupational Outlook" is published by the San Diego Consortium & Private Industry Council, (619) 238-1445, and is available at libraries.

Here are some of the major employers in San Diego that offer employment in positions from custodial and non-professional, to clerical and professional jobs.

Major employers with 10,000+ employees in S.D. . . . Personnel Phone
San Diego Unified School District . . . . (619) 725-8150
Scripps Health . . . . (800) 376-0088
Sharp Healthcare Corp. . . . . (858) 499-5627
University of California, San Diego . . . . (858) 534-2812
County of San Diego . . . . (619) 531-5764
City of San Diego . . . . (619) 682-1011
U.S. Postal Service . . . . (858) 674-0577

Major employers with 5,000-9,999 employees in S.D. . Personnel No.
Kaiser Permanente . . . . (619) 528-3071
National Steel & Shipbuilding . . . . (619) 544-8512
QUALCOMM, Inc. (Telecommunications) . . . . (858) 658-5627
San Diego Community College Dist. . . . . (619) 584-6580

Major employers with 3,000-4,999 employees in S.D. . Personnel No.
City of S.D. Police Department . . . . (619)531-2126

Cubic Corp (Electronics manufacturer & developer . . . . (619)505-1540
Foodmaker, Inc. (Restaurants) . . . . (619) 571-2481
Solar Turbines, Inc. (turbines-industrial gas) . . . . (858) 694-6046
Home Depot USA, Inc. (building materials) . . . . (877) 967-5443
Naval Aviation Depot, North Island (aircraft maint./repair) . . . . . . (619) 545-3100
Pacific Bell (telecommunications) . . . . (800) 559-7442
Palomar Pomerado Health System . . . . (848) 675-5155
Costco . . . . (619) 490-5400
San Diego Gas & Electric . . . . (858) 654-1600
San Diego State University . . . . (619) 594-6404
Science Applications International Corp. (technology services) . . (858) 826-6000
UCSD Medical Center . . . . (858) 682-1001

Excerpted from the Greater San Diego Chamber of Commerce publication, "Major Employers San Diego County." Other major employers are also listed. Available at public libraries and from the Chamber of Commerce, (619) 232-0124.

Job Hotlines The following employers have 24-hour job hotlines that list all the jobs that are currently available:

Federal Government . . . . (912) 757-3000/ (800) 688-9889
This is THE central federal job hotline for *all* of California, including San Diego. Listen carefully to directions. Jobs for San Diego area listed by occupation. You may also hear listings for all over the country, by occupation. The Federal Government Walk-in Job Center, is located at 880 Front Street, Room 4280, downtown. No phone. You can also check federal job listings on the Web site: www. usajobs.opm.gov.

State of California . . . . (619) 237-6163
Post Office . . . . (858) 674-0577
San Diego Unified Port District . . . . (619) 686-6599
San Diego County . . . . (619) 531-5764
City of San Diego . . . . (619) 682-1011
City of Escondido . . . . (760) 432-4585
City of Chula Vista . . . . (619) 691-5095
City of Coronado . . . . (619) 522-7807
City of El Cajon . . . . (619) 441-1671
City of Imperial Beach . . . . (619) 423-8300x134
City of La Mesa . . . . (619) 667-1183
City of National City . . . . (619) 336-4306
City of Poway . . . . (619) 679-4300
City of Lemon Grove . . . . (619) 464-6934
City of Santee . . . . (619) 258-4100x4

UCSD Medical Center . . . . (858) 682-1001

Schools, Colleges & Universities . . . . **Personnel Number**
San Diego Community College District 584-6580x6580

San Diego County Office of Education . . . . (858) 292-3500
Grossmont/Cuyamaca College . . . . (619) 465-1700
San Diego State University . . . . (619) 594-6404
University of California (UCSD) . . . . (858) 682-1000

All elementary and secondary school districts are listed in the *Yellow Pages*. See the green section in the front for Schools, Academic. All colleges, universities and vocational schools are listed there, too.

While you have the *Yellow Pages* in hand, call all hospitals, which hire hundreds of employees from administration to custodial + medical staff.

Thumb through the *Yellow Pages* for other ideas. Who knows. You might create the ideal job match for you. Check the editions for San Diego, North County, Inland, East County, South Bay, etc. Public libraries have them all.

The Employment Development Department (State of California) has job listings posted in the lobby of their offices. Call for further information. All listings for the county . . . . (800) 300-5616

The *San Diego Business Journal* publishes an annual list of top employers by occupation (manufacturing, health maintenance organizations, real estate) with the name and phone number of the personnel directors. They publish another list of top general employers. The publications are about $65, but you can get a copy of the page you are interested in for $5 at their offices at 4909 Murphy Canon Rd., Suite 200, (619) 277-6359.

San Diego Career Center, 8401 Aero Drive, (619) 974-7620, offers a job leads room with hundreds of job postings for anyone looking for a job. Also, you can take advantage of free career planning and assessment at any adult school. Free job counseling. You get a lot of help here. The program includes a two-day job search workshop, career exploration, assessment, developing job leads, applications and resumes. Stay motivated and energetic during your job search with their professional networking group. Free faxing, telephone room, computer room. You will be assigned to case manager to help you get your career goals met.

Job Search Assistance Workshop, a free one-day workshop held almost every Friday , San Diego Career Center, 8401 Aero Drive, (619) 627-2553.

Job Placement Preparation/Civil Service Review is a *free* three-hour workshop on preparation and practice for the civil service test, West City Center Continuing Education, Point Loma Campus, 3249 Fordham Street, near the Sports Arena, (619) 221-6973. Ask about other locations, too.

If interested in leaving the area for a job, ask the librarian for the directories of jobs in other cities, with titles such as: *Job Banks: Los Angeles; Job Banks: Orange County; Job Banks: Chicago,* etc.. I was surprised at all the titles I found in the downtown library, including *101 Ways to Find An Overseas Job.*

If you want to earn big bucks, consider employment in Iraq, Saudi Arabia or South Korea for a year or two. You can earn two to three times the salaries paid here. Many young people are going abroad for a few years and come back with enough money to buy a house and set themselves up for life. Book stores and libraries have many books on seeking employment abroad, complete with names and addresses of American companies who are hiring for employment overseas. U.S. companies are hiring construction workers to help rebuild Iraq, and they will pay you very well. Boy, I would do it in a heartbeat. You only have to do it for a year or so to come back well-healed. My uncles worked on the Panama Canal retrofit, the San Juan, Puerto Rico airport, and the St. Thomas airport. They have lots of tales to tell. Take a computer and/or set of encyclopedias with you and catch up on your reading because there's not much else to do there. A friend whose daughter and husband are both registered nurses are headed to Saudi Arabia and will make several times as much as they can here.

Web site: www.overseaswork.com; email: research@overseaswork.com.

Peace Corps Recruiting Office . . . . (800) 818-9579

For anyone and everyone: each community college has a job placement board with jobs countywide posted. Walk on campus, ask where the job placement board is, and take a look. You don't have to be enrolled to do this, but if you enroll in a class, you can get free job counseling, etc.

Look for these books (or books similar titles if these titles are no longer available) in libraries or book stores: *Jobs In Paradise, Work and Sail Your Way Around the World, Directory of Overseas Summer Jobs, How To Get A Job On A Cruise Ship, How To Get A Job With The Airlines, Summer Jobs in Britain, How to Make Money in Music, Art, Photography, How to Get an Overseas Job, International Directory of Job Opportunities, Job Seeker's Guide to 1000 Top Employers, Job Seeker's Guide to Socially Responsible Companies, etc.* New titles along this line are available every year. Here are some web sites for job hunting:

Software Industry Council - 225 employers . . . . www.sdsic.com
City of San Diego . . . . www.ci.san-diego.ca.us
San Diego Union job source . . . . www.uniontrib.com
Career . . . . www.careermosaic.com

Monster Board .... www.monster.com
Head Hunters .... www.headhunter.net
Online Career Centers .... www.occ.com
JobWeb.. www.jobweb.com
American's Job Bank .... www.ajb.dni.us
Job Trak .... www.jobtrak.com
Overseas Jobs .... www.overseaswork.com
or email to: Research@overseaswork.com
Europe's Best Jobs .... www.taps.com

Free Job Training/Career Change

The ROP Program (Regional Occupational Program) offers quality free job training for anyone in the County, all ages, no tuition, for all income levels, in all areas from accounting to welding, with computer, construction, medical, insurance, interior decorating, food service, travel and other occupations. Call San Diego, (619) 292-3611, for further information.

Community College Continuing Education (adult education program) offers dozens of free business skills classes including all office skills (computers, desktop, accounting, data entry, business math, medical office skills, shorthand and typing.) They also administer tests for 10-key adding machines; typing and shorthand tests, plus courses for entry-level opportunities in insurance, clerical and accounting, career assessment, career planning, resume writing and interviewing techniques, and more. Vocational courses include appliance repair, auto body paint and repair, auto mechanics, electronic assembly, basic electronics, construction, landscape construction, pipefitting, sheet metal, shipfitting, blueprint reading, plumbing, heating, air conditioning, printing, graphic arts, upholstery, VCR/TV repair and welding. For a schedule of free classes, call (619) 527-5242; web site: communitycollege.net.

Don't know what kind of work you want to be in? The library has *hundreds* of books written on how to enter careers in art, fashion, advertising, public relations, health, catering, human services, animals, outdoor careers, law enforcement, high tech, real estate, how to make money in music, freelancing, mail order, retailing, franchising. They also have books on alternative careers, working from home, self-employment opportunities, starting a word processing service, getting money to start a business, temporary employment, freelancing, career guides, career assessment, resume writing, interviewing techniques, job hunting guides, plus financial aid for college, etc. (How I wish *I* had known about all these options and alternatives when I was in a career change!!)

Start Your Own Business

If you're interested in starting up your own business or home based business, here are some resources you may want to look into. Drop by a newsstand or major book store and look over the magazines on money-making opportunities including *Venture, Entrepreneur, and Spare-Time Money Making Opportunities.* These magazines are actually catalogs of mail-order books that cost about $75 or more on how to start various business including home-based businesses (hot right now are personal services and home care for older adults!), how to start a business on a shoe string, etc. They are great for ideas, but you can do better and save money by looking over the books with similar titles in libraries, book stores, or the SBA Business Resource Center (see below).

Free counseling on how to start up a business is available from S.C.O.R.E (Service Corps of Retired Executives) at the U.S. Small Business Administration, located at 500 West C Street, Suite 550, downtown, (619) 557-7272, 9-3pm only. The SBA Business Resource Center offers a free *Business Start-Up Kit*, and their library contains many references including "how to" manuals for 186 different kinds of businesses, business planning software, business publications, video tapes and CD-ROM databases. They can provide you with information on potential new customers, do-it-yourself marketing, management, etc. All services are free. Government loans are also available from the U.S. Small Business Administration to start up or expand a small business for those who have been turned down by two banks. Call (619) 557-7250x4 for further information. Micro-loan programs, up to $25,000, sponsored by the SBA, (800) 8-ASK-SBA. Web site: www.sba.gov. Web site for business startups sponsored by Wall Street Journal: http://startupjournal.com

Chapter 8
LEGAL GOOD DEALS
& CREDIT INFO

Having a legal problem is like having a serious illness: it can consume and drain you of your health, sanity and bank account. If you need a first, second or third opinion, the following resources could be helpful and save you a lot of money!

Legal

Every family will probably eventually need a **legal reference guide**. The Reader's Digest's *Family Legal Guide* is an excellent reference covering everyday legal problems: how to select an attorney; buying, selling and financing real estate; pensions; condemnation; landlord/tenant; insurance; marriage contracts; divorce; income tax; social security; wills; laws of intestacy; estate taxes; estate administration; employer/employee; consumer; defamation; auto accident; personal injury, etc. Easy to understand. Other similar titles are available at libraries and bookstores.

For a free catalog of **do-it-yourself legal books**, reference guides and software (living trusts, wills etc.), call Nolo Press, (800) 992-6656. Titles include: employees rights, family law, homeowners, landlords, tenants, harassment, bankruptcy, patents, how to buy a house/sell one, neighbor law, homestead your house, legal guides to living together, small claims court, superior court, fighting tickets, do your own divorce, domain names, copyrights and many more. These books and software contain usable legal forms, and are also very useful in helping you understand your case even if you are using an attorney. Save yourself some money and arm yourself with a little knowledge before you step into your attorney's office so he/she doesn't have to charge you $150+ per hour to explain things to you that you can read about in your $25 Nolo legal guide. Frequently recommended by attorney Bill Handel of Handel on the Law, KFI Radio, (see below). Nolo software is available at CompUSA, Computer City, Borders and Egghead. Nolo's self help law center on the web is at nolo.com where you can download ebooks, eguides, forms. Legal tools you can use, legal dictionary, Ask Auntie Nolo questions, look up state and federal statues and lawyer jokes!

American Bar Association Web site offers information on legal topics that affect your daily life, from 'Family' to 'Your Job' to 'Buying and Selling' to 'Finding a Lawyer.' Go to abalawinfo.org

Most attorneys will give you a **free initial legal consultation** (over the phone) to determine if you have a case. However, if you call the San Diego County Bar Association Attorney Referral Service, (619) 231-8585, they can refer you to an attorney who specializes in the type of law you need. They will usually refer you to three. Check with the Bar to see if there are complaints against the attorney. Most complaints are settled out of court, but if you want to see what cases have been filed against the attorney, go to the court house and look his/her name up at the research desk.

San Diego Mediation Center . . . . (619) 238-2400
A *free* service to help you handle disputes concerning neighborhood, domestic, juvenile, landlord-tenant, consumer-merchant, employee-employer, small claims, etc. Web: mediate.com/sdmc

San Diego Small Claims Legal Advisory (Free) . . . . . (619) 236-2700
Recorded information on how to file and collect a small claims court action.

Free Law Day/Week . . . . (619) 231-0781
San Diego County Bar Association members offer free informal consultations on a one-on-one basis at six area shopping malls around the county as a part of Law Week. An annual event in April or May, including seminars with questions/answer sessions. Call for exact dates.

San Diego Volunteer Lawyer Program . . . . (619) 235-5656
Free legal advice on specific matters for low income individuals. Contested custody, divorces, immigration, special education, HIV and AIDS-related cases. No criminal, DUI, personal injury or landlord/tenant.

University of San Diego Legal Clinic . . . . (619) 260-7470
Services for low income: civil, juvenile, environmental, immigration and mental health cases. Small claims, too. New entrepreneur clinic. Available September to November and January to May.

KOGO AM600 sponsors a live local legal show on Saturdays, Primerus Law Hour, 1-2pm. Call in and ask for **advice on your personal legal problem**, (858) 569-TALK or (800) 600-KOGO.

Bill Handel, attorney and very entertaining talk show host, is on KFI (L.A.) radio (640 on your AM dial) every Saturday morning from 7-10 a.m. offering **free legal advice** to those who call in. I love listening to him on the car radio every Saturday morning when I'm out yard "sale-ing." Get your question and thoughts organized, and call (800) 520-1534 about 10 minutes before the show starts. Let the phone ring until someone picks up. Who knows how long he will be doing this, but for now, take advantage of it. And, what a character he is. He has a call in line for referrals to associated attorneys in Southern California, and for do-it-yourselfers and those who want to know something before paying an attorney, he highly recommends Nolo Press (see above).

Lawyer referral service of the **Legal Aid Society** of San Diego, (619) 262-0896, for low income individuals.

A **Legal Services Plan**, about $11.^{95} a month, (800) 323-4620. No attorney legal fees for consultation and advice by phone and one face-to-face consultation, etc. More than 7 local attorneys participate in this plan; discounted rates for representation, $75 per hour.

Here are a few **legal web sites**. Current codes for California, all other states and federal law: sdlawlinks.com, internetlawyer.com or findlaw.com; nolo.com; uslaw.com; fastsearch.com/law; calbar.org

We The People Fast preparation of legal documents. No lawyers, saves money. Divorce, $189-289; bankruptcy, $199; living trust, $399. (619) 422-4599.

A class on **Basic Legal Research** is sponsored by the San Diego County Public Law Library, $12, from time to time. Call (619) 531-3900.

Hire a **law student** to do leg work for you, look up things at the Court House, etc. Call Thomas Jefferson, Cal Western or USD law school.

Funerals (your very LAST legal issue!)

The national average cost of a funeral is around $5000, not including cemetery and monument expenses. Immediate cremation or burial can be around $500. Individuals may obtain permits to handle all death arrangements themselves at a considerable savings. For a wide range of funeral options and cost saving consumer tips, call the Funeral and

Memorial Societies of America, (800) 765-0107. Lifetime membership about $25. Web: funerals.org/famsa

```
Caring Cremation Services, $595 includes transport and all (619) 282-0505
Direct Cremation, $585, includes all; no other charges  ..  (800) 845-4821
      Telophase Cremation Society . . . . . . . . . . . . . . . .  (619) 299-0805
      Caskets & Urns For Less (offers discount coupons)  (619) 467-1200
      Alvarado /Casket Outlet . . . . . . . . . . .  (619) 427-8517/ 628-1112
            Payments, layaway, savings from 40-70%.
```

Credit & Credit Cards

Following is information on credit cards with the lowest rates, building a better credit line, and more, but *your goal is to pay off your debts and get on a cash basis.* Instead of monthly payments to pay off debt, your goal is make monthly payments into investments that will EARN money. Don't just work for your money, make your money work for you! Would you like a 30-40% pay raise? Well, the average American pays about 30-40% of a paycheck to pay off credit card debt, so if you want this pay raise, pay off your credit cards and get on a cash basis.

Every time you open an account for a credit card or loan, your creditor keeps tabs on your repayment record and reports this information to the credit bureaus. Your credit report is simply a compilation of your bill-paying history. It is important to obtain a copy of your credit report to see if the information is correct. Errors sometimes occur in reporting: lending institutions may fail to report that your debt has been paid and negative credit information could be in your file that belongs to some one else. Get a copy of your credit report from the three major credit reporting agencies below. Send your request with your full name including "Jr.," maiden name, current address, and addresses for the past five years, social security number, and date of birth to:

```
Experian ($8.50)  web: experian.com . . . . . . . . . . . . . .  (888) 397-3742
Equifax ($8.50 charge) web: equifax.com . . . . . . . . . .  (800) 685-1111
Trans Union ($8.50 charge)  web: transunion.com . . . .  (800) 888-4213
```

Privacy Guard (800) 374-8273 will check all three credit bureaus for you and send you a copy of your credit reports. They will check your driving records and health records to see what public information is on file for you. You will receive a quarterly report of inquiries into your credit report, unlimited copies of your credit report, information about who is checking your credit report, and you are notified if anything negative has been put into your file. Annual fee, $79.95. You will also receive a newsletter and a financial profile with your FICO score. You can input information into your credit file. Web site: Privacyguard.com

Your credit score is known as your **FICO score**. It is a complex evaluation of your creditworthiness. Your credit score doesn't just report your payment history. It uses a formula that assigns a weight to factors such as your bill repayment habits, percent of available credit used, and even your employment history. This credit score is used in almost every mortgage decision and loan. Fair Isaac & Co. Peioneered the concept of scoring. A FICO score ranges between 300 and 850. About 39% of the population scores above 750, and a score below that level is a warning signal. This score is based on the length of time your accounts have been open, your bill-paying habits and the percentage of your credit limit that you are using on each card. You want to pay your accounts on time, before due, and keep the balance well below the limit.

Credit Card Tips

For a list of the **ten lowest-rate credit cards** available and those with no annual fee, check the Personal Finance Section of the *Union-Tribune* on Mondays. For rates on the web, check bankrate.com, getsmart.com or consumer-action.org. If you carry a balance, switch to the best deal. Making only a minimum payment on your credit card can be very costly. It would take 33 years to pay off a $2000 debt paying only a minimum payment. You would repay $9,125.98! You can **request a lower interest rate on your major credit card** and ask them to waive the annual fee. Always send more than the monthly minimum, make your payments on time and establish a good credit history with them. You can pay most credit cards online, and it would be wise to pay them as soon as you can afdter you get a bill. Then, call and ask them to drop the fee and lower the rate. Suggest that you're considering switching to a no-fee/lower rate card company. Some of the "apple pie" institutions have the highest **interest rates** on their accounts: JC Penneys, 21%; Mervyn's, 21%; Home Depot, 21%; bank cards charge less interest, some introductory rates, as low as 2.9%. Or even 0.0%.

Mission Federal **Credit Union** (with numerous San Diego locations) is open to membership by any parent of a student in school, any alumni of a local college or university, any senior citizen or retired person, in addition to educators and school employees. They offer a Visa Card at 12.9% interest, with no annual fee. (Interest varies) Secured cards available, processed normally, 12.59% interest, 150% on deposit. Call (858) 552-6860. The San Diego Teachers Credit Union is also open to any student of parent of a student in San Diego County. Call (619) 495-1600. Membership benefits include low auto loans.

Credit Repair The City Attorney's Consumer Fraud Unit has prosecuted a few San Diego credit clean-up clinics who have taken fees, but failed to deliver the services they promised. Typically, what they do is charge $75-$300 or even $6000 up front and promise to clean up your bad credit and obtain credit cards for you regardless of your past credit. If they do obtain credit cards, it is usually done through a bank that issues "secured" credit cards, where your credit line is the same amount or greater than the amount you are required to place on deposit as "security." Erasing bad credit is a questionable promise and rarely successful since only information that is outdated or erroneous can be eliminated from your credit report. Using the Fair Credit Reporting Act (FCRA), the credit repair company will dispute everything in your credit report in the hope that something inaccurate will show up, or the credit reporting agency will not be able to confirm the information. If it cannot be confirmed, it must be removed. California law states that a credit reporting agency does not have to reinvestigate disputed information if "it has reasonable grounds to believe that the dispute by the consumer is frivolous or irrelevant." Since credit repair companies investigate *everything,* items are frequently dismissed as "frivolous." Inaccurate and outdated information is best remedied directly by the consumer. For a copy of *Credit Repair Clinics: Consumer Beware*, send $1 to Bankcard Holders of America, 560 Herndon Parkway, Suite 120, Herndon, Virginia 22070. A new law now prohibits credit repair outfits from taking consumers' money before services are performed. The law also mandates full disclosure and gives consumers a right to cancel after three days.

Here's essentially how to **clean up your credit** yourself: First, get your credit report (see Credit Reporting Agencies above) and dispute everything on it that is negative. Send by certified mail. They will either: 1) remove items as requested, 2) tell you they won't change your credit file and give reasons, or 3) if the party involved fails to respond within 30 days, the information you want removed will be removed. Many companies can't be bothered to go through back records, so this can work for you. If not, you are allowed to send in a 100 word consumer explanation which will be included in your credit report. If you have unpaid debts on your credit report, determine an affordable plan to pay off your debts, and contact your creditors with your proposal. Send an explanation of your repayment plan to the credit bureau. This will let potential creditors know you are satisfying the debt. Bad credit stays on your record for seven years, after which it can no longer be reported. Pay your credit card bills and loans on time for six months, then get a secured credit card. (Utility bills are not reported on your credit, unless you fail to pay after they cut you off.) If your bills are paid on time, you can improve your credit rating. Having too many credit cards is a "red flag" with lenders. Close inactive cards. Check the library and book stores for more information on how to solve your credit problems and clean up your credit, or go to Money Magazine online at moneymag.com or Microsoft at msn.com and click on Personal Finance, and everything you need will pop up. Information on all aspects of finances. This is awesome.

If you have *no* credit, get started with a **secured Master Card or Visa**. Even if you've been turned down for credit due to divorce, bad credit or bankruptcy, you may be eligible for a "secured" credit card. Here's how secured credit works. "Secured" in this case means that your credit limit will be established by the amount of money you place on deposit in savings with the credit card company as "security." Most bank cards require $1 on deposit in a savings account for every $1 of credit you want. If you want a $500 credit line, you'll need $500 on deposit. Their interest rates may be higher, but some banks offer lower rates because you have cash on deposit with them. Your credit line will be increased automatically as you establish a good credit history with them by paying your bills on time, and always paying more than the minimum required. Secured credit cards are offered from Mission Credit Union (above) and some banks.

Debt Consolidation: If you want free advice and free assistance in consolidating your bills, get help from Consumer Credit Counseling Services, 1550 Hotel Circle North, Suite 110, San Diego, (619) 497-0200. All services are free at their five local offices. These services can run as high as $100 a month elsewhere. They also offer classes in credit repair. Do not get involved in paying someone to help you consolidate your debts. There are many complaints that the money you pay doesn't go to pay off your debts, but to pay the people who are helping you. The Debt Relief Institute in Washington, DC, a public interest group, offers a Debt Relief Kit at institute-dc.org.

Loans/Credit Banks give "A" loans to those with perfect credit histories, good salary/debt ratio. Other financial institutions and private investors offer "B" and "C" and "D" loans. Those who have late or missed payments or have bankruptcies a few years old, but have recent good credit, may be eligible to secure these loans despite being turned down by a bank. Interest rates vary, some are very high, so be sure to shop around for the best deal. Check several sources. Look under "Mortgage Loans" in the *Yellow Pages*, or check online. Search for "mortgage loans." And, you can go to bankrate.com on the internet, or msn.com or moneymag.com and they all have connections to mortgage calculators, current rates, etc.

Chapter 9
CONTINUING EDUCATION
Lifelong Learning: Academic and Leisure Classes

Some people like to play golf or play bridge, but me?? I like to play *school!* I'm a class and seminar junkie! Just love to hear a good speaker! And there are classes, workshops, seminars, lectures and speakers all over town offered not only by traditional learning institutions, but book stores, hospitals, museums and art galleries. Yes,Yes,YES!!! They are wonderful and exhilarating and motivating and fun and informational and all those good things. And, many listed in this chapter are free!! You'll also find valuable information on going back to school for credit through adult schools, community colleges, colleges and universities, their fees, and a section on money for college, much of which you don't have to repay! So long as you keep learning, you'll never grow old. . . .think about it!

Continuing Education/Adult School/College

California offers the best system of traditional continuing education classes for adults in the country, putting more tax dollars into the system than any other state. Here in San Diego, you can return to school at any age and earn a high school diploma at an adult school free of charge. You can work toward a community college credential (still a deal at $11 per unit, but it may be increased soon), or pursue a bachelors or advanced degree at a college or university. The fees are listed later in this chapter. You can take vocational courses, many of which are free, that lead to a certificate, enroll in job search and career counseling for adults *(free)*. Or learn computers for fun or profit.

Free and low-cost leisure and credit courses are offered through adult continuing education in every school district in San Diego County, funded by local, state and federal tax dollars. County residents can attend any adult continuing education school in any district; there are no boundaries. If you don't know where the nearest adult school is, your local high school office should be able to tell you. Continuing ed (adult) classes are available in every school district.

Within the city limits, the San Diego Community College District Centers for Education and Technology offer more than a thousand classes at 300+

locations including enrichment, vocational and high school credit classes. They also offer classes at off site locations, including churches and senior centers. For a free class schedule, call (619) 527-5242 or check the web at communitycollege.net. Among the **free classes** offered within the city limits are:

Internet and computer training	Health education
Word-processing and desk-top	Home Planning
All job search classes	Introductory ceramics
Civil Service Review	Jewelry Making
Resume & interviewing classes	Landscape
All job training classes	Literature Survey
All academic classes leading to a diploma	Machine Shop, Welding
Appliance Repair	Management classes
Assertive Parenting	Menu Planning
Building Maintenance	Microwave Cooking
Cake Decorating, Bread making, Pastries, Desserts	Most Senior Classes
Child Development	Music: Chorus, Orchestra
Childbirth Preparation	Musical Experiences
Desk-top Publishing	Music Appreciation
Effective Writing	Office Skills
Electronics	Plumbing, Heating, Air Conditioning
English as a Second Language	Sewing, Wardrobe Planning, Tailoring
Financial planning	Typing Certification
Floral Design	Upholstery
	Writer's Workshop

Free computer classes are offered seven days a week at the San Diego Metro Career Center, 8401 Aero Drive, Kearny Mesa, (858) 627-2545. Classes include Windows 95-XP, Intro to Computers, web page, Microsoft Office, Internet, Photo Shop, QuarkXPress, DreamWeaver, and many more. Hours are from 6:30 a.m. to 9 p.m. M-F, and until 4 p.m. on Saturdays and Sundays! Check schedule at communitycollege.net. There are four other career centers offering free computer classes: El Cajon, Encinitas, Escondido and South Bay. Certificate programs available.

ROP - Regional Occupational Program

The San Diego County Regional Occupational Program offers a variety of free job preparation classes for adults leading to careers in areas from agriculture to welding, including animal care, telecommunications, travel/tourism, commercial art, woodworking, computers, food service, manufacturing, electronics, engine repair, child care, banking, office professions, etc. To listen to recorded information and descriptions of dozens of courses, call the 24-hour information line, call the toll free line at (800) 479-4900x5. Classes are held in El Cajon, Linda Vista, Coronado, Chula Vista and North County. Over 50,000 enroll per year in SD County.

College One-Day Workshops (& Trips!)

Most colleges now offer short-term, non-credit workshops for personal enrichment or career advancement and credential programs. You may enroll at any of the colleges regardless of where you live. Most also offer one-day short trips to regional sights (Laguna Arts Festival, plays in Los Angeles, Getty Museum, etc.) To get on the mailing list to receive their free schedule of workshops, call the following numbers. I receive them all! I took a class on Tijuana at UCSD extended studies in the mid-70's and loved it. Am still taking classes, and teaching them, too.

Grossmont Extended Studies .... (619) 670-1980 x350
Southwestern Continuing Education .... (619) 482-8376
Mira Costa College Community Services .... (760) 757-2121x485
Palomar College Continuing Education .... (760) 744-1150
UCSD Extension (Web: extension.ucsd.edu) .... (858) 534-3400
SDSU Extended Studies .... (619) 594-5152
CSUSM Extended Studies .... (760) 750-4020
National University Community Education
   Mission Valley...... (619) 563-7292; Vista .... (619) 945-6292

Other Classes & Seminars For Fun & Learning

Learning Annex (downtown) .... (619) 544-9700
The Learning Annex is a private corporation with affiliations in Los Angeles, San Francisco, New York and Washington, DC. They offer a large variety of three-hour, low cost classes for fun or business. Hear nationally known speakers and authors. Call to be on the mailing list. I have taken MANY classes here. Taught many, too. Wanna free Learning Annex class? Volunteer to check in students at classes and earn credit for future classes.

For **free lectures**, check the *Reader's* "Guide to Local Events: Lectures" each Thursday. Lecture junkies follow this column with a passion, and head out to hear the free speakers at book stores, churches, etc. Also, check the Books section of the *Union-Tribune* on Sundays for the calendar of lectures by authors, book signings and other special author events including beer demos, food demos by cook books authors, workshops on how to publish your book, occasional musical performances, etc, plus many children's events. Barnes & Noble stores, Borders, Warwicks in La Jolla and Bay Books in Coronado host many author events. Many of the new book superstores have a Calendar of Events, listing classes, workshops and other happenings for the month. Ask for a copy at the register. Some stores have a mailing list.

Barnes & Noble University is offering free online classes ranging from Introduction to Jazz Music to How to Plan a Wedding.

Older Adult Workshops can usually be attended by anyone of any age, provided the 51% attending are seniors. Get on the mailing list of the senior center nearest you; watch for workshops in the Senior Scene column of the *Union-Tribune,* and check out *San Diego Seniors* calendar of events. Lots of free classes! I discovered and started attending senior classes in my neighborhood when I was 30! The La Mesa Senior Center has nonstop classes daily, mostly free, including self-healing, exercise, writing, Schedule of classes, call (619) 464-3761. For writing classes, call (619) 466-0622.

Free Education on the Internet a <u>free-ed.net</u>. This site offers free online courses, tutorials, study guides and lessons in 120 academic and vocational/technical topic areas including basic physics, or how to fix your car's engine, or how to write your own Web page. The courses are simple and straightforward.

Local College $Fees

San Diego ranks in the top 10 largest cities in the U.S., and ranks fourth in percentage of population age 25 years or older holding a bachelor's degree. San Francisco area ranked first with 37.3%; Washington, DC was second with 37.2; Boston was 3rd with 34.4, and San Diego was 4th with 34.0

Community college tuition fees are $11 per credit, or under $350 for one year of college for California residents (this may be going up); $110 per unit for non-residents. The California community colleges serve 1.7 million students at 108 campuses. California has the lowest fees in the nation! In New York, comparable fees are $2,557; in Texas, $931.

Mesa College Over 25,000 students   Web: <u>sdmesa.sdcc.cc.ca.us</u> ..... (619) 627-2600
City College (Downtown) Web: <u>city.sdccd.cc.ca.us</u> .... (619) 230-2400
Educational Cultural Complex (E. San Diego) .... (619) 527-5258
Miramar College, Web: <u>miramar.sdcc.cc.ca.us/</u> .... (619) 536-7800
Grossmont College, Web: <u>grossmont.gcccd.cc.ca.us</u> .... (619) 465-1700
Cuyamaca College, Web: <u>cuyamaca.net</u> .... (619) 670-1980
Palomar College (San Marcos & Escondido), Web: <u>palomar.edu</u> .... (760) 744-1150
Mira Costa College (Oceanside & Encinitas) Web: <u>miracosta.cc.ca.us</u> .... (760) 757-2121
Southwestern College .... (619) 421-6700

San Diego State University (SDSU) Web: <u>sdsu.edu</u> .   (619) 594-5200
California State University, San Marcos .... 760) 750-4000

Annual tuition and fees are about $1,500-$2,000 per year for residents. (There are 23 CSU campuses with over 400,000 enrolled.) Financial assistance available. Food and housing in university housing at SDSU will average about $6000 a year. Estimated standard total costs of one year at SDSU including tuition and fees, books and supplies, food and housing, transportation, miscellaneous and personal expenses:

Living with parents . . . . $9,500+
Living in university housing . . . . 14,900+
Living Off-Campus . . . . 14,500+

University of California, San Diego (UCSD) . . . . (619) 534-2230
UCSD ranks in the top 10 public universities. Web:.ucsd.edu
Annual tuition fees: about $3,834. Financial assistance available.

University of San Diego (USD) . . . . (619) 260-4600
Annual tuition and fees: about $21,988. Financial assistance available.

Point Loma Nazarene University (PLNU) Web: ptloma.edu 221-2200
Annual tuition: about $16,260. Financial assistance available.

Check with the above colleges and universities regarding their online education programs, distance learning, and other new programs.

There are a number of other private colleges and universities in San Diego where you can pick up a degree on weekends while holding down a full time job. Many financial aid packages available.

National University . . . . (619) 563-3100
Chapman University . . . . (619) 549-6021
United States International University . . . . (619) 635-4595
See Colleges, Universities /Schools in the Yellow Pages for more institutions

The cost of college text books averages around $600 or more per year. The cost of tuition and living on campus at Stanford, Yale, Harvard, Vassar and Bryn Mawr is about $30,000 a year, plus books, personal expenses and transportation. According to a recent College Board survey, two-year public college costs run about $1,394; four-year public colleges and universities, tuition and fees average $4,000; four-year private colleges and universities, tuition and fees average $30-50,000.

Other college information
Online classes are offered through local community colleges including Mira Costa, Palomar and the San Diego Community College District thru

Edu2go.com. Choices include computer, internet, small business and personal enrichment classes. Fees vary. Courses are non-credit; no letter grades are given. Students receive either a "complete" or "incomplete." Most courses run six weeks.

Over 5000 classes are offered through the **Open University at SDSU**. Gain college credit without the admission process. Anyone may attend any class without prerequisites. Apply for admission to the university simultaneously or later, (619) 594-5152. Web: ces.sdsu.edu

Seniors over age 60 may attend any class at SDSU for fun or credit towards a degree, free of charge; $3 processing fee per semester. Call (619) 594-6590 and ask for the **SDSU Over 60 Program**. YES!!! And, seniors over age 65 may attend Pt. Loma Nazarene College's SPICE (Senior Persons in College Education) Program free of charge. Take classes for credit or enjoyment. Call (619) 849-2273 for more information.

Online Education Universities are now offering a course of instruction online. Check these out: California Virtual U: a clearinghouse for online courses at UCLA, Berkeley, Stanford, etc., california.edu ; California State University Extended University, gateway.calstate.edu; San Diego Mesa College, sdmesa.sdccd.cc.ca.us;; Golden State University, cybercourses.ggu.edu. Take **free online courses at MIT** (Massachusetts Institute of Technology). Check current offerings at ocw.mit.edu/index.html

The College Board reports that bachelor degree recipients earn eighty percent more than high school graduates. Those holding law and medical degrees earn $5,000 or more a month than college graduates, on average. About 2/3 of full time undergraduates receive financial aid averaging $18,000 in federal loans.

Good web site for college students: collegeclub.com, millions of registered members. Everything from homework help to chat rooms, dating service, info on scholarships, lecture notes from university classes throughout the country, discussion on books, student auctions, etc. College Board Online, collegeboard.org; SAT and GRE test prep, Peterson.com.

Money for $College$

Millions and millions of dollars in grants and scholarships that don't have to be repaid is available every year for college students of all ages. Much of it is never awarded because no one applies for it, or it is applied for after the deadline, which is usually early in the spring prior to the fall semester.

Grant money and college loans are available to all American families, whether you earn $20,000 or $100,000. Home equity is no longer a factor in determining eligibility for free and low cost federal grants and loans. The federal government wants to grant or lend you money to get your education. The more education you have, the more society will benefit.

Grant money is a gift assistance with no obligation for work or repayment. Scholarships can be awarded for merit, heritage, occupational major, etc., and do not have to be reimbursed. Loans require a future obligation for repayment.

AmeriCorps is a federally funded agency founded by President Clinton for young people in their late teens and early 20s who volunteer their time to community improvement projects fighting hunger, poverty, illiteracy, homelessness and pollution. The program is like a domestic Peace Corps. They live in dorms with room and board and a stipend for expenses for ten months and perform community service. At the end of the year they are granted a $5,000 tuition scholarship from the federal government. How many kids can SAVE $5,000 in one year toward school tuition? Great opportunity. For more information, contact AmeriCorps at (800) 942-2677. There headquarters were here in San Diego at NTC for seven years until moving to Sacramento. Web: americorp.org.

Most scholarships have nothing to do with high scholastic grades. Many, many are available from industries to entice you into majoring in their field (Pillsbury has scholarships for those interested in the food industry, IBM offers scholarships for those entering the computer field; Tylenol offers scholarships to those entering the health field, etc); many are available to women and minorities to encourage them to compete in the academic world. You can save thousands if you're willing to do some legwork to gain the free money that is available for you. A woman told me she made $1000 a month from grants and scholarships while attending college.

Scholarships are available from a huge number of organizations: the **American Association of University Women** (AAUW) distributes about $4 million a year in fellowships, grants, and other educational awards. Check their web at: aauw.org. The **San Diego Women's Network** gives four $500 scholarships every fall and spring to women who are going to Palomar, Mesa and Grossmont Community Colleges. **Soroptomists International**, Optomists, Kiwanis, Lions, Rotary, the Assistance League and many other local civic and social organizations offer scholarships based on need or certain requirements. Major corporations and local businesses offer scholarships and grants: Target, Mervyns, Nordstrom, Nike, Vons, Ford Motors, Gateway, Qualcomm, Best Buy, Union Tribune, McDonald's, women's clubs, Padres, Chargers and hundreds *more*. Billions of dollars in grant and scholarship money goes unclaimed. Where do you find them? They will be listed in scholarship books at libraries, book stores and college financial aid offices, and online (see below).

Here is a GREAT tip: Contact the **Funding Information Center** at the **San Diego Foundation**, 1420 Kettner Boulevard, Suite 5500, San Diego, 92101, (619) 239-8815. They have a library with sources of various grants and scholarships of all sizes. The staff will personally assist you in locating grants appropriate to your needs on Mondays and Wednesdays (as of this writing). Check their web site for more information: sdfoundation.org. Most community college extended study programs offer a three-hour **workshop on scholarships**, grants and loans for higher education, for about $35, at least once a year. Call the colleges listed above. FastWeb.com's scholarship search will automatically match available scholarships to your personal profile.

The *Student Guide: Financial Aid Programs*, and *Funding Your Education* are free publications which describe federal grants, loans and work-study programs for college, vocational and technical school students. For information or to request a free application, call from the U.S. Department of Education **Student Aid Information Center** at (800) 433-3243, 7 days a week. the largest source of student aid in America, providing over $60 billion a year in grants, loans, and work-study assistance. At this site you'll find help for every stage of the financial aid process, whether you're in school or out of school: ed.gov/offices/OSFAP/Students/sfa.html. Also available on the web at: ed.gov.or pueblo.gsa.gov. Fill out the online application for federal student aid, fafsa.ed.gov. **California Student Aid Commission** information and applications at their web: csac.ca.gov/default.asp. **Federal Pell Grant** ($400 to $4,500), depending on your family's contribution (must be $2,100 or less to be eligible), does not have to be repaid, available to all undergraduate students including those attending college less than half time. For information, call (800) 433-3243. **Cal Grants** up to $5,200 per year are available from the State of California for qualifying individuals. If you are a California resident, your grade point average is better than 2.0, and your family income qualifies, you are eligible. Forms are available at all high school counseling offices and at college financial aid offices. Cal Grants are available to students graduating from high school who have submitted the Free Application for

Federal Student Aid (FAFSA) and the Cal Grant Grade Point Average Verification forms. Cal Grants cover full tuition at California State University or University of California and up to $8,832 at a private college. To students attending community colleges, grants of $1,551 pay for living expenses and educational-related supplies. Cal Grants are awarded based on family income levels and a high school grade point average of at least 3.0 for those students attending a four-year university. **Federal Supplemental Educational Opportunity Grant** (FSEOG) is based on financial need. Priority given to Pell Grant recipients. For further information, call (800) 433-3243. The American Council on Education, 1 Dupont Circle, NW, Washington, DC, (202)-939-9300, publishes the *Complete Grants Sourcebook for Higher Education,* which should be available at libraries and financial aid offices of high schools, community colleges, or directly from the American Council. *Bear's Guide to Finding Money For College* (Ten Speed Press) by John Bear, Ph.D.: offbeat, creative ways to finance your education. **Student loans**: Nellie Mae (New England Loans), the largest nonprofit provider of college loans in the country, offers free up-to-date information on low cost government loans and other loans for students and parents, (800) 634-9308. **Stafford (Federal) student loans**, formerly called Guaranteed Student Loans, are for dependent undergraduate students and are based on need. Students can borrow up to $2,625 for freshmen, $3,500 for sophomores, $5,500 for juniors and seniors, $8,500 for graduate students. Interest well below current rates. No interest while in school, no family income limits. For further information, call (800) 433-3243. **PLUS (Federal) student loans**, capped interest rate. No adverse credit history. For further information, call (800) 433-3243. **Perkins (Federal) Loans**, formerly known as national direct student loans. Borrow up to $3,000 a year, for a total of $15,000 for undergraduate study; $5,000 a year for graduate study. Interest is only 5 percent and doesn't start until the student leaves school. Inquire at the Financial Aid Office at any college. Check libraries and book stores for the *Directory of Financial Aid for Women* by Gail Ann Schlachter (Los Angeles Reference Service Press, Inc.).The Business and Professional Women's Foundation (BPWF) offers hundreds of thousands of dollars in semester scholarships of up to $100 for women seeking education for entry into or advancement in the work force. Last year, they awarded over 430 such scholarships. To be eligible, you must be a woman 25 years or older, a U.S. citizen, in need of financial assistance, be in an accredited program and be graduating within 24 months. For an application, send SASE, business size with two first class stamps to: BPW Foundation, 2012 Massachusetts Ave. NW, Washington, DC 20036. For tons more info on financial aid, calculators, and more, visit finaid.org. Under the new tax laws, you can deduct $3,000 for annual college tuition. The deduction will increase to $4,000 in 2004-5 for singles who have income below $65,000 and married below $130,000. Also, student loan interest has dropped to 5.5% or lower.

Other helpful information:

Golden Rule Insurance of Lawrenceville, Illinois offers **student medical insurance** for about $400 (depending on age) for a six-month policy, and pay 80% with a $500 deductible. Time Insurance of Milwaukee offers Student Select, with major medical coverage up to $100,000 for full time students for about 1/3 the cost of regular insurance. Check with your insurance agent on the above. Send your kid to **college for *free*** at one of the military academies: Naval Academy, West Point, Air Force Academy. Contact the academies directly for requirements at their website: nationalacademies.org. This works best if you have your heart set on going to an academy by the time your kid gets to junior high so you can cultivate the right elected officials for nomination. Free tuition, room and board and they give the students over $700 a month for expenses. Start **saving for your children's education** when they are young. Invest in a Coverdell or State 529 college savings plan, or both (tax free). The maximum annual contribution is $2000. See more at collegesavings.org. Check with your financial advisor about avoiding taxes on your child's investment income. Check into **prepaid, guaranteed tuition** at the university of your choice. Don't overlook going into the military to get the **G.I. bill**. I know a young gal who went into the army for four years and paid into her G.I. bill so that she got $48K for college when she got out. There are various options for paying in, and she chose the max so she could get the max. She said it wasn't easy to live on so little money for the first year she was in the army, but she has $1,200 a month FREE MONEY coming in for college now.

Chapter 10

HOW TO RAISE QUICK $CASH

Could you use a little extra cash for doing very little or next to nothing? Wanna fatten your wallet while having a good time? Well, you'll never get rich with the following ideas but you *can* raise come quick cash to ease the crunch, pay off some bills or just treat yourself to something nice. Try some of the following ways you can create extra cash:

Participate in **Market Research** focus groups and get paid for your opinion. Earn approximately $40-75-$150 cash (sometimes more!) for a one-time shot (usually two hours) of your time, sharing your opinion. Market research companies are paid by a client to find out YOUR opinion of their product or service. Qualified volunteers (each study has its own requirements) can participate in a variety of studies: taste-test new food products, fast foods, or restaurant meals; evaluate products, evaluate the effectiveness of products; evaluate product advertising; and more. You can share your opinion, meet interesting people, have a lot of fun, enjoy gourmet snacks and make a few bucks! (Some don't pay, but give free products to use (soap, diapers, etc.) A friend participated in a mock jury for three hours and was paid $75; another jury was 6 hours for $150; another discussed ordering fitness wear from a catalog for two hours for $50; another taste-tested cereals for $50; another evaluated new car advertising for $50; another friend discussed ordering postage stamps through the mail for $75; another gave recommendations for services wanted by small business owners for $75; another evaluated five kinds of vanilla ice cream for $35 in 20 minutes. For opportunities to participate in market research, check the *Reader* classified ads ("Notices" or "Personals") and display ads on Thursdays. Also check the *Union-Tribune* classified ads ("Personals"), usually on weekends. Here are a few companies to call to inquire about how to get in the data base to participate in their market research focus groups: (see next page)

Analysis Research . . . . . . (only occasional focus groups		((858) 268-4800
Answers Research Corp . . . . Email: info@answers.com		(760) 792-4660
Directions in Research		(619) 299-5883
Flagship Research		(619) 849-1111
Fogerty Group (register at Kobey's Swapmeet)		(619) 718-7500
Jagorda . . . . N. County & Kearny Mesa		(888) 569-0424
Luth Research . . . . . . Call recruiter after 4pm daily only/		(619) 234-5884 x8028
San Diego Surveys . . . . Call after 4pm (800) 895-1225/		(619) 265-2361
Taylor Research . . . . Register at taylorresearch.com or		(619) 299-6368

Following are several more creative ways to pick up a few extra bucks, some of which could turn into full time careers:

Audition for acting in TV commercials and bit parts. Check the *Reader* classified ads ("Stage Notes") for places and dates to audition. Check the library for books on how to get a job in movies or modeling. **Be An Extra** in movies and TV shows that are filmed in San Diego. You won't get rich, but you could have a lot of fun. Don't I wish I had been in "Titanic." Call the casting hotlines for their casting interview dates. Some will want pictures, so get pictures. Don't let them take photos for you as that is often a scam. Get a friend to take a couple rolls or get some made by Glamour Shots (see Photography).

Background San Diego, 4775 Ruffin Road, Kearny Mesa	(858) 974-8970
Tina Real Casting, 3108 5th Ave, Hillcrest	Hotline (619) 298-1766
Screen Actor's Guild (SAG) Hotline	(858) 278-7695
(SAG Membership, about $1360+) Web: sag.org	

The Learning Annex offers classes in how to become an extra in movies and TV. Call (619) 544-9700 for more information. **Show Biz Jobs** Check out some show biz jobs at showbizjobs.com **Get Free Rent** Become an apartment manager. Apartment complexes offer managers a discount on rent, free rent or free rent plus salary. **Host A Student** Be a host parent (married or single, OK) for international students who come here to study English at language schools (not local colleges) for varying lengths of time. In the summer, many students come for short periods of two weeks to a month or two; the rest of the year, the students are here for about a month to several months. A private room is required by most schools, with a private or shared bath. Most students want half-board, which includes a light breakfast and a full dinner with the family, although an occasional student will want only breakfast, or no meals. The home must be in a convenient location for the student to take public transportation to school. Check "Language Schools" in the *Yellow Pages*. and look for schools with host programs that are in your area or convenient by bus to the school. Or, post a notice at the International Student Center at a local college. **Participate in Medical Research** Participate in medical research and get paid. One study paid $100 a night to sleep hooked up to a brain wave machine, etc. A student did it 30 times for $3000, which really helped with his tuition. Recently, they were paying $200 a night!! See chapter on Health for more on participating in medical research/clinical studies. Be a **mystery shopper**. (I am very pleased with myself for what I found on this topic!) Stores and businesses need mystery shoppers (paid shoppers who evaluate employees the quality of customer service, quality of merchandise, cleanliness and price, etc). It's done for improving service and/or sales, research and price comparison. Companies that need this service include Fortune 500 companies, retail stores, airports, apartments, banks, grocery outlets, golf courses, amusement parks, entertainment, and other businesses. You can apply to a "mystery shopping service" that acts as an agent for the above businesses. After signing up, you will receive assignments based on your application and interests. As a beginner, you won't be assigned the deluxe jobs like shopping at Nordstrom or visiting a posh spa or five-star hotel. You'll have to work your way up and prove yourself reliable and capable. A typical first assignment may pay only about $15 or so for a visit. You will be given a check list of items to evaluate, which you will email to the mystery shopping company you work for. Some companies may require you to have a laptop and a digital camera. Airlines use shoppers on board flights, real estate companies want to know if singles are being treated the same as couples, luxury hotels need to evaluate their services, etc. A restaurant may want you to dine, then fill out a several page questionnaire regarding everything from how you were greeted upon entering to the temperature of your soup (warm, hot, not so warm, etc.) to the cleanliness of the restrooms. Some chain restaurants get "shopped" a half dozen times a month. Caution: Don't get involved with a shopper company that requires you to call a 900 number or a long distance number or requires any money up front from you. They are usually SCAMS and make money off YOU. The Learning Annex, (619) 544-9700, offers a class in mystery shopping from time to time, and there are several books on Mystery Shopping (check amazon.com, used bookstores, libraries) that list companies that will hire inexperienced shoppers. Check the *Yellow Pages* under "Shopping Service-Protective, Price Comparison" for local companies that are hiring "shoppers" including the Bass Co. Shopping Service, (619) 440-3563. Also, check out this locally-owned Web site: professionalmysteryshoppers.com. For a fee, one gets lifetime enrollment in the program and direct access to over 400 actively working mystery shopping services. The owner of this site, whom I've met, gets some very fancy assignments! La Quinta Spa and Resort, La Costa Spa, Dick's Last Resort downtown, Rock Bottom in La Jolla, Ruby's Diner and El Torito's Friday night margarita. She says: "Hands down, the best lunch was at Zodiac in Neiman Marcus at Fashion Valley. I've gotten free clothes from the Limited, sinful chocolate from Godiva, and train trips all along the coast." Mystery shopping is a costly service for businesses and many are starting to use a customer feedback system where the customer fills out a questionaire and turns it in by phone, internet or mail, and receives a discount coupon or other small compensation. Next, have a **yard sale**. If you advertise in the classified ads of the *Union/Tribune*, the *Reader* or your neighborhood newspaper, you'll end up with tons of cars in front of your house very early in the morning! Put up good signs at nearby intersections with date, time, address and arrows pointing in the direction of the sale. Print your signs with an inch-wide felt pen (really easy to read from a distance), available at office supply stores and drug stores. Price everything about 10-20% of original retail value. Take more expensive things to a consignment store or sell them through classified ads. Most sales net $200 or more, often $600+, depending on how much accumulation you have to sell. Get your neighbors to join in. The more the merrier. Have an annual event. Do as a lot of people are doing: attend yard sales, rummage sales, estate sales and auctions and buy up the great buys to resell. Take them home, mark them up, and have a yard sale of your own every few months (or sell your stuff at the swap meet or at a consignment store). Hold **garage sales for others** for about 20-25% of the take. **Sell Your No-Longer-Wanted Clothing** Clean out your closet and sell your unwanted clothes at Buffalo Exchange in Pacific Beach or one of the consignment stores that pay cash up front for used clothing. (If you leave things on consignment, you usually get about 60% of the selling price, but if you want cash today, you will only get about 40% of the agreed-upon price. So, if you take in a sweater that you and the store determine will sell for about $10, you'll get $4, today.) They are "picky" about what they will take, so call first and tell them what you have. A smart move is to ask: "What are you looking for?" They sometimes drive a hard bargain, so be prepared. See chapter on "Resale and Consignment" for stores that pay cash up front, etc. **Consign It** Take your surplus/unwanted furniture, decorator items and dinnerware to a furniture consignment store. You usually get 60% of the agreed-upon selling price, the store gets 40%. You usually sign a three-month contract, and the price gets lowered 10% at the end of each month until it sells. Most items sell, but some things do get returned at the end of 90 days, if unsold. **Ebay** Sell your surplus stuff on Ebay. I read an article that said everyone should be selling on Ebay, and that eventually, everyone WILL be selling on Ebay. You can find someone to sell for you at pages.ebay.com/tradingassistants. People are buying up new overstocks and selling them on ebay. (See Internet Shopping for more on this.) Look for books on *How to Start an Antique or Used Furniture Biz, How to Buy & Sell at Swapmeets*, etc. **Swap Meets** Think of something to sell at the swap meet. Stop by a swap meet office and ask for their free publication on how/where to buy wholesale, and info on how to sell at swap meets. Book stores and libraries have additional information on how to sell at flea markets and where to get wholesale merchandise. Go to google.com and type in "wholesale merchandise" and up will come thousands of sources. Refine it from there. I was impressed with the wholesale resources they have in the downtown library's Business Book section. People sell goods at swap meets to supplement incomes, to make a living or for the social aspect of it. **Plants** Grow house plants or tomatoes or lemons or avocados, etc., in your yard for profit. Sell them on weekends at your own yard sale or become a local supplier for a nearby restaurant or small grocer. You can make a career out of tending plants for rich people or offices. **Pets** Breed pedigreed dogs or cats or tropical fish or birds. Pick up a "how to" book at the library or book store. Some breeds sell for several hundred dollars! For a list of sweepstakes to enter, got to ragstoriches.com, sweepstakesonline.com, redhotsweeps.com. **Cook** Make homemade soups or desserts to sell to local restaurants and pick up some extra bucks. I have a friend who makes and sells hot sauce for chicken wings. He sells it by the gallon to restaurants. You'll need to take a class at a community college/adult school (just a few hours) to get your food handler's certificate. **Moonligh**t Get a part-time job in a retail store, restaurant or business at night or on weekends. Millions of Americans have second jobs. **Seasonal Jobs** Get a seasonal job (summer, Christmas, etc.) Work at the post office or UPS during the holiday crunch. (Good pay, too.) Do **free-lance** work in your field. Advertise your services in the neighborhood newspaper: typing, carpentry, accounting, resume writing, etc. Look into **overtime** work at your job. **Move Up** Consider getting a better job, with more pay, more benefits. **Rent A Room** Rent a spare room, or get a room mate. **Provide A Service** Do housecleaning, child care, painting, pet care, hauling, yard work, sewing, running errands. **Catering** Sign up for part-time work with a caterer. **Petitions** Get people to sign petitions at stores. See *Reader* classified ads for job listings. **Work Conventions** Sign up to work part-time at conventions. Call the San Diego Convention Center and ask about opportunities. Be a **cash winner** by listening to local DJs on the radio. I have a friend who is really into this and won cash, a cruise for four to Puerta Vallarta, Padres t-shirts, movie tickets, theater tickets, dinners at restaurants and much more, just by listening to the radio (or TV), and signing up at station's Web sites, earn points, etc. Get on the e-mailing list of local radio and tv stations (& the Union-Trib) for great contests, giveaways, tickets, etc. I heard someone won a JAGUAR ($80K) from one of the local stations. Where was I on that one? Prepare Taxes Learn to prepare tax returns and make extra money during tax season. Instruction is usually provided by the employer, free, and takes only a few weeks. Look in the *Yellow Pages* for tax preparation agencies. **Work At Polls** on election day and earn about $30-40 a day. Call the Registrar of Voters, (858) 565-5800. **Deliver Flowers** Deliver flowers on special occasions such as Valentine's Day, Mother's Day, etc. Call a major florist near you. **Day Care** Start a day care center. Get a "how to" book at the library or book store. **Deliver newspapers** for the *Union-Tribune* or other publication. I know a mom who delivered newspapers to help pay her law school tuition. **Elder Care** Become an elder sitter. Many elderly need attendants. Take a short course at an adult school on how to care for the elderly(it's just a few weeks long). I know a flight attendant who slept at an elderly woman's house every night and was relieved by the next attendant in the morning, for $125 a night. There are many elderly job opportunities as this is one of the fastest growing professions. Call ElderHelp and inquire, (619) 284-9281. **Be A Driver** Transport elderly people and pets. People who can't drive would gladly pay for transportation. Mothers who work need someone to drive their children to band practice, take pets to groomers, or someone to be at home when the repairman comes. Post your services at a local church or nearby laundromat. **Board Pets** Care for cats and dogs in your own home while owners are away. **Census Taker** Counts heads for the Census Bureau every ten years. It's a federal job, with good hourly pay.

Get that lined up well in advance of 2010. **Apply For Grant** or student loan and head back to college. (See previous chapter). This is a real good bet. **Borrow money** from friends or relatives who may be more willing to give you a low or no interest loan and a flexible repayment schedule. Borrow on your whole **life insurance** policy which has a cash value if it has been in force for any length of time. **Baking Contests** Enter the Pillsbury Bake-Off Contest. The grand prize is $1 million, the largest ever awarded. Head for the library or a book store and ask for a book on how to enter cooking contests and others. Be a **surrogate mother** or egg donor. Contact the Center for Surrogate Parenting, (800) 373-9525. They pay very well! If you want to earn big bucks, consider employment in **Iraq.** They are rebuilding there after the war. You can earn two, three or more times the salaries paid here in San Diego. There are many job listings abroad in construction, electronics, health, teaching and all the support services in the *Union-Trib* and *L.A. Times*. Many young people are heading overseas for a few years to make and save enough money to buy a house when they return, and set themselves up for life. Book stores and libraries have many books on "seeking **employment abroad**," complete with names and addresses of American companies who are hiring abroad. Take a computer and/or set of encyclopedias with you and catch up on your reading (because there's not much else to do in some countries.) A friend whose daughter and husband are both registered nurses headed to Saudi Arabia where they made several times as much money as they can here. Another option for making extra bucks: Drive an 18-wheeler (truckers make LOTS of money). This isn't a life sentence, it's a short term opportunity to make a lot of money! **Making Money At Home** Head for the business book section of the library or book store, and find a book on ideas for home-based businesses you can start on a shoe string. There are dozens of titles available in this field, especially how to make money with your computer. There are also guides for young people that contain useful advice to help ambitious teens start profitable business enterprises. There are many titles to choose from, and it's never too early to have your kids learn about making money!

Plasma Centers Earn varying amounts: possibly $20 + $10, first visit; $45 second, $20 on third, or more (up to $200) by selling your blood plasma to blood centers. They draw whole blood, separate the plasma, and return the red blood cells to you.

```
Alpha Plasma Centers  . . . . . . . . Natl. City (619) 474-4644 / SDSU area (619) 265-7550
Pyramid Biologics . . . . . . . . . . . . . . . . . . . . . . . . . . . . . . . . . . . . . (619) 298-4011
Bayer Corp  . . . . . . . . . . . . . . . . . . . . . . . . . . . . . . . . . . . . (619) 233-7763
```

Some restrictions apply. Certain antibodies are worth more hepatitis B. Qualified Rh negative mothers can earn up to $300 a month.

Chapter 11
RESTAURANTS FOR LESS

Since dining out is the Number One Pastime these days, here are a bunch of restaurants where you'll get our money's worth and then some! Check out the opportunities for half-price dining, the fun "all-you-can-eat" restaurants, Sunday brunches that won't break the budget, great seafood finds (because I wanted to know about them!) and some fabulous happy hours deals.

Half-Price Dining

Give this a try for three months: DON'T EAT OUT WITHOUT A TWO FOR ONE COUPON. PERIOD. (That's what they're for, Silly! Use them!)

Your local neighborhood newspaper has a number of "two-for-one" (buy one/get one free) coupons every week. My local paper, the *Beacon*, always has several, and the beauty of it all is, of course, they're all nearby! Also, check the coupons in the "Night & Day" section of the *Union-Trib* every Thursday, and the *Reader* has many every Thursday, as well. Check your junk mail, too. There are usually three or four coupons in the mail every week along with the *Pennysaver*. Don't overlook the discount coupons that are in the back of the *Yellow Pages*! And, do you know about restaurants.com? Go there, click on San Diego, and you'll find TONS of $25 restaurant gift certificates for half off. An even better deal is to go to Ebay.com, click on "gift certificates," then refine it to "restaurant gift certificates" and voila. You will find some restaurant.com certificates that are being auctioned. I have gotten three for the Princess Grill on India for only $5.25 and a little more. When you win, you pay and they send you an email with an address to go to where you print out the certificate, so you can use them tonight. No waiting. Don't bid over 10 bucks because you can buy them outright at restaurant.com for half price anyway. The concept of "buy one/get one free" coupons works for restaurants and they want you to use them. An empty table yields nothing. They enjoy the business they wouldn't have otherwise, so no one should feel guilty about using them.

Then, there is the awesome *Entertainment* coupon book, ($40; see chapter on Resources for where to purchase them), with hundreds of "buy one/get one free" coupons and some with 25% off, etc. The *Entertainment* book is divided into three sections for food: Fine Dining, Casual Dining, and Informal Dining & Carry-out. For fine dining restaurants, no coupon is required. You use your Entertainment membership card (and get $20 off the bill!) while dining at some of San Diego's best known great restaurants like Tom Ham's Lighthouse and the Boathouse on Harbor Island; Humphreys La Jolla, Torreyana Grille; Passage to India in Rancho Bernardo, Neimans in Carlsbad; plus many others all over the county. The *Entertainment* book has coupons for casual dining, (Sammy's Woodfire Pizza, Sports City, Panda Palace, and many more. The fast food & carry out section includes coupons for Krispy Kreme, Fins, Dominos, Del Taco, Baskin Robbins, Cold Stone Ice Cream, Subway and most major hamburger chains. Coupon books pay for themselves by using them just a few times. Tipping on the total bill is expected; the restaurant has given you a discount, so treat the employees well, because "what goes around, comes around. . ."

Many restaurants offer "early bird specials," usually between 4-6 p.m. before the regular dinner crowd crunch. You'll like the price, and you can be off to get your half price theater tickets at ArtsTix. If you're a senior, don't forget to ask if there is a "senior" special. See which is the better deal.

All-You-Can-Eat Restaurants

Whether you want American, Italian, Chinese, Polish, Thai, Greek, Indian, Middle Eastern, Polynesian, Afghan, Japanese cuisine or just a great fresh salad bar, you'll get your money's worth at the following:

Acapulco Restaurants, 2467 Juan Street in Old Town, (619) 260-8124; big Mexican buffet lunch called the Pronto Buffet with taco station, salads, soups, enchiladas, many menu items, desserts, $6.99. Other locations in Clairemont, San Marcos, Rancho Bernardo and Escondido.

Azul, 1250 Prospect, La Jolla, (858) 454-9616; lunchtime buffet, Tues--Sat, 11-2:30pm. California cuisine with a Mediterranean flare. Delicious crusty breads, humus and dips, grilled veggies, salads and a hot entree. The gorgeous view of La Jolla Cove is free; the buffet is $11.95. Very special.

Bahia Café at the Bahia Hotel, 998 W. Mission Bay Drive, (858) 539-7635. All-you-can-eat prime rib buffet on Saturdays with potatoes, fresh vegetables, pastas and salads, $16.95. (Whadda deal.)

Bali Hai, 2230 Shelter Island Drive, (619) 222-1181, serves a luau buffet luncheon with Polynesian and American dishes, three main entrees, chicken and beef. One day a week they have fish; call Monday morning to find out which day. Salads, desserts, Monday-Friday, 11:30-3pm, $8.95. Seniors, $6.50. The view of the bay and downtown is to die for, and definitely a favorite spot because of it. In the bar, try the Blue Mystique drink that is huge and gorgeous; two share and sip with two straws.

Buffalo Joe's, 600 Fifth Ave, downtown, (619) 236-1616; All-U-Can-Eat Ribs on Sundays, 4-10pm, $9.95 per person. Fries, more. Popular place.

Café India, 3760-5 Sports Arena Blvd., Pt. Loma, (619) 224-7500. Vegetarian buffet, 4 entrees, curries, soup, bread, dessert, lunch weekdays, $6.95; 11-4p.m.; Sat. and Sun., all day, $9.95; buffet dinner nightly, $9.95.

China King has a 16 course Chinese buffet for $4.95 lunch at 1041 4th Ave, downtown next to Horton Plaza, (619) 233-3389; dinner, $5.95.

Cottage Café, 2351 5th Ave, downtown, (619) 696-0071. Polish buffet includes pirogies, potato pancakes, stuffed cabbage, stroganoff, polish sausage, mashed potatoes, chicken paprikish, borscht, salads; lunch, Mon-Fri, $8.95, 11:30-3pm.

Dragon House, 2662 Garnet Ave., Pacific Beach, (858) 272-8788, has a 40-item menu oriental buffet with soup, hot entrees, salads, desserts, $5.30 lunch until 3pm; dinner $6.29 until 9pm.   Seven days.

Fairouz Café, 3166 Midway Drive, (619) 225-0308. All you can eat vegetarian lunch, 7 days, til 5pm, $6.99, and menus vary with salads, humus, beans, eggplant, rice, marinated vegetables, tabouleh, spinach, lentil and chicken lemon soup. Dinner includes chicken, lamb, beef, eggplant, and other regional specialties for $11.99, or vegetarian for $9.99.

Godfather Pizza has an all you can eat lunch buffet with pizza, salad bar, potato wedges, breadsticks, dessert pizza & beverage, $5.49 for lunch daily; $6.49 for dinner, Mondays and Tuesdays only.

317

Greek Town 345 West Main, El Cajon, (619) 442-9708. All you can eat Greek buffet with lemon chicken, spanikopita, pastitsio, grape leaves, lamb shanks, skewered sticks of meat, 50 items; Lunch, $6.95; dinner, $7.95.

Home Town Buffet, 9 locations including 5881 University Ave. at College, (619) 583-7373, plus Santee, Clairemont, San Marcos, Chula Vista, Oceanside, National City, El Cajon. Full buffet with standards like meatloaf, chicken & dumplings, fried chicken, baked fish, ham, whipped potatoes, beverage, dessert. Lunch, $7.32; dinner, $10.01. Senior discount, too.

Mandarin Plaza, 3760 Sports Arena Blvd, Pt. Loma, (619) 224-4222; has a 20-foot lunch buffet bar with over 25 items plus soup & salad bar; $5.25, seven days, 11-4 pm. Early bird special 4-6pm daily except Sunday, $5.99. After 6pm and Sundays, $7.29. No MSG.

Mandarin Szechwan, 3373 Rosecrans (Midway & Rosecrans) Pt. Loma), (619) 224-3838, oriental buffet luncheon with beef, chicken and seafood dishes seven days, 20 items plus salad bar, $5.49 til 3pm; dinner, $6.99.

 Sizzler, with many locations in San Diego including Midway & Rosecrans, Pt. Loma, (619) 224-3347, has an all-you-can-eat salad bar for lunch or dinner that is enormous, with over 50 items to choose from including hot dishes, chicken wings, onion rings, soups, hot pasta, taco bar, pasta salads, fruit and vegetable salads, and desserts. Menu items such as steak or chicken are available for an additional charge but you don't need anything more!   Monday through Friday, $4.99 for lunch, 11-4pm ; $8.29 dinner and all day Sunday. Seniors, $ 6.99 includes drink.

Soup Plantation, located at 3960 W. Pt. Loma Boulevard, (619) 222-7404, 6161 Mission Gorge Road, (619) 280-7087; 9158 Fletcher Parkway, (619) 462-4232; Rancho Bernardo, several other locations. Great salad bar includes Caesar and won ton chicken salads, build-your-own salad items, six assorted soups and chili, baked potato works, a bread bar with assorted freshly baked muffins and brownies, pasta bar, and a fruit and yogurt bar. Lunch until 4 p.m. for $6.99 includes soup and salad; dinner is $8.49. AAA discount, 10%. Senior discounts: 10%; 20% between 4-5 p.m. The best deal is their coupons in the slicks in Sunday's *Union-Trib*.

Thai Café, 4722 Clairemont Mesa Blvd., (858) 270-8303. Fresh salads, Pad Thai, sauteed shrimp, glass noodles, peanut chicken, stir fry, roast pork w/egg, orange chicken, curries, pork with peppers, eggplant, Thai green beans; seafood items, tofu, etc. Delicious variety. Lunch, $5.99; dinner, $7.99, Mon-Fri; Sat, Sun and Holidays, all day, $7.99.

Todai, 2828 Camino Del Rio S., Mission Valley, (619) 299-8954; 200 foot Japanese seafood buffet, sushi, lobster thermidor, shrimp cocktail, fresh salmon, scallops, mussels, oysters, shashimi, tempura shrimp, fruit bar, $12.95 lunch, $22.95 dinner, seniors, 20% discount on dinners only. Sunday lunch, $14.99; dinner buffet, $23.95.

Tom Ham's Lighthouse, 2150 Harbor Island Drive, (619) 291-9110. Beautiful harbor view, big buffet, good value, $18.50; Seniors, $6.95.

Sunday Buffet Brunches

So many of the all-you-can-eat brunches in San Diego fall into the extravagant category, costing well over $20 (**Humphrey's**, $24.95, (619) 224-3577; **Aviara Four Seasons**, $35; (760) 603-6800; **Hotel Del**, $39.95, (619) 435-6611; **Westgate Hotel**, (619) 238-1818, $32.95). But, here are several wonderful ones that are beautiful, bountiful but not that pricey.

Acapulco Restaurants, 2467 Juan Street in Old Town, (619) 260-8124; big Mexican buffet brunch with omelet station, taco station, salads, soups, enchiladas, many menu items, desserts, $13.99.

El Torito, 8910 Villa La Jolla Dr, (858) 453-4115, 445 Camino Del Rio S., (619) 296-6154; also in La Mesa, Mission Valley, Mira Mesa,, Oceanside, Rancho Bernardo & Chula Vista). Buffet from 9-2 p.m. includes 12 Mexican specialties, ceviche, corn cake, tamales, enchiladas, fish of the day, barbecue ribs, chicken ranchero, hot vegetables, omelet bar, sausage, waffles, sundae bar, Mexican pastries, fruit salads, tossed salads, carnitas, fresh taco bar, beans, rice, champagne, desserts, $12.99.

Bali Hai, located at 2230 Shelter Island Drive, (619) 222-1181, a favorite restaurant because of the incredible view of the city and bay, serves a Sunday buffet brunch until 2 p.m. for $16.95 includes champagne, ham, eggs, sausage, pastries as well as a variety of oriental and traditional buffet specialties in a tropical setting.

Bay Club, 2131 Shelter Island Drive, (619) 224-8888, serves a buffet breakfast in an elegant marina setting, daily til 10:30 a.m. and Sundays til ll a.m., with omelettes or eggs to order, fruit, potatoes, breakfast meats, Danish or pancakes, cereal, coffee, juice, $9.95.

Fairouz Café & Gallery, 3166 Midway Drive, (619) 225, 0308; Vegetarian buffet lunch 7 days a week including Sundays, $6.99, 11 a.m. - 5 p.m..

After 5p.m., vegetarian dinner buffet is $9.99; buffet with meat, $11.99. Frequent discount coupons are in the *Reader* and the *Union-Trib*.

Ginza Sushi/Shangai, Hazard Center, Friars Road at 163, (619) 297-8282. Fresh sushi and Chinese specialties and champagne, $11.95, 11-3pm.

Chuey's Café, 1894 Main St, under Coronado Bridge, (619) 234-6937. Famous old place with Mexican brunch including egg station, bacon sausage, hash browns, French toast, enchiladas, rice, beans, tortillas, coffee and soft drinks, $7.50; children, $3.50.

Hamburger Mary's buffet brunch 308 University, Hillcrest, (619) 491-0400; omelet, meats, salads, pasta, fruits, desserts, $16.95 10-1:30pm.

Pacific Beach Bar & Grill, 860 Garnet, PB, (858) 272-4745. Great Mexican buffet; outdoor dining on patio, $9.95, 9-1pm; $8.95 before 10am.

Quails Inn, 1035 La Bonita, San Marcos, (760) 744-2445. Award winning buffet includes seafood salad bar, lamb, ham, pastas, eggs, the works, $14.95, 9:30am-3pm. (Weekdays, $11.95).

Tom Ham's Lighthouse, 2150 Harbor Island Drive, (619) 291-9110. Big buffet, good value, beautiful harbor view, $15.95.

Sheraton Four Point Hotel, 8110 Aero Drive, (858) 277-8888, really a fabulous spread, carving table, tons of food, for $16.95, 10-1:30pm.

Todai, 2828 Camino Del Rio S., Mission Valley, (619) 299-8954; 200 foot Japanese seafood buffet, sushi, lobster thermidor, shrimp cocktail, fresh salmon, scallops, mussels, oysters, sashimi, tempura shrimp, fruit bar, $12.95 lunch, $22.95 dinner, seniors, 20% discount on dinners only. Sunday brunch, $14.99; Sunday dinner buffet, $23.95.

Troy's, 10450 Friars Road, (619) 281-7741. Eggs plus about 20 Greek items including Baklava, and American items, $11.95; Sundays, 10-2pm.

Viejas Casino, 5000 Willows Rd, Alpine, (619) 445-5400; fabulous spread, very deluxe gourmet items, desserts, for $10.95, 9am-4pm. In the Sunrise Diner, they have steak & eggs for $4.99, 24 hours a day.

Barona Casino, 1000 Wildcat Canyon Rd., Lakeside, (619) 443-2300; all you can eat buffet, Sundays, 10am-10pm; omelets, breakfast meats, pastries, plus soups, carving station, seafood, meatloaf, several cooked vegetables, salad bar, dessert bar, tons of food, $12.99.

Sycuan Casino, 5469 Dehesa Rd., El Cajon, (619) 445-6002; Sunday brunch with Belgian waffles, seafood, carving stations, etc., $12.95, all day.

Great Seafood Finds

For you seafood lovers, here are deals you won't want to miss:

Todai, 2828 Camino Del Rio S., Mission Valley, (619) 299-8954; 200 foot Japanese seafood buffet, sushi, lobster thermidor, shrimp cocktail, fresh salmon, scallops, mussels, oysters, sashimi, tempura shrimp, fruit bar, $12.95 lunch, $22.95 dinner, seniors, 20% discount on dinners only. Sunday lunch, $14.99; dinner buffet, $23.95.

Boathouse, 2040 Harbor Island Drive, (619) 291-8011, offers lobster night for $9.95 every Wednesday from 5pm on but they run out by about 8:30pm, so go early for this one. Not a huge lobster, but all is delightful. Also, they have prime rib night for $9.95 every Friday from 5pm on.

Onami Seafood Restaurant, Mission Valley Shopping Center next to Robinson-May (619) 295-9774; Carlsbad and Escondido, too. Unbelievable, large seafood buffet with lobster, jumbo shrimp, snow crab, fresh clams, salmon, tempura, teriyaki, sushi and sashimi, oriental salads, desserts, beverages. Lunch, $12.95; dinner, $21.95.

Barrett Café (since 1946), 34 miles southeast of San Diego on California 94 at the corner of Barrett Lake Road, (619) 468-3416. This is a popular eatery that serves an all-you-can-eat fish dinner daily, from 11-8 p.m., which includes cod fish, hush puppies, wheat pilaf, refried beans and salad. Natives and tourists from all over the world come to sample this fish fry at $12.95; $10.95 seniors.

Lael's at Hyatt Regency, Harbor Dr. & Market St., downtown, (619) 687-6066; All-you-can-eat deluxe seafood buffet, loaded, every Friday, $23.95.

Rolfy's Bistro at the Sheraton Four Point, 8110 Aero Drive, (277-8888-x7090, has an all you can eat seafood buffet every Friday night, $32, featuring smoked salmon roulade, smoked oysters, shrimp, smoked trout, mussels plus mahi mahi, crab legs, clam chowder, bouillabaisse, seafood pastas, salads, carving station with pepper steak.

Rubio's Baja Grill, 35+ locations including 3555 Rosecrans, (619) 223-2631. The originator of the fish burrito was Rubio himself. A real San Diego success story. Fish burrito and fish taco plate with rice and beans, $4.79 includes tax. Fast food environment, but the food is usually good and the salsa is supurb.

Brigantine, 2725 Shelter Island Drive, (619) 224-2871, and other locations including Old Town, Del Mar, La Mesa, Coronado and Escondido. Special happy hour prices in the lounge/bar on seafood items including jumbo shrimp cocktail, $5.95; fish taco, $2.50; raw oysters, $5.98; Calamari strips, $4.95; clam chowder, $2.95; garlic bread, $1.25 Tuesday through Saturday, 4-7p.m. Sunday & Monday, 3 p.m. to closing! Love it!

Humphrey's, 2241 Shelter Island, (619) 224-3577; happy hour is 4:30-6:30 p.m., Monday-Friday. One dollar off most drinks; two fried shrimp or oysters for $1; ceviche, $1; fish taco, $1; 2 roast beef cocktail sandwiches, $1; plus other specialty hors d'oeuvres in a lovely marina setting. Saturday happy hour offers half off the appetizers menu. Sundays are Jazz Sundays with a $6 cover charge in the bar after 4pm. Jazz starts at 7:30pm and there in no additional charge for the happy hour buffet, free from 5:30-6:30pm.

Torreyana Grille, Hilton La Jolla Torrey Pines, (858) 558-1500. Beautiful seafood buffet including peel & eat shrimp, exquisite cuisine with gourmet dishes including salmon, swordfish, crab legs, shrimp, mussels, halibut, calamari, baby lobster, pasta station, marinated veggies, fruits, desserts, on the last Friday of the month only, special price: $31.95. The **Westgate** and **Aviara** have deluxe seafood buffets on Fridays, too.

Life is not complete until you've tried the fried fish sandwich or a *fresh* tuna sandwich on the greatest sour dough fresh-baked bread at **Point Loma Seafoods**, 2805 Emerson St., Pt. Loma, (619) 223-1109. Great chowders, seafood platters and salads, and a complete fresh fish market with live lobsters. Eat outside by the boats in the marina or in the covered area.

Hudson Bay Seafood, 1403 Scott Street, Pt. Loma. Great small casual restaurant on the bay with clam chowder, crab cakes, calamari, scallops, fish tacos, etc. Popular place. Indoor eating or on the patio on the bay.

Special prices on many oyster bar items during happy hour at **Quiigs** in Ocean Beach, 5083 Santa Monica, Ocean Beach, on the ocean, (619) 222-1101, 4 -7 p.m. Great view, great sunsets, great place to watch the ocean during storms, $3.25 champagne; great clam chowder, $2.95 bowl; jumbo shrimp cocktail, $5.95, oyster shooters, $1.50; garlic bread, $1.75. Calamari strips, $3.95; artichoke & shrimp, $4; Margarita, $3.25; wine,$3.75.

World Famous **Puerto Nuevo** Mexican style lobster is served with rice and beans (and limones) at several restaurants in a group off the right hand side of the road a few miles south of Rosarito Beach. Ask for broiled or boiled, because most of them cook the lobster in *oil*. The best view of the ocean is from the Lobster House, with a 180-degree ocean view.

Some of the best seafood restaurants in San Diego offer "two-for-one"coupons in the *Entertainment* coupon book!! (See *"Resources."*)

Happy Hours

Happy Hour is a special period in the afternoon, generally too late for lunch and too early for dinner, when restaurants offer reduced prices on drinks and an array of complimentary (or low cost) hors d'oeuvres. Happy Hour is usually held Monday through Friday from about 5-7 p.m., or 4-6 p.m. A few restaurants offer happy hour on weekends, but they are truly few and far between; however, the Brigintine has happy hour til closing on Sundays & Mondays, and Humphrey's has a Sunday happy hour (see below). Here are some great happy hour bars in San Diego.. Nothing is cast in stone, so call first.

Rockin' Baja Lobster, 3890 Twiggs, Old Town, (619) 260-0305; Drink specials, beer $2.25, and appetizers are half price from 3-7 p.m, Mon-Fri. Also in San Marcos, Bonita, Oceanside.

Boathouse, 2040 Harbor Island Drive, (619) 291-8011; doubles are $1 extra, $1.99 Margarita and $3 appetizers (shrimp cocktail, quesidillas, nachos) plus bar menu, from 2:30pm to 5pm. Ends early, but beginning at 5pm on Wednesdays they have their $9.95 lobster night, and on Fridays they have prime rib for $9.95. Also see Birthday Freebies below.

Brigantine, 2725 Shelter Island Drive, (619) 224-2871, and other locations including Old Town, Del Mar, La Mesa, Coronado and Escondido. Half-price on selected seafood bar items like clam chowder, $2.95; shrimp cocktail, $5.95; fish taco $2.50; calamari, $4.99, garlic bread, $1.25 Tuesday-Saturday, 4-7pm; Sunday & Monday, 4 p.m. to closing! Love it!

Humphrey's, 2241 Shelter Island Drive, (619) 224-3577, Monday through Friday, 4:30-6:30pm. The "California Riviera" view plus hors d'oeuvres buffet with 2 shrimp, $1, fish taco, $1, 2 small roast beef sandwiches, $1; , special drink prices. Big Margarita, $7.75. Piano bar 5:30-8:30 p.m., **Saturday** happy hour, ½ off appetizers; **Sunday Happy Hour & Jazz**, $6 cover includes complimentary buffet from 5:45-6:45 p.m. and jazz concert begins at 7:30pm.

Jake's, 1660 Coast Blvd., Del Mar, (858) 755-2002. Happy hour prices on drinks and 50% off bar menu bistro; Mon-Thurs, 4-6; Friday, 4-closing.

Tio Leo's, 5302 Napa at Morena Blvd , (619) 542-1462, offers great free happy hour eats: 2 warm entrees, sometimes tostadas, or burritos, wings or quesedillas, salsas, and the best bean dip & chips in town, Monday-Friday, 4-7pm. $3 wells. On Thursday-Fridays, music and dance lessons dance lessons are Monday & Tuesday at 6 p.m.; at 6333 Mission Gorge, (619) 280-9944 but no music.

Bertrand at Mr. A's, 2550 Fifth at Laurel, (619) 239-1377; 4-6 p.m., 12th floor. There is no happy hour any more here, but it is worth the price of a drink to see the view. Drinks from $6 up. Coffee, $4. They will fax you a drink menu. No jacket required. The most beautiful view of the sunset, and a wonderful place to go around the holidays to see the city dressed up in lights at night right after the sun sets.

Old Bonita Store/Rockin' Baja, 4014 Bonita Road, (619) 479-3537; best happy hour in South Bay, 3-7 p.m. free food on Friday, plenty of people. Margaritas, $3.50. A deal.

94th Aero Squadron, 8885 Balboa Ave., Clairemont, (858) 560-6771; outdoor patio on the airstrip, 3:30-6:30p.m., Mon-Wed, free buffet spread on Thursdays & Fridays + special prices on bar menu. $2 house wine; $2.50 draft, $2.75 happy hour well drinks.

Quail's Inn on Lake San Marcos, 1035 La Bonita Drive, (760) 744-2445; special priced happy hour menu and drink specials, Monday through Friday.

Acapulco Restaurants, 4060 Clairemont Mesa, (858) 483-9222, and 2467 Juan Street in Old Town, (619) 260-8124; little complimentary buffet with chimichangas, bean dip, tacitos, veggies, chips. Order from appetizer menu, half price. Drink specials, festive atmosphere, 4-7 p.m. Mon-Fri.

Most of your better hotels have good complimentary happy hour food and drink specials in the bar, altho most charge $1-3 a plate Whadda deal.)

Birthday Freebies

Many restaurants offer **free champagne or dessert** to the birthday celebrant. The **Brigintine** and **Chart House** often give mud pie for two (YUM!). **Todai** (above) offers a free birthday dinner with three paid dinners (party of four). **China Camp** offers a free birthday dinner when another is ordered during Chinese New Year (February/March). You can go any time during Chinese New Year if you birthday falls in that time; you don't have to go on your birthday. Call and ask for the dates this year. The **Boat-house** at 2040 Harbor Island offers a free-prime-rib-birthday-dinner-night once a month, usually on the last Thursday, for anyone whose birthday is in the current month. Must how ID, and purchase another dinner. If your birthday is February 2nd, the free night will be the last Thursday in February, but call a week or so ahead to find out the exact date, (619) 291-8011. Dinner starts at five, and then you can go to the theater for half price (see ArtsTix). You clever devil. **Yakatori**, (619) 223-2641, offers a free birthday dinner with the purchase of another meal on your birthday, or the day before or the day after. Aren't the Japanese nice about birthdays?

Chapter 12
RESOURCES

WHERE TO FIND MORE BARGAINS
& OTHER HELPFUL INFORMATION

"Two-For-One" Coupons

If you want to save 50% on leisure activities including eating out, here's the deal for you: the *Entertainment* book. Whether you're young or not so young, married or single, if you like to get out and about, you'll save a bundle with *Entertainment* book. It contains hundreds of discount coupons, mostly two-for-one, but some are for half off, or even 20% off. **Fine Dining** at the Boathouse restaurant and Tom Ham's Lighthouse on Harbor Island, Bay Club & Grill on Shelter Island (and many more in La Jolla and all over the county) **Casual Restaurants**: (Sammy's California Woodfired Pizza, Baja Brewing Co., Su Casa, World Curry, and many more), **Informal Dining & Carryout** restaurants: (Burger King, Round Table Pizza, Baskin Robbins, Subway, Incredible Cheesecake Co., and many more), plus theaters, harbor cruises, whale watching, fishing, sailing, sports, zoo, Wild Animal Park, Legoland, Padres, hotels, car rentals, airline discounts and much more.

Thousands of editions are sold every year commencing in August; coupons expire 14 months later (you have plenty of time to use them!) Many working couples and families eat out on a regular basis using the coupons. Some families buy two or more coupon books!

The *Entertainment* coupon books sell for $40, and are used as fundraisers by non-profit organizations and are available for purchase from Cystic Fibrosis, hospital gift shops, local schools, youth groups, churches. About $8+ goes to the organization selling them. Last year, San Diego groups selling the book raised $1.6 million. For more information on where to buy a coupon book, call *Entertainment Publications* at (858) 554-1080.

Entertainment publishes dozens of coupon books for other major U.S. cities and several cities in Europe, and are available at a discount after you have purchased the local book (see order form in the back of the local book) or call *Entertainment,* (800) 374-4464. The Hawaii and Las Vegas editions are carried at the local office. QVC was selling them in the spring for $10 + $5 postage, and they were still good for at least another 5 or 6 months.

The Reader has several "two-for-one" coupons for dining every week, as does your neighborhood newspaper. You can also get a few from the back of the *Yellow Pages!*

Valuable Resources

Here are a number of interesting, valuable resources that may benefit you: *San Diego Union* home delivery, about $14 a month, (619) 299-4141; *San Diego Magazine*, $16 per year, (619) 230-9292; *San Diego Home/ Garden Lifestyles,* $16 per year, (619) 571-1818. Ask if there are any specials when you call! Also, gift subscriptions make a very nice gift.

At Paras Newsstand, near the corner of 30th and University in North Park, you can pick up a copy of the *New York Times*, the *Washington Post,* the *London Times* and other out-of-town newspapers plus hundreds of magazines for every interest. Also at the Newsstand at University & 6th.

The *Pennysaver*, a free weekly publication mailed to residences, distributes 84 different neighborhood booklets in San Diego County. It's a good source of discount coupons for dry cleaning, smog check, pet supplies, restaurants and more.

Transportation sdcommute.com is the site for all public transportation information including fares and transfers for the **bus, coaster, trolley for day trippers, monthly passes, disabled and senior passes**. The direct line for calling for personal trip planning for Southern San Diego is (619) 233-3004. For Northern County, call (800) 266-6883.

Here are some interesting and helpful web sites: **SanDiegoInsider.com** offers online San Diego entertainment, recreation, sports, community, money, travel, marketplace, news, guide to arts including movies, entertainment, business, classifieds, more. **SignOnSanDiego.com** is the *San Diego Union-Tribune* web site with today's newspaper online, plus archives, event listings, restaurants, bars/clubs, shops, professional services, real estate, etc. **Sandiego.gov** is the city of San Diego's new award-winning site with online services. **Co.san-diego.ca.us** is the County's growing site offering all the online services available. **Governmentguide.com** provides information on your national, state and local representatives by typing in your ZIP code. **Hicitizen.com** has forms and government information for local, state and federal. **Firstgov.com** is a major government website with links to all federal and state government agencies and information. At this site you can apply for jobs or student loans, renew drivers licenses, apply for passports and buy stamps. Businesses can check laws and regulations, file patents and trademarks, and look into contracting opportunities. Links to hundreds of government services and agencies. At **usbluepages.gov**, you'll find a virtual help desk with government toll-free numbers, more. **Fedforms.gov** contains the top 500 forms requested by the public. **LowerMyBills.com** is the site for lowering all your monthly bills from Internet Access to Auto Insurance.

San Diego Eldercare Directory is a 120+ page countywide guide to independent living and long term care, hailed as a invaluable resource for San Diego caregivers. It contains hundreds of countywide listings for services and products. It's free at libraries, or call (800) 960-4040. The directory can also be accessed online at signonsandiego.com.

I discovered that if you have any questions about San Diego and it's services, the **Mayor's office** is available to answer them. They have a large staff of volunteers to serve callers, (619) 236-6330. Hotline for calling in suggestions to the Mayor's office: (619) 570-1000.

If you are interested in getting funding for college, or forming or getting funding for a non-profit organization and/or acquiring grant money for your idea, visit the Funding Information Library at the **San Diego Foundation**, located at 1420 Kettner Boulevard, Suite 500, downtown, at Ash Street (The San Diego National Bank Building). There you will find comprehensive information on government, corporate and philanthropic funding sources. The staff will assist you in locating resources appropriate to you. Use of the library is free, and classes are offered monthly on how to write a grant proposal. In the last 25 years, they have granted over $124 million within the community. For more information, call (619) 235-2300 or visit their web site at sdfoundation.org.

For grants and low interest loans for home repairs within the city of San Diego, call the Housing Commission Rehabilitation Department at (619) 231-9400. Household income must be below national average.

Investing for Rookies, a monthly 8-page newsletter, is written by George Chamberlin to help rookie investors make the transition from saver to investor through impartial and independent financial education. George is not a stockbroker, rather a full time financial journalist whose goal is to take the mystique out of investing (Host of Money in the Morning, AM600 KOGO on Sunday mornings and Money advisor to NBC TV 7/39). One year (12 mo.) Subscription, $29.95. Send to: Investing for Rookies, POBox 1969, Carlsbad, CA 92108 or check his web site at investingforrookies.com Free step-by-step financial guides to understanding stocks, bonds and mutual funds, building a portfolio on a shoestring, adding to your portfolio, what you should buy as a beginning investor and more are available online at moneycentral.com, yahoo.com/financial, cnnmoney.com, and msn.com Most investment houses won't work with you unless you can commit a substantial amount of $$$ monthly for mutual funds or stocks. Here are three companies that will invest as little as $50-$100 a month by automatic withdrawal: T. Rowe Price, (800) 638-5660; American Century (800) 345-2021; Scudder (800) 225-2470.

Free Stuff for Kids ($9.^{95}). Published annually, this little book contains over 250 free and up to $2 things kids age 5-11 can send for by mail: decals and bumper stickers, story magazines, maps, coloring books, comic books, fun games, booklets, colorful posters, exotic stamps and more. Makes a great gift for the child in your life, and I swear it will raise your child's IQ 10 points! Great gift from Grandma. By new or used at book stores or amazon.com *Consumer Reports*, a monthly magazine (about $24 per year). Subscription includes a copy of the Annual Buying Guide ($8.^{95} value, 400 pages) with products rated by brand name, domestic and foreign cars, kitchen appliances, stereo, cameras, tools, paints, TVS, cleaning products, and personal care products. You will also receive a 314-page guide to everyday health problems and health products ($8.^{95} value), and the Annual Auto issue, free with subscription. On newsstands everywhere, or call (800) 529-0551, or check their web site at consumerreports.org (fantastic info). Similar info is at consumerguide.com

Wholesale by Mail Catalog, by the Print Project, St. Martin's Press. You can buy almost anything at 30-90% off retail prices. Available at bookstores and libraries.

Contest Newsletter, P.O.Box 58637, Boulder Co 80322-8637; $15.97 a year. Sweepstakes Online, contains mail-in, website, radio & TV, phone in and retail drop in sweepstakes and contest information. For sample newsletter, send $3 to P.O.Box 146, Redmond, WA 98073-0146.

Bargain Hunting in the Bay Area, by Sally Socolich, Chronicle Books, $13.^{50} includes tax and postage, P. O. Box 144, Moraga, CA 94556. (Please say I recommended you!) Available at new or used bookstores or amazon.com.

Voice your opinions on current issues through the White House Comments Line, (202) 456-1111. Responses are tallied and delivered to the President twice daily.

For a free photo of the President or President and First Lady, send request for photo with your name and address to: Office of Correspondence, Room 94, The White House, Washington, DC 20500. Vice Presidential photos available, too.

The *President of the United States* will send a note of congratulations to any citizen celebrating their 80th or subsequent birthday or any couple married 50 years or more. Send request to Greetings Office, The White House, Washington, DC 20500.

Web sites with money-saving including super frugal tips, debt control, etc. quicken.com, thefrugallife.com, miserlymoms.com, pinchingpennies.com, frugalfamilynetwork.com Great money-saving ideas.

Enroll in any school: adult, community college and others and you will get a student ID card that entitles you to endless discounts on goods, services, software, admissions, travel, movies and more.

If you need certified copies of birth, death, marriage and divorce certificates, call the library and they will look up the address of the vital statistics office in any state for you. You can also access this information online at the government web sites above.

Privacy web sites: Privacy Rights Clearinghouse, privacyrights.org. Online Privacy Alliance: privacyalliance.org; Privacy Inc: privacyinc.comlocate If you are receiving anonymous telephone calls and hang-ups, call the SBC

 Annoyance Call Bureau at (800) 698-7223. They can put a trap on your phone for 14 days; prosecution of the annoyer is available. Available at other telephone companies, too.

Federal Government Telephone Information Center Get in touch with any federal government agency including social security, grants, copyrights, government publications, passports, job hotlines, etc. Put this one on your Rolodex, (800) 688-9889, Monday-Friday, 8-8pmES; Web: firstgov.com.

Identity theft is on the rise. How can someone steal your identity? By taking your name, Social Security number, credit card number, or some other piece of your personal information for their own use without your knowledge, and using it to commit fraud or theft. The following government site describes various ways that identity thieves work along with consumer alerts, and how to file a complaint. Go to consumer.gov/idtheft

For a free **Consumer Information Catalog** listing dozens of free and low cost consumer publications, call toll free (888) 8PUEBLO, or send your request to: Catalog Request, Consumer Information Center, P. O. Box 100, Pueblo, CO 81002. Sponsored by the Federal government. View it online free at pueblo.gsa.gov.

Find out how much **social security** you will receive at retirement at (800) 772-1213. Check several years in advance because your records may not be accurate, and it may take social security years to straighten things out. Women who were married a minimum of 10 years before divorce are entitled to a social security claim based on their ex-husband's benefits. An ex-wife is eligible to receive her own entitlement, or she can receive an amount equal to half her ex-husband's entitlement, which ever is greater, as long as he is alive. This does not affect his entitlement in any way. The way social security is set up, any and all ex-wives of 10 years of marriage are entitled to receive an amount equal to one half his entitlement as long as he lives. Upon his death, each ex-wife of 10 years is entitled to receive an amount *equal to his full entitlement*. Be sure to check this out.

If you have a problem getting your social security check, or any kind of problem with ANY city, state or federal government agency, write a letter to your CONGRESSPERSON. Your Congressperson will act on it. And, boy, does a government agencies ever *dislike* hearing from a Congress-person. You will get prompt action on your request from your representative. The list of local, state and federal representatives in listed the second Wednesday of every month in the *Union-Tribune*, Section B. A dear friend was offered a $5,000 refund from IRS after asking her representative to take action at the highest level possible. Another started receiving social security disability checks after her congressman took action on her behalf.

Seniors: go to benefitscheck.org and see what's available to you. Some have age and income requirements.

Unclaimed Cash/Abandoned Property

Property and cash estimated to be worth billions of dollars is sitting in federal and state treasuries waiting for the owners to make claim. Outdated bank accounts, lost checks, unpaid dividends, unclaimed interest payment, forgotten security deposits, utility deposits, uncollected insurance benefits and uncashed tax refunds are turned over to the state and federal agencies' abandoned property divisions. Unclaimed money and properties (usually the result of a death with heirs unaware of assets, or a move where people forget to close an account) is held until a claim is filed. Call the California Administrator of Abandoned of Unclaimed Property's "Claim What's Yours" line at (800) 992-4647 or check these web sites: unclaimed.org or foundmoney.com.

Chapter 13

VISITORS
Hotels, Auto Rentals, Weather, etc..

Welcome to San Diego. I hope your stay is absolutely fabulous and that you find the area to be enticing with it's 70 miles of gorgeous coastline and beautiful sunsets. The people here are friendly, there are tons of things to do, and the shopping is great. Please don't be disappointed if we don't have sunshine 365 days a year. The coastal clouds are a reminder that we are very close to the Pacific Ocean. This chapter contains some great ways to save money on hotels, auto rentals, weather info, and more.

Save on Hotel Rooms & Accommodations
* The average room rate is about $110 *

Inexpensive Hotels $30-$60
Downtown Inn Hotel, Gaslamp
La Pacifica Hotel, downtown
Old Town Inn, Old town
Padre Trail Inn, Old Town
La Pacifica, downtown
Super 8 Bay View, downtown
Surf & Sand, Mission Blvd.
Vagabond Inn, Hotel Circle
Village Lodge, Gaslamp

Moderate Priced Hotels $60-$100
Arena Inn, Midway & Rosecrans
Best Western Bayside, downtown
Best Western Posada, Pt. Loma
Best Western Seven Seas, Hotel Circle
California Suites, Clairemont
Comfort Inn, downtown, Ash Street
Comfort Inn, Hotel Circle
Days Inn, Mission Bay
Days Inn Suites, Rosecrans
Grovesnor Inn, Ash St., downtown
Holiday Inn, Sea World area
Holiday Inn Harbor View, downtown
Holiday Inn, Sports Arena
La Pensione, Little Italy downtown
Pacific Shores Inn, Mission Blvd.
Quality Inn & Suites, 7th Ave., downtown
Ramada Plaza, Hotel Circle
Vagabond Inn, Hotel Circle
Super 8 Motel Harborside , Pt. Loma
Vacation Inn, Old Town

You can **get hotel rooms for less** by asking a few questions. As a major city, San Diego ranks in the top ten with the highest room occupancy rates (about 68%), but that means on average that about 30% are unoccupied. So, start asking: Are there any special promotions? Are there are any two-for-one coupons available? Do they honor AAA membership? Do they use a "frequent flyer" program (earn mileage)? Do they give senior, student or military discounts? Do they give a discount for professional, employment, organizational, credit union or other membership? Are there any cheaper rooms? Does it make a difference if you're there on a week day or weekend? How much is a room with a view versus one without? Call for rates on their 800 toll free number, then call directly and see if there is a difference in room rate. According to a national publication, many hotels quote a higher rate over the toll free line! If you want a deep discounts at a hotel, negotiate-negotiate-negotiate. You'll do best with advance reservations, advance purchase and a minimum stay. Keep asking questions about discounts, and add one final question: "Is that your lowest rate?" They will tell you. Ultimately, ask "Who gets the lowest rate?" (if you think they won't throw you out for asking!!) Another tip: you can *ask* for the corporate rate even if you don't work for a corporation. Or, say you're on a budget. Whine a little . . . . it can work for you! Also, I like to ask for an upgrade (view room, hmm?) Schmooze a little with the clerk. **Priceline.com**: bid the hotel room rate you want to pay. Stay at deluxe hotels or economy; name your discount. See Travel for more info. The **Entertainment** coupon book has coupons for 20-50% off the rack rate of hotel rooms, moderate to deluxe. See Resources for more info. **Print coupons online** at roomsaver.com. **Costco** Travel offers Costco members discounts on hotels in San Diego (and many other cities.) See the Costco travel brochure available at warehouses, or online at costco.com For an alternative to hotel rooms, consider a **Bed & Breakfast Inn**, (800) 619-ROOM. Call for a referral to one of 30 B&B's in San Diego County. Rates, $49-$350. Weekly, monthly rates. If you're staying for an **extended time**, check hotels listed in the *Yellow Pages* for those with weekly and monthly rates, refrigerators and microwaves. Or, check the *Yellow Pages* and *Union Tribune* classified ads for short-term furnished apartments. **Cheap Sleeps**: Consider staying in a **Youth Hostels** (NOT for youth only). Hostel International, 521 Market, (619) 525-1531; 134-bed hostel, near to the trolley, buses and train; $16 members, $19 nonmembers; private rooms available. No age limit. With Hosteling International membership card, you get discounts on car rentals, restaurants, museums, air fares, more. Hostel International San Diego-Pt. Loma, 3790 Udall St., (619) 223-4778 has 61 beds, $16mem, $19 nonmembers. Ocean Beach International Hostel, 4961 Newport Ave., (619) 223-SURF. Historic, 60 bed hostel near the beach. $16/bed. Banana Bungalow San Clemente Youth Hostel, 233 Avenida Granada, (714) 492-2848. 40 beds, $14. The Inn at the YMCA, 500 W. Broadway, 234-5252, offers a weekly single rate of $155 and $175 for two people. Nightly rates are $40 for single; $50 for two. Check the web at usahostels.com and hiayh.org more information.

Ways to Save on Car Rentals

Discount coupons for major car rentals are in the *Entertainment* book (see Resources), and you can find them in free tourist publications at hotels and tourist information centers. **Costco** offers Costco members a discount on car rentals. Inquire about discounts for AAA membership, seniors, students, professional groups, AARP, etc. Ask: *"Are there any discounts I might qualify for or any coupons I should know about?"*

Enterprise Car rental offers a weekend special at $9.99 per day for a three-day weekend ($29.97 total), from Friday afternoon to Monday morning, except on three-day weekends. This is for compacts only and includes 100 miles per day. Additional miles are at 25 cents a mile, or for an additional $10 per day, you get unlimited miles. If you reserve a compact and they are out, they will give you a free upgrade. Not available at the airport office. Their Balboa Avenue location almost always has compact rentals. Check the white pages for other locations. I use the one in Pt. Loma ((619) 225-0848. Enterprise will come get you!

There are a number of cheaper car rentals listed in the *Yellow Pages* including Dirt Cheap Rent A Car that charges about $499 a month, or $400 a month with your own U.S. insurance coverage which covers ANY car you drive. Be sure your personal car insurance coverage is sufficient to cover the value of your rental car. Remember, most major credit cards offer insurance coverage on auto rentals that are charged on the credit card. Some have discontinued this policy, so check with your credit card company first. "Gold" cards usually provide this coverage.

Make reservations early. It can be VERY difficult to rent a car in San Diego at the last minute on holiday weekends or during special events because they are usually sold out. If sold out, however, keep checking back because people turn in cars, or a cancellation may come in, so one may become available for you. Call a car rental inland (La Mesa, El Cajon) if you find they are sold out in the city. Also, negotiate the price!

Cheaper auto rentals include Bargain Auto Rentals, (619) 299-0009, $18.95 up; Rent a Wreck, (619) 260-1673, $19.95 up.

Visitor Information & Weather

Pick up free maps and information at the International Visitor Information Center, First and F St., downtown, (619) 236-1212. Check the San Diego visitor web site at sandiego.org.

Here's a monthly chart of the **weather** conditions in San Diego from the National Weather Service. For a recorded weather forecast, call (619) 289-1212.

Month	Temp. High	Average Low	Humidity	Days of Rain	Sunshine
Jan	65	48	63	2.11"	72%
Feb	66	50	66	1.43"	72%
Mar	66	52	67	1.60"	70%
Apr	68	55	67	0.78"	67%
May	69	58	70	0.24"	59%
June	71	61	74	0.06"	58%
July	76	65	74	0.01"	68%
Aug	78	67	74	0.01"	70%
Sept	77	65	72	0.19"	69%
Oct	75	60	70	0.33"	68%
Nov	70	54	65	1.10"	75%
Dec	66	49	64	1.36"	73%

More Visitor Information & Tips:

Taxis: Average rate for one to five persons is $2 a mile. **San Diego Transit** One day bus/trolley pass, $5; two day, $8; three day, $10; four-day pass, $12. The pass is good for unlimited access to buses, the trolley . Bus fare is usually around $1.50-$3.50. Direct line for personal trip planning in Southern San Diego County is (619) 233-3004. Northern County, call (800) 266-6883. Unlimited monthly bus and trolley passes, $54 for adults age 18-60. One ride, $1.50 up. Seniors, disabled: $13.50 a month; youth pass, $24.50; half-month passes available. Located at lst & Broadway, (619) 234-1060. Inquire about Super Saver fares, "3-for-1" weekend cheap seats, airport shuttle bus, Coaster train, etc.. Check their Web site at sdcommute.com for routes, time schedules, prices **Passport to Balboa Park**, (619) 239-0512. Visit thirteen Balboa Park attractions for $30 ($70 value). Good for seven days. Purchase coupon from the Balboa Park Visitors Center, any participating museum or at the Times Arts Tix booth in Horton Plaza. For $55, you get a San Diego Zoo pass included. **Times Arts Tix**: Horton Plaza, 3rd & Broadway, (619) 497-5000. Here is where you get half-price, day of performance tickets for theater, music and dance performances. Sunday events are available for half-price on Saturday. Closed Sunday/Monday. Cash only. Also available: discount admissions for San Diego Zoo, Wild Animal Park, Sea World and Gray Line Tours. (I'm available for **personally guided tours**. Send email request to Sally at sallygary@aol.com.)

The End ☺

INDEX

INDEX

INDEX

INDEX

INDEX